What's a Landlord to Do?

DEDICATION

This book is dedicated to Dario, AKA "Papa," who answered my own many questions about landlording patiently and wisely when he was asked and who let me be stupid without comment and learn on my own when he wasn't asked.

ACKNOWLEDGEMENTS

Many people submitted questions through the landlording.com website. Some of those questions reached me and some did not. Some I answered within hours and some I answered within years.

Thanks to all of you who asked!

THE USUAL CAVEAT

This publication is designed to provide accurate and authoritative information in regard to the subject matter covered. It is sold with the understanding that the publisher is not engaged in rendering legal or accounting service. If legal advice or other expert assistance is required, the services of a competent professional person should be sought.

> — From a declaration of principles jointly adopted by a committee of the American Bar Association and a Committee of Publishers and Associations

What's a Landlord to Do?

Landlording Q & A's

Written by
Leigh Robinson

Illustrated by
Jan Brown

Published by

P.O. BOX 1639
EL CERRITO, CA 94530-4639
landlording.com

FIRST EDITION   January, 2005

COPYRIGHT 2005 by Leigh Robinson

INTERNATIONAL STANDARD BOOK NUMBER: 0-932956-28-9

Jan Brown drew the cartoons.

David Patton drew the timid landlording family, who appear at the beginning of each chapter, the scrupulous landlording family, who appear on the last page of this book, and also the unscrupulous family, who appear on the ExPress order form.

Leigh Robinson designed the cover, and Joe Fletcher rendered it.

PRINTED IN THE U.S.A.

The LANDLORDING SERIES™, of which this is Book Three, is a trademark of ExPress and Leigh Robinson.

Preface

This book is full of questions from wannabe landlords, newbie landlords, accidental landlords, experienced landlords, frustrated landlords, puzzled landlords, and troubled tenants. It would not exist except for the variety of challenges landlords and tenants face regularly and the urge they have to ask questions about those challenges in their search for good answers.

You might very well want to ask me a number of questions about this book, that is, if you had the chance. Take a look at the ten questions below, and see whether they resemble the questions you have on your mind as you contemplate whether this book you have in your hands is worth your time.

1) What qualifies you to write a book consisting of answers to people's landlording questions?

2) Why didn't you include the information in this book in your *Landlording* book?

3) How did you come to write *What's a Landlord to Do?*

4) Did you rewrite the questions submitted to you?

5) Why didn't you put the questions and answers (Q&A's) into a computer database so that anybody with a specific question could query the database for an answer to their question and go directly to it?

6) Do your answers apply to every state?

7) I have what I think is a unique question. How can I get my question to you and be sure that you receive it?

8) Why did you include a chapter consisting of nothing but questions from tenants? Don't they belong in a book entitled *What's a Tenant to Do?*

9) Where can I find information about errors in the book and about revisions and updates?

10) Will you take responsibility if I try one of the ideas you mention in the book, and it doesn't work?

Here are my answers to those questions.

1) For years I was a tenant. For many more years, I have been a landlord. I have owned all kinds of rental properties, both residential and commercial, from a single-family house to apartments to mobilehome parks to self storages and motels, and I have owned them in more than one state. I have owned properties in urban and rural areas and in shoddy and prime neighborhoods. I have been a hands-on and a hands-off landlord. I have myself handled every conceivable landlording task, from fixing fixer-uppers to evicting unscrupulous tenants, from jumping on overflowing garbage containers to solving mold problems, from setting up a workable bookkeeping system to devising a pet agreement. I have studied landlording. I have taught landlording, and I have lectured on the subject. I started with nothing except personal savings and determination. I have done well in the business through hard work, resourcefulness, creativity, dedication, luck, and marrying the right woman. I have been told that I have more than a lick of common sense, and I have answered more than one difficult landlording question posed by friends and strangers who had their troubles and misgivings about something.

2) At 500 pages, the *Landlording* book is already too big. Think of this book as its mate, a book full of examples of the teachings and techniques described in the *Landlording* book, all taken from real life.

3) One of the many things I wanted to do through my landlording.com website was give landlords the opportunity to ask me questions, and so I solicited questions. I would mull them over, write answers, email my replies, and put both questions and answers up on the website for all to see. I continued that routine for quite some time. People submitted so many questions that I couldn't keep up with them all, and the Q&A

page on the website grew and grew to be so long that it became unwieldy. It was disorganized as well. When people asked me to organize the Q&As, I decided to do just that and make a book out of them, a book organized by subject and thoroughly indexed. This is that book.

4) Before I became a landlord, I was a high-school English teacher. I taught grammar and punctuation and vocabulary and style. At least that was my mission when I was confined inside a classroom with youngsters whose hormones were raging and who were much more interested in the opposite sex and fashion and music and sports and cars and gossip than in English. I left the classroom behind after a dozen years, but I didn't leave my red pencil behind. I still have it, and I couldn't help myself when reading people's landlording questions. I had to mark them up with my red pencil and make the changes and corrections myself. I had to try to make the questions more explicit, more understandable, more readable, and more applicable to others who have similar questions. I had to rewrite them. Believe me when I say that not every landlord paid attention in English class as a teenager and can write clearly today.

5) The Q&As in this book could have been entered into a searchable database and distributed on a CD-ROM, and some day they may well be. Right now, when most landlords are more comfortable reading a book than using a computer to search a database, a book, especially one with some organization to it, will reach more people who might have these same questions and who don't know where to go to find the answers.

6) A landlord in one state can become a landlord in another state without much trouble because landlord/tenant laws vary little from state to state. They do vary, of course, and wise landlords learn all they can about the laws in every state where they have rental properties. In this book, you will find no mention of the specifics which vary from state to state, such as the notice requirements for a nonpayment-of-rent eviction and the length of time allowed for the return of a deposit. Instead, you will find common-sense answers about things such as the calculation of deposit deductions, alternatives to pursuing evictions through the legal labyrinth, handling of surly

tenants, picking good tenants, and fixing wobbly toilets. Those Q&As apply equally to rental properties in Alaska, Hawaii, and anywhere in the lower forty-eight.

7) Although I cannot guarantee that your own unique question will reach me if you send it via email to mail@landlording.com, I can guarantee that it will reach me if you send it via U.S. Mail to the publisher (ExPress, P.O. Box 1639, El Cerrito, CA 94530), and refer it to my attention.

8) There are two sides to every story, and the other side to landlords' questions are tenants' questions. Including tenants' questions in a book devoted to landlords' questions gives the book a broader perspective. Landlords need to consider a tenant's point of view and develop a broader perspective themselves. Tenants are not the enemy, and we need to know what they're thinking about their landlords in order to become better landlords ourselves. The tenants' questions included here are not rants about despicable landlords who prey on their poor, defenseless tenants. They're substantive questions, and they raise legitimate concerns.

9) Check the landlording.com website periodically for the latest information pertaining to the books and software published by ExPress.

10) You are on your own if you try one of the ideas in this book and it doesn't work. Use me as a scapegoat if you'd like. I play that role well. But don't come crying to me and expect me to take responsibility for something you did that went awry after you followed what you read here. Nope, that won't happen. You have to take responsibility for your own actions as a landlord. You have to interpret what you read here and apply it to your tenants, your property, your community, and your state. No advice works everywhere every time, certainly not landlording advice from me. Should you try an idea you read about here and find that it didn't work, please do let me know what happened in your case and why the idea didn't work. I'd like to share your story with future readers of this book so we can all learn something from your experience.

If you're satisfied now that you might learn something more about landlording from these Q&A's, keep reading.

Table of Contents

Introduction

Invariably, landlording questions consist of some questions about buying rental properties, some about selecting tenants, some about settling tenant disputes, and many about evicting deadbeats and undesirables. Questions on these subjects appear here, as well they should, because landlords are always looking for answers to these questions. They're important questions. *What's a Landlord to Do?* includes many variations, enough for you to find a question similar to the one you would have asked had you had the opportunity.

Questions on other aspects of landlording surface often enough in an even wider variety and appear here in great number. Whereas you will never encounter every one of these situations, you will encounter some of them sometime. They come with the job, and no amount of insulation between you and your tenants is enough to keep you from having to find answers to them.

Let's say that you want to kick back and do some traveling after diligently managing your rental properties yourself for twenty years, but you don't want to liquidate your three highly appreciated and highly depreciated twenty-unit buildings because you know you'd have to pay as much in capital gains taxes as you originally paid for the buildings. You have done well. You seek and you find a seemingly honest and reliable property management company to look after your properties, and you give them a free rein. You tell them not to bother you with problems. All you want is a check from them every month. Things go well for six months. You get no phone calls from anybody, and you get the expected check every month. Then the checks stop coming. You have to call the property management company to ask them what's happening, and they give you a song and dance about why the checks are late and why they're smaller than expected. The next thing you know, one of the on-site managers calls you to ask why the property management company is not answering their phone. You discover that they have gone out of business and left town with the funds in your discretionary account, and you have to cancel your thirty-day cruise around South America.

You have a question. *What's a Landlord to Do?* has an answer.

Let's say that your tenant's grandson has moved in with his grandmother and smokes dope in his room. She doesn't mind. The downstairs tenant does. She cannot abide the smell of the smoke and calls the police to make him stop. They stop by, but they don't stop him from smoking. They say they can't. That's a job for the landlord. That's a job for you.

You have a question. *What's a Landlord to Do?* has an answer.

Let's say that your tenant submits a maintenance request, and you send your maintenance man around to her apartment to fix her malfunctioning plumbing. When he gets there, he discovers that she is Ms Piggy herself. Her apartment is a mess. There's litter everywhere. There's spoiled food everywhere, and there's a stench worse than camel's breath everywhere. He calls you in to witness for yourself how the tenant lives. You wonder what you ought to do. She pays her rent on time and never bothers her neighbors.

You have a question. *What's a Landlord to Do?* has an answer.

Let's say that your tenant calls a plumber to come out and repair something you could have repaired yourself had you known about it. The tenant deducts $400 from his next month's rent to pay the bill. You let the matter slide rather than get into an argument. Then he moves out, and you get a bill directly from the plumber for the $400. The tenant never paid the bill, and the plumber comes after you to pay it. You know you never should have paid the bill the first time, and now you're being asked to pay it twice.

You have a question. *What's a Landlord to Do?* has an answer.

Let's say that you have a friend who's handy and wants to rent from you in exchange for working around your property. You have plenty of work for him to do to work off his rent and can't foresee any problems. He moves in and works when he pleases. He won't account for his hours. He calls in other workers when he isn't available to do a job, and then sends you their bills. You'd like to evict him, but because he's a friend, you don't want to.

You have a question. *What's a Landlord to Do?* has an answer.

Real landlords posed these questions and many more to me over the landlording.com website. Real landlords needed answers, and I came up with answers. They may not have been the most desirable of answers, but they may have been the only realistic answers, and even battle-tested landlords need to get a reality check now and then. With its realistic answers, *What's a Landlord to Do?* is just that, a reality check.

Oddly enough, real landlords weren't the only ones visiting the landlording.com website and asking questions. Tenants, parents, adult children, roommates, and prospective landlords were asking questions as well. Tenants' questions especially can be instructive for landlords who may not have walked in tenants' shoes for a long time. These questions also give *What's a Landlord to Do?* a balance it would not have otherwise.

There are two sides to every story. We all know that. The tenants' questions are here to remind us. Although they appear in a single chapter, you might want to consider what kind of a question a tenant would ask when her landlord poses his question in the other chapters. In a better book than this, there would be a corresponding tenant question beside every landlord question, and you could ponder each person's point of view fully. Lacking those corresponding questions, you will have to use your imagination and visualize the second question to get the other side of the story.

Good landlords have good vision. My hope is that *What's a Landlord to Do?* will help sharpen your good vision.

1
Investing in Rental Property

He wants to become a multi-millionaire.

Q. What suggestions might you have for somebody who is twenty-five years old and wants to become a multi-millionaire investing in real estate?

—R.R., New York

A. Here's my formula for success as a real estate investor.

Be prepared to work 24/7/365, longer when necessary. Be willing to do menial work when necessary. Find a mate who shares your goals and will work as hard as you will to reach them. Avoid having a family before you make your first $250,000. Seek out someone local who has achieved more than a modest success in real estate investing; treat that person to a fine meal; ask for advice; listen; and learn. Waste no money on expensive tapes and seminars promoted by hucksters with get-rich-quick promises. Study William Nickerson's classic *How I Turned $1,000 into Five Million in Real Estate in My Spare Time*, and adapt its techniques to fit your circumstances today. Avoid partnerships unless the partner has expertise, experience, or connections which you lack. Understand that your lack of money is no reason to form a partnership with someone who has money. Learn how a professional appraiser appraises a property. Study and follow the market for different kinds of properties. Identify any number of fixer-upper properties, and make offers based upon location, financing, condition, current income, and potential income. Avoid becoming attached to any property before, during, or after ownership. Fix up and trade up again and again. Borrow for investment purposes only. Pay your debts on time. Learn how the time value of money affects your business dealings. Take fewer risks as you accumulate more assets. Cultivate relationships with an accountant, an attor-

ney, a banker, an insurance agent, a loan broker, a real estate agent, and a Jack or Jill of all trades. Hire on-site management. Handle off-site management yourself. Hire help to do those things which somebody else can do for you equally as well as you might do them yourself so that you can concentrate on doing those things which you alone can do to achieve your goals. Stay out of court except for evictions. Learn how to evict, and evict promptly. Expect setbacks and take them in stride. Be unflappable. Keep your word. Be fair. Be available. Be tough. Be patient. Be flexible. Live beneath your means. Complete a financial statement every six months to take stock of your assets. Give back to your community.

Good luck! Self-made millionaires need a little bit of luck, too.

She's determined to become a landlord.

Q. I am nineteen years old and a college student. Currently I'm unemployed, but only because I'm taking a full load of classes and have a partial scholarship and some savings from having worked at fast-food restaurants all during high school. I'm a worker. Right now, I'm determined to become a landlord of a $164,000 building in Atlanta, Georgia, where I grew up. What can I do to convince the people I need to finance me that I will pay them back?

—T.W., Georgia

A. Even at your age and with little or nothing in your purse, you can become a landlord, but you will need to demonstrate that you are mature enough, honest enough, industrious enough, and dedicated enough. In other words, you will need to demonstrate that you have the makings of a good landlord.

You do that by first reading whatever you can on the subject of rental property management and then answering classified ads which seek rental property managers for properties with ten to thirty units. Look for a position with someone who has owned a property for a long time and might want to sell it within the next year or so.

Tell the owner straightaway that you are interested in buying a building yourself and that you want to learn what you can about being a landlord from down in the trenches.

As soon as you feel both competent and confident, approach your boss about buying the building you have been managing on a workable lease-option arrangement which would enable you to begin an ownership role without having to come up with any cash. The lease-option itself needs to be worded carefully to protect you and the owner, enabling each of you to reach your goals. Pay a real estate attorney to draw it up for you. You can indeed become a young landlord if you will go all out to become one.

He has masters degree and nest egg and wants to be a landlord.

Q. Although I earned a masters degree recently, I'm thinking about pursuing a career in rental properties because I would like to be my own boss. I've been working at various jobs for the past ten years, and I've accumulated a nest egg of over $125,000. In addition, I have $75,000 in a 401k. I've read your book and several others, and I've done my homework on the subject.

Here is my question. Will a bank finance me if I don't have a job, but I do have an adequate down payment and some reserves?

I'm thinking, of course, about properties which have good numbers. I plan to manage the properties myself and do most of the small jobs. I'm fairly "handy." I would pay myself roughly $20,000 per year, and that would be my primary income. Any advice you have would be appreciated.
—D.G., Kansas

A. Anybody who has managed to save as much as you have sounds like a good risk to me. Still, not every banker will look at what you have done and what you plan to do and lend you the money you need to buy income property. Some are willing to lend only to people who have a secure income, people similar to themselves.

With as much money as you have salted away,

bankers should be courting you as a customer, that is, once they know what your assets are. Take advantage of your position. Visit a number of bankers and tell them about your assets and your plans. Tell them that you'd like to do business with a single bank if possible, one where they know you and will work with you. You should find a banker who is eager for your business, a banker who understands that an income property loan depends more on a property's fundamentals than on the borrower's personal income from outside sources, a banker who is just as happy to lend you $300,000 on a $425,000 property as keep your $125,000 on deposit.

Should you fail to find the right banker, however, you needn't abandon your plans. Banks are not the only lenders around. They aren't even the best lenders around. The best lenders are sellers.

Sellers don't demand fees and appraisals and more fees. They lend on the property they're selling you, which they know is worth at least as much as you're paying them for it, and they lend at reasonable rates, too. When you're looking around for a property to buy, ask about seller financing. Consider it to be an important asset of any rental property you're thinking about buying.

You're in a better position to begin a career of owning and managing rental properties than most people are when they first get into the business. You have a nest egg. Take advantage of it.

He wants cash flow.

Q. After reading the *Landlording* book, I'm excited about the idea of working for myself in the landlording business.

I'm 26 years old and currently have a good job and about $120,000 in savings. I will be working abroad for the next two years, but I want to get started in landlording on a part-time basis when I return to the U.S. and have only a year left on my employment contract. After my contract ends, I would like to become a full-time landlord.

Most of what I have read about real estate investments in general says that the cash flow is meager from rental property investing and that the return comes mainly from appreciation and tax benefits. I have read that many rental property owners look after their properties on the side while working at another job. I don't want to do that, but I am concerned that if I do devote myself to working on my rental property full-time, I won't have enough cash flow to live on.

How can rental properties provide me with enough cash flow to live on?

—C.A., Texas

A. You sound like a good candidate to become a good landlord. You know how to save your money. You understand that landlording pays off in more ways than one. You want to work for yourself, and you are schooling yourself before buying your first rental property.

What you have been reading about many landlords being moonlighters is true. Many landlords are moonlighters. They hold down full-time jobs while looking after their rental properties in their spare time. They think of their rental properties as nest eggs which will help them enjoy a better retirement later in life.

What you have been reading about the cash flow from rental properties being meager is only half-true. Landlords may or may not be getting any cash flow. That depends upon what they paid for their properties in relation to the properties' income and expenses and how big of a debt they have to service.

Let's look at debt first and see how it affects cash flow.

Let's say that you took your entire savings and bought a duplex for $120,000 in cash. If each unit generated $500 per month in rent for a total income of $1,000, and if your expenses amounted to $400, you'd have cash flow of $600 per month.

Now let's say that you bought the same duplex for the same price and had the same income and expenses, but you put 20%, or $24,000, down and secured a $96,000 loan to finance the balance. Let's say that the loan had a fixed interest rate of 7% payable in equal monthly installments over 25 years. The $679 payment would more than wipe out your cash flow. You'd have negative cash flow of $79.

In the first instance, you would have positive cash flow. In the second, you would have none. The property is the same. The income is the same. The expenses are the same. Only the debt is different.

Buying rental property with a large down payment or with all cash is one way to insure cash flow. The other is buying the right property for the right price.

Anybody can open a multiple listing book,

check the attractive rental properties for sale in the good neighborhoods, and see that they would produce a meager cash flow, if any, after a normal down payment. Those are pride of-ownership properties which anybody would be proud to own and crow about, but they aren't the properties anybody who is interested in generating cash flow ought to own. They don't deliver the dough.

Trophy properties have low capitalization rates (cap rates), some even as low as three or four percent. You want to own properties with higher cap rates than that, or else you'll be working another job to support your properties rather than owning properties that support you.

A property's cap rate, by the way, is a measurement of how much net operating income (NOI) a property generates in relation to its price. Properties with higher cap rates generate more net operating income.

To calculate a property's cap rate, you add up all of its annual expenses except debt service and subtract them from the annual income. That number is the property's NOI. Divide the NOI by the price of the property and you come up with the cap rate.

In the duplex example above, the NOI is $7,200 (the property's monthly net income of $600 multiplied by 12 months). Divide $7,200 by the price of the property, $120,000, and you get a cap rate of 6%. So long as the income and expenses remain the same, the cap rate remains the same, no matter how much of a down payment you make on the property.

If the income goes up, and the expenses remain the same, the cap rate goes up, sometimes way up.

Let's say that you saw some potential in that duplex for increasing the rent. You bought it at a 6% cap rate. You evicted the owner's brother-in-law and cousin, who were paying substantially below-market rents. You redecorated the two apartments and rented them to new tenants for double the old rents. You experienced no increase in annual expenses, so you saw your NOI jump to $19,200 and your cap rate jump to 16%. Wow! Now that's something to crow about! You'd be in a position to pocket some real cash flow.

Buying problem properties and correcting the problems is the best way to make the cash start flowing. Perfectly normal people who are more aggressive and energetic than others who are speculative and sedentary have been making very good money for years by searching out properties which have problems and owners who are eager to unburden themselves of those problems.

Once the new owners correct the problems and the property starts to generate more income, the new owners can jump for joy and even choose what they want to do next. They can hang onto the property and enjoy the increased cash flow. They can hang onto the property, refinance it, use the proceeds to buy another similar problem property, correct its problems, and continue doing more of the same. Or they can sell the property for a considerable profit and buy another, much larger, problem property, correct its problems, and continue doing more of the same.

In order for a buyer to profit most from correcting property problems, the problems must be correctable with little time and little money. Examples of such problems are below-market rents, drab interiors, drab exteriors, overgrown landscaping, and tenants who need to be evicted. Examples of problems requiring too much time and money are soil subsidence, foundation cracks, bad neighborhood, and a carpenter ant infestation.

You may have to look at a hundred properties for sale before you find the right one, the one with the right problems, the one you can turn into your very own cash cow.

They exist in every market in every part of the country. They're the properties most people won't touch because most people don't want to deal with property problems. They want to buy a beautiful property right out of the multiple listing book.

Every day, perfectly normal people buy these beautiful rental properties with zero or negative cash flow. They expect to make their money from appreciation and income tax benefits. They're optimists because they're expecting to get their biggest return from appreciation. They're hoping that they'll be able to sell the duplex they bought for $120,000 to somebody else in five years at a price of $150,000. They may or may not be able to do just that. Nobody can say for sure. If they take their initial $120,000 and buy five such duplexes with five such loans and sell them all in five years at a profit of $30,000 each and turn their initial $120,000 into $270,000, they'll look like geniuses. If their properties decline in value even $5,000 each over five years

and their initial $120,000 becomes $95,000, they'll look like dunces.

People who buy beautiful rental properties with negative cash flow are speculators. They sometimes do well, and they sometimes do poorly.

People who buy ordinary rental properties with positive cash flow are investors. They get their cash flow regularly and take their appreciation as it comes, if it comes at all, but they don't count on getting any appreciation. It's strictly a bonus.

Many rental properties do generate enough cash flow to provide a good livelihood for their owners. Find them, buy them, fix them, maintain them, and you can declare your independence from the lockstep, lunch-bucket, briefcase-toting, 9-to-5 world.

They want to ask sellers the right questions.

Q. I'm seriously interested in becoming a landlord. Because I have no experience in the field whatsoever, I recently purchased your *Landlording* book along with a couple of other books on the subject. My wife and I are thinking small (five units or so) until we get some experience under our belts.

My primary question right now is this: What questions should we ask the current landlord who is selling the property? I know the obvious, common-sense questions like how the utilities are covered and whether the tenants are cooperative. What else should we ask? I want to be certain to cover all aspects of the property before making a purchase so we're not blindsided later by something we failed to ask about. I am very determined to get into the business because I'm tired of working long hours at an unfulfilling job just to make someone else rich.
—D.S., Michigan

A. You are already on the right track to becoming a successful landlord. You have a goal. You have a willing spouse. You have good work ethics. You have a thirst for knowledge. You have an inquisitive mind. You have common sense. You have an independent streak in you. All in all, you appear to have good landlording potential.

To realize that potential, you must be willing to close your ears to the naysayers who tell you that you cannot succeed today as a landlord for one reason or another. You must be willing to scoff at the scam artists who spin fantasies about becoming rich quickly by investing in real estate if only you will pay them to divulge their secrets. You must be willing to accept your mistakes and learn from those mistakes. You must be willing to be socked by criticism now and then and turn the other cheek. You must be willing to work long and late hours when necessary. You must be willing to put your landlording life ahead of your personal life in order to work on your properties yourself for a few years at least. You must be willing to clean other people's toilets and pick up other people's trash over and over again. You must be willing to be patient, very patient, until you wake up one day to the realization that you're a "millionaire next door" and you can stop eating so much tuna and beans right out of the cans.

When you're looking to buy your first rental property, you'll be apprehensive all right. Everybody is. Becoming a landlord is a big step, one fraught with responsibilities and obligations such as you have never known before. Don't worry. You'll get used to the frantic calls at dinner time. You'll get used to the excuses for late rents. You'll get used to playing the role of human trash compactor, jumping up and down on stinking garbage in overflowing trash cans. Every landlord with staying power gets used to those things.

To ease your apprehension when buying any rental property which strikes your fancy, whether it's your first or your last, ask the seller some or all of the following forty questions, whichever ones you consider relevant to your deciding whether to purchase a particular piece of property.

1. Do you have written rental agreements? If so, provide copies.

2. Are any tenants on leases? If so, when do the leases expire?

3. Who are the building's problem tenants? What problems are they causing?

4. Are there any tenants who are currently being evicted? Why?

5. Are there any tenants who should be evicted? Why aren't they being evicted?

6. Are there any authorized pets in the building? If so, provide copies of the pet agreements. Are there any unauthorized pets?

7. How do you collect rents?

8. Who pays the utilities–gas, electricity, water, and garbage–the landlord or the tenants?

9. Are there any tenants in arrears?

10. How do you handle late rents?

11. When were the rents last raised or lowered?

12. What are the current rents for each of the units? How were they determined?

13. What are the market rents for each of the units? How do you know?

14. How much of a security deposit are you holding for every tenant?

15. What's the current occupancy?

16. When was the last vacancy?

17. How long was the last unit vacant between the outgoing and incoming tenants?

18. How do you advertise vacancies?

19. Has there been any criminal activity in the area? Has there been any drug activity in the area?

20. What furniture and appliances go with the property?

21. Whose laundry machines are in the coin-operated laundry?

22. What long-term service contracts or equipment leases, if any, affect the property?

23. How do you handle maintenance requests?

24. Whom do you use for plumbing, electrical, painting, roofing, gardening, and general maintenance?

25. When was each of the units last painted inside?

26. When was the outside of the building last painted?

27. How old are the water heaters? Who installed them? Are they properly braced?

28. How old are the heaters and air conditioners? Who installed them?

29. How old is the roof? Who installed it? Has the roof ever leaked?

30. How old is the carpeting in every unit? Who installed it?

31. Does every unit have adequate, working smoke alarms? How do you handle the smoke alarm battery replacements?

32. Where are the fire extinguishers located? When were they last inspected by a professional?

33. Do you have keys to every unit? If not, why not?

34. What is the parking situation? Are the garages billed separately?

35. Have you had any mold problems? If so, where? What remedies have you tried?

36. Is the property subject to any natural calamities? If so, what are they and when did the last one occur?

37. What income and expenses did you re-

port on your last tax return? Provide a copy of that schedule.

38. Have you delegated any management tasks to someone who lives on the premises?

39. How much time do you spend looking after the property?

40. Why do you want to sell the property?

Honest answers to these questions will give you a pretty good idea whether the property will be troublesome to look after and whether it will make you any money while you own it and when you sell it.

Of course, you have to be the judge of the honesty of the person supplying the answers, especially if he sells snake oil or used cars for a living.

She wants to know about rental house and apartment investing.

Q. Should my husband and I be investing in rental houses or apartments?
—B.B., Alaska

A. Market, math, and mindset determine the answer to your question. Let's look at market and math first.

The housing market and the rental market are decidedly different. People will pay big bucks to buy a house of their own because they're buying into a dream, the American dream. Their dream house doesn't need to have a white picket fence out front and Mr. Rodgers for a neighbor. It needs only to be something they can call their own. It could be a cottage on Long Island, a farmhouse on the outskirts of St. Louis, a little ticky-tacky box south of San Francisco, a log cabin near Anchorage, a classic bungalow on Cape Cod, or any of the millions of other domiciles available anywhere across America. No matter what or where that single-family dwelling is, investors must compete with buyers who want to buy it and live in it, and its price is likely to be higher than warranted by the rent it will generate.

There are times and places when a local housing market makes good sense for investors who want to buy rental houses for cash flow, but that's more the exception than the rule today. The exception would be when the rental market is so brisk and the housing market is so sluggish that a house will rent for 1% or more of its market value per month. That's when buying rental houses makes good sense, but that's an exception. The rule is another matter.

Let's say that the market value of a desirable detached three-bedroom house in your area is $180,000. That house would have to rent for $1,300 or more per month in order for it to make good sense as an investment. If the rental market for that house were $900 per month, you'd have to dig into your pocket every month to keep the house because the rent wouldn't even be enough to make the loan payment, let alone pay the taxes and upkeep.

Investors will buy houses for $180,000 and rent them for $900 per month when they're speculating that the houses will appreciate in value and more than compensate them for any monies they have had to pay out of their pockets every month.

Here's the math.

If an investor buys a $180,000 house and keeps it for three years, during which time it appreciates 8% per year, the house is worth $226,750 at the end of three years. That's an increase in value of $46,750. Would that the increase were all profit! It's not.

If the investor puts 20% ($36,000) down on the house and rents it out for $900 per month, there would be an expenditure shortfall of approximately $400 every month. That's what people commonly call "negative cash flow." Deduct three years of negative cash flow ($400 x 36 months = $14,400) and sales costs of 6% ($13,605), and that leaves a profit of $18,745. Take into account the equity buildup ($4,713 on a 30-year loan of $144,000 at 7%), and an annual rent increase of 5% for the second and third years ($1,647), and the investor stands to make a profit of $25,105, which still represents a good return on a cash outlay of $36,000.

The problem with such investing is this: Real estate values are unpredictable. Erase that increase in value of $46,750, and the investor loses money on the house after owning and managing it as a rental property for three years. In fact, the investor loses $21,645.

Now let's look at a four-unit apartment building costing the same amount as the house, $180,000. It will have greater rental income than the house because its market value as a real property investment bears some relationship to its rental income. Also, its pool of buyers is smaller, so there's less upward pressure on the sales price. Instead of competing with all those buyers who want to buy into the American dream, plus all those investors who believe that a rental house is a good investment, apartment building buyers are competing almost exclusively with other investors who believe that apartments are a good investment.

A $180,000 fourplex will generate monthly rents greater than $900. Depending upon the rental market, the aggregate rents will be as low as $1,000 and as high as $2,200. Taking a figure between the low and the high, $1,600, we come up with an entirely different set of numbers than we did for the house.

Here's the math.

If an investor buys a $180,000 fourplex and keeps it for three years, during which time it appreciates 4% per year, half as much as the house, the building is worth $202,475 at the end of three years. That's an increase in value of $22,475, hardly worth bragging about compared to the appreciation in the price of the rental house example.

If the investor puts $36,000 down and rents the units for $1,600 per month, there would be a cash flow of $200 per month. Add up three years of cash flow ($200 x 36 months = $7,200) and deduct sales costs of 6% ($12,149), and that leaves a profit of $17,526. Take into account the equity buildup ($4,713 on a 30-year loan of $144,000 at 7%) and an annual rent increase of 5% for the second and third years ($2,928), and the fourplex investor stands to make a profit of $25,167, almost identical to the rental house investor's profit of $25,105.

Whereas those profit figures are almost identical in an inflationary market, they're very different in a flat market, very different indeed. If neither property appreciates or appreciates at a slower rate, the fourplex investor comes out far ahead of the rental house investor because the fourplex investor has cash flow every month.

Here's the math.

If neither property appreciates at all, if the rents stay flat, and if neither investor sells at the end of three years, the rental house investor loses $400 per month ($14,400) in negative cash flow and gains equity buildup of $4,713, for a loss of $9,687, while the fourplex investor pockets $200 per month ($7,200) in positive cash flow and gains equity buildup of $4,713, for a gain of $11,913. Because the one figure is negative and the other is positive, the difference between them amounts to a significant amount, $21,600.

Of course, these examples are simplifications. Any number of factors, such as evictions, vacancies, unforeseen capital expenditures, deferred maintenance, income tax brackets, market variables, available financing, and sales costs, will tilt the figures one way or the other. They make every rental property investment unique, whether it's a house or a high-rise apartment building.

Having looked at the market and the math, let's look at mindset, your mindset. Some investors would rather put their money into rental houses than apartments because they believe that houses require less management and that houses will continue to appreciate forever. Some investors would rather put their money into apartments because they aren't bothered by management, they like the numbers, and they don't want to rely on appreciation triggered by inflation to make their investment pay off.

Which are you?

Many investors have made piles of money investing solely in rental houses. I am not one of them. I'm a more conservative investor. I'll take appreciation when it comes my way, but I don't want to count on it to make my investment pay off.

He wants to know something about portfolio mix and city size.

Q. I'm 37 years old and thinking about retiring early from my current job to invest in real estate full time. I expect to have approximately $400,000 available for rental property purchases and expenses, as well as $200,000 invested elsewhere for retirement and emergencies.

What approach would you recommend for someone who is just starting out? Should I buy a fourplex? Or should I buy something either smaller or larger? I don't want to start with something too big and make a monumental mistake, nor do I want to start too small and waste precious time accumulating a portfolio of properties. I want to manage my own property for a few years, even longer if I enjoy it, but I envision turning things over to a property management company eventually.

Next, is it easier to trade up to larger complexes over time rather than continue buying a number of smaller units?

Finally, I intend to relocate to a smaller city (50-100,000 population), somewhere cooler than where I currently live in Texas, to start this new career. Is it much more difficult to buy bigger properties (possibly even commercial) in such a limited market or is city size of minor importance? —R.G., Texas

A. Start small, by all means. Landlording is not for everybody. It may not be for you, and you won't know for sure one way or the other without putting your tender feet to the landlording fire.

Anything from four to twelve units in a blue-collar neighborhood will test your mettle. Give yourself twelve months.

If you find yourself cringing every time the phone on your property line rings, if you find yourself procrastinating about pursuing tenants who are late with their rent, if you find yourself resenting the visits you have to make to the property for one reason or another, if you find yourself feeling uncomfortable about being called a greedy landlord, if you find yourself begrudging the money you have to spend to maintain or improve the property, if you find yourself troubled about what to do when tenants tearfully tell you their hard-luck stories, then put your rental property up for sale and put your investment monies elsewhere.

SHIRLEY REALLY BECAME INTERESTED IN RENTAL PROPERTIES WHEN SHE BEGAN WATCHING THE LANDLORDING CHANNEL

If you find yourself taking the role of landlord in stride and maybe, just maybe, enjoying it a little, start looking around for more property. You're landlord material.

Anyone who is landlord material and has had landlording experience, knows better than to hire a rental property management company to look after things. Such companies never do as good a job as the owner. That's right. They never do as good a job as the owner. They don't have an owner's mindset. They throw money at problems rather than study each problem carefully to determine the best and most cost-effective solution.

Owners who don't want to, or can't, do everything themselves do better by hiring out specific jobs, such as the on-site management, the gardening, the maintenance, and the bookkeeping, and retaining for themselves the job of overseeing operations.

When owners want to expand their operations, they generally trade into larger properties because larger properties are easier for an owner to manage than a scattering of smaller properties, and they yield a greater return. A forty-eight-unit property takes just as much of an owner's time as a twelve-unit property. Each has one on-site manager and one set of problems to deal with, but the larger property, given that the two have similar rents, will yield four times the gross income and more than four times the net income. Also, because there's a greater pool of buyers for smaller properties and because these buyers tend to be less sophisticated than the buyers of larger properties, smaller properties typically sell for more per rent dollar than larger properties. Hence, smaller properties yield a lower return per purchase dollar.

As for city size, it's important all right, but more important is diversity. You want to invest in areas which have a diverse income base. You don't want to invest in areas which depend upon a single employer or a single industry, either of which would affect your income dramatically during one of their downturns.

In general, you will find that areas with greater populations will have more investment opportunities than areas with smaller populations, but I have long invested successfully in communities with populations around five thousand and can recommend them so long as they have diverse economies. Areas with populations of 50-100,000 are plenty big enough to have investment opportunities so long as they, too, have diverse economies.

You are wise to give landlording a try, and you are wise to be inquiring about some of the business's many aspects before you ever give it a try. Go ahead now and study it some more. Then do give it a try.

He'd like to buy a duplex and live in half.

Q. I am considering the purchase of a duplex. I would live in one unit and rent out the other. This would allow me to build equity in the property while lessening my mortgage payment. Further down the road, I would move out of the duplex, finance a home, and rent out the entire duplex. Essentially, I'm trying to buy a home and begin investing in real estate simultaneously.

I was wondering whether this scenario makes any sense at all. If so, are there any resources (books, periodicals, etc.) that you are aware of which describe this situation? I already have a copy of *Landlording*. Any help would be greatly appreciated.

—W.E., New Mexico

A. Your scenario makes all the sense in the world. Americans have been breaking into the real estate market for years using just this technique.

Since you already have a copy of *Landlording*, you have many clues as to what you face in becoming a landlord. The only other book I would recommend that you read is the William Nickerson book, *How I Turned $1,000 into Five Million in Real Estate in My Spare Time*. The book's numbers are out of date, but its good advice still holds true (though out of print, you will find it at libraries and at used-book stores).

As for periodicals, subscribe to the *Robert Bruss Real Estate Newsletter* (bobbruss.com).

They want to buy house across the street to use as a rental.

Q. Our neighbor across the street is planning to sell her house this summer, and my wife and I are considering buying it from her to use as a rental. The house can easily be switched from a single-family dwelling to a duplex and would bring in $900-1,000 per month in rent in either configuration. Purchase price would be in the $125,000 range. We have several questions as we consider this possibility.

1) Is there a typical minimum financial position considered advisable before embarking on such a course? We can probably pull together about $10,000 as a down payment, with no debt other than the $65,000 mortgage on our home, which is worth around $95,000. Our annual income is around $45,000. Are there ways that people in our position can structure things to make landlording workable? Are there any general banking guidelines on this as there are on purchasing a primary residence? Are there any books we should read on the subject?

2) We work, attend church, and generally hang out with a large number of college and post-college young adults, and thus think we would have little trouble finding fairly reliable tenants without advertising. Is it possible to rent entirely by word-of-mouth without triggering anti-discrimination laws? For instance, because our tenants would also be our immediate neighbors, we hope to be renting to folks we already know. Would we be required to rent to any qualified person who inquires even if we are not advertising?

We're pretty handy with repairs, etc., and the house is within plain sight of ours, so we think it would be relatively easy to look after. What potential pitfalls do you see in our scenario?

—M.B., North Carolina

A. Whew, to answer your many questions in full, I could write a book or two. I'll try not to. I'll restrain myself and give you my short-answer version.

Understand upfront that landlording is a business. It's not something you get into for pride or health or recreation. Indeed, it can rob you of your pride and your health and your time for recreation. You must make money at it, or you should never go into it.

You can make good money at landlording only if you buy right, that is, if the potential rents will justify a rental property's price. Buy wrong, and you'll be suffering losses every month.

Rental houses and duplexes do not produce the cash flow which larger rental properties produce because their prices do not depend upon income at all. Their prices rise and fall according to the demand for owner-occupied residences. As a consequence, a house which is worth $100,000 to someone who plans to buy and occupy it may be worth only $500 per month to someone who plans to rent and occupy it. An investor who buys such a house would lose money every month because the rent wouldn't cover the cost of owning it.

In your case, the numbers indicate that you would be losing money every month. The monthly rent for a house costing $125,000 ought to be 1% of the market value, or $1,250, rather than $900 to $1,000. The down payment for a rental house costing $125,000 ought to be 20%, or $25,000, rather than 8%, or $10,000.

Let's look at other relevant numbers. If you can get a $115,000 mortgage at 7% for 25 years, the payments would be $813 per month. Let's say that property taxes are $100 per month, insurance is $50 per month, and maintenance costs average $50 per month. We're now at $1,013, and we haven't even addressed sewer, water, garbage, or yard service, which admittedly you might get the tenants to pay.

If you're getting $1,000 in rent for the house, whether in a single-family or a duplex configuration, you'd have to lay out at least $13 from your own pocket every month to support your landlording business.

In return, you would be getting some equity buildup, some tax benefits, and maybe some appreciation.

The investment would be better if you could buy the house for $100,000, put $10,000 down and get the seller to carry back a $90,000 note at 7% with payments of $636 per month for 25 years. After collecting rent of $1,000 per month and paying taxes, insurance, and maintenance, you'd have close to $165 in positive cash flow. That's much better than a negative cash flow of $13.

Even then, the acquisition has an element of risk. How much risk are you willing to take?

You could have unexpected tenant troubles, roof troubles, heater troubles, air conditioner troubles, water heater troubles, or vacancy troubles which prove to be costly and beyond your means. What then?

People do buy rental houses every day for $125,000 with minimum down payments in markets where the rent for those houses is $1,000 per month. They expect luck to bail them out. They expect luck to provide them with so much appreciation that they can sell the house within a few years for considerably more than what they paid for it.

That's speculation. That's not investment.

Rather than buy the house across the street with its marginal investment numbers, look for a nearby property which needs some work you could do yourself in order to increase its value. Look for a fixer-upper house on the market for $80,000 in a neighborhood where similar houses in good condition sell for $125,000. Spend two months and $10,000 fixing it up, and then rent it out for $1,000. That's a sure way to make money investing in rental houses.

As for using word-of-mouth advertising exclusively for your rental property in order to avoid anti-discrimination laws, you could, but you shouldn't, that is, you shouldn't if you plan to use word-of-mouth advertising strictly to keep from having to abide by anti-discrimination laws. Use word-of-mouth advertising only if it's the best advertising vehicle to use for your particular rental property.

Don't worry about anti-discrimination laws. Learn them and follow them all the time, and you eliminate the worry of being successfully sued for illegal discrimination.

You put yourself in just as much jeopardy by limiting your potential renters to friends and acquaintances who respond to your word-of-mouth advertising as you do by renting to complete strangers, Joe and Jill Blow, who meet your standards and respond to your wider ranging advertising. Some landlords who rented to relatives and friends thinking that all would go well, have some mighty sad stories to tell.

Landlording has its pitfalls. No matter how careful you are, no matter knowledgeable you are, no matter how experienced you are, no matter how bright you are, you'll fall into a few of them. Those landlords who pick themselves up and go on will always do well.

Novice investor wants to know more about financing.

Q. Although I bought my first rental property almost two years ago, I still consider myself to be a novice investor. There's so much I don't know about this business. I'm always learning something new. Recently I found another property that I'd like to buy, but I haven't been able to find the right financing to buy it. All the lenders I've approached have wanted large down payments and are quoting high interest rates. A friend told me that I could get better terms if I told lenders that I was going to occupy the property myself, but I don't want to lie about something like that.

Is there some way to buy rental properties on reasonable terms with only a modest down payment?

Every so often I see ads in my local paper for a free seminar where they teach you how to buy properties for no money down. Is there any truth to those ads? Is there something I'm missing about financing?

—F.M., Pennsylvania

A. You are wise not to lie about occupying a property you want to buy just to get better financing. Lying on an application for a loan at a federally regulated lender is a federal offense. It's fraud, and it could cost you significant legal fees, fines, and anguish if you were ever to be found out. Don't commit fraud for any reason, certainly not to buy another rental property. You want to live out your days knowing that you won't have to spend any of them in a federal penitentiary, no matter how comfortable it is, no matter which scofflaw celebrity might become your cell pal.

There are any number of perfectly legal ways to buy another rental property on reasonable terms with a modest down payment.

Don't expect to learn all there is to know about them by attending the "free," heavily advertised "seminars" given by hucksters who travel the country teasing the gullible and twisting their arms to buy costly follow-on seminars. These hucksters put on a well orchestrated show, make outrageous claims, display great conviction, tell graduates' success stories, and offer guarantees, but they don't deliver on their promises. Try to get your money back when you discover that their techniques don't work in real life, and they will blame you for failing to succeed. They will say you didn't pay close enough attention or you didn't work hard enough or you didn't apply the techniques correctly. They will say that the failure is yours, not theirs, and your failure doesn't qualify for their money-back guarantee.

The hucksters claim to possess buying and financing secrets which they will divulge only to a select few who shell out thousands of dollars for the information. They are stretching the truth. They have no secrets, no proprietary information. They put powder and paint on old terms and old techniques. Don't waste your time attending their pitch sessions. Don't waste your money buying their costly follow-on seminars.

Instead, look around for a local real estate investors group which holds regular meetings featuring speakers with areas of expertise relevant to real estate investing. Some speakers will be hawking expensive materials, to be sure. Listen to them and ask them questions, but beware of paying an artificially high price for their materials because of claims that you are paying hundreds to make thousands. Other speakers will share freely what they have learned from experience, expecting nothing more in return than applause and recognition. Listen and ask questions.

Better still, spend your time reading material on financing written by reputable experts like Bob Bruss (bobbruss.com) and John T. Reed (johntreed.com), each of whom has written knowledgeably about real estate financing.

Subscribe to the monthly *Robert Bruss Real Estate Newsletter*. At $35 per year, it's the biggest real-estate-advice bargain there is, and it regularly covers real estate financing. For a paltry $4 each, you may purchase back issues, such as #04359, "Secrets of Buying Your Home or Investment Property for Nothing Down" and #01328, "Tips and Tricks for Profitable Mortgage Refinancing."

John T. Reed publishes clearly written, nononsense booklets of sixty to a hundred pages on a number of real estate topics. The booklets, with titles such as "Fundamentals of Real Estate Finance" and "Real Estate Finance Techniques," sell for $29.95 each through his website.

You won't find these experts recommending that you borrow cash using a dozen low-interest credit cards and that you then use the money to make a down payment on a rental property. You won't find them recommending that you focus on buying houses from vulnerable FSBO (for sale by owner) seniors who know only that they need to sell the family home at any price and on any terms in order to move into a retirement home. You won't find them recommending that you hoodwink lenders with bogus or quasi-truthful information. Cockamamie approaches such as these flow freely at the huckster seminars and can get you into all kinds of trouble.

Financing is the key to making real estate acquisitions. That's for sure. The more you know about it, the better. After all, financing is what gives us investors the leverage we need to make the real money there is to be made in real estate.

When we buy a property for 10% down, and it appreciates 5%, our equity doesn't increase by 5%, it increases by 50%! When we buy a property for 20% down, and it appreciates 5%, our equity doesn't increase by 5%, it increases by 25%! When we buy a property for 30% down, and it appreciates 5%, our equity doesn't increase by 5%, it increases by 17%! The leverage provided by financing makes these good numbers multiply greatly in our favor.

Contrary to what many investors believe, real estate financing is much more than loans from institutional lenders on inflexible terms. It's loans from sellers, from private parties, from insurance companies, from syndications, from Wall Street, and from hard-money lenders. Each source has its place, and each source has its terms, depending upon the collateral and the borrower and the attendant risk. Each source wants to get paid back over time with interest and without hassle.

As a real estate investor, you should be developing a reputation for yourself as a good credit risk. You should be working to improve your FICO® (Fair Isaac Corporation) credit score. You should be demonstrating that lenders ought to give you better terms than they give the average borrower because you will repay the money you borrow from them no matter what happens. You will shoulder the burden if your rental property collateral has a vacancy problem and fails to produce enough cash to repay the loan. You will sell your Harley. You will rent out rooms in your house. You will pull your children from their private colleges and put them to work at a Starbucks. You will take in laundry. You will do whatever you have to do to repay the loan.

Unless you're a Walter Shorenstein, a Donald Trump, or a Sam Zell, you won't count for much at a big bank. You'll never become known there.

Move your bank accounts to a local bank, a bank where loan decisions are made locally rather than at a corporate headquarters a thousand miles away. Make yourself known personally to the president of that local bank, and keep applying for larger and larger lines of credit so you can pounce on good real estate deals as soon as you hear about them.

The people at that local bank will listen to you when you come to them for money and will give you favorable terms, all because they know you and know that you will pay it back as agreed.

Besides identifying a good local source of institutional financing, look for real estate which comes with its own financing. The physical property and the financing, whether seller financing or assumable financing, make up a package which is more attractive than a physical property in need of financing.

Seller financing is the best financing you can get, and you should always try to get it. You don't have to qualify for it. You don't have to submit bundles of paperwork for it. You don't have to pay points for it. You don't have to pay high rates for it, nor do you have to wait for it.

Ask the sellers of the property you want to buy whether they will carry the loan themselves, and give them a few reasons why they should. They will get a higher interest rate than they would get if they put their proceeds in a savings account or certificate of deposit, they will have a reliable income stream, and they will pay capital gains taxes on the payments rather than on the entire amount of their gain. Those are powerful reasons for them to carry the loan.

Keep attending local real estate investors meetings, keep reading about financing techniques, keep making all of your loan payments on time, keep getting yourself noticed at your local bank, and keep looking for properties to buy with seller financing, and you will be getting the best financing available when you go to buy your next rental property.

He wants to know how to avoid paying capital gains taxes.

Q. I own a rental house here in Michigan and have heard that I can sell it and reinvest my equity in another income property without paying capital gains. Is this true? Would I be able to sell this house in order to build a duplex for the same purpose somewhere else? If so, how much time do I have to reinvest? —M.K., Michigan

A. You may indeed sell your income property and reinvest the proceeds in another income property. Income property owners "out West" here use this technique all the time, and it's catching on elsewhere rapidly because it's such a good deal for investors who want to build equity and avoid paying capital gains taxes every time they move up to larger properties.

Before this procedure made its way into the tax code officially, it was known as a "Starker exchange," after the man who tested its legality in tax court and won his case. Now these exchanges are commonly known as 1031 delayed exchanges, after the IRS Code number.

The procedure does have a strict timetable, which you must follow religiously to reap the benefits. Fail to follow the timetable, and you'll wind up writing a big check to the IRS for the capital gains taxes you were trying to avoid.

Basically here's how the procedure works. Arrange to sell your property and put the entire proceeds into a bank account controlled by a trustworthy intermediary ("facilitators" have sprung up to act as advisors and intermediaries in these transactions, but they charge too much for what is essentially some simple paperwork and paper shuffling; read the regulations yourself; they're clear enough and helpful enough to guide you through the entire procedure; or else read "How to Do a Delayed Exchange" by John T. Reed; then enlist the services of a trustworthy friend who qualifies to be an intermediary according to the code, and take the friend out for a "night on the town" once the exchange is complete). Within forty-five days of closing on the property you sold, identify up to three properties you want to acquire. You may exchange into any one or all three, but whatever you acquire must be worth more than the property you sold, and you must put all of your sales proceeds into your acquisition(s), or else you will have to pay the taxes on that portion of your capital gain which you didn't put into your acquisition(s). After identifying what you want to acquire, close the transaction within six months.

It is simple. It does save you bundles of tax dollars. Do it. You'll see.

No-money-down boot-camp grad is waiting for the money to roll in.

Q. A year ago I saw a full-page ad in my local daily newspaper advertising a free wealth-building seminar. It said I would learn no-money-down techniques I could use to become a millionaire by investing in real estate. It said I would learn how to buy properties with no money down, and it gave testimonials from ordinary people who had used the techniques to make a lot of money in real estate in just a short period of time.

I'm a hard-working single mother, and I would like to quit my day job to work for myself. I've never enjoyed working for other people and have never had a job which paid very much or was very fulfilling. When my husband ran off with his young secretary and left me with two kids, I didn't have much in the way of skills and had never held a good job. Before we were married, I worked as a waitress and a bank teller. That was the extent of my work experience. My husband

always wanted me to be a stay-at-home mom, and I agreed to stay at home for the benefit of the children.

I can't live on the alimony and child support he pays. Even though he pays regularly, it's not enough for us to have any sort of a life, and I haven't been able to convince a judge that we ought to get more. After not working for ten years, I took a job as a bank teller, but I know that I can't progress to a good-paying job at the bank unless I go back to school and get at least an AA degree from the local community college.

I don't have the time or the inclination to go back to school for years. I decided that I needed something quicker to help me make more money, so when I saw the newspaper ad for the seminar, I was interested. I read every word in the ad and thought that real estate investing might be my ticket to a more independent life.

I went to the free seminar and got caught up in the excitement. They talked a lot about people who had taken their weekend "boot camp" for $3,000 and had made twenty thousand dollars, fifty thousand dollars and more on their very first deal. When they offered to cut the price of the boot camp by fifty percent and charge it to my credit card, I signed up. Most of the people in the room signed up, too. It seemed like a good deal.

The boot camp did teach me a few things. I know it wasn't worth $3,000, and it probably wasn't worth the $1,500 I paid because I have since learned that the same information is available in books on the subject of real estate investing, but what the boot camp did was give me enough confidence to try investing in real estate.

The boot camp leader told us that one way to do a no-money-down deal is to use a double lease-option. Take out a lease-option on an ugly house for as long a term as possible, make the house attractive, rent it out on another lease-option for a higher amount, sell it to the tenants during or at the end of their lease for the amount of their option, exercise the original option at the same time, and pocket the difference. Of all the techniques they gave us at boot camp, that one sounded the best to me, so I tried it.

I was so eager to make some money that I went "whole hog." I tried it with three houses. I know now that I should have been more patient and tried it with just one.

Here's my problem. One of these deals worked

out so well that it could be used as a success story for advertising the boot camp. It made me $12,000. The other two have given me nothing but trouble, and I'm wondering what I ought to do about them because I'm losing money every month. One of the tenants turned out to be a deadbeat and had to be evicted. He cost me $2,000 in lost rent and $1,500 for the eviction. The other tenants I still have are okay, but they told me they're not interested in exercising their lease-option.

What should I do with these two houses? The one's empty, and I'm having to pay the rent to the original owner every month as agreed. That's costing me $950 per month, and I tell you it's money I hate to part with. Should I let it go back to the original owner and make nothing for all the work I've done there? Should I put it on the market and see what I can get for it? If I have to pay a real estate commission of 5 or 6%, I think I may lose money on this one. If I sell it myself, I may make a little money.

Should I keep the other house a little longer and try to get new tenants who will want to exercise a new lease-option?

I don't know where to turn. I was so optimistic after boot camp. The techniques they taught us seemed foolproof. I never thought I'd have so much trouble. After my first deal worked out so well, I began to think that I was on my way to easy street. Now I'm in the dumps and thinking that these other deals are going to drag me down.

Please help!

—S.S., Oregon

A. Life is full of examples of expectations which turned out differently from the expectation. Your marriage is one example. The expensive boot camp you attended is a second, and two of your three lease-option houses are a third.

Expensive real estate investment boot camps are as much of a scourge as are timeshares. Both are so overpriced that they have to be sold through high-pressure operations designed to make coal look as valuable as diamonds.

Tough is the person who can resist being worn down by the sales pitches. You weren't tough enough to resist the pitch thrown at you, but you were at least bright enough to absorb the boot camp's lessons and motivated enough to give one a try.

Let your experience with two of the three houses you lease-optioned be another lesson, a lesson you didn't learn in boot camp: Not every real estate deal turns out as expected. Real estate deals are not sure things. Besides not being sure, they are not easy, not quick, not simple, and sometimes not profitable. They can be some of those things, or even all of those things, some of the time but not often enough to be labeled sure, easy, quick, simple, and profitable. Be surprised when you encounter a deal which is all of those things. Feel fortunate that one of your deals was.

Having said that, I want to commend you for trying a technique you learned in boot camp and for trying it three times. You have smarts and you have guts and you have motivation enough. You will succeed. Focus on the one textbook deal you did rather than on the two duds, and tell yourself that you can repeat that textbook deal. You can, you know, and you can go beyond it to make more good deals and bigger good deals. Tell yourself that you can make the duds work, too, and then make them work.

Evictions are downers. I know. I've done enough of them myself to know the procedure well, well enough to write a book about them. Now that you have been through one yourself, you have become inoculated against them, and you'll be more aware of potential eviction problems when you're still selecting tenants and can reject those applicants you believe would have to be evicted later.

Whatever you do now with the two houses you still have, don't panic and try to dump them, and don't let them keep you down in the dumps. Consider your options. There are many.

Start by getting a free internet appraisal of the houses. One source is ditech.com, which offers no-strings-attached appraisals as its second option under "Calculators." These appraisals are not carved in granite or even pounded into sheet metal. They're rough figures based upon comparison sales. They will help you decide whether to buy, sell, hold, extend, or abandon.

That's right. You have five ownership choices as a lessee-optionee. You may buy (buy the house), sell (sell the house), hold (continue the lease-option), extend (secure an extension of the lease-option), or abandon (return all rights to the legal owner).

As with any other business transaction, you must always keep your eyes on the money. If you're going to make any big money on the two houses, you're going to make it by taking advantage of the spread between your option price and the sales price. You're not going to make it by renting to tenants. In fact, tenants may be a hindrance.

Tenants are a hindrance if they don't pay their rent, if they don't exercise their option, if they don't let you have ready access to fix up the house, if they don't let you show the house when it's ready for sale, and if they don't move when you have a ready buyer.

Tenants are an asset to you if they pay rent while you're doing the fix-up, if they are otherwise cooperative, and if they exercise their option to buy at a price which assures you a profit. If they exercise their option, you'll save paying a sales commission of 5% or 6%, and that alone could be the profit you make on your deal.

Think about selling that empty house without even bothering to find more tenants. Check its appraisal value, and if you think you can break even or make a profit from selling it, make it presentable, and put it on the market. If you have committed to a long lease-option and you don't think you can break even or make a profit from selling it, then find new tenants or call the legal owner and negotiate a return of the property. You may discover that the legal owner would be glad to get the property back in much better shape than it was when you took it over.

The second house is less of an urgent concern because you have tenants who are paying rent and are on a lease. You may want to offer them the equivalent of a month's rent in cash if they will let you put the house on the market and if they will move out when a new buyer wants to move in rather than at the end of their lease. By all means, put any such agreement in writing and give them the cash only when they have fulfilled their commitment as agreed. If they won't agree, bide your time until just prior to the end of their lease. Give them notice, and put the house up for sale.

Yes, the two houses do have their complications for you, but they're not insurmountable complications. Fortunately, you are working with appreciating assets, not depreciating assets, and you have added value to the houses by fixing them up. Selling them should net you a profit.

The next time you do a similar deal, you might want to forego finding tenants entirely. Negotiate a good lease-option on an ugly house, make it presentable as quickly as possible, and sell it as quickly as possible. That's where the money is.

Buyers want tenant info and pet policy before they take over.

Q. We are not landlords yet, but we have made an offer to buy a triplex which has tenants in two apartments and none in the third. The vacant apartment needs renovating before it can be rented.

The real estate agent hasn't shown us any rental agreements but said she can get them for us. She told us that the one tenant has been there for over eleven years and the other for seven years. Should we just wait to see if our offer is accepted and we become owners before we have these tenants sign new rental agreements?

We in no way want to do anything to make these tenants leave. They are older folks and seem to be set in their ways. The current owner isn't taking care of the property, so we are sure that if we show them that we are willing to make improvements, they will want to stay. We still want to make sure we have agreements with them in writing.

Should we find out from the real estate agent right now if the tenants are current with their rents?

Also, once we fix up the empty apartment, can we specify that there will be no pets allowed there, even if the other tenants have them? The existing tenants have cats, fish, and hamsters. Because they've been there so long, we would not ask them to get rid of their pets. We definitely do not want dogs on the premises, and we don't want any animals in the apartment which we'll be renovating.
—W.K., Pennsylvania

A. Your offer on this property should include a clause stating that prior to closing you must be provided with current rental agreements and with copies of the last year's rental receipts or some other proof of the current tenants' payment history. You certainly do not want to take possession of a rental property and then have to evict the tenants because they aren't paying the rent.

You do not have to accept pets in a rental if you don't want to, but when some tenants have grandfathered pets and you no longer allow pets, you must expect problems. Before renting to anybody, have a heart-to-heart talk with them and explain your pet policy clearly. Make sure that your rental agreement covers the policy as well.

"As is" property has more problems than they bargained for.

Q. My wife and I are buying a five-unit rental property consisting of a house divided into three units plus two free-standing cottages. Although we knew the buildings needed some obvious repairs, the seller indicated that he did not want to fix anything. He wanted to sell the property in an "as is" condition.

We agreed to buy "as is" with contingencies based upon the results of a physical inspection and a termite inspection. The house is a 100-year-old Victorian, so we expected a few problems. Overall, the physical inspection went pretty well, but some plumbing and electrical code deficiencies surfaced. The termite inspection revealed certain non-structural termite problems, which, according to the termite inspector, must be fixed before escrow closes. There were also a few other problems that aren't code violations as such but would cost quite a bit to remedy. We didn't know about any of these problems until the inspections, and now we feel our "as is" bid was a little high.

Is the seller responsible for bringing the building up to code before close of escrow, or is he off the hook because he wants to sell it as is?

We are getting estimates for the work and plan to confront him with the cost to try and get him to bring the buildings up to code or lower the purchase price accordingly. We're not sure whether he'll fix anything out of the goodness of his heart, but if he were at least required to bring the building up to code, it certainly would save us money and headaches.

—A.P., California

A. Consider yourself fortunate for having learned about these building deficiencies before taking possession. You're in a much better position to negotiate with the seller now than you would have been after taking possession, when he might have taken his proceeds from the sale and committed them to some frivolity or other investment.

Now that you know more about the buildings than you knew when you submitted your offer, you can revise the offer accordingly. That's why you had contingencies in the offer to begin with. You are well within your rights to revise it, too. Don't be shy. You have to look after your own interests. Nobody else will. The seller isn't going to fix anything out of the goodness of his heart. You have to tell him what you want, and you have to be willing to walk away from the deal if he won't give you what you want.

Good real estate agents learn what's important to the buyer and the seller in every transaction, and they try to satisfy these primary concerns.

In this case, for whatever reason, the seller's primary concern appears to be to sell the buildings "as is." Fine. You can buy the buildings "as is," but you must adjust the price to reflect their condition or have funds held in escrow to pay for the work which needs to be done.

You're in a strong position, stronger than you think. You don't have to buy the buildings. You can walk away. The buyer needs you or else he's stuck with buildings he no longer wants and work he doesn't want to do. If he can't satisfy you, and you can't satisfy him, there should be no transaction.

You certainly don't want to be stuck with buildings which aren't worth what you paid for them, buildings which will drain your resources and make you unhappy. Determine what will make you a happy buyer and negotiate until you get it, or put this deal behind you and start looking for another property.

2
Facing Life
as a Landlord

New landlord has
questions and more questions.

Q. I am a first-time landlord with a nine-unit apartment complex. I have had some tenants ask me for lots of repairs, and I'm not quite sure how many of these repairs I should be taking care of myself as the landlord and how many they should be taking care of themselves as tenants.

Can you provide me with a list of repairs that are reasonable for tenants to take care of themselves? I'd like to put them in the rental agreement I plan to start using as the new owner.

One repair item some tenants asked me to take care of was their plugged garbage disposer. They jammed the disposer with spoiled meat, and it stopped working. They didn't even try to clean it out. They called and asked me to fix it. When I arrived, I almost gagged at the disgusting mess of rotting meat I found. I replaced the disposer for them because it was rather old anyway, and I figured that removing their foul food and coaxing the old disposer back to life would be more time-consuming than replacing it. Do you think I should have asked them to remove the jammed mess of meat themselves instead of taking over the whole job myself?

Another thing they have complained about are cockroaches. I had their apartment and the two adjoining apartments treated by a pest control company. The pest control worker said that he had been there many times before we owned the complex and that he was never able to rid this particular apartment of roaches. He said that he could kill the roaches running around when he was there but that the tenants needed to keep their apartment cleaner so the roaches wouldn't return.

I must say that I was horrified by how dirty their apartment was. When I was replacing the disposer, I noticed crumbs and bits of food all over the place, on the counter, on the stove, on the kitchen floor, and even on the carpet.

How should I handle their lack of cleanliness? How can I rid their apartment of cockroaches in the midst of their uncleanliness? Can they or the other tenants stop paying rent and sue me if they have cockroaches and claim that their apartments are uninhabitable as a result?

These same problem tenants, who are on a month-to-month agreement, also have never put up a security deposit. Can I legally require them to give me the same security deposit which all the other tenants have paid? I am worried that they might claim I am retaliating against them because they have made so many complaints.

I have been requiring my new tenants to come up with a $500 security deposit and have stated in the contract that $200 of that amount is non-refundable. Should I require these old tenants to come up with a $500 deposit as well? I am not certain whether I can require them to pay the $200 nonrefundable portion since they already occupy their apartment.

I read in my state's landlord-tenant law that I can ask for a security deposit from existing tenants but that I have to give them three months to pay it if they have been there a year or more, and these tenants have. The statute also says that a "security deposit" must be refundable unless items are damaged, so what should I call the non-refundable part? Can I consider it a "cleaning fee"?

The problem tenants have told me that their apartment was in really poor shape when they moved in and that they fixed it up better than it was. I have my doubts about that. It is poorly cared for and very dirty. How would I determine what to give them back out of their deposit since I never saw the apartment when they moved in?

I'd like to raise the rent on my problem tenants now in hopes that they would move out, but how can I do it without seeming to be retaliating? I plan to raise everybody's rent in another couple of months, when they will have had a full year since the previous landlord raised their rents.

I am pretty frustrated with these particular tenants and am not sure what to do other than to give them a notice to terminate tenancy.
—J.F., Oregon

A. When you bought that nine-unit apartment complex of yours as a first-time landlord, you may not have realized that you were also enrolling in Landlording 101 at Hard Knocks College. You were, you know. Most of the classes there are taught by tenants, and the teaching and learning never end. The best of the teachers are problem tenants, and you should be grateful that you have some. You're learning some valuable lessons from them, lessons which will help you become a better landlord as you travel down landlording's bumpy road.

Your questions about repairs, roaches, nonrefundable deposits, cleaning fees, and retaliation have all surfaced because of your problem tenants. They're good questions, and you need to know the answers so you can stay out of trouble.

You already know that your state's landlord-tenant laws provide some of the answers to landlording questions, and you must know that those laws are now available for everyone to consult over the internet. No longer do you have to visit a law library or an attorney's office to consult them. Access is easy for you. It's also easy for your tenants, so you ought to assume that your tenants know as much about the laws as you do, and you won't be too surprised when they quote a law correctly now and then.

Landlord-tenant laws cannot circumscribe every possible circumstance landlords face because there are so many variations in circumstances, and for that same reason, neither can a handbook. You asked for a list of repairs tenants might be expected to perform for themselves. That's something you will have to write yourself because there are far too many variations in properties for such a list to be useful at every property. Heaters differ from property to property, as do air conditioners, toilets, faucets, sanitary waste systems, locks, floor coverings, windows, window coverings, appliances, wiring, electrical panels, light fixtures, roofs, fireplaces, yards, walk-ways, fences, and pest problems. An all-inclusive list of repairs for every property would require forty pages, whereas a list you prepare for a particular property might require only one page. Begin writing that page as follows:

"We want to keep your dwelling in good repair. That's our job as landlords. We know that pipes burst, pests appear, light switches break, roofs leak, and faucets malfunction all on their own sometimes, and when they do, nobody may be at fault. We also know that pipes burst because tenants sometimes fail to leave the heat on when the temperature drops below freezing. We know that pests appear when tenants leave food around to attract them. We know that light switches break when children play with them or adults hit them wrong. We know that roofs leak when tenants poke something through them. We know that faucets malfunction when tenants manhandle them. In other words, sometimes nobody is at fault when something breaks, and sometimes you as tenants are at fault when something breaks. When nobody is at fault, we will fix what's wrong at no cost to you. When you are at fault, we will fix what's wrong and charge you for the repair.

"Only in an emergency and only after trying several times to contact us first should you ever contact a repair person to fix something. If you do contact a repair person without contacting us first, you will have to pay the repair bill. We will not pay it.

"You should know where to shut off the water, the electricity, and the gas to your dwelling so that you may shut them off in an emergency. You should also know the location of the nearest fire extinguisher. If you don't already know where these things are, ask us and we will show you.

"We expect you to keep your dwelling reasonably clean inside and out. Keeping a clean house costs nothing. Even a prairie family living in a log cabin could keep a clean house. There is no excuse for a dirty house. Besides, a dirty house attracts pests and mold and causes illnesses."

Continue writing that page by citing specifics related to your particular rental property.

Know that you face the same dilemma every landlord faces. You want to keep your property in good repair, and you want your tenants to notify you whenever there's a problem because you don't want that problem to become a big problem. At the same time, you don't want to be bothered by too many little problems, problems they should be handling themselves.

That spoiled meat you found in the problem tenants' garbage disposer is something they should have handled themselves before you ever diagnosed the disposer. They put the meat there. They could remove it. At the very least, they could have helped you remove it while you made sure that the job was handled safely. When it was removed and you'd rinsed the disposer, you could have shown them how to reset the overload switch, and if that didn't work, you could have shown them how to check the breaker or fuse. If nothing worked, you would be saddled with the job of replacement. That's a job for you, not them.

Their messy apartment is something they should definitely be handling themselves, and you shouldn't tolerate it. Tell them what you expect in the way of cleanliness, and tell them why. Tell them that their mess is attracting roaches, not only to their apartment, but also to the neighbors', and there is no way to get rid of roaches when tenants are providing an endless source of food for them. Tell them what the pest control worker told you. Tell them that you can do only so much to exterminate the roaches. The rest is up to them. They must keep their apartment cleaner, or you will have to give them notice.

By the way, I would give their apartment and the adjacent apartments a boric acid dusting. Boric acid works slowly to kill roaches. Unlike chemical sprays, it does not kill on contact. It kills roaches gradually, and it keeps on killing them for a long time to come, so long as the powder is present and remains powdery.

Boric acid has such residual strength that builders in roach-infested areas will put it inside wall cavities before closing up the walls. Roaches passing through the powder get it on their feet. When they clean themselves just as house cats do, they ingest the boric acid, develop a killer case of indigestion, and die. Drug stores have boric acid powder. Hardware stores have a product called RoachPruf®, which works the same way. Unless ingested in large quantities, it is not harmful to children or domestic animals.

Your tenant transition checklist should have a boric acid item on it to remind you to check whether the powder has caked or disappeared. If it has, reapply it.

Checking the boric acid powder in a rental dwelling is only one of many items on a transition checklist. Completing the checklist so that a place is ready for a new tenant takes time and money, and landlords always try to cover those costs by charging new tenants for them.

You mentioned that you want to charge a non-refundable deposit. Don't.

"Nonrefundable deposit" is an oxymoron. Like the terms deafening silence, bittersweet, dry rain, freezer burn, holy war, working vacation, plastic silverware, true lies, and sweet sorrow, it contradicts itself. Unlike these somewhat amusing examples, however, "nonrefundable deposit" is not the least bit amusing. It's serious. It's serious because it's about money, and people aren't amused when money is at stake, especially if it's their own money and they're tenants. Money on deposit is supposed to be money refundable provided that certain conditions have been met. Long after most states have banned its use in rental agreements, "nonrefundable deposit" still appears in some landlords' agreements. Don't use the term in your agreements unless you want to risk being taken to court by a tenant who knows your state's landlord-tenant laws.

You could use the term "cleaning fee" to refer to those upfront monies you collect from tenants before they move in and have no intention of returning to them after they move out, except that it, too, has been banned in some states.

A better way to collect nonrefundable monies when tenants move in is to set the rent higher for the first month, or even for the first two or three months, than it will be later when the tenants are established and you are no longer incurring transition costs. Landlords know and tenants do, too, that rent is not refundable.

If you want to try collecting a deposit from your problem tenants, you cannot expect them to pay you anything to cover your transition costs. You don't have any. The tenants were there when you bought the property. The most you could ask them to pay as a deposit would be $300, since that's what you required the other tenants to pay, and you have every legal right to ask them for that since they haven't paid a deposit yet and all of your other tenants have. You certainly aren't discriminating against them by asking for it.

Even so, I would not ask them to pay a deposit because they aren't likely to pay it, and then what do you do? Threaten to evict them? You are only creating problems for yourself by asking them to pay you a deposit now.

The same goes for trying to determine what their place was like when they moved in. You could try to make a determination, but since it would depend almost entirely on what the problem tenants tell you, you are wasting your time. You might as well wait until they move out and then listen to them. You already know that their place is a mess, and it will be a mess when they move out. Don't waste your time going to the trouble of getting a security deposit and making a determination because when they move out, you'll have to return the whole deposit anyway because they will argue that they actually improved the apartment while they were living there, and you won't be able to prove otherwise.

As for a rent increase, I wouldn't bother giving them one sooner than you give the other tenants theirs. They could consider it retaliation for their having made so many complaints. You'll be giving them a notice to vacate soon enough because they aren't going to clean their apartment well enough to keep the roaches from returning. That notice would not be retaliation. It would be for cause, and yet you don't have to, and shouldn't, state the cause in the notice.

Yes, dealing with problem tenants is frustrating, but you're a landlord now, and frustration is something landlords have to get used to. Get used to it.

He's wondering whether he's cut out for this business.

Q. I'm a new landlord with a rental house in the state of New York, and I'm beginning to wonder whether I'm cut out for this business. Month after month I have trouble collecting the rent, and it's become a nagging worry for me. My tenants are again behind in their rent. This time they're behind a month and a half.

They have two infants, and they lean on me hard for sympathy. The husband is a great scam artist, and the wife isn't far behind. They used to own a collection agency, but it went bankrupt (that should have told me something). Now he's out of work again.

I'm afraid that I'll never get another dime out of them and I'll never get them to move without evicting them. I don't know how to begin eviction proceedings, not even the first step (you'd never know that I am fairly successful in the business world). Please tell me where to begin and what my basic rights are. Everything I have read so far indicates that tenants are hard to evict in New York.
—D.B., New York

A. Even New York has a legal procedure for evicting deadbeats. The playing field may not be level, but you can evict for good cause and you should. You cannot afford to allow a tenant to live in your rental house without paying you the rent you need to collect in order to pay all of the expenses of owning and maintaining a rental house, and the sooner you begin eviction proceedings, the better.

Although every legal jurisdiction has its own procedure, timetable, and forms for evicting deadbeats, the basics are the same. You wait until the rent is delinquent. You serve the tenants a notice stating that they owe a specified amount of rent (nothing other than rent should be included in this figure), that their rent is delinquent, that they have a certain number of days to pay, and that you will take them to court to evict them if they don't pay within the time allowed. If they don't pay, you take them to court and you pursue them doggedly there until you receive the right to reclaim possession of your property. Then you have a legal officer enforce your right to reclaim possession by removing the tenants from the property.

You may handle the entire procedure yourself using a guidebook or you may handle it through an attorney.

For tips on how best to pursue an eviction for nonpayment of rent in your area, search the internet using Google or Yahoo and then contact your local rental property owners association.

Tenants try to scare off buyer.

Q. I am about to acquire my first rental property, a four-unit building. During the acquisition process, the real estate agent and I made five attempts to enter the units so we could see the layout and condition of the interiors. Every time, the tenants either slammed their doors in our faces or they just wouldn't answer. The tenants do not want the property to change hands because their rents are well below market and they pretty much have free rein of the premises since the current owner lives three states away.

My offer to purchase was accepted, but the seller was not keen on my request to have all four tenants evicted before I take possession. In our state, an eviction is simple. It's a low-cost court proceeding, and it doesn't even require a reason other than just wanting the tenant to vacate. These particular tenants are all "at will" on a month-to-month basis. The seller is not going to bend on evicting them before closing, other than to clear out the one unit I plan to occupy myself.

My first order of business after the closing is to get rid of these already troublesome tenants and clean up the units to prepare them for new tenants. How do I manage to live on the same premises for up to thirty days with these unreasonable people? I sense that there will be much hostility toward me and some resentment, maybe even destruction of the units, once the tenants are served. Do you have any advice on how to make the transition go somewhat smoothly?
—S.A., New Hampshire

A. For someone who has never before owned rental property, you have some good landlording smarts. You know enough to ask the seller to clear the building of its uncooperative tenants before you take possession, and you know enough to realize that any tenants who are being evicted are likely to cause trouble, especially for a new owner living on the premises who has just displaced one of their own.

My stovepipe hat is off to you for persisting in buying the property when you know that you're going to be facing people problems straightaway. You have the right landlording stuff.

I believe that you can minimize these problems by using the right approach, but first you should recognize that the reception you received when you tried to gain access to the tenants' units was an attempt to scare you off. Now that the tenants know that they can't scare you off so easily and that they have to answer to you as their new landlord, their attitude toward you should change.

Here's the right approach. Determine the market rent for each unit. Prepare a letter introducing yourself as the new owner and telling the tenants what changes you intend to make. At the same time, give them a rent increase to market and give them at least a sixty-day notice. Tell them that you are giving them the extra time so they can look around and decide for themselves whether they can get a better deal elsewhere. Also tell them that if they do decide to move, you will give them a good recommendation so long as they are cooperative and current with their rent.

Some of them may move. Some of them may not. If they do move, they will feel as if they are moving voluntarily. They won't feel as if they have been forced to move, and they will likely behave themselves in order to get a good recommendation from you, something which is of greater value now that more and more landlords are doing complete background checks on applicants before accepting them as tenants. If they do not move, you will have brought the rents up to market and you can begin improving the exterior of the building, biding your time until they do move and you can fix up the interiors of the units one by one.

Eviction notices grate on tenants. They feel as if you are giving them no choice, and they may try to retaliate against you. They hate to feel powerless.

You will accomplish your primary objective of increasing the property's value by giving the tenants rent increase notices rather than eviction notices, and you will save yourself much grief using this approach. It's the right approach.

They want to empty the building and start fresh with new tenants.

Q. We are in the process of buying a building with three rental units. We plan to live in one of the units and rent out the other two. This will be our first experience dealing with tenants and the whole rental process as landlords, so I am trying to find out as much information as I can about doing things correctly.

Currently all three units are occupied. We would like to start fresh when we take possession, that is, we would like to get rid of all the old tenants and get new ones. Can we do this, and if so, how should we go about notifying the current tenants that they must leave?
—C.R., Wisconsin

A. Unless the building is in a rent-controlled jurisdiction, you may give the tenants a notice to terminate tenancy within a specified number of days, generally thirty, and hope that they will indeed heed the notice and vacate. If they don't, you'll have to evict them through the courts. That's one method.

Another method is to give the tenants a substantial rent increase. The rent increase method works better than the notice-to-terminate method because tenants feel that they're in control of their decision to move. They feel that they're going to show their greedy landlord a thing or two. They're going to move out. Moving out is their decision, they believe, not their landlord's. Consequently, they tend to vacate in a better frame of mind and tend to leave the unit in better condition.

In your situation, you will want to give the tenants in one of the units a notice to terminate tenancy because you want to occupy that unit yourselves. You want them to vacate, period.

As for the other units, you should ask yourselves whether you stand to gain anything by removing the existing tenants. At least you know something about them. You know whether they are clean and quiet, whether they follow the rules, and whether they pay on time. If they are clean and quiet and follow the rules and pay on time, why get rid of them and take your chances on getting new tenants who may not be as good? Good tenants lay golden eggs for you. Keep them. Treasure them. Make them happy.

If the existing tenants are troublesome tenants, get rid of them, by all means. Getting rid of them will make you happy.

Eviction in progress will be new owners' first order of business.

Q. We will be closing escrow on a foreclosure soon. Come to find out, one of the tenants is being evicted. If we close escrow prior to the completion of the eviction, do we need to start the eviction over, or can we continue where the buyer left off?
—A.Q., Oregon

A. Good question!

You may want to make the completion of the eviction a part of the contract for you to take over the property, or you may want to go ahead with the closing and withhold $1,000 from the sale until the eviction has taken place. By withholding some funds from the sale, you will insure that the original plaintiff will cooperate with you.

Whatever happens, you do not need to start the eviction over. You may continue with the action and add yourself as a plaintiff or substitute yourself for the plaintiff who first started the action. For specific details, you may want to get some legal advice from an attorney who specializes in evictions. Contact your local apartment owners association for a referral.

Tenants trash beautiful unit before she bought the building.

Q. One of the units in an apartment building I purchased recently is in horrible condition. The previous owner said that everything was new there when the tenants moved in. Can I charge them for the cost of the repairs even though their unit was a wreck when I bought the building?
—M.E., Maine

A. Whether the unit was or was not a wreck when you bought the building doesn't matter. What does matter is what the unit was like when the tenants moved in. If you can dig up some proof besides the word of the previous owner, proof such as photos or signed documents, which show that the unit was in good condition then, you should charge the tenants for the cost of repairs when they vacate. Don't try to charge them before then. You'll only aggravate them and make trouble for yourself.

Very first rental property is giving him headaches already.

Q. I recently purchased a four-unit building. It's my first property, and I'm having some problems with it.

The previous owner designated one of the tenants as the manager, and this tenant has been very persistent about remaining as the manager. I have told him and the other tenants that I don't need a manager. I can handle the place myself. Right away, though, I've got a problem about whose responsibility it is to roll the garbage cans out to the sidewalk for pickup. The tenants think that it's my responsibility to roll the trash cans out since this is something the former manager used to do. Whose responsibility is it anyway?

Also, I raised the rent shortly after I took over the property. I understood that 3% was the only amount it could be increased within California, but I want to increase it again after I do some renovations. How do I go about this?

I have been having some trouble renting one of the units. Where can I advertise to get good tenants? I'll admit that the outside of the building is not the most attractive, but I have to get it rented. Would you recommend Section 8 tenants?
—N.H., California

A. Congratulations on acquiring your first rental property! You have taken a giant step forward, a step which will either make you or break you both financially and spiritually.

Recognize straightaway that landlords must be optimists and problem solvers. Do your best to think of the big picture as you solve the many problems facing you in your new role.

Let's consider the problems and concerns bedeviling you now: the former on-site manager, the garbage-can rollout, the rent raise, the renting of a unit in an unattractive building, and the Section 8 tenant.

As for an on-site manager, even at a fourplex, I believe in them wholeheartedly. They cost little for what they do in saving you time, money, and aggravation. A good one will keep the grounds around the building cleaned up, the plants trimmed, collect the rents doggedly and on time, handle minor maintenance, and keep the tenants in line. If the former tenant-manager was doing that much for the former owner, I'd seriously consider rehiring him.

Whose responsibility is the garbage? Ultimately it's the responsibility of the landlord. It's one of those tasks which tenants expect somebody else to do for them. You might offer a monetary incentive to those tenants who roll their own garbage cans out to the curb as one way of handling the matter.

How much can you raise rents? That depends on your location. You need to apprise yourself of the laws which apply to your fourplex's specific location. California, as a state, has no rent control and no limits as to what you can raise rents. Some places in California do have rent control, and you must comply with it. You have no choice. Ask somebody who's knowledgeable, such as the staff at your local rental property owners association, rather than take the word of somebody who claims to know.

How can you rent a unit in an unattractive building? You can't, that is, you can't unless you want to rent to lowlifes who don't care what their home looks like. Fixing the place up on the outside is just as important as fixing it up on the inside. You can't attract decent tenants to a run-down building, no matter how hard you try. They presume that the inside looks as bad as the outside, so they won't even bother taking a look at the gem of a unit you've painstakingly remodeled. It'll go begging. Fix the place up on the outside as soon as you can and put out a "for rent" sign. That's the best advertising you can do.

Should you rent to Section-8 tenants? Like any other tenants in the general population, Section-8 tenants are both good and bad. The big advantage in renting to them, though, is the government's guarantee that the bulk of the rent will be forthcoming even if the tenants turn out to be deadbeats. Section-8 certificates are so hard to obtain that most people who do obtain them will struggle to protect them. These people may not be model tenants, but they may be very good tenants. Learn what you can about the Section-8 program before you participate.

Persevere!

New landlord wants old tenants to increase their reserves.

Q. I am in escrow on a triplex and will need to raise the rents to market levels, $175 higher than current rents. One tenant has been there for ten years, and the other has been there for three years. Nobody is living in the third unit.

I plan to move into the vacant unit myself, and I plan to ask each tenant to fill out a rental application and a new rental agreement. I plan to propose that they make payments to increase their reserves so there will be enough to cover last month's rent and a security deposit. Each tenant's reserve is very low right now.

Is this the correct action to take? Am I missing anything?
—L.M., California

A. You are correct as a new owner in adjusting the rents to market or to something slightly below market (after all, these people are long-term tenants), but you should give the tenants at least sixty days notice that you are raising their rents. That will give them plenty of time to look around and see that they have a good deal right where they're living. They won't be so anxious to move if you give them plenty of time. If you give them thirty days notice, they'll feel that they have to make a decision now whether to stay or leave, and they may leave just to spite you.

Try to get them to complete a tenant information form (see *Landlording* book) rather than a regular application form. Many existing tenants will refuse to complete a regular application and challenge your authority to make them do so. Don't undermine your authority by asking them to do something which you can't really make them do. What're you going to do if they refuse to complete a rental application? Evict them?

You should try to get them to sign a new rental agreement. Whether they sign it or not, it will become effective with proper notice at some time following the expiration of their old agreement.

As for getting a higher last month's rent and security deposit from existing tenants, don't even try. You're more likely to antagonize the tenants and frustrate yourself with the effort. Consider the existing deposits, small as they are, sufficient for tenants who have a good track record.

New landlord battles tenant over agreement, rent, and deposit.

Q. After taking control of a family business which includes a piece of commercial property that my absent-minded grandfather rented out to a woman with only a verbal agreement, I presented the woman with a new lease and a rent-increase notice.

She insists that she does not have to pay the increase for the upcoming month because I did not give her thirty days' notice. From what I know about our state's landlord-tenant laws, I don't have to give her a thirty-day notice. Should I give her thirty days' notice anyway? If so, is the notice I already gave her sufficient enough to raise her rent for the month following the upcoming month, or do I have to give her another notice?

When I gave her the rent-increase notice, I also requested that she put up a security deposit equal to one month's rent. She never paid my grandfather any deposit when she rented from him, and she was quite insulted that I would ask for a deposit. She said that she has been in the building for quite a long time and has never been late with her rent, something I cannot verify for certain. She said that if I am increasing the rent, she should not have to pay a security deposit, too.

I just want to do what's right. I'm trying to be the kind of landlord I would like to have if I were in this woman's shoes. I feel comfortable asking for the rent increase and for the security deposit. They seem to me to be reasonable requests. Would you recommend that I "stick to my guns" or let this tenant have her way?
—J.S., Pennsylvania

A. You may be a new landlord, but you have the right attitude to be a successful landlord. You are trying to be fair and proper, just as fair and proper as you would like your own landlord to be. Too many new landlords think they can boss their tenants around and treat them with disrespect. Not so. Those landlords do not succeed because they don't understand that they have to please their tenants in order to keep their tenants.

This tenant of yours, whom you inherited from your grandfather, needs to be pleased at the same time you give her the triple whammy: new rental agreement, rent increase, and security deposit request. Naturally, she's balking. She was used to having a lackadaisical landlord who let her be and trusted her completely. Now you come along and introduce changes. She's upset, and you can't blame her for being upset. You have to win her over to your way of doing business.

To win her over, you have to bend somewhat and show your humanity while still pursuing your objectives. Tell her that you'll postpone the rent increase for a month so that it will become effective on the first of the month following the upcoming month. Tell her that she's really getting more than thirty days' notice at that. Don't give her a new notice. Tell her to correct the one she received to reflect this change. Legal or not, the changed notice and its consequences become a win for her. She'll pay the increased rent when the time comes, and she'll pay it without question.

The security deposit is another matter. Push for it, all of it. Remember, this is a commercial property, not a domicile. Tell her that the increased rent and the security deposit are different matters entirely. A justifiable rent increase has nothing to do with a justifiable security deposit request. Just because you're raising the rent to reflect market conditions is no reason why you ought to drop your request for a security deposit. Tell her that the security deposit is something your grandfather should have requested a long time ago. He didn't, and not paying it then was to her advantage. She's had that advantage ever since she moved in. All you're doing is requesting that she pay what she should have paid a long time ago. Tell her that she as a business person should understand why every landlord should collect a security deposit from every tenant and that she should understand that you are now merely correcting your grandfather's oversight. Tell her that you want to reward her for having been such a good tenant for your grandfather over the years. You'll let her pay the security deposit over the next five months, twenty per cent each month. That will soften the blow for her and make you appear to be more reasonable.

The new written rental agreement you want to introduce appears to be acceptable to her. Go ahead and get it signed and be done with the fair and proper changes you as the new landlord recognize that you need to introduce.

New landlord discovers that 10-day grace period is too long.

Q. I am new at being a landlord and find that I'm learning things the hard way as I go along. I rented my house to a couple and made their rent payments due on the first of the month. I allowed them a ten-day grace period and told them they would have to pay a late fee if they paid on or after the eleventh day.

Their first check was returned because of non-sufficient funds, and their second and third payments have both been late. Each time they have paid the late fee without question.

When I talked with them about being habitually late, they said that they have a ten-day grace period and can pay it on the tenth rather than on the first of each month if they want.

I disagreed with them. I called their attention to the paragraph in their contract that says I can evict them for anything deemed reasonable that couldn't be worked out. It states I have to give them only a ten-day notice. They said they would get an attorney if I tried to evict them. They said that they are paying their rent, even though it is admittedly late. Who is right here?

Can I evict them for making late payments every month?
—S.B., Wisconsin

A. Your tenants are right when they say they aren't late until the eleventh of the month. You gave them a ten-day grace period in their agreement, and you must abide by it. If you want to evict them for nonpayment of rent, you cannot even give them a notice to pay rent or quit until the eleventh.

You are not obligated by law to give your tenants a grace period of even one day. When you wrote that ten-day grace period into their agreement, you were being overly generous, and your tenants are now taking advantage of your generosity.

You could give them a thirty-day notice of change in terms of tenancy, changing, or even

eliminating, the grace period if you wanted to. I wouldn't. You would be withdrawing a privilege you gave them when they moved in, and you'd only antagonize them. Don't antagonize them.

You should, by all means, give them a notice to pay rent or quit whenever they're late. That's not antagonizing them. That's doing what's expected of you. If they don't comply with the notice, you may continue legal eviction proceedings immediately. Giving them the notice not only begins eviction proceedings, it keeps them from using an estoppel argument in court, that is, claiming that you were allowing them to pay their rent late as a matter of course, and as a consequence, you couldn't expect them suddenly to pay by an earlier date, even if that date is the one specified in their agreement.

The next time you write an agreement, don't be so generous with your grace period. Give the tenants a four-day grace period. That's my standard grace period. It keeps me from having to worry unnecessarily about my rent collections every month.

As for evicting your tenants because they're habitually late, don't. Pursue them every month when they're late. Either they'll slip up and get evicted or they'll shape up and start paying on time.

Heir wonders about licensing and registration.

Q. I inherited a house and want to rent it out rather than sell it. Are there any specific things I need to do to become a landlord? Are there any licenses I need? Do I need to register it as a rental property, or do I just start renting it?
—R.G., Michigan

A. You don't need a license to become a landlord. You would need one to manage rental properties only if you were handling the off-site management for other owners. Managers who live on the premises of the property they manage, sometimes referred to as on-site managers, don't need a license either.

State laws dictate licensing requirements. If you have any questions about licensing in your state, go to its legislature's website and check the licensing laws there.

Cities and counties dictate registration requirements for rental properties. Generally, properties don't need to be registered at all unless there's rent control or an inspection program in place, and even then, rental houses may be exempt from registration. There's a simple way to find out whether your rental house needs to be registered. Call city hall and ask.

Licensing and registration requirements may be the first of a new landlord's concerns, but they are the least of a seasoned landlord's concerns. There are so many other things for a landlord to be concerned about, starting with the laws governing rental housing itself. There are plenty of those, covering everything from habitability requirements to notice requirements. These are state laws, and they're available through your local law library, your local rental property owners association, and your state legislature's website. Become familiar with them.

Equally important are the procedures you should follow to get good tenants and the forms you should use to outline in writing the relationship you have with your tenants. Consult my *Landlording* book for both the procedures and the forms.

You could just start renting out that house of yours and see what happens. You wouldn't be the first person to jump into the landlording business that way. You might get lucky and find model tenants who never give you trouble and always pay their rent promptly. You might. You might get unlucky and find tenants so abominable that your life will never be the same again, too.

Remember, the landlording business is a risky business. It's fraught with pitfalls. Be careful. Be very careful. Every time you rent to tenants, you're "betting the farm" on them. They could destroy that rental house of yours and usher you into the poor house, or they could turn that rental house of yours into a neighborhood showplace and increase its value substantially.

Do your homework. Learn as much as you can about the business as quickly as you can and keep right on learning as you go. Pay close attention to what's happening with your tenants and your rental house, and you'll have reason to expect a payoff every time you "bet the farm."

3 Renting to Friends and Relatives

Long-time friend done them wrong.

Q. We have a four-bedroom house in Silicon Valley which we rented some time ago to a long-time friend, her husband, and daughter (mistake #1). For the first two years, either my husband or I checked on the house every three months or so and made minor "wear and tear" repairs as needed. Since this friend and I spoke regularly, and her response about the shape of the house was always "everything's fine," my husband and I stopped doing our quarterly walkthroughs (mistake #2).

Last May, our tenant sent us a letter advising us that she and her family had decided to purchase a house in a nearby city and that if approved, they would be moving within two months. At the time, my husband was very sick, and we were in no condition to be involved with the move-out. The tenant sympathized and said, "Don't worry. We'll clean everything." On the very date she promised, she brought me the keys with a nice letter thanking us for allowing them to rent our house. She even said she would pray for my husband's health.

In the letter, she listed several things that were in need of repair: the dishwasher, the shower in the master bath, the garage door, and the garbage disposal.

The very next day I visited the house to check things out and was shocked by what I found. The house was almost destroyed. The dishwasher was broken. There had been a fire in the oven. There was food caked two-and-a-half inches thick on the stove top. The fireplace in the living room was burned and had broken bricks. There were huge crankcase oil spots on the carpet. The kitchen floor was warped. There was a hole in the master bath subfloor so big that I almost fell through it. There were huge nails in the walls and in the wooden doors. There were rusted tools and worthless stereo equipment in the garage, as well as castoff clothes and luggage in the shed. Not even the swimming pool equipment escaped destruction. It had been taken apart and was lying about here and there in pieces.

We have had to lay out approximately $16,000 for the repairs and have lost more than the usual amount of rent between tenants. I might add that we had just consolidated our bills and were doing fine, but since these tenants left us with this mess, our debts are higher than they have ever been.

Four months after these people moved, the house is now ready to rent. It looks so good that I've been trying to talk my husband into selling the house we live in, taking our capital gains, and moving into the rental, but I haven't made much headway.

We're going to rent this house out again, but this time we know what we're doing. We have established some definite tenant standards, and we are being extremely picky about selecting tenants. We've learned our lesson from experience, and we've been reading your *Landlording* book for tips on selecting good tenants.

I still cannot understand why this woman and her husband left the house the way they did. As of now, they have disappeared, and her family members won't return my phone calls.

This woman killed us with kindness. She helped my parents when they were sick. She always paid the rent on time, even delivering it in person. She took pictures of a neighbor's new fence and brought them to our house to show us, and she was always sending us flowers and gifts and the like.

Now I know what she was really doing. She was strengthening our trust in her at the same time she was stabbing us in the back. At present we cannot afford the cost of a lawyer to go after

her and her husband. Is there anything we can do to stop them from doing to someone else what they did to us?
—H.S.W., California

A. Too bad you had to learn such hard lessons the hard way! Experience is the toughest teacher there is, and as you discovered, it's the most expensive, too!

In order to mark these people as the tenant traitors they are, you might want to subscribe to a credit reporting agency or join your local rental property owners association so that you can insert a derogatory remark on their credit report. Suing them for money damages might bring you some satisfaction, but it's not likely to get you any money. Then again, you might be surprised.

Husband's father and brother won't vacate house.

Q. My husband and I are not really landlords, I suppose, because we don't rent housing out to just anybody, but we do have a landlording problem. We own a house occupied by our immediate family and by my husband's father and brother. For the past eight years, we have been living in the attic of this house with our children, and they have been living in the rest of the house. Four months ago, we asked the father and brother to find themselves another place to live so we could spruce up the house and put it on the market. Despite repeated requests and several conferences, they have made no effort to move. We want them out as soon as possible and would like to know what course of action we ought to take.
—A.S., Massachusetts

A. Your husband's father and brother are considered "lodgers" because they have full run of the house, and the procedure for evicting them is the simplest available. Here's the way we would evict them in California, and I'd be willing to bet a buck that Massachusetts has a similar procedure.

First, serve them with an appropriate notice. In your case, it would be a thirty-day notice to terminate tenancy because we're assuming that you have no contract with them and that they pay whatever "rent" they do pay you once a month.

Second, if they haven't moved within the thirty days, you change the locks and make a citizen's arrest should they refuse to leave.

Unfortunately, there is a wrinkle in your case, and you'll need to research Massachusetts law to determine exactly what it says. California's non-judicial procedure for evicting lodgers applies only when there's one lodger, not two. When there are two or more, the owner must use the judicial eviction procedure used for ordinary evictions. No matter which procedure applies, however, it always begins with an appropriate notice. Serve that notice immediately, and you'll have a month to determine which procedure actually applies.

Once father and brother see that notice, they'll know you mean business. They'll likely clear out within the thirty days, and you won't have to concern yourself about which procedure applies.

Daughter-in-law won't vacate in-laws' house after separation.

Q. I have a different kind of question.

About nine months ago, my son and daughter-in-law asked if they could live with us in order to save up enough money to move to another state. Their plans called for them to be moving in six months. We agreed. In the meanwhile they decided to separate, but no divorce papers have been filed. We asked our daughter-in-law to move out, but she declined, indicating that we would have to go through the full landlord-tenant eviction procedure to remove her from our home. Neither my son nor daughter-in-law pays any rent or utilities. In fact, they have paid us nothing at all during their stay. What laws apply here, and where could I get some information on this situation?
—T.S., California

A. Your daughter-in-law sounds like a real sweetheart! Since she insists upon taking advantage of your generosity until you boot her out legally, you should get started with the procedure for evicting lodgers immediately.

The procedure is outlined in California Civil Code Section 1946.5, which you will find in its entirety on the California Legislature's website (use a search engine and search on "California Codes.") My book, *The Eviction Book for California*, also has several pages about evicting a lodger, including some information about the procedure's quirks.

Basically, the procedure is simple. All you do is give the daughter-in-law a notice to vacate. If she hasn't vacated by the end of the notice period, you may make a citizen's arrest. You do not need to go to court.

There are any number of wrinkles in your situation, including your having allowed both your son and daughter-in-law to move in with you. To take advantage of the lodger eviction procedure, you must not have more than one lodger, so you may want to tell your son to stay somewhere else while you're evicting the daughter-in-law, although a court would probably rule that the son was immediate family and would not be considered a tenant.

Were I you in this situation, where you don't have a rental agreement and aren't accepting any rent, I would give the daughter-in-law a seven-day notice to vacate (use the same wording as a standard thirty-day notice and change the time period). If she's not out by the eighth day, I would wait until she has left the premises, and I'd change the outside locks.

Changing locks in normal landlord-tenant evictions is absolutely *verboten*, but yours is a different situation entirely.

Old boyfriend's kinfolk want to report her for illegal housing.

Q. A year and a half ago I was dating a guy and planning to marry him. At the time I was living in a mobilehome I owned on five acres. There was another mobilehome on the site, too. My fiance's brother and new wanted to rent the other mobilehome, and I agreed. They moved in along with their daughter and her boyfriend.

In the end, I didn't marry this guy and no longer live in the mobilehome we occupied together. His brother and wife moved out of the other mobilehome, leaving the daughter and boyfriend still there wanting to rent it. We had no written agreement. Everything was verbal.

I have asked them to do a few things to keep the place up because I drive truck and cannot do the upkeep myself. They have refused to do anything. Now they're telling me that it is illegal for them to live there since they are not family and are living on the property, and they have threatened to call the housing authority on me.

I was unaware that it is illegal for them to live there, and I don't know what to do.

What are my rights since there is no lease or deposits or anything? I would just like to move back into my own place. What are my rights as a landlord?
—A.B., Washington

A. I can't understand why the daughter and boyfriend would want to turn you in to the housing authority for renting to them illegally because all the housing authority would do is tell you to stop renting to them. Your "tenants" would gain nothing. They'd merely be put out of the place where they're living.

If I were you, I'd approach the daughter and boyfriend and tell them that they have five days to leave. You won't force them to pay you anything. You won't ding their credit. You won't begin eviction proceedings against them, so long as they pack up and leave within five days and turn the keys over to you.

If they don't leave, you should begin eviction proceedings immediately by serving them with the proper notice for your state. You may or may not be able to proceed with the eviction yourself, that is, without having an attorney do the work for you, but I tend to think that you ought to have an attorney do the work because as a long-distance truck driver, you aren't around enough yourself to deal with the paperwork when it has to be dealt with.

Regardless of your not having a written contract and your having a strange relationship with these "tenants" of yours, you are in a strong position for getting rid of them and reclaiming your rights of possession.

Friend doesn't live up to agreement.

Q. Last year we bought a house with an older mobilehome on the property. The mobilehome needed work such as carpet, ceilings, underpinning, and other repairs. We offered it to a friend, telling him he could stay there rent-free for a year if he would fix it up. We discussed this at length and then signed a simple agreement.

Well, after a year he had done nothing at all to fix the trailer, so we drew up another agreement with very specific things for him to do, i.e., replace certain floor coverings, fix unsightly ceilings, strap frame to eyebolts in concrete pad, etc. In this second agreement, we set his rent at $100 a week. He never signed the agreement, but he has paid on time, though he has done none of the things we have asked him to do to the mobilehome. We want him OUT! Do we have to file eviction papers, or can we just tell him to leave since he never signed the lease?
—D.B., Nevada

A. Now that you want this "friend" to vacate, you should first ask him to vacate by a particular date. Be reasonable and be prepared to put in writing whatever you agree upon, say, that he has ten days to vacate before you begin eviction proceedings. Because you cannot be certain that he will vacate and because you don't want to waste any time if you do have to evict him, you should also serve him with whatever notice you need to serve him in order to begin eviction proceedings in your area for the kind of eviction you wish to pursue, likely failure to vacate rather than breach of contract or failure to pay rent.

In the future, be especially wary about renting to friends. Always outline the terms of every tenancy in writing as completely as possible.

Classmates clash when one changes his mind about rental.

Q. I needed to move and was looking around for a house to rent. I wasn't going to be able to move for another thirty days, that is, not until the beginning of the next month. I told every landlord I approached just when I expected to move so there would be no misunderstandings.

While shopping around, I ran into somebody from high school who has a rental house. He showed it to me and said that everyone who has looked at it has wanted it, but he was excited about renting it to me since I am a former classmate.

I filled out his rental application and faxed it over to him so he could check my credit and references. He called me later and said that I checked out okay and that he wanted to rent his house to me if I still wanted it.

He said that he could wait until the beginning of next month to rent to me, but he wanted me to give him a $500 deposit and sign a six-month lease. I told him that I wanted the house but that I probably wouldn't be able to give him the deposit for another two weeks.

I continued looking at rentals to satisfy my curiosity about the rental market and found a much better deal a week later. When I called to tell him I had changed my mind, he was pretty upset and demanded that I pay him the $500 deposit anyway.

Even though I offered to give him $200, which was all I could afford at the time, he insisted that we had a verbal rental agreement which I had broken, and he wouldn't take less than $500. He said he would take me to court if he didn't get the money, and he would sue me for the $500, plus the cost of placing his ads and running all the previous credit checks for the other applicants (he didn't ask me for any money when he ran my credit check).

As I see it, when I told him I had changed my mind, there were still three weeks left to go until the date I was planning to move in. Isn't that the same as giving him three weeks' notice? Can he sue me over our broken verbal agreement?
—S.I., California

A. This former high school classmate of yours is no friend. He should be wishing you happiness in your new home, getting together with you over a cup of coffee to chat about old times, and calling the best of the other applicants one by one to offer the place to them. Instead, he's trying to squeeze money out of you and talking about suing you if you aren't forthcoming. How petty! How greedy! How mean!

He can sue you if he wants, but he'd never convince a judge that you owe him anything. You don't owe him anything. You didn't have a contract with him. You would have had a contract with him had you actually paid him something. You didn't. You merely gave him your word, your promise, that you would rent the house, and he took you at your word. He foolishly took the house off the market and waited for you to sign the paperwork and give him a deposit. He assumed that you had rented the house. You hadn't.

When you changed your mind, he foolishly assumed that you owed him the same deposit you would have paid him had you entered into a contract to rent the house. He's completely wrong in this assumption. He's also completely wrong in his malicious approach to force you to pay. Poor fellow, he wronged you and lost a potential friend.

You can hold your head up because you at least called him as soon as you changed your mind. You didn't leave him dangling. You enabled him to continue his search for a new tenant without wasting any time. A week did go by when he thought you were going to rent from him, and he likely did pull his ads and did lose other good applicants, but he was prepared to wait three more weeks for you to move in, and that was going to cost him a lot more in lost rent than reinserting his ads and renting to somebody else who was prepared to move in right away.

You needn't feel sorry for him. He did all the wrong things in this episode. You did one wrong thing in reneging on your promise, but you did the right thing in contacting him promptly once you made your decision.

Tell him to go ahead and sue you because you want to see him laughed out of court.

Verbal agreement with cousin makes for misunderstandings.

Q. Three months ago I separated from my husband and asked my cousin, who is a real estate agent and a landlord, if she had anything to rent. She said she did. I looked at her available rental house and agreed to rent it from her. She said she wouldn't ask me to sign a lease in case my husband and I decided to get back together. That way I wouldn't be tied down, and I could leave at any time without further obligation. When I asked to pay my rent biweekly to coincide with my paychecks, she agreed. We discussed nothing else about our rental arrangement and agreed on nothing else.

Assuming that this arrangement was a favor from a relative, my mother-in-law and I painted the whole house out of gratitude for her kindness. Well, last week I purchased a mobilehome and told her I would be moving out of the house by the fifteenth. She proceeded to tell me that legally I was a month-to-month renter and had to give her a month's notice and I would have to pay rent for the rest of the current month and all of the next month.

I never agreed verbally to be a month-to-month tenant. She knows that. I understood that she would let me leave at any time without further obligation. I can't believe that she misled me so much, and I can't believe that the landlord-tenant laws in our state require me to pay so much rent when I want to move out.

What are my obligations to her? Do I really have to pay her all the rent she's asking for? I must admit that I have to wonder whether we even had a valid verbal agreement in the first place because we never shook hands on it.
—D.I., Kansas

A. Your cousin ought to know better than to rent a house to anybody without putting the terms of the rental agreement in writing. After all, she's a real estate agent and a landlord. She's a professional. Selling properties and renting properties are her business. A verbal agreement to rent a property is perfectly legal and binding even if you don't shake hands on it, but it's no way to conduct business. People cannot remember exactly what they agreed upon yesterday, let alone months ago.

She was wrong in renting her house to you a few months ago on a verbal agreement, and she is wrong now in making three assumptions. The first is that you are a month-to-month tenant. The second is that a month-to-month tenant has to give notice on the first of the month. The third is that you as a month-to-month tenant owe rent for more than a month following the day when you gave notice.

You are not a month-to-month tenant. Unless a landlord and tenant agree otherwise, a tenancy is the same as the rent interval. A tenant who is paying monthly is a month-to-month tenant. A tenant who is paying semimonthly is a semimonthly tenant. A tenant who is paying biweekly is a biweekly tenant, and a tenant who is paying weekly is a weekly tenant. You are a biweekly tenant because you are paying your rent on a biweekly basis. You and your cousin never agreed otherwise.

A month-to-month tenant does not have to give a thirty-day notice of intention to vacate on the first of the month. Many do, but it is not required. A month-to-month tenant may give a 30-day notice of intention to vacate on any day of the month, and it takes effect thirty days hence, not forty-five days or fifty. You as a biweekly tenant do not have to give your notice of intention to vacate on the first of the month or on the day when your rent is due. You may give it on any day of the month you choose, and it takes effect fourteen days later.

A month-to-month tenant does not have to pay rent for more than thirty days following a 30-day notice of intention to vacate. Even if you were a month-to-month tenant, you wouldn't owe the amount of rent your landlord claims you owe, that is, for the balance of the current month and all of the next month. You would owe rent for only thirty days following the day you gave notice. In your case, you owe rent for only fourteen days following the day you gave notice because you're a tenant who pays her rent every fourteen days.

Let's say that you gave notice on the fifth of the month, and your rent was paid up through the fifteenth. You would owe rent through the nineteenth, which is fourteen days after the fifth. On the sixteenth, you would pay your landlord rent for four days. That's all the rent you would owe her.

Be pleasant but firm when you tell your cousin what you have learned about your obligations to her, and tell her to consult an attorney on the matter if she doubts you. Tell her that you were so grateful for the help she gave you to begin with that you went out of your way to paint the house for her at no charge. Say that it's in better shape now than it was when you moved in, and say that you want to be fair to her now in paying her what you're supposed to pay her, but you want to be fair to yourself as well. You don't want to pay her more than what you're supposed to pay her.

Tell her that unless she can show you chapter and verse to prove that she is right and you are wrong, you will pay her exactly what you are supposed to pay her and nothing more.

Friend promises to trade fix-it work for a year's rent.

Q. Last year we bought a house with an older mobilehome on the property. The mobilehome needed work and things such as carpet, ceilings, underpinning, and bathroom repairs. We offered it to a friend of ours, telling him he could stay there rent-free for a year if only he would fix it up. We discussed the arrangement with him at some length and then signed a simple agreement.

After a year there, he had done nothing to the mobilehome, so we drew up another agreement listing very specific things for him to do, e.g., replace floor coverings in the bathroom and kitchen, fix unsightly ceilings in the two bedrooms, etc. The agreement also stated that he has to pay us $100 a week in rent.

He never signed the second agreement, and he still hasn't fixed up the mobilehome, but he has been paying the rent on time. We don't care so much about the rent. We care more about fixing up this eyesore on our property. We're tired of dealing with him and want him to leave. Do we have to file eviction papers, or can we merely tell him to leave since he never signed the lease? —D.B., Colorado

A. This "friend" of yours sounds as if he's just plain lazy. He doesn't sound as if he needs to be evicted through the courts. He sounds as if he will vacate if you tell him to vacate.

So, tell him to vacate. Tell him to vacate by a particular date. Be reasonable. Give him something like ten days or two weeks or whatever length of time you can agree upon.

Have him sign and date a "notice of intention to vacate" stating that he will vacate on or before the date you agree upon. This notice is nothing more than a statement directed to you as the landlord. Since he won't know how to write it himself, you should prepare it for him. Word it something like this, "Please be advised that on [date] I intend to vacate the residence I have occupied at [address]. I will pay the rent I owe through that date."

You know from experience that agreements on paper don't mean much to this guy, but you will be able to put this signed statement to good use if you have to evict him and show a judge that he failed to vacate as promised.

If he doesn't vacate as promised, talk with him and find out when he will be leaving. Tell him he must vacate by such and such a date or you will begin eviction proceedings the very next day.

If you do have to begin eviction proceedings, you won't have to serve him a notice of your own before you file the court papers because you already have a notice from him. That's the notice you can use as the basis for the eviction. He didn't vacate when he said he would, so you can use the power of the courts to force him to vacate.

Evicting him should not be complicated, and you may want to do the job yourself to avoid having to pay an attorney. Ask the librarian in your local law library to direct you to relevant materials, and ask for help from the clerk in the office where you go to file the papers.

In the future, be especially wary about renting to friends, and always outline the terms of every tenancy in writing.

Parents want to reoccupy their home alone.

Q. My husband and I are in big trouble. A year ago, we let our son, who can't seem to hold a job, and his wife, who was pregnant at the time and can't hold a job either, and their three-year-old child move in with us for the third time. He has since found a job and she had her baby four months ago. My husband was laid off work in May and drew unemployment until August. The company he worked for then offered to let him work for them in another state until the local affiliate called him back to work. We are out of state now and are returning home to my husband's old job in another month. When we left our home four months ago, we were gone only two days and our daughter-in-law's mother moved in.

All the utilities are in our name. We are paying the bills, and we are making the house payments. We want our house back one month from now, but we don't know what to do. They have paid us nothing. They have no lease and no rent receipts.
—D.C., Missouri

A. Ouch! You want to help your son and his family. That's only natural, but you also don't want to be taken advantage of, and you are being taken advantage of. You know that.

Because of the circumstances, you might want to take a cautious approach to the matter, one which takes into account your future relationship with your son, daughter-in-law, and grandchildren, one which hides a steel fist inside a velvet glove.

Here's that approach. Send your son a friendly letter stating that you are planning to return to live in your home on such and such a date and that you want to give him and his family thirty days to find another place to live because you and your husband want to occupy the home without other people around.

You hope that the letter will get them moving. If it doesn't, you move back into your home anyway and help them find another place to live.

Brother encroaches on property shared by two houses.

Q. My husband and I own two houses on the same lot. Behind the front house are a patio and a garage. Further back are a carport and the other house. My brother lives in the front house and has always had the run of the entire property. The tenants in the rear house have never needed the carport between the garage and the rear house. He took it over and has stored a bunch of his stuff there.

We are getting new tenants in the back house and would like them to have the carport. We'd also like to put up a fence between the two houses.

How do we ask my brother to remove his stuff? He has never been told that he couldn't use this area, and his rental agreement doesn't mention it. What is our legal obligation to him? Do we serve him a written notice requesting that he remove his property from the carport?
—J.R., California

A. Family members renting to other family members must recognize that they have to be uncommonly fair in their landlord-tenant dealings with relatives. Dealing with strangers as tenants is easy in comparison because you can always tell them to move on when there's a problem, and you can avoid ever seeing them again if you choose. You can tell family members who are your tenants to move on, too, but you can't avoid seeing them again. They appear at every family gathering and tell their stories about how you mistreated them when they were your tenants. Because you can't get rid of them, you must treat them right or you'll never hear the end of their grumbling.

In your case, I would offer to buy a portable shed for my brother on condition that he move all of his stuff out from under the carport into the shed. Erect the fence between the two houses and locate the shed on his side of the fence. Make your offer to him in person if possible. If not, make it over the telephone.

Judging from his reaction, you will know whether you need to "take a legal stand" and draft a notice of change of terms of tenancy defining the property he is renting from you. If you do, you might word the notice something like this: "The extent of the property at [address] being rented by [brother's name] under a rental agreement dated [agreement date] has been unclear. As of [thirty days from the date of the notice] and thenceforth, the property rented by the party in the front house shall be defined as being from the [example–North property line to the South property line and from the East property line to a point midway between the front and back houses on the lot]. The carport between the houses is part of the property which goes with the back house."

Once you and your brother resolve this matter between yourselves, make sure that the rental agreement you sign with the tenants in the back house defines the extent of the property they are renting from you.

Friends agree to stay temporarily and refuse to leave permanently.

Q. A friend of mine recently allowed friends of hers (a couple) to move into the apartment in the basement of her home. The apartment is not

legal. She allowed them to move in because they needed a place to stay temporarily. They do not pay rent. They just pay part of the utilities. My friend wants to sell her home now and has asked them to move out. They have refused. There is no lease or contract. Does the couple have any rights? What can my friend do to get them out?
—L.N., Massachusetts

A. Contract or no contract, your friend will have to evict this couple who are taking advantage of her. Because she has been letting them stay for nothing, the fact that the apartment is illegal should not be an issue. She might be able to make a case for their being lodgers in the basement rooms and subject to a streamlined form of eviction. To determine exactly how she needs to proceed with the eviction, she will need good legal advice.

Before she goes to an attorney for that advice, however, she ought to offer the friends some money to leave. If they still refuse to leave, she should contact an attorney who specializes in landlord-tenant law and proceed to evict them promptly.

Brother-in-law's friend makes poor tenant and poor handyman.

Q. My parents own a house and two rentals in a rural community. Recently they rented to one of my brother-in-law's friends who wanted to do work on the property to help pay his rent. They agreed to hire him, but they chose not to give him any credit towards his rent. Instead, they said they would pay him directly for the work they asked him to do.

They asked him to rebuild the broken door on a detached garage, and he did it, but two months later the hinge broke off the frame. He began working on the frame without first asking my parents whether they wanted him to do the job. While securing the hinge, the bolts sheared off and the door closed on him. I heard the loud crash and heard him holler, and my mother and I ran outside to see what had happened. He showed us where the bolts broke and said the door brushed by him and pushed him down on the ground. He said he was fine and would get some help to fix the door.

Later that day he stopped by to tell us that he was going to the hardware store to see if they could determine why the large carriage bolts failed. He also told us that he had gone to a doctor for a checkup and that the doctor had given him a clean bill of health.

This tenant has been late with his rent before, and he's late now. He's three weeks behind. I have a bad feeling about him and have told my parents that they shouldn't let tenants do any more work on the property, that they should hire a company with insurance and workers compensation.

Are they liable for injuries on their property when a tenant does work for them even if the work does not directly affect the rental property? Can we evict this guy for failure to pay rent and cut our losses?
—D.D., Idaho

A. Your parents are liable for work-related injuries when they hire tenants or anybody else to work on their properties, rental property or home property. You are giving your parents good advice. They ought to be hiring people who are knowledgeable, bonded, licensed, and insured. This tenant of theirs is none of the above, and he could cost them plenty because he isn't.

Bolts don't just shear off unless they're stressed beyond their stress limits. They're no longer made by hand with wide variations in quality. They're made by machine to high standards. This tenant must have badly miscalculated the bolts' stress limits and nearly killed himself as a result. He is not only "an accident waiting to happen," he is an accident.

He's a poor handyman and a poor tenant. Your parents should give him a notice to pay rent or quit today to begin eviction proceedings. At the same time they should tell him that they do not want him to do any more work for them, period.

4
Renting to Roommates

He wants subtenant's deposit to pay for rent and damages.

Q. I am a tenant who had a verbal monthly rental agreement with a roommate subtenant. Two months after this woman moved in, I gave her a 30-day written notice to vacate. She was very angry with me for giving her the notice, but I had no choice. She had violated the terms of our agreement. She moved her teenage brother into the apartment and concealed his presence from me even though she specifically agreed not to allow anyone else to live with us (she had previously been evicted for the same reason). She also installed a lock on her bedroom door without permission and gave me and my landlord (the owner) keys which would not open the lock. When confronted, she refused to give the owner and me keys which would open the lock, so I had to hire a locksmith to make us keys for emergency purposes.

After she moved in, I learned from her previous landlord and her parents that she's basically a small-time con artist, a liar, and a difficult person to deal with. Little things started happening. She pushed me hard enough to leave bruises. She called the police twice to report me for completely trumped-up charges. She let the police enter my bedroom late at night while I was sleeping (each time the police said they believed my account of the situation). She stole small objects from me, things which are ridiculous to report to the police. She gave keys to the house to other people, allowing them access to all of my belongings. She threatened me with lawsuits and with arrest. She threatened to report for child abuse of her brother if I didn't comply with her wishes. She repeatedly denied me the right to show the apartment to prospective new tenants even with a 24-hour notice.

I figured I was in for a long, contentious eviction, but I got lucky. Her brother's social worker called me to say that she was told she needed to move out if she wanted to retain guardianship of her brother.

After that, she left, but she did not pay the last twelve days of her rent or her utility bills. She took three pieces of my furniture that were in her room, and she left a mess behind. After three days, the only things left in her room were some cleaning supplies and a few clothing castoffs.

She refused to communicate with me when I tried asking her any questions. I was worried that she might take more of my belongings, but I wanted to get the place ready for a new roommate, so I changed the locks on the door to the apartment. I left her a phone message right after I changed them to let her know, asking her to call me when she wanted to pick up the rest of her stuff. Instead of calling, she broke into the apartment, claiming that her brother's medication was inside. It wasn't, and she knew it wasn't.

Here's my question. Can I use her security deposit for the rent she owes, for the locksmith charges I had to pay to provide me with a key to the lock she installed on her bedroom door, and for the value of the furniture she took?
—A.M., California

A. Yes, you may use her security deposit to pay for the rent, the locksmith charges, and the furniture. If there's anything left, you may use it to pay for the damage she did to the apartment, especially the front door. You should send her a full accounting of how you used her deposit, and you should return to her any unused monies.

You should also have this former tenant of yours arrested if she tries to break and enter again. Breaking and entering is a crime. This woman no longer had any tenancy rights after she moved out. In fact, because she was actually a lodger, all you really needed to do was give her a notice appropriate to the situation, in this case, a 3-day notice to perform covenant based upon her having allowed her brother to move in, and if the brother's still there after three days, you could have the tenant arrested. You don't need to go to court.

That said, let's consider what you ought to do the next time you sublet to anybody.

Always use a rental application and always check out every applicant before you make a commitment to rent to her. You want to learn about a person's faults from her previous landlord and her parents when you can still reject her as an applicant. You don't want to learn about a person's faults after you have already rented to her and you have to deal with those faults yourself.

Always put your agreement with the tenant in writing. Written agreements hold up better than verbal agreements, especially when you're dealing with somebody whose brain doesn't quite know the difference between fiction and fact.

Always get a security deposit from her just as you did. You may need it to settle accounts when the tenant moves out.

Having had such an appalling landlording experience as you just endured, many people would throw up their hands and say, "Never again will I be anybody's landlord." Too bad for them! What they should be saying is this, "Never again will I rent to anybody without checking them out thoroughly first." Good for you for wanting to keep going!

Boyfriend has got to go.

Q. My question is a simple one, but I can't seem to find the answer anywhere. I hope you can help.

I live in Arizona, where I am renting an apartment on a six-month lease. I am current with the rent. My boyfriend of three months moved in with me two months ago and has paid half of the rent directly to me.

At this time, we can no longer live together in peace, and I want him to leave. He is very loud. He yells and screams and slams doors and has done this almost every night for the past two weeks. He has put holes in the walls and has totally demolished one inside door. Even though he has never hit me, I have had to call 911 twice because he has become rough with me, and I thought I was in danger. I gave him a week to move out, but he won't leave because he says that he has nowhere to go.

What are my rights? What are his rights? What can I do without having to involve anyone else? I am afraid he is planning something on a larger scale to "get" me. In his mind I am the bad guy.

The apartment complex likes me and I have had no problems as of yet. I like living here and don't want to leave, but I feel that the only way I can get rid of this guy is to leave. Please advise. —T.S., Arizona

A. You have all the "rights" here because you are the tenant as far as the apartment complex and the law are concerned. Your boyfriend has no right to possession even though he has been helping you out with the rent. He is not on the contract, and he is not paying the rent directly to the landlord. He is your guest, and guests are supposed to leave when asked.

That said, there's the practical matter of getting the guy out of your apartment since he doesn't seem to understand that he's no longer welcome there.

Were I in your socks, I would wait until you know he'll be gone for two or three hours, and I would change the locks. I would box up his stuff and take it somewhere safe, somewhere neutral, somewhere accessible, where he can retrieve it right away. I would advise the apartment manager of my plans because some managers will change the locks for their tenants free of charge under these circumstances. If your manager won't, call a locksmith to do the job, or if you're a handy person, buy new locks and replace the old ones yourself (buy the same brand, if possible, so you won't have to change the latches or make any modifications in the holes to accommodate the new locks). Give the apartment manager a copy of the key and say that neither the key nor access should be given to anybody without your permission.

In addition, I would contact the local police department to alert them that you may be calling them soon if your ex-boyfriend becomes boisterous when he returns to find that he has been locked out of your apartment.

Do not let this guy cross your threshold after you have changed the locks. Do not even open your door to him. If he asks for his rent money back, don't give it to him. Tell him he owes you even more money because you have to pay to repair all of the damage he did to the apartment.

Getting him out of your apartment is the easy part really. Getting him out of your life is the hard part. You're on your own there. Just don't feel sorry for him. He made your life miserable, and he would continue making your life miserable if you let him. Be glad that you can "evict" him and "divorce" him without having to put yourself through our very expensive and very imperfect legal system.

Police threaten to arrest woman who locks out live-in boyfriend.

Q. Your response to the young lady who wanted to evict her live-in boyfriend was to have the locks changed while he was out. Well, I live in New York City and I'm in the same situation. I changed the locks, but when the guy returned and couldn't get in, he called the police, and they insisted I let him in and give him a set of the new keys or they would arrest me.

Image my surprise and disgust, especially considering that this is my co-op apartment. I pay the mortgage and all the bills. This guy has been out of work since he moved in and hasn't helped with the bills in the past year and a half that he has been living with me (except for two months when I insisted that he pay the phone and light bills). He's been living with me and off me. Do you have any advice for getting rid of this leech? I don't know where to begin.
—W.B., New York

A. My advice remains the same. Change the locks when your live-in boyfriend has left the apartment. He has no legal right to stay there. You aren't married to him, nor have the two of you lived together long enough for him to be your common-law husband. He has no ownership interest in the apartment, nor does he have any tenancy rights as a result of his having paid you rent. He has no legal claims on you or on the apartment. In other words, he has as much right to live there as a cat burglar. He might have the right to collect his belongings, but that's it.

If this guy were to show up on his parents' doorstep and ask for shelter, his parents would likely give it to him for a time, but if he lingered there without getting a job and if he treated them as shabbily as he is treating you, the parents would lock him out just as you did. As an adult, he has no legal right to stay with them because of a blood relationship or with you because of an earlier romantic relationship.

As for the police, they may be "the long arm of the law," but they are not the law. They're peace officers, and in that role they dispense street justice which they hope will keep the peace. The boyfriend must have fed them a line and they must have swallowed it. Had you called their bluff and told them that they might as well take you to jail and book you because you weren't letting the guy back in, methinks they would have backed down. What criminal act could they have booked you for? You broke no law in locking the guy out. You weren't disturbing the peace.

If you are wary about following the same change-the-locks scenario a second time, and I wouldn't blame you if you were, you might next enlist the help of the district attorney for assistance in the matter, or you might enlist the help of an attorney who specializes in landlord-tenant law, or you might enlist the help of some burly male friend. Ask him to move some of his things into your apartment temporarily and pose as your new boyfriend. He will convince the old boyfriend to leave permanently. Then change the locks.

Get this beast out of your castle. He belongs in a dungeon, and his jailers should throw away the keys.

Lesbian roommate puts the moves on the teenage daughter.

Q. I live in a rental house with my 14-year-old daughter. To help pay the bills, I took in a young couple as roommates. After they moved in, I learned that they were not a couple. They were just friends. The girl turned out to be a lesbian. I don't have a problem with that except that she made sexual advances on my daughter. After finding out that she had climbed into my daughter's bed and was rubbing her back, I pretty much lost it. I told her to get out and she did. A few days earlier, the guy moved out in the middle of the night without giving any notice. They were not under any sort of a lease, and they left some furniture behind. Now the guy who moved out is calling me and threatening to call the police to come and get the furniture. After what happened to my daughter, I am ready to file criminal charges against them. I need to know what rights I have. I was planning to sell the furniture to cover some of the money they owe me.
—P.S., Georgia

A. You could make life miserable for these young people if you wanted to. You could file charges against the girl for the advances made on your daughter. You could file a small claims court action against them for the monies they owe you, and you could keep the furniture and wait for the outcome of your court action. They, in turn, could make life miserable for you and your daughter if they wanted to. They could file a small claims court action against you unless you let them come and get their furniture. The girl could plead innocent to the criminal charge and make your daughter undergo the rigors of an attorney's examination in court.

Unless you are bent on getting some revenge against these people and you don't care what the costs are to you and your daughter, negotiate the return of the furniture. Give the people an itemization of what they owe you, and tell them you will let them have the furniture if they pay you what they owe. If they pay, let them have the furniture and let that be an end to the matter. If they won't pay what they owe, tell them to put an offer on the table and tell them that you will consider it. Be reasonable.

You needn't worry about the police coming to get the furniture or even supervising the removal of the furniture. Police don't do such things nowadays. The young people would need to get a court order to retrieve it.

The next time you take in roommates, get them to fill out an application, check out the application thoroughly, complete a rental agreement, and get their full deposit and rent monies before you allow them to move in with you. Don't risk putting yourself and your daughter in jeopardy again with complete strangers.

Automatically renewing lease trips up roommates.

Q. My roommate and I leased an apartment in Greenville, NC. The lease was for a year, and apparently it stated that we had to give sixty days notice that we would be vacating or the lease would renew automatically. I don't have a copy of the lease, and neither my roommate nor I can remember anything about such a requirement. The landlord is saying that we are stuck because we signed it and it's a legal document. I found all this out when I called to give a 30-day notice. She said that she had taped notices on our door, but neither of us saw them. She said she would let us terminate the new lease if we pay three months' rent, but that seems unfair. She has also raised the rent by ten dollars. Is this legal? Should we agree to her terms or should we seek legal

counsel. We have already applied to rent another apartment in Little Rock, AR. Will this have a negative effect on our chances of getting a new apartment?
—B.G., North Carolina

A. You should seek legal counsel to determine what your rights and responsibilities are under the lease and under North Carolina's landlord-tenant laws. Leases say whatever their authors want them to say, but they are not necessarily legal. Your state's laws take precedence over any lease wording wherever there is a conflict. Get a copy of the lease from your landlord, a copy of the very lease which you signed originally, and take it for review to an attorney who knows landlord-tenant laws.

When you seek legal help, learn all you can about lease legalities and illegalities from the tenant's point of view and from the landlord's, and ask the attorney for practical advice as to what you ought to do under the circumstances.

Having been trapped myself by an "evergreen clause" in a laundry machine lease, I have felt the misery you are feeling. Such clauses are grossly unfair and devious and should be illegal in any kind of lease, especially in a lease for rental housing.

Landlord refuses to release roommate from rental agreement.

Q. Please provide me some insight into this debate I'm having with a former landlord.

My ex-roommate and I signed a joint one-year lease agreement on an apartment in Virginia with an option of renting month-to-month at the end of the agreement. We filled out separate rental applications and were both named on the lease. Thirty days before the lease ended, we notified the landlord in writing that we wanted to stay there on a month-to-month basis. The landlord verbally agreed. Three months later, I decided to move out. I notified the landlord in writing thirty days before vacating that I was leaving and that I wanted my name removed from the lease. I also informed him that my roommate would remain.

Upon receipt of my notice, the landlord informed me that even though I was vacating the premises, he was refusing my request to take my name off the lease and that I would continue to be legally responsible for the apartment (rent, late fees, etc.) until my former roommate signed a new lease or moved out. Now, five months later, the ex-roommate still resides in the apartment, pays rent, and has a new roommate, all of which the landlord knows, but the ex-roommate has avoided signing a new lease and now the landlord wants to evict him.

First question: Am I still legally and financially bound to the lease?

Second question: If the landlord chooses to evict, can I be named on the eviction notice even though I don't live there?

Third question: How do I get my name removed from the lease and end this nightmare?
—A.A., Virginia

A. You did all the right things. You stayed through the end of your fixed-term lease. You continued your tenancy on a month-to-month basis with the consent of your landlord. You gave thirty days notice in writing that you intended to vacate. You informed the landlord that your roommate wanted to remain, and presumably, you also made sure that the rent was paid through the date when you moved out.

Because you complied with the fixed-term lease to begin with and then with the month-to-month lease after that, you have no further legal or financial responsibilities to the landlord. Those responsibilities now belong to your ex-roommate and to your replacement. The landlord has been accepting rent from them since you vacated, and that's tantamount to having an agreement with them.

The landlord may name you in an eviction action if he chooses, just as he may name Mickey and Minnie Mouse if he chooses. If he does name you, respond and go to court. Whatever happens with the other tenants, he won't prevail against you. You are already off the lease.

By the way, my *Landlording* book includes a "Roommate Agreement" which addresses seven primary problem areas. Yours is one of them. Here's what the agreement says about departing roommates: "Roommates who move out while this agreement is in effect continue to have financial responsibility under this agreement unless owners release them from this responsibility in writing or unless they are replaced by substituted roommates approved by owners. Upon being relieved of financial liability, departing roommates relinquish all rights to the deposits."

Under this agreement, which is designed to clarify the roommate relationship for all parties, you would be relieved of liability because the landlord gave tacit approval to your tenant replacement by accepting the rent month after month following your departure. Even without this agreement, you should have no worries. The landlord knows about your departure and the substitution of another roommate and has been accepting rent now from the two existing roommates for five whole months. Had the landlord wanted to oppose the substitution of another roommate or evict your ex-roommate for some reason other than nonpayment, he should have done so long ago.

Go on about your life and don't look back.

Roommate may or may not be liable for paying all the rent.

Q. My roommate and I are tenants in a condominium. He has been out of the country lately and has had difficulty paying his portion of the rent. He and the real estate agent for the owner have been talking on the phone about his situation, and now she wants to talk to me. The fact that she wants to talk to me is a little alarming. Actually, she didn't just call me. She showed up when I wasn't home and told the doorman that I should call her as soon as possible. Before I speak to her, I need to know what my responsibilities are. I've been paying my rent diligently. Can I still be evicted because my roommate hasn't been paying his rent?
—E.T., Ontario, Canada

A. The rental agreement you have with the owner of the condominium addresses your responsibility for paying the rent. If the agreement entitles you to occupy the condominium for a certain rent and gives the owner the right to rent the place to another person to share with you, then you have no responsibility to pay the roommate's portion of the rent.

On the other hand, if the agreement includes both you and the roommate as co-tenants and quotes the rent as a lump sum, no matter how it is paid to the owner, then you do have a responsibility to pay the roommate's portion of the rent. Most rental agreements are like the latter. They obligate every roommate to pay the entire amount of the rent, so that if one moves out, the remaining roommate(s) will continue paying.

You need to read your agreement closely and discuss your roommate's situation with him before contacting the agent. If you are obligated to pay the entire rent yourself and your roommate no longer has the wherewithal to pay his share, you might want to ask the agent to give you several weeks to find a new roommate who can help you with the rent. If you can't pay the entire rent by yourself and the agent or the existing roommate won't let you get another roommate, you'd better start packing.

One roommate pays late while the other pays promptly.

Q. We have a tenant who became chronically late with her rent after she lost her job. We allowed her to catch up because we hadn't had any other problems with her. When she finally did catch up, we thought she'd get better about paying on time, but she hasn't improved much. Incidentally, she has a roommate who is a model tenant and who always pays on time, sometimes even ahead of time.

Their utilities are included in the rent. We feel that one recourse for us when the rent is late would be to have the utilities shut off, but we also realize that shutting off the utilities would not be fair to the good tenant.

What do you suggest we do?
—B.J., Indiana

A. Whatever you do, don't shut off the utilities. Don't ever shut off a tenant's utilities. Doing so can get you into big trouble with the law and cost you big dollars.

Although you may be frustrated by this late-paying tenant, you are wise to be patient and flexible with her just as you have been because she's a good tenant otherwise.

There are two things you might consider doing to help the situation.

First, ask her whether changing her rent due date and/or the frequency of her rent payments would help her pay on time. Perhaps her income source pays her twice a month, on the first and the fifteenth, and she has a difficult time setting aside enough out of the money she receives on the fifteenth to add to the money she receives on the first to pay you a lump sum on the second. If you accept two rent payments from her, say, one day after she gets paid, she may find that paying you on time is easier.

Second, increase her late fee to its legal limit. Find out what the legal limit is in your area, give her proper notice that you are increasing the late fee, and see whether this added incentive to pay on time does any good.

By the way, you should increase the late fee on the other tenant at the same time so that the tenant who is chronically late can't accuse you of discrimination because she's left-footed or has uncommon religious beliefs.

Roommate wants deposit returned in spite of agreement.

Q. We own three flats in Chicago. We rented one to two roommates for a year. Their lease contained a clause stating that if one roommate moves before the lease expires, that roommate is still responsible for the rent through the end of the lease and forfeits any claim to the deposit.

Five months into the lease, one of the roommates moved. We were lucky enough to find a replacement for her, and this new tenant has given us a deposit equal to half of one month's rent (the same amount as the roommate who broke her lease). The new tenant also signed an agreement stating that she will take over the remainder of the lease from the other person, which effectively lets the lease breaker off the hook as far as her obligation to pay rent through the end of the term is concerned.

All of that is fine with us, but now the lease breaker wants her full deposit back. What do we owe her? What are our rights? What are her rights?
—J.H., Illinois

A. Return the deposit minus any out-of-pocket expenses you incurred to find the new tenant.

Remember, you collected the deposit initially as insurance against any losses you might incur in renting to the roommates. Had they damaged the property, failed to pay the rent, required the hiring of an attorney, or vacated prematurely and caused an income lapse, you could have used the deposit as compensation.

None of those things happened. One roommate moved out. Another took her place. Ho hum! Life in your flats goes on. You suffered no loss of income. You paid little or nothing to find the replacement tenant.

In spite of what your agreement says about keeping the deposit, I doubt whether it's enforceable because you suffered no harm.

Don't force your former tenant to sue you to get her deposit back just so you can test the agreement in court. Return the deposit to her with a smile. You lucked out in finding a replacement tenant promptly, and the tenant who broke her lease lucked out, too.

5
Listening to Tenants

Landlord gives no grace period and charges $50-per-day late fee.

Q. Is there a grace period for rent payment? Our landlord charges us $50 for every day our rent is late. He says it's in our lease, and we should look there if we have any questions.

Assuming that he knows what he's doing, I interpret the lease to say that there is no grace period. I find that hard to believe. If there is a grace period, what can we do if our lease says there is none?
—K.K., Illinois

A. No state requires a landlord to give tenants a grace period except when the rent due day occurs on a weekend or a holiday. In those cases, the tenant has until the following banking day to pay the rent.

Forget about the grace period which your landlord doesn't allow and doesn't have to allow anyway, and look at his late fee instead. It's ridiculous. It's unreasonable. It's unconscionable. A late fee is supposed to represent the amount of the damages caused by the late payment. It is not supposed to be a punishment for the tenant or a revenue source for the landlord.

Your rental agreement may stipulate a late fee of $50 per day, but no court in the land would enforce such a fee. Your landlord does not know what he's doing.

Landlords who know what they're doing might charge a late fee of $3-$5 per day up to a maximum of $50. Landlords who really know what they're doing might charge a lump-sum late fee of 5% of the rent, up to a maximum of $50. Even then, these landlords would include a provision in their rental agreements stating that landlord and tenant agree that the actual damages of a late payment are difficult or impractical to establish but that they agree to the late fee provision in the agreement as liquidated damages.

Landlords who know what they're doing will collect a nominal late fee from tenants who are late. They will also give every delinquent tenant a notice to pay rent or quit and then initiate eviction proceedings straightaway.

Landlord wants double rent.

Q. I'm a tenant in Massachusetts. I sent my landlord a letter terminating my lease because of an unbearable and persistent noise disturbance from new tenants who moved in next door (I tried unsuccessfully to work things out with them myself). In my letter, I gave sixty days' notice but indicated that I might be out in thirty days if all went well (I paid a month's rent and told him to use the last month's rent for the last month). He agreed to my moving out and told me in conversation that if I did get out in thirty days and the apartment was re-rented, he would return the last month's rent to me.

I am getting out in thirty days and the apartment has been re-rented as of the first of the month. Everything seemed fine until I received a letter from him stating that in consideration of my early termination, he was keeping the last month's rent even though he is sustaining no loss of rent on the apartment.

I was not required to pay a security deposit when I moved in, and the lease does not designate the last month's rent as a security deposit. Is he entitled to keep the last month's rent?
—T.W., Massachusetts

A. Tell your landlord that collecting double rent is the kind of thing they do in hot-sheet motels, not in apartment buildings with good reputations.

Your landlord would be entitled to keep your last month's rent only if the apartment were vacant the last month. A landlord is not entitled to collect double rent.

Since the lease says that the last month's rent you originally paid is for last month's rent only, he cannot use it for anything else, nor should he.

Were I in your slippers, here's what I would do. I'd draft a simple handwritten agreement to be signed by the landlord. In it I would say that he promises to return my last month's rent within seven days of my vacating the apartment on or before the last day of the month so that new tenants can move in.

Next, I would meet with him face to face. I would remind him of the verbal promise he made to return the last month's rent if he re-rented the apartment. I would tell him that his letter really upset me because I thought that he was a good landlord and an honorable man. I would tell him that he should return the money to me because he promised he would and because he is not entitled to collect double rent. I would tell him that I would like him to sign the simple agreement I brought with me or one with similar wording which he writes up himself. I would tell him that I have two alternatives if he doesn't agree to return the last month's rent. I could throw a screwdriver and a monkey wrench into the transition process from one tenant to another by refusing to vacate the apartment completely and refusing to turn in my keys so that the new tenants could not move in when they're supposed to, or I could vacate the apartment completely and then haul him into small claims court to get the money out of him. I would tell him that the judgment I would get will go against him on his personal credit report even if paid immediately.

When you meet with him to tell him all this, try to be calm. You're playing a card game with your landlord, and you're holding a very good hand, much better than he thinks. Look him straight in the eye when you tell him you've always thought of him as a good landlord and an honorable man. Look him straight in the eye when you remind him of what he told you before about returning your last month's rent if he were able to re-rent the place. Look him straight in the eye when you ask him to put on paper what he already promised to do. If he blinks, take the pot. Go no further. You'll get your money back. If he doesn't blink, look him straight in the eye and show him your two aces, those two alternatives you have to force him to yield the pot.

Landlords don't know it all. My guess is that your landlord wrote you that letter when an un-informed friend told him that he had a right to keep your last month's rent and that he had nothing to lose in doing so. You need to show him the errors in all that.

House she rents is for sale, and people tour it all the time.

Q. For the past two-and-a-half years I have been renting a house in the Sacramento area on a month-to-month basis. The house is forty years old and has severe cosmetic damage. It has neither fans nor air conditioning so it gets uncomfortably hot inside during the summer.

When I moved in, the property manager explained that after two years I would have the option to purchase the house if I chose. I declined, and now the house is on the market. It's been on the market for about five months, and the current manager said that because touring the house is an inconvenience to my family, the owner would pay us $10 per tour. We agreed and asked for a 24-hour notice from the agents.

Since the house first went on the market, we have had problems with people coming over for a walk-through whenever they pleased. The real estate agent in charge of selling the property has even told people to take the house key from the lockbox and come in if they can't reach us by phone.

Isn't it illegal to enter without a 24-hour notice or the tenant's consent unless there is a health or safety hazard?
—S.P., California

A. A landlord may enter an occupied rental property only with the tenant's permission or upon providing notice of at least twenty four hours or in case of an emergency. Them's the only three circumstances, period.

Insist to the property manager that nobody enter your home under any other circumstances, no matter who they are unless they have prior permission from you. Tell the property manager that you expect a compensation of $50 for every time somebody enters your home upon short notice or $100 if they enter without your permission. Otherwise, you will abide by your agreement for compensation of $10 per tour.

Meddlesome manager perturbs tenants.

Q. My ex-wife and I are good friends. She came to me for help in dealing with certain issues she's having at the apartment complex where she and a co-worker moved only a short time ago. They rented an unfurnished apartment and split the security deposit of $1,050 right down the middle, but because my ex-wife has poor credit, she had to come up with an additional deposit of $1,050. In all, they paid $2,100 in security deposits, plus $35 as a deposit on the remote control for the garage door opener, plus their first month's rent of $1,050, for a total of $3,185.

At first the two of them were happy to be living right across the hall from the manager. He seemed pleasant enough and concerned about the comfort and safety of two single women living alone. Little did they know how overbearing and meddlesome he would turn out to be!

For starters, he has been calling my ex-wife several times a day on her cell phone while she's at work. He calls with odd little reminders and trivial questions. He called to tell her she should break down any cardboard boxes she wants to throw away. He called again to tell her that her neighbors work nights, and as a consequence, she must be quiet during the day. Note that he made these calls before my ex-wife threw away any cardboard boxes and while she was still at work. She isn't home to make any noise during the day. He called again to ask her whether she had a home phone yet and to ask her to give him the number as soon as she got one. My ex-wife never said she would be getting a home phone and likely won't. She uses her cell phone for everything.

The first few times he called, my ex-wife was appreciative that he cared so much. Now, she's perturbed, especially because he disturbs her at work several times a day.

Here's another example of his overbearing behavior.

One evening at 7:30, my ex-wife hammered a picture hook into the wall so she could hang some artwork. The light hammering lasted no more than ten seconds. Seconds later, the apartment manager was knocking on her door. He came to chide her about the hammering and to remind her of the sleeping neighbors. He told her to do any noisy work during the afternoon from then on, in effect contradicting what he had told her before about being quiet during the day to avoid waking the neighbors.

My ex-wife is not one to make waves, nor is she unaware of other people's rights, needs, and preferences. She is kind and cooperative to a fault.

She feels that making a little noise at a reasonable hour while hanging some artwork is a reasonable thing to do and not something which would bother anybody. After all, the neighbors didn't complain to the manager. The manager complained to her on his own behalf, not on behalf of the neighbors. Even if they had been bothered, the neighbors didn't have enough time to complain to the manager before he came knocking on her door.

She is beginning to resent the manager's intrusion into everything and is also beginning to suspect that he is entering their apartment to intrude further into their lives when she and her roommate are gone for the day. Several times when they have returned to their apartment after a day's work, they have noticed things out of place. They want to protect their privacy and would like to change the locks, but they don't know whether they can legally change them without giving the manager a new key. What good would that do when he's the one they want to keep out of the apartment? He has no business entering the apartment when they're gone.

There's one more issue my ex-wife has. It concerns her cat. I've been looking after the cat for her because she wasn't able to keep it where she was living before. She wants to take it now, and according to her rental agreement, she can have a cat. The kicker is that the manager says she has to put up an additional $200 pet deposit, and he says it's not refundable. She and her roommate have already put up $2,135 in deposits.

A landlord friend of ours told us that landlords may not require more than the equivalent of three months in rent for unfurnished apartments before people move in. That's for rent and deposits and last month's rent. My ex-wife and her roommate were required to pay more than that before they moved in, and now the manager is requiring still more money and is saying that the pet deposit is not refundable. That's not right.

Keep in mind that my ex-wife loves cats, and we've had this particular cat for two years. She wants to take the cat, but she still wants to cultivate a good relationship with the manager.

How would you suggest she handle the cat issue? Would you recommend she pay the additional deposit now and argue later? What would you suggest she do about the manager's other bothersome behavior?

—N.L., California

A. Your ex-wife has a manager who must think he's above the laws regulating landlord-tenant relationships, or else he's just plain ignorant. He sounds like a rogue manager who wants to control the apartment house and everybody in it as if it were a federal prison.

Some tenants would tell the guy to get lost when he perturbs them by acting like a prison warden, but since your ex-wife wants to accommodate him, she needs to take a low-key approach in her dealings with him.

She can put an end to the petty phone calls at work by telling him that her boss has complained to her about taking personal phone calls on company time. She should tell him that she is not in control of her own time when she's at work and that she can no longer take his calls there. If he persists, she should subscribe to caller ID and let him leave her a message when she knows he's on the line. He'll soon get the message, her message.

She can put an end to his pretending to represent the neighbors with complaints about noise by getting to know the neighbors, those neighbors who supposedly sleep during the daytime, as well as those neighbors who sleep during normal nighttime hours. They will be glad to tell her when they need their quiet time. This information will serve her well when she's hammering the rest of her picture hooks into the walls and the manager appears at her door.

She can put an end to his entering the apartment when she and her roommate are gone by installing a wireless security alarm system which will sound an alarm or call her cell phone number whenever the system is armed and somebody enters the apartment. Her system could cover the primary door only or all the doors and windows. It could have a motion detector sophisticated enough to detect an ambient temperature change caused by a person entering the room while at the same time it ignores pets roaming about that weigh less than forty pounds. Such alarms cost around $200, install in minutes, and are easily removable for installation elsewhere.

Another, less-expensive, way for her to put an end to his entering the apartment when she and her roommate are gone is to install a keyed chain door lock. This secondary lock is just like a basic chain door lock except that the user can lock and unlock it from the outside with a key by reaching through the partially open door. Locking and unlocking it from the inside requires no key. If the apartment already has a chain door lock, a keyed chain door lock will replace it neatly. They're available for $10-25 from locksmith shops. Locksmiths, by the way, may have other suggestions for dealing with a nosy manager.

She can put an end to the pet deposit issue by paying it cheerfully now in order to move her cat in with her and making an issue of it later when she and her cat move out.

In addition to taking these measures to foil her overbearing manager in low-key ways, she should ask the neighbors to share with her what they know about the manager. She'll get more than an earful from them. They'll tell her how they handle him. Maybe he's just a henpecked husband married to a shrew who dominates him so completely that he cannot help but take out his frustrations on the tenants. Maybe they know how to get to the shrew and thereby get their way with the manager. They'll know what makes the guy tick and why he acts the way he does.

Your ex-wife might want to ask the neighbors whether they know of any instances where the manager has entered tenants' apartments while they're gone. She might want to tell them that she has her suspicions and ask them to keep an eye on her place when she and her roommate are gone.

As a very last resort, that is, before your ex-wife decides that she has to move in order to get this manager out of her life, she should find out who owns the apartment building, contact the owners, and tell them what's really happening at their building. The owners will want to know, and they may decide to change managers as a result or change the way this manager manages.

Your ex-wife has options for dealing with this guy. Acquaint her with her options and help her exercise them.

Manager rents tenant's trailer space to somebody else.

Q. I am staying temporarily in my travel trailer in Arizona, while I determine whether trailer living is really for me.

My question is this: I am a tenant in a campground and my rent is paid up for thirty more days. The manager of the park has just informed me verbally that he has rented my site to some snowbirds who are arriving eighteen days from now. He is making me move to an undesirable location in the park so he can accommodate these snowbirds.

How can he rent and accept monies for a space that has already been rented and paid for?

Thank you for any help you may offer me as I am not a happy camper. This change of space will cost me a reconnect charge with my phone company. It hardly seems fair.
—B.D., Arizona

A. Check your rental agreement, if you have one, and look for a reference to a space number. Lacking an agreement, check your last rent receipt for a space number.

If either of them mentions a space number, then you are paying for a PARTICULAR space in the park, not just for ANY space in the park, and the manager of the park cannot make you move.

Because the period in dispute is only twelve days, however, you might want to cooperate with the manager in moving to the less desirable space if you plan to stay in the park beyond that period anyway and if you want the manager to treat you well in the future.

Fire sprinklers damage tenants' belongings.

Q. Who's responsible for putting fire extinguishers into rental units, landlords or tenants? How about fire alarms?

Some friends of mine had a cooking oil fire in their kitchen and couldn't put it out themselves. The fire did damage to the kitchen, but it didn't burn the building down because the sprinkler system went off and put out the fire. The trouble is that it also ruined their belongings in the kitchen and elsewhere in the apartment. Who's responsible for the damage?
—S.P., Georgia

A. Few residential buildings have fire sprinklers. They're the best of any equipment available for putting out fires and saving buildings because they're always on the site ready to do their job, and they require no human intervention. They're completely automatic.

On the other hand, they're definitely not the best equipment available for putting out fires and saving the contents of a building threatened by fire.

As your friends learned, fire sprinklers cannot distinguish between what needs dousing and what

doesn't. In the course of extinguishing the fire which activates them, sprinklers douse everything. They keep the building from burning, but they saturate the building's contents wherever they spray and they ruin whatever things water will damage.

Fire codes give special consideration to any building equipped with sprinklers. This building occupied by your friends may not have been required to have alarms and extinguishers because it was sprinklered. Required or not, they should have been installed in order to warn people of the danger and give them the opportunity to put out the fire before the sprinklers turn on.

In any case, this example emphasizes the importance of having renters insurance.

Because the tenants caused the fire, they are responsible for the damage. If they had renters insurance, it would have paid to repair the damage to the building and replace the damaged items.

Landlord wants to displace tenants during fumigation.

Q. My landlord wants us to vacate our apartment (2 tenants, 2 bedrooms) for two nights and three days to fumigate. We pay a total of $1,095 in rent per month. Could you suggest a reasonable amount of compensation and perhaps a reasonable time for notification prior to the fumigation?
—A.G., California

A. Given the fact that your rent is $36.50 per day (twenty-four hours) and that you will have to find temporary accommodations either with friends or at a lodging facility nearby, I would say that adequate compensation would be double the figure you're paying for rent, or $73 per day, but this figure presumes that you have little to do in preparation for the fumigation and little to do afterwards. If you have to spend hours and hours preparing and hours and hours cleaning up and reorganizing afterwards, then you should be compensated something for your time as well.

Reasonable time for notification prior to the fumigation would be seven days or more.

Fumigating for termites raises some questions.

Q. My wife and I have been renting the house we are in now for eleven years. We are responsible tenants and are thoughtful of our landlord's property.

Our landlord is getting ready to have the house fumigated for termites. This is fine with us, but it will remove us from our home for approximately two days. Is it our landlord's responsibility to cover our expenses if we have to stay in a hotel? Also, who's responsible for moving the furniture and taking care that the food does not spoil in the refrigerator? Who's responsible for any damage that is done, if any, or any vandalism? My primary concern is the relocation because we have two kids.

—A.R., California

A. At the very least, the landlord should give you rent credit for two days, but more than that, the landlord should give you a lodging allowance sufficient for you to spend the two nights in modest overnight accommodations near the property. This allowance should be agreed upon in advance and should be paid to you in advance so that you might spend it wherever you choose.

As for moving and safeguarding things, you and your landlord should cooperate with one another to the extent that you can in order to make sure that all goes well. The end result of a termite-free house is in both your interests.

Whatever damage might occur as a result of the termite work should be covered by the termite company's insurance policy, the landlord's insurance policy, or your own renters insurance policy, which is something I strongly urge every one of my tenants to secure.

Previous tenant's fleas bug new tenant even after extermination.

Q. After I signed a rental agreement for an apartment, the landlord told me that she had taken care of a flea problem caused by the previous tenants' pet. She said she had shampooed the carpets and felt confident that the fleas were gone.

When I walked into the place, I learned that shampooing the carpets had not eliminated the fleas. They attacked me. I called the landlord, and she bombed the place with foggers she bought at a hardware store.

Thinking that the flea problem had been solved, I moved in my belongings. I paid the movers $140, and because there was no refrigerator provided, I bought one for $340 and had it installed. I never got a chance to spend the night there before I found fleas again, or more accurately, they found me.

I called the landlord and asked for an exter-

minator. She refused and promised to spray instead with a home remedy. She sprayed her home remedy, and I spent the night with friends. Twenty-four hours after the spraying, I returned and found lots of fleas there happy to see me.

This time I called the landlord and demanded an exterminator, and she agreed to call one. He came and sprayed and said that since I didn't have a pet of my own, the fleas' life cycle would be broken in a few days. He told me his chemicals would kill only the adult fleas and that I should vacuum everything thoroughly every day for three days to remove the flea eggs.

I did as instructed and found their numbers greatly reduced, but they weren't gone. I called the landlord and asked her to replace the carpet. She refused and called the exterminator out for the second time. He came and sprayed again, and I vacuumed again, and still there were fleas.

I called the landlord and demanded that she replace the carpet and have the exterminator spray for a third time while I was away for a few days.

I returned five days later and found that she had replaced the carpet, but the place was still infested. In a matter of minutes, ten fleas jumped onto my ankles.

This whole series of events has all occurred within two weeks after I signed the rental agreement. I've tried to cooperate with my landlord in her efforts to get rid of the fleas, but I'm frustrated. I haven't been able to spend a single night there yet, and the welcome at my temporary quarters has worn out. I am a young woman concerned about my appearance and am ashamed to show my legs now. They're grossly bitten and marked. As if that weren't enough, I have had to spend money on oral and topical medications because I'm allergic to the bites.

I have had enough. What are my rights?

—L.W., Washington

A. Your landlord has tried and failed to rid your apartment of the flea infestation, and she deserves high marks for having tried so hard, but she hasn't eliminated the fleas. They're still using you for their meals, and as far as you're concerned, the apartment is uninhabitable.

Whenever a rental dwelling is uninhabitable and the tenant has had nothing to do with making it uninhabitable, the tenant has no obligation to pay the rent. You shouldn't be paying any rent for the time you have been unable to live in your apartment. Those pesky fleas have definitely made it uninhabitable, and you didn't bring them with you.

Decide now what you want to do. Do you want to move somewhere else, or do you want to wait a little longer for the landlord to eliminate the fleas?

If you decide to move somewhere else, you face going through the search and selection and application procedures again, and you may or may not find a good alternative place to move to. You face the daunting task of packing and moving, and you may find after the move that some of those hardy fleas have hidden themselves in your clothing or furniture and have followed you to your new apartment. You also face the unpleasant task of trying to convince your landlord to reimburse you for your moving expenses and return your rent and deposit, and you may have to go to small claims court to get anything out of her.

If you decide to wait for the landlord to eliminate the fleas, you will have to find somewhere else to live, perhaps in an extended stay hotel for several weeks, but you won't have to endure another move and all the attendant hassles, and you'll be living in an apartment with new carpet when the landlord has eliminated the fleas and you can return.

Your apartment isn't the first one to have been overrun by fleas. Its fleas will be eliminated when your landlord tries the right combination of remedies. So far, she's been unlucky, but she will prevail. She knows that she has to rid the apartment of the fleas or else she'll never be able to rent it to anybody other than to someone who wants to move in with a flea-bitten dog and doesn't care about the fleas, and you know she doesn't want any flea-bitten dog's paws on that new carpet.

Get together with your landlord and talk the matter over with her. She may have been looking for the most inexpensive solution to the infestation when you were working with her before, and she may have seemed like a difficult person, but you'd have done the same thing had you been in her position. You wouldn't have spent the money to replace the carpets before trying the self-administered remedies and the exterminator first.

You may find that she's eager to work with you now because she wants to keep you as a tenant. Tell her what you have decided and why. She may try to convince you to change your mind if you have decided to move. Listen to her. She may have some good arguments, and she may give you more of what you want than if you were to leave without giving her one more chance to eliminate the fleas while still expecting her to refund everything you've paid her, plus pay your moving expenses.

Month-to-month agreement requires 60-day notice-to-vacate.

Q. My husband and I are tenants in an apartment complex in North Carolina. We have found a house to buy and are planning to close in thirty days.

When we called the apartment office to notify them that we would be moving, they said that we were required to give them 60 days' notice or else we would be responsible for the rent until they found a new tenant or until sixty days passed, whichever came first.

Our original lease was for six months and was converted to a month to-month rental agreement after that. We have been living here "month to-month" for over a year now. We have always paid our rent on time and have never made any trouble. After the six-month lease expired, the office sent a new "agreement" for us to sign, specifying a month-to-month status and I think it stated the 60-day policy. Then, a couple of months ago, they sent another agreement over for us to sign for the new year, but we never did. By still continuing to live there even without having signed the latest agreement, did we unofficially accept the terms of the previous agreement, including the 60-day notice policy?
—S.S., North Carolina

A. Gather up all three agreements and take them to an attorney or paralegal who knows something about North Carolina's landlord-tenant laws and ask your question of that person.

Without seeing those agreements and knowing your state's laws, I cannot give you a definitive answer.

Off the top of my head, I would say that a month-to-month agreement which requires a 60-day notice to vacate is not a month-to-month agreement at all. It's a two-month agreement. If the agreement calls itself a month-to-month agreement, then it must be a month-to-month agreement, and it must not contain a clause which would require sixty days notice to vacate.

What I would do today, if I were you, is give the rental property management a notice of intention to vacate in writing rather than rely upon a verbal notice. State in the written notice the date when you gave verbal notice and to whom you gave it and indicate when you plan to vacate. Also state in the notice that you are under a month-to-month agreement and that a month-to-month agreement cannot require you to give sixty days notice. Put them on notice that you believe the thirty days' notice you are giving them is sufficient and that you believe you are not obligated to pay rent for any longer period. I believe you would be on solid ground in taking this approach. What do you have to lose?

Tenants need an extra ten days to move into their own house.

Q. We have been renting a house from friends of our family for a year and two months. When we moved in, the house needed a lot of cleaning and painting. We offered to do the work in lieu of paying a full deposit, and they agreed to accept a deposit of only $200 rather than six times that amount. After we did the work, the house was awesome. We have continued to take good care of it and have been putting money into caring for the yard as well. We have never signed a written contract.

When we moved in, the porcelain sink in our bathroom was cracked. We mentioned this to the landlords because we knew that over time it would continue to crack even more and eventually become unrepairable. About two weeks ago, it finally cracked beyond repair. They were upset with us and said we must have dropped something on it or broke it intentionally. Of course, we didn't. The crack just grew over time into a full-fledged break.

Our landlord is a handyman on the side and always comes himself to fix everything. We calculate that he has had to spend approximately $300 to fix things since we have been here, and that includes replacing the sink. We think that's only normal.

Some time ago, we decided that we were going to buy a house. We found one and it is in escrow now. It will be ours in forty-five days. We had planned to give our landlords a 30-day notice soon. Then we found on our doorstep a 30-day notice from them stating that we need to be out by a date which is ten days before our escrow closes. We're upset because we have nowhere to go until escrow closes.

Do we have the right to contact the landlords and tell them we need an extra ten days? Can they evict us, or do they have to work with us on this? We don't want an eviction on our credit record. We have always paid our rent on time and are not now in arrears. We feel that they are retaliating against us because they think we broke the sink, and we aren't happy about it. What should we do?
—S.H., California

A. In your situation, ten extra days is not much time to ask for. 99.9% of all landlords would happily give you the extra time, provided that you contact them in writing and explain yourself.

Do not sit and stew. Write a letter of explanation to your landlords and ask them to extend the time for your departure. In your letter, tell them that you have bought a house and plan to move there as soon as you can after escrow closes. Because escrows too often take longer than expected, give yourself an extra five days after the closing date. Tell them that moving before then would be an extra burden on you, requiring that you find temporary accommodations for yourselves and temporary storage for your belongings and that you move everything twice. Assure them that you will pay the rent through the day you intend to move out and that you will leave the house in good shape. Keep the letter non-confrontational. Say nothing about your feelings or suspicions.

If they have any idea what they face should you refuse to move out when they want you to move out, they will grant your request. You see, their 30-day notice is only a first step in forcing you to move out. If you don't move, they must follow a very specific procedure to get you to move, and that procedure will cost them dearly in time, money, anxiety, and aggravation.

Get busy with that letter right now.

Tenants who survived two break-ins want to break their lease.

Q. We have had two break-ins in the past six weeks, and now my son and I no longer feel safe living where we are. We're afraid that one of the intruders may return and harm us. Under these circumstances, do you think we can get our landlord to let us out of the lease?
—J.D., Tennessee

A. So long as the break-ins were reported to the police, you have a reasonable and verifiable excuse to break the lease. You should take the initiative and tell your landlord that as a result of the break-ins you and your son no longer feel safe there. Tell him that you have decided to move and that you want him to let you out of the balance of the lease. Tell him that you are giving him 30 days' notice as of now and that you will pay the rent through the end of this thirty-day period. Tell him that you will leave the place clean and undamaged and that you expect him to return any deposits and excess rents (last month's rent, if paid) owed to you. See how he responds.

If possible, put something in writing to this effect. Modify it as you and the landlord see fit, sign it, and get him to sign it as well, so you have something to show a judge later should the matter wind up in court.

Your landlord likely doesn't have to let you out of the lease, but he would be wise to do so after what you've been through, and you might indeed be able to convince a judge that the place is not safe for you and your son and that you ought to be released from further lease obligations.

Reformed tenant is haunted by her wayward past.

Q. Okay, I know that this question will generate a chorus of boos and hisses from some landlords out there, but I do have a serious question.

I was a problem tenant in the past. I did drugs, destroyed apartments, had to be evicted, and was generally a nuisance wherever I lived. For the past three years I have been living with relatives and have been getting my life together. When I applied recently to rent an apartment, I was rejected because of my past rental history. How long should I expect to be penalized (not that I don't deserve to be penalized) for my past behavior? I can't live with relatives forever. In fact, the relatives I've been staying with are starting a family and want me to move out soon.

How does someone like me rent an apartment? How long do landlords keep a tenant's history on record? I'm desperate and need some answers.
—L.E., Illinois

A. "Someone like you" used to have no problem finding another place to rent because landlords were notoriously lax in checking applications. A tenant's rental history remained pretty much buried in the memory and records of each affected landlord, resurrected only when a diligent landlord happened to be checking an application and contacting previous landlords.

Nowadays most landlords check applications thoroughly because checking them is easier, cheaper, and less time consuming than ever before. Thank the internet for that. Also, because evictions cost more and tend to take longer than ever before and because rents are higher than ever before, so that more money is at stake whenever a tenant stops paying rent, landlords want to know in advance whether an applicant is going to be a good tenant who will be quiet, cooperative, clean, and prompt with the rent, or a bad tenant who will make the landlord's life miserable and will have to be evicted at great cost.

A tenant's rental history is the best predictor there is of a tenant's future behavior, and landlords rely more on this history than on anything else when determining whether they will rent to a certain tenant. Because this history is scattered rather than concentrated, consisting of factual and anecdotal data from individual landlords, court records, and creditors, it doesn't simply vanish after a certain period of time. It lingers a long, long time, like the stink of a skunk.

Although you cannot expect your appalling rental history to vanish anytime soon, you can do something about it. You can counterbalance it by being frank with prospective landlords about your past and telling them that you want to prove you have matured over the past three years. To prove yourself, offer to put up a higher security deposit than required, offer to secure a co-signer who will vouch for you and pay for any of your misdeeds, and offer to sign a statement saying that you will move as demanded by any notice the landlord should give you for nonpayment of rent or breach of contract without compelling the landlord to evict you through court action. Many landlords will give you the chance to prove yourself under those circumstances.

If you seriously want to redeem yourself, contact the previous landlords you wronged and tell them you are sorry you caused them grief and cost them needless expense. Tell them that you have reformed and want to compensate them for what you did to them. Offer to pay them a reasonable sum of money, or ask them what they would consider fair compensation. Then pay them. They will be so overwhelmed that they will revise their opinion of you as a person and will tell any landlord who calls them for a recommendation that you do appear to have reformed and ought to be worth considering now as a tenant.

You can get back into the rental market, but you cannot expect the mere passage of time to remove the blemishes in your collective rental history. You must do something to prove that you are not the same person you were three years ago. You know that you have changed for the better. You know that you would make a good tenant today. So, prove it to the landlord who holds the keys to the dwelling you want to rent.

21-year-old worries about bad rental experience 3 years ago.

Q. I'm twenty-one and very responsible. I've been gainfully employed since I was sixteen. I've been living with my mother for some time now, but we both know that I need to move into my own apartment soon. The problem is that when I was eighteen I leased an apartment for a year, and four months later I had a car accident and was unable to work. I was a waitress at the time and unfortunately had no savings. I tried to make arrangements to pay my rent in a timely manner even though it would be late, but the management imposed impossible conditions on me. I knew I couldn't meet their conditions, so I decided to move out without paying any more rent. I was not in arrears when I moved. After I moved, I again attempted to make arrangements to pay off the rest of my lease, but they still wouldn't be reasonable. Even though I moved willingly, they considered me evicted and turned my account over to a collection agency within days after I moved. The agency said I owed $3,000 and dogged me for the money. I never paid, and now I have that blotch on my credit report. I'm worried that I won't be able to rent because of it. What can I do?
—L.P., Texas

A. Shame on the management at the apartment complex where you were once a renter! You acted sensibly. They did not. Their being uncaring and unreasonable cost them whatever payment you and they might have negotiated. Too bad for them that they failed to collect anything! Too bad for you that you now have to concern yourself with clearing your credit!

Don't despair. You're not the first person who's had financial problems as a result of something beyond your control. There are things you can do to make yourself creditworthy once more.

Start by ordering a copy of your credit report. You need to see whatever negative information it contains so you will know whether it's accurate. Perhaps the report doesn't even mention your little misfortune from three years ago. You won't know unless you check.

You may order a copy of your credit report from any one of the three major credit bureaus, Equifax, Experian, or TransUnion, by phone or by mail, but you'll get it more quickly by ordering it over the internet. In fact, you'll get it within seconds after you place your order. The cost is around $10.

If there's nothing negative in the report, rejoice. Somehow your unfortunate episode as a teenage renter either was never reported originally or was deleted later. In either case, stop your worrying and go find yourself a pleasant place to rent.

If the episode does show up, read carefully what the report says about it and write an explanation to submit to the credit bureau. You have a right to tell your side of the story, and if you make a good case, the credit bureau will include it in your credit history.

Whatever you do, don't fall for one of the credit repair services' pitches claiming that they will erase your bad credit and create a new credit identity for you legally. The Federal Trade Commission (FTC) has been warning people about these scam artists for years in a brochure called "Credit Repair: Self-Help May Be Best," also available on the "ftc.gov" website as part of the consumer information they provide. The brochure says, "Do yourself a favor and save some money, too. Don't believe the [credit repair services'] statements. Only time, a conscious effort, and a personal debt repayment plan will improve your credit report."

You're on track. You're doing what the FTC says you ought to be doing to repair your credit. Long ago you offered the apartment management company a payment plan, only to have it rejected. You tried. You did the right thing. You deserve credit for trying.

Now you're wanting to make a conscious effort to improve your creditworthiness. Good! You have both time and maturation on your side, that is, your episode occurred three years ago when you were only eighteen years old. In credit-history terms, three years is a very long time. What you did back then is ancient history. Credit providers are more interested in whether you're paying your bills now. If you're paying your bills now, they're content and will extend you credit. If you're not paying your bills now, they'll deliberate about extending you any more credit and will increase your cost of borrowing.

In your case, you were a teenager when you had that car accident and had to move out of your apartment under a black cloud. Teenagers in our society are entitled to make a few mistakes as they mature. You're twenty-one now. You're an adult. You have no current credit problems. You're a pretty good credit risk, and to a landlord with a vacant rental, you should look pretty good as a prospective renter.

After you have done all you can do to make yourself more creditworthy, you'll still have to face some worrisome questions on rental applications, and you'll be wondering whether you should fess up to the trouble you encountered with your previous landlord. The truth is that the truth will come out whether you want it to or not. Don't tell a landlord lies and half-truths in order to get an apartment. If you do, you'll worry that the landlord might find out about your past from a source which doesn't know what really happened, certainly not the way you do. Fess up to what happened. Tell your side of the story before the landlord learns about it from another source, and tell it as if it were ancient history. It is. Say that even though you were but a teenager when you had a car accident which kept you from fulfilling your lease commitment, you still acted responsibly by moving out voluntarily while your rent was paid up. You didn't have to be evicted. You moved and made the apartment available for renting as soon as you knew that you couldn't pay the rent. Stress the facts that you were a teenager, that you were working and paying the rent on time until an automobile accident kept you from working, that you tried to negotiate an end to your lease, that you moved of your own volition, that you tried again unsuccessfully to negotiate with the apartment management, and that you have been living at home for the past three years and saving your money so that you could afford a nice apartment and have a cushion just in case something unexpected keeps you from gainful employment.

You'll find a good landlord who will listen to you and give you a chance to prove yourself once more.

Landlord's suicide worries tenant.

Q. Last week I rented a room in someone's house and moved all of my things there. I was so pleased with everything about it, the neighborhood, the neighbors, the light, the quiet, the spaciousness, and the rent, that I signed a one-year lease. Yesterday came the shock of my life when I learned that my landlord had committed suicide. He was separated from his wife and must have been more despondent than anybody knew.

I'm worried now that the estranged wife will take over the house and force me to move. I have a signed agreement entitling me to rent the room for a year at the current rent, and when I signed it, I paid the first and last month's rent. Everything's in the agreement.

What are my rights?
—I.L., Montana

A. You have the same rights you had before your landlord committed suicide. Whoever becomes your new landlord must honor the agreement, every word of it. Should you receive a notice to vacate, respond to it with a copy of the agreement and say that you intend to stay for the duration.

Do your best to cooperate with the new landlord and prove yourself to be a good tenant. You could be evicted for failing to pay your rent on time or for some other breach of the agreement. Those provisions apply now just as they did before.

If the new landlord insists that you move, insist that you be compensated for moving prior to the expiration of your agreement, and negotiate a fair compensation amount.

New managers loosen security and tighten security deposits.

Q. Before I ask my two questions, I'd like to give you some background on my situation.

Six months ago the owners of the building where I live changed property management companies. The new company has just now sent me a letter saying that they are raising my security deposit from $300 to $600. They say that their policy requires this higher security deposit from every tenant. They have given me thirty days to come up with half the money and another thirty days to come up with the balance.

When I moved here two years ago, I signed a

lease. That lease expired and became a month-to-month agreement. I have not signed a new lease or a new rental agreement with this new company.

Under these circumstances, do they have the right to raise my security deposit?

My second question relates to security. Since the new management company took over, the locks on the gates have been inoperable and the intercom system doesn't work. I rented under the impression that the building was secure. Do they have an obligation to make adequate repairs to make the building secure again?
—M.L., California

A. Upon giving you a 30-day notice, the property management company may request an increase in your security deposit, but they would be hard pressed to make you pay it if you chose not to. To avoid a confrontation and avoid being marked as a problem tenant, pay the increase. If you need more than two months to pay it, tell the management company. They may give you more time to pay.

As for the decrease in security since the new management company took over, you have every right to expect that they maintain the building's security at the same level it was in when you arrived. Send them a letter stating your concern and tell them exactly what you want them to do about it. If they ignore you, send a letter directly to the owner. It will get results.

She's in a family way and wants to leave bad neighborhood.

Q. I began renting a small one-bedroom apartment four months ago. It's in a bad neighborhood, but I could live with the neighborhood because it's close to my school and very convenient.

I have recently become pregnant with twins. My boyfriend and I are going to get married and have the children, but the apartment is a bit small for one person. Soon we will be four people. The apartment is not in any condition for two newborns. The carpet needs to be replaced, the walls have cracks in them, the windows are drafty, and the rooms aren't rooms at all. They're more like spaces separated by folding shutters. My car window has been broken twice, and a man four houses down was murdered recently. I would really like to get out of my lease and move into an apartment that will suit us better. I have talked to my landlord, and he said that he would not let me out of the lease early but that I could try to find someone to sublease the apartment. What would you do in this situation?
—J.T., Missouri

A. Since your landlord won't let you out of the lease, you have to ask yourself what is more important, staying in a place which is too small and potentially dangerous for you and your family strictly to comply with a lease or breaking the lease and moving to safer quarters.

If I were you, I would break the lease. You even have grounds for breaking it because you were the victim of a crime on the premises. Your car window was broken twice. The neighborhood is simply not safe.

Give the landlord 30 days' notice in writing that you are moving and pay your rent through that date. Don't look for someone else to sublease the apartment because you will still be responsible for their fulfilling the obligations of the lease, and you don't want to guarantee that they will.

Clean the apartment after you move and take photographs to show that it was clean when you left it. Then send a letter to the landlord asking for a refund of your deposits.

Likely you will receive nothing from him other than a demand for rent to cover the balance of your lease, and you will have to take him to small claims court to get your deposits back. He is obligated to try to rent the apartment after you move and to credit you for any rent he gets through the end of your lease. He may not collect double rent. Be aware of that fact when you go to court because you may get a judge who is unsympathetic toward you and will require you to pay the entire balance of the lease. Ask the landlord in court whether he re-rented the apartment after you moved out and when he did so. If the judge makes you pay anything at all, it should cover only the period when the apartment was vacant. Make your best case before the judge. Tell him about the two times you were the victim of crimes, and hope that he will understand your position and award you the monies you deserve.

They want to take unscrupulous landlord down a peg.

Q. I'm a stay-at-home mom, and I'm home-schooling my children. My husband holds down

Chapter 5: Listening to Tenants

a regular job. We have been living in the same rental unit for three years. Our landlord doesn't care about his property or his tenants. I made a videotape showing all the things wrong with this place. The floor is falling through, the walls are bulging out, and the closet has both mushrooms on the floor and mold on the walls because it stays wet all the time for some unknown reason. Our neighbors are having problems, too.

The old landlord signed the property over to his son last month, and the son made us sign a lease with him. They both know about the problems we're having and have done nothing about them. We know that the insurance company sent our old landlord a check to have the floor fixed, but he pocketed the money and never did anything about it.

We have always been about a week late with our rent, and it was never an issue until now. When I handed the son the rent check the other day, he told me that if we were late again, we would be evicted. That remark got to me, so I took the check back from him. If he's going to be that impertinent to tenants who have lived here for three years and always paid the rent, and if he's going to be an unscrupulous landlord to boot, then we won't give him another penny.

We're fed up with this son and his father and are looking around for another place to live where the owner cares about the property and the tenants. In the meantime, we're wondering about a few things. Can we get our landlord in trouble with the housing authorities by showing them how bad this place is? We only need to show them the video. It's all there. How long can we stay here without paying rent before we have to move? Someone told us it can be as long as ninety days, and you have to be served twice by an officer of the law. Is this true?

Our new landlord is just like his father. The father told our neighbor when their septic tank was full that he would die and go to hell before he paid a penny to have it pumped. He said that they could deal with it or get out. They stayed there three months rent-free and then took off. Who could blame them? The son needs to learn that he can't treat people so callously. He deserves his comeuppance. What can we do to teach him a lesson and stay within the law?
—C.B., Alabama

A. "Unscrupulous" is the right word to describe your landlord. He is "second-generation unscrupulous" and came to be just like his father by careful observation, I'm sure. Father and son are ignorant, shortsighted scrooges with all four of their feet in the 19th century, completely oblivious of 21st century landlord tenant laws. As a favor to scrupulous landlords everywhere and to the tenants who will replace you in the dwelling you currently occupy, you ought to drag this landlord of yours kicking and cursing into the 21st century.

Every rental dwelling in the United States today comes with an implied warranty of habitability. It must meet certain health and safety standards and be fit for human habitation. Hazardous floors, moldy walls, bulging walls, and volunteer mushrooms inside closets all make a dwelling uninhabitable and violate the warranty.

As a tenant living in an uninhabitable dwelling, you need to alert the landlord to the deficiencies first and give him enough time to make repairs. If he fails to make the repairs, as yours has, you should gather evidence, invite the county health and building departments to inspect the place, stop paying rent, and take him to small claims court requesting that he repay you the rent monies you have already paid him while the dwelling has been uninhabitable and that he pay you damages as well.

He may have ignored you when you requested repairs, but he won't ignore you when you withhold rent. He'll badger you for it and threaten you with dreadful consequences unless you pay. Be firm with him. Tell him that you won't pay him another dollar in rent until he makes the repairs. Sooner or later, he will begin eviction proceedings against you. He will try to convince the judge that he has been responsive to your complaints and that you should be evicted because you have no good reason for failing to pay the rent. You will have an opportunity to tell your side of the story and convince the judge that your landlord is lying. Show the judge evidence of an inspection by a public agency, show him photographs and the video (chances are that the judge will not take the time to watch the video, so you do need to have photographs), and tell him that you have brought a case against your landlord in small claims court. You may or may not prevail in the two lawsuits. Your success will depend upon your preparation, your evidence, your appearance, your presentation, your landlord's behavior, your landlord's connections, and the judge's inclinations.

The legal case to evict you requires two or three visits from someone charged with the responsibility of serving you with court papers and finally removing you from the premises if the landlord succeeds in court. This person may be a police officer, a sheriff, a marshal, or a process server.

You will be served with paperwork outlining the landlord's case and summoning you to court. Read the paperwork thoroughly and respond to it appropriately. If it tells you to file an answer to the complaint within a certain number of days, do so. If it tells you to appear in court on a certain day, do so. Do whatever it says, and if you don't understand what it says, take it to legal aid, and ask for help.

If you win the eviction action, the landlord won't be able to evict you until he complies with the terms of the judgment, nor will you owe him any rent. If he wins the eviction action, you will be served with a notice giving you a certain number of days to move, you will be removed bodily from the premises if you haven't moved within the time allowed.

No matter what happens with the eviction action, pursue your case in small claims court because it may result in a money judgment against the landlord, and you know how much he hates to part with his money.

In any event, prepare to move elsewhere. You won't want to endure the wrath of a scrooge of a landlord who feels he has been fleeced and taken for a fool.

Landlord changes screen door policy.

Q. Friends of mine have lived in an apartment in a California beach community for the past nine years. This week the owner removed every front door and screen door on the entire building and installed new front doors. The new doors look good, but they have three clear window panes along the top, and someone tall enough can easily see through them into the apartments. To protect their privacy while their doors are closed, the tenants have to buy and hang curtains on the window panes. That's no big problem. They can handle that, but it's not the only problem. When they open their front door to let in the cool outside air, they let in flies as well, and also, they are exposed to intrusion.

All the tenants want their screen doors back so they can open their front doors for cool air and continue to enjoy a semblance of privacy. My friends and their landlord signed the usual month-to-month rental agreement a long time ago, but it doesn't address anything like this. The owner has flat-out refused to allow screen doors. One tenant complained so much that the owner told him he could get out if he's so unhappy with the new door arrangement. My friends have told me other things about the owner, things indicating that he is not a reasonable person to deal with.

The tenants want the owner to allow them to get their own screen doors and have the doors installed at their expense. They feel imprisoned and almost suffocated when their doors are closed, and at risk to intrusion when they're open. They want their screen doors back.

My friends are at a point now where they are considering moving out of their apartment if they can't have a screen door.

I live in a building where the owner allows us to have a screen door so long as we pay for it ourselves. I have a screen door myself and would definitely not live here if I couldn't have one.

What, if anything, can my friends do about this situation?

—C.D., California

A. There are at least six things your friends could do.

1) They could experiment with air flow through their screened windows and rearrange their furniture so they could use the windows to let the cool air in and still keep flies out.

2) They could install an instant screen on their front door, a screen which requires no tools, nails, or screws.

3) They could ask other rental property managers in the area about their screen door policies and then arrange a meeting with the landlord to discuss his policy.

4) They could move elsewhere.

5) They could install an ordinary screen door themselves in defiance of the owner.

6) They could file a lawsuit against the owner, either on their own or with the other tenants in the building, for stripping them of a right which they had when they moved in.

These alternatives are in the order I would consider them if I were in your friend's two tennies and trying to solve this vexing problem. Let's take a look at each of them in turn.

1) Because your friends were used to opening their front door to admit the cool ocean air, they may have overlooked opening screened windows to do exactly the same thing. We open doors all the time to go in and out of buildings and rooms. We're so used to opening doors that opening one to admit cool air is a perfectly natural thing to do. We don't open windows all the time, and we sometimes forget that we could open a window to admit cool air. Whereas screens are optional on doors at rental properties, they are not optional on windows. Windows must have screens. Landlords have been sued successfully for not having screens on their windows when crimes occur. Assuming that your friends' windows have screens, I would advise them to experiment with the air flow through their windows and try to duplicate the same flow they get from opening their door. This alternative is the first one I would try because it's simple, it's free, and it's nonconfrontational.

2) Fortunately enough, there's a screen on the market now which is tailor-made to solve the very kind of problem your friends are facing. Its inventor came up with the idea in order to give apartment and condo dwellers a functional screen-door where they aren't permitted to have a standard framed screen door. This unframed screen door is called Bug Off™, and it attaches to the top of a doorframe with a spring tension rod and to the bottom with Velcro® adhesive strips. It has a two-inch overlap in the center where it parts to admit people passing through. Gravity closes the screen after a body passes through, and magnets keep it closed. It does a good job of keeping bugs out, and it also closes off the opening so that there is at least some barrier to intrusion. Somebody coming up to a door with a Bug Off™ screen door installed would be inclined to knock or ring the doorbell before entering, whereas an open door would be an open invitation to enter. A Bug Off™ screen door is not as good as a closed and locked framed screen door in discouraging intrusion because it cannot be locked, but then the latches and locks on framed screen doors are flimsy things, hardly sufficient deterrents to anybody intent upon entering. To see what a Bug Off™ screen door looks like, go to bugoffscreen.com.

3) Although your friends' landlord has a reputation for being unreasonable, maybe, just maybe, he would listen to them if they would meet with him and talk calmly about his screen door policy and the policies in force at other apartment complexes in the area. They should listen to him explain why he adopted his own policy. They should tell him what they learned from polling managers at other complexes, and they should tell him why they believe he ought to rethink his policy in order to please all of the tenants in the building. Dialog sometimes works miracles, and they should not do anything drastic until they have tried dialog. As a last resort while trying this alternative, they might give him a copy of a letter signed by all the tenants stating that they plan to move unless he changes his policy. It might wake him up to the fact that his policy will empty out his building and interrupt his income, and he'll have to find all new tenants in order to restore that income.

4) Moving elsewhere is always an alternative for tenants who have encountered an unreasonable landlord. Your friends' landlord is being unreasonable by refusing to allow screen doors when tenant after tenant is pleading with him to let them install one. Since this unreasonable position of his is not the only manifestation of his unreasonableness, your friends might want to consider moving somewhere where they can have a screen door and where they can put some distance between themselves and this unreasonable man.

5) Installing a screen door in spite of the landlord's specific prohibition against it is an alternative which only intrepid or desperate tenants ought to try. It's a drastic measure. In this case, the best way to try it would be to convince all the tenants in the building to try it at the same time, so that the landlord would understand that he is facing a mutiny rather than a single defiant tenant. Tenants who defy their landlord must know that they are throwing caution to the sea breezes. It's a risky business and requires uncommon fortitude because it may result in their eviction. They must know that the landlord will react when he feels his authority has been undermined, and there's no telling how this landlord will react, for he has already shown himself to be unreasonable.

6) Filing a lawsuit against an unreasonable landlord for stripping your friends of a right they had when they moved in is no simple matter and should be the last resort they consider, if they consider it at all. It would require good money,

good records, good witnesses, a good attorney, a good judge, and good luck, and even if they were to win a judgment, they might find that they actually won nothing at all other than a courtroom victory because the cost in terms of their time and money was high and because they would have poisoned their relationship with their landlord altogether. He would be more of an ogre to them then than ever.

Tell your friends to consider the alternatives above and try one. Neither keeping their front door closed and moping around in a hotbox of an apartment all day nor keeping their front door open and swatting flies is the best way for them to respond to their landlord's dictum denying them a screen door. There are alternatives, and one of them will work.

They think worn-out carpet should be a habitability issue.

Q. We have been renting an eighteen-year-old house for the past twelve years from landlords who live five-hundred miles away. Currently, we are paying a rent of $1,800 a month, which is maybe a hundred dollars below market for a house like ours. As long as we have lived here, our landlady has come to see the house twice and our landlord has come once. There is no property management company or local person we deal with. We deal with them directly.

Whenever something needs fixing, we call them and eventually they get around to fixing it. For example, when the stove conked out, we called and told them about it. Five months later, without telling us anything about their plans, they had a new stove delivered and installed.

We have painted all the rooms in the house ourselves over the years. The landlady never reimburses us. She told us that she paints the home where she lives, and she feels we should do the same to the home where we live, even though it belongs to her and not to us.

Right now the carpet is coming apart. It's the original eighteen-year-old carpet, and it was of poor quality to begin with. We've called carpet cleaning companies for estimates to clean and fix it, but they won't touch it for fear that it will come apart even more and they'll be blamed. We've rented a steam cleaner from the local supermarket several times ourselves, and we can get it reasonably clean, but in the traffic areas, it's worn right down to the backing, and we can't

do anything about that. It looks awful. The seams are split, and the padding is disintegrating. We have sent our landlords photos to show them how bad the carpet is, and they are aware that we have tripped on the split seams and the large wrinkles, but they don't seem to care.

When the husband was here on his one and only visit four years ago, he agreed then that it was in horrible shape and needed to be replaced, but the wife calls the shots in their family, and she refuses to replace it.

We want to stay here. We're in a nice neighborhood, and we're raising our children to think of it as their neighborhood. We want them to have a childhood of continuity rather than one of change. They have friends here they have known all their lives, and they go to neighborhood schools. We don't really want to move, but we're frustrated with our landlady.

What can we do to get our stingy landlady to install new carpet? We know that every rental property comes with an implied warranty of habitability, and we're wondering whether we can force her to replace the carpet under this warranty. Does worn-out carpet ever become a habitability issue?
—G.R., California

A. Carpet never becomes a habitability issue. Carpet is a floor covering, and like window coverings, it's superfluous to habitability. It's pleasing to the eye and it's comfortable under foot, but it's not essential. A dwelling with bare plywood or concrete floors would be just as habitable as a dwelling with luxurious, pillow-soft carpet. A leaky roof, a plugged toilet, a broken front-door lock, a cockroach infestation, and a nonfunctional heater are all habitability issues. They make a dwelling uninhabitable. They come under the warranty of habitability. Worn-out carpet does not.

Carpet like yours could be a liability issue if it should cause a trip-and-fall accident, but bad as it is, it's still not a habitability issue.

Even so, there are some things you may do to make it look better and some things you may do to get your landlady to replace it.

To make it look better, rent a knee kicker and try removing the wrinkles yourself, or hire a carpet installer to restretch it carefully and release him from liability for any damage he might cause to the carpet. Then buy some inexpensive area rugs and put them here and there to cover the worst-looking areas, arranging them to look as if they were put there to decorate rather than to conceal.

To get your landlords to replace the carpet, try plan A first. Become a squeaky wheel. Take some photos from angles which make the carpet look even worse than it is if that's possible, and enclose a photo and a short note with every rent check. Remind them that your carpet still needs to be replaced and that you and your children would be most relieved if you no longer had to worry about tripping and falling on the old carpet. Mention that the contract carpet installed in a new house has a useful life of five to ten years and that the life of the carpet in your home is all used up. It's eight years beyond its useful life expectancy. It's shot.

Because your landlords live so far away and certainly don't want to travel five hundred miles to shop for carpet in your vicinity, do some groundwork and legwork for them to make a carpet purchase easy. Draw a diagram of your home and measure the carpeted areas. Learn what you can about carpet, pad, and installation just as if you were the homeowner. Then go shopping for carpet just as if you were the homeowner. Get three bids for similar carpet from local firms, and submit them to your landlords together with a letter explaining what you have learned about carpet and giving them your color preference. After that, wait six months, all the time, of course, reminding them when you send them your rent check that the carpet needs to be replaced.

As you already know from experience, your landlords move slowly, but they should have responded within six months to your carpet replacement campaign with a yea or a nay. If the answer is nay, resort to plan B or plan C if you're tired of seeing area rugs on top of the unsightly wall-to-wall carpet and you still want them to replace it.

Plan B is simple. Offer to pay some of the cost. Remember, you are renting the house for less than market rent. You could justify to yourselves paying some of the cost of the replacement carpet, and doing so might be enough to make your landlords understand how serious you are about replacing the embarrassing carpet you have to live with. "Some of the cost" should be specific and should not be a dollar amount or a percentage of the total. They're too subject to negotiation. Instead, offer to pay for the carpet pad or the installation. You know from the bids you obtained

earlier approximately how much they would obligate you to pay.

Plan C is more complicated than plan B. It requires some legwork. You have already given your landlords three bids for new carpet. Now give them a bid for used carpet installed by a freelance installer.

Used carpet can be a great deal for anybody who wants carpet with life in it at a rock-bottom price and doesn't mind purchasing something used. Think of it as being in the same league as buying a used car. There's no stigma attached. Besides, you may be saving landfill space by installing used carpet.

Installers come by perfectly good used carpet every so often when homeowners are redecorating and want to change their carpet, not because it's worn, but because it doesn't match their new color scheme. The installer gets the carpet at no cost and wants to get rid of it as quickly as possible so he doesn't have to store it or haul it to the dump.

Contact several carpet installers who advertise in the "services available" section of your newspaper or list themselves on the internet. Tell them what you're looking for, especially the quantity and the color, and ask them approximately how much such carpet would cost, including a new 3/8-inch rebonded pad and installation. You might even tell them that you would take two or three different colors and styles for the different rooms in your home if there isn't enough yardage of a single carpet available.

Next, phone your landlords and tell them what you have learned about used carpet, and ask them if they would approve such a purchase. Tell them that you would have to move quickly to buy it when it becomes available, so you would need their advance approval of the purchase because there might not be enough time for you to get hold of them when an installer calls to tell you what he has available. Tell them that you would pay for the entire cost out of your own funds because installers want to be paid on the spot for such jobs and that you would deduct the amount from your next rent check. If they give you the go-ahead, contact the installer and wait for his phone call. Rather than accept the carpet sight unseen, take a look at it and decide whether it's right for your home and is priced right. If it isn't, give it a pass and wait for another phone call.

Unfortunately, you have landlords who are not

savvy about the landlording business. They don't seem to understand that things at their rental house wear out and require replacement periodically in order for it to attract and keep good tenants. As long-term, good tenants, who are neither rough on the house nor demanding, you have spoiled them. You have lulled them into thinking that they can keep collecting rent month after month, year after year, without their having to visit the house regularly, without their having to pay a property management company to look after it, without their having to do much to keep you as tenants, and without their having to spend much to keep the house maintained.

Savvy landlords would have replaced the worn-out carpet long ago. Lacking savvy landlords, you have to prod your landlords into action. Go ahead now. Prod them.

6
Working
with the Neighbors

Neighbor from hell costs landlord the perfect renter.

Q. For some time I had the perfect renter in a single-family home. She paid her rent early, never bothered me with complaints, kept the interior immaculate, kept the lawn looking better than any in the neighborhood, and even sent me other good referrals. Then my nightmare began.

The house next door was purchased by a guy who has completely destroyed his own property and in so doing has effectively destroyed mine. There are junk cars in his yard and a huge dog pen that contains several dogs. Beer cans are everywhere, and the loud parties never seem to stop. He has cut trees down and left the mess all over the ground. My renter called the police on him, then the city, and finally me. There was no reasoning with him. Finally, she gave up and moved out. I can't rent this house now because every prospective renter has been frightened off by the mess next door. This small town doesn't have the resources to handle such a nuisance, and I am sitting on a very nice, but empty, house. I need help. I can't afford to lose the rental income.
—R.F., North Carolina

A. Short of doing something to the guy which you might regret while sitting in a prison cell for twenty years, you still have options. By all means, do check county records to see whether he really owns the property or whether he says he owns it and is actually renting. If he's renting, contact the owner about the problem. If he owns the place, find out who holds the mortgage and contact them about the property's condition. They'll be interested because their loan isn't much good without good collateral behind it, and a badly maintained property is not good collateral. They likely have clauses in their loan papers about his maintaining the property in good condition, and they could call the loan due if he isn't maintain-

ing it.

Keep the pressure on the city to do something about the problem. Whether they have sufficient resources to handle it or not, you need to be a squeaky wheel around city hall. Eventually they'll tire of your squeaking, and they'll do something. O, and don't forget to contact the county to get your property taxes reduced. The property isn't worth what it was when last assessed. Why should you continue to pay high taxes when the local authority supported by your tax money won't help you solve this problem. Hit them in their pocketbook.

Assuming that you have already contacted the guy directly about the problem, but to no avail, you could sue him in small claims court for the loss of rents you've suffered and whatever else you might think of, or you could hire an attorney to go after him for bigger bucks.

If you have the bucks available, you could offer to buy the guy out for a fair price, or if you have the bucks available and you think a solid fence would do some good, you could build a solid fence along the side of your property contiguous to the nuisance property.

Don't adopt a victim's mentality here and mouth the mantra, "Woe is me. Woe is me." You have a major problem. Unless you tackle it head on, it will continue until you eventually lose your rental house.

Slumlord tree owner won't help neighbor with driveway damage.

Q. When I purchased my rental property approximately four years ago, the driveway was in good condition. I have a photograph showing what it looked like then. Over the past year, it has developed bigger and bigger cracks. I believe the neighbor's tree, which is at least fifty feet tall, is the cause. The driveway is approximately thirty feet from his tree.

A certified nurseryman told me that the roots of this particular elm tree will spread out one-and-a-half times its height. That's a radius of 75 feet, which is more than enough of a spread to damage my driveway.

I have written the owner of the neighboring property and talked to him on the phone about this problem. At first he seemed interested in helping. He did cut three above-ground roots heading in the direction of my driveway, but now he says he won't do anything more. He wants to sell his duplex and says he will let the next owner deal with the problem.

This guy is a slumlord. His tenants dislike him because he doesn't look after his property. The roof leaks, and he hasn't done a thing about it. He has tried to tell me that he's a businessman who must watch how he spends his money on a rental property.

What should I do? How can I prove that his tree is breaking up my driveway? He has only a post office box and doesn't accept certified mail. I don't know where he lives, but I know that his wife works as a teacher in town somewhere.
—E.W., Washington

A. Like tenants, landlords come in all varieties, some good, some mediocre, some terrible. This landlord appears to be of the terrible variety. He won't cooperate with you, a neighbor, to help solve a mutual problem, and he won't maintain his rental property according to minimum standards. What he doesn't realize is that his miserliness is costing him more than he could ever be saving. His duplex is worth less and less every day because he isn't maintaining it.

As for you, don't despair. There are ways to deal with people who think they can shirk their responsibilities as rental property owners and neighbors.

First, document your case in words and photos. Your "before" photograph is a good beginning. Second, get at least two bids from certified arborists for severing the roots causing the damage to your driveway. Third, get at least two bids from concrete contractors for repairing the driveway. Fourth, send a letter to the neighbor telling him that you intend to have his tree's roots severed on your property to protect your driveway and that you intend to have the driveway itself repaired as necessary. Tell him that you expect him to pay for this work by a certain deadline (don't get your hopes up that he will be forth-

coming). Fifth, order the work to be done and pay for it out of your own pocket. Sixth, file a small claims action against the neighbor for the entire amount.

Trying to be as wise as Solomon, the judge will likely award you half of what you request. Take it. At least the problem will be solved.

As for locating your antagonist and serving him with papers, you need only check county records for the owner of the parcel in question to get his address. If the wife is listed as a co-owner, you may want to serve her at the school where she teaches. That will suffice. You needn't serve them both. If you want to serve him and you haven't been successful in serving him by mail, hire somebody to deliver the summons in person at his residence or do it yourself in the presence of a witness.

Don't let the problem continue to vex you. Do something about it.

Also, consider buying the property to take care of the greater problem of having a slumlord doing business next door. Contact him with an offer to purchase based upon an appraisal from an appraiser acceptable to both of you. Tell him that if both of you accept the appraisal as a realistic value, you will split the commission he would otherwise have to pay a real estate agent and pay him that amount for the property. Besides the benefit to you of buying a neighboring property should you consummate the transaction, you may find that if he considers you a buyer, he will cooperate more fully with your proposal to deal with the tree damage.

Unknown property line causes neighbor concern.

Q. The neighbor next door to my rental house poured a concrete landscaping border on or near our common property line, and he wants to put up a low fence along it, too. We can't tell where the property line is because the contractor pulled the survey pin at one corner when he put up the boundary fence, and the other pin was lost in the course of the landscaping work during construction.

The neighbor, who is a difficult person, thinks that he messed up and may have encroached slightly on my property with his concrete border. He called me over and tried to convince me that he's not really encroaching, but you can't tell without a new survey. I told him that I'd talk it over with my wife and get back to him.

My concern is that a new survey might show an encroachment when I go to sell the property, and it could mess up the sale. I think that I should at least write him and tell him that we give permission for the encroachment for now, but in no way do we relinquish our rights to our property. An alternative might be to ask him right now for a quitclaim of any improvements encroaching on our property. What do you think?
—D.C., Idaho

A. You and your neighbor are guessing about the exact location of the property line, and you shouldn't be. You should know its exact location. Because it's an issue now and could become a bigger issue later when you sell the property, you should have the line surveyed. You'll likely have to get it surveyed when you sell the property anyway. Don't wait until then.

Call several surveyors and get an idea from them how much the survey would cost. Then contact the neighbor and offer to split the cost with him.

Once you know where the line is, you and the neighbor can make a more rational decision about what to do.

Neighbor wants to replace property management company.

Q. My neighbor next door had to leave the state for her work. She decided to keep her house and rent it out. She hired a property management company to look after it in her absence, thinking that they would know what they're doing. What a mistake! What a nightmare! They don't seem to know what they're doing, and they seem to be dishonest to boot.

The tenant they selected moved out prematurely because of a death in the family, and she agreed to forfeit her last month's rent and deposits as compensation for moving early. The management company told my neighbor that she wouldn't see any of that money because they had used it all up to fix the house before the tenant moved in. Their story is hard to believe because they were paid separately for all the interior painting and outside work they did before the tenant moved in.

My neighbor wants to sever her relationship with the management company and have me look after the property. I'm willing. I've already been helping her get quotes to fix up the house for new tenants. The tenant who moved out told me that she had asked the management company to repair certain things that were wrong with the house, but they never did anything. As a result, the house needs more repairs than it would otherwise need after somebody moves out.

My neighbor will be giving me funds up-front to pay bills, and I will be giving her work orders for the repairs, maintenance, and cleaning so that she can decide for herself what work she wants to have done. Together we'll decide upon whom to hire to do the work she chooses to have done, and I'll pay for the work from the funds she entrusts to me.

I'm a little concerned about my relationship with my neighbor. I like her and don't want our relationship to sour if I do something wrong while I'm looking after her rental house. Do you have any suggestions for how we can preserve a good relationship while we're doing business together?
—C.T., California

A. Your neighbor is fortunate to have a good neighbor like you who is interested in looking after her rental house. You are the best person for the job. You care about her. You care about the neighbors. You care about the neighborhood. You care about the house. The property managers she had working for her cared only about themselves.

You are right to be concerned about your personal relationship with your neighbor as the two of you enter into a business relationship. Where money is concerned, people often lose their perspective and wind up becoming estranged if even the slightest thing goes awry or if they begin to doubt one another's honesty.

Follow these four fundamental precepts and you will greatly increase the chances of having a successful business relationship with your neighbor:

1) Minimize your handling of the neighbor's money.

2) Communicate with the neighbor whenever you feel the need.

3) Make important decisions together.

4) Settle upon a fair compensation for your work.

In order to minimize the handling of your neighbor's money, structure the way you handle it when it comes in and when it goes out so that you couldn't pilfer much even if you wanted to. Train the tenants to pay their rent with checks or money orders made out to the neighbor and mailed directly to her or else given to you so you can mail them to her. Never accept cash. You don't want to have access to the money coming in, and you don't want to have access to the money going out. You should have only a small amount of petty cash available, perhaps a hundred dollars, for buying miscellaneous items you need immediately and for paying casual laborers who insist upon being paid on the spot as soon as they finish their work. Advise anybody else doing work at the house that the owner will pay them directly by check, and make sure that the owner pays them promptly. Tell her that you won't be able to hire help in the future if she puts off paying the bills. To expedite payment, you might want to communicate with her soon after completion of a job to give her the bill's particulars and urge her to pay it right away.

In order to communicate with your neighbor whenever you feel the need, arrange to communicate with her by fax or email as well as by telephone. You will want to review all written documents with her, especially rental applications, rental agreements, and bills, as quickly as possible so the two of you can make appropriate decisions about them together, and neither of you will have to wait by your mailbox for postal workers to ferry the documents back and forth physically.

In order to make important decisions together, discuss with your neighbor which subjects she considers important enough for you to confer with her about. Selection of tenants ought to be important enough. Expenditures above a certain amount ought to be important enough. Building deterioration ought to be important enough. A local news story about rent control ought to be important enough. In discussing these subjects, you may find that she wants to be more or less involved with property decisions than you think. No matter how much or how little involvement she wants, insist that you want her to help you make tenant selection decisions at the very least because you know that they are always important and you don't want to be making them alone.

In order to settle upon a fair compensation for your work, discuss in advance exactly what your neighbor wants you to do as the caretaker of the property and what you are willing to do. Estimate how many hours the work ought to take you during a normal month when you don't have to deal with a tenancy transition, and add two hours per month as compensation for merely taking on the responsibility of looking after the house. Multiply that number by a rate pegged several dollars higher than the minimum wage, and use it as the monthly base pay. Use a time sheet to keep track of the time you spend looking after the property every month, and request extra hourly compensation whenever you exceed the normal number of hours. Write up an informal letter of understanding listing your responsibilities and compensation, give a copy to your neighbor, and review it with her every six to twelve months.

Following these four fundamental precepts will help you and your neighbor remain on good terms throughout your business relationship, but you still must learn all you can about the landlording business so you will be a good substitute landlord. Get a copy of the *Landlording* book and follow its common-sense advice.

Neighbor wants floodlight removed or shaded.

Q. Next door to my fourplex is a two-story, owner-occupied duplex. The owner lives in the upper flat and has built a deck onto her unit where she entertains regularly. For some time now, she has been asking me to remove a pole-mounted floodlight I installed on my property long before she bought her place. She says it shines onto her deck and bothers her and her guests. I have told her that I installed the light to illuminate my property and protect my tenants from predators after dark. It's there for safety and security. I have also tried to tell her that she benefits from it as well as my tenants and I do, and she doesn't even have to pay anything for its benefits.

I want to be a good neighbor, but I also want to be a good landlord, and I don't want to be sued by a tenant of mine who suffered somehow because I removed the light. I don't want to remove it, and I have told her more than once that I don't want to remove it.

She doesn't seem to want to take "no" for an answer. She is one persistent lady, and she mentions the offensive floodlight every time she sees me. It really does appear to be a mote in her eye.

Today I received a letter from her asking me to consider shielding the light. She said that she had contacted the manufacturer and learned that there is a special shield available to restrict the light to a certain area. She said that she would like to discuss with me the possibility of installing this shield sometime soon.

She's pushing me into a corner, and I'm not sure how to respond to her. Do you have any ideas?

—S.M., Virginia

A. Good neighbors are to be treasured and accommodated whenever possible. Treat a neighbor badly, and you'll be sorry later when you want the neighbor to do something for you. That time will come. Count on it.

Your floodlight is "trespassing" on your neighbor's property, and it's really bothering her. It's bothering her enough for it to have become a recurring topic whenever you meet and enough for her to have researched alternatives. Now that she thinks she has found an alternative, you should listen to her and consider using her alternative, but before you meet with her, you might want to look into various other alternatives which won't compromise your safety and security objectives.

Because your floodlight predates your neighbor's purchase of her duplex, it's likely to be as obsolete and inefficient as a blunderbuss. It is not what is known today as "quality outdoor lighting," that is, lighting which isn't wasted, isn't too bright, isn't too glaring, and isn't too inefficient. Quality outdoor lighting is directed downward, where it does some good, rather than upward or sideways, where it does no good. Your floodlight goes every which way, and it likely uses an inefficient mercury vapor lamp, which was the first bulb type used in pole lighting fixtures made available for exterior residential use.

You could buy or make a light-directing device like a shield, visor, or hood for your old floodlight, and it would surely be enough to satisfy your neighbor and illuminate your property sufficiently, but you'd still have an old, ugly, and inefficient fixture. Think instead about taking this opportunity to install an entirely new, up-to-date, quality outdoor lighting fixture which would be attractive and efficient.

One such fixture is the flat-lens "shoebox" fixture with a metal-halide bulb. The bulb fits up inside the fixture directly under a reflector, and the fixture has a horizontally aligned, flush-mounted lens. Placed twenty feet above the ground, this fixture produces minimal glare and minimal light pollution, and it would make your

neighbor a happy neighbor. Instead of being blinded by an ugly mercury-vapor lamp, she'd be seeing light directed downward from a modern fixture, and she wouldn't even be able to see the source of the light.

Because your neighbor is begging you for a solution to that blinding floodlight of yours, you might as well ask her to help you pay for a solution which would please you and her. Show her how attractive the shoebox fixture is, tell her what it will do for both of you, tell her why you think it's better than a light directing device added to that old eyesore of a fixture she hates so much, and ask her to split the cost.

If she agrees to split the cost, go ahead and install the new fixture. If she says she'd rather split the cost of a light directing device, tell her you'll have to think about that for a while. Give yourself a week and ask her again to split the cost of the new fixture. If she won't, go ahead with the light-directing device. Either way, you'll satisfy her, and you can point later to the solution you decided upon as an instance where you did her a favor.

Neighbors' overwatering concerns landlord and tenants.

Q. My rental house is in a shady glen. It gets less sunlight on a good day than the house next door, which sits on a hillside and gets enough sun for the neighbors to grow a productive vegetable garden every year. They raise everything from tomatoes to squash to sweet corn.

The neighbors are good about sharing the produce from their garden with my tenants and even with me when I come around. They are bad about overwatering. They use a well to irrigate their garden so they're not concerned about the cost of water when they irrigate. They will turn on the sprinklers in the morning before they leave for work and not turn them off until they return in the evening.

My tenants and I have told the neighbors that they're overwatering and that we're concerned about the runoff because it collects in the glen and under my house and makes the house cold and dank. My tenants have told me they're concerned about the muddy soil around the house all the time and about the cold air inside the house, but they haven't said anything to me about mold, at least not yet. I'm worried about mold because I know that it thrives in areas of high humidity and will certainly appear one day and cause me a lot of trouble.

The neighbors are nice people. They've listened to me when I've talked to them about the overwatering, and they've cut back on their watering somewhat.

Cutting back did help. There's less water standing around the house, but the ground is still wetter than it ought to be, and the air inside the house is still chilly and damp.

What more might I do to dry out the ground, dry out the house, make the house more comfortable for my tenants, and reduce the chances that mold might appear?
—F.G., Washington

A. You are fortunate to have neighbors who will listen to you and who will make some effort to cut back on their overwatering. Their cooperation is important to solving the problem. You want to maintain good relations with them because you want to feel that you can approach them whenever you come up with a fresh idea to try something which involves them and you also want to keep those fresh vegetables coming your way.

Since you have good neighbors and they have helped you already, go ahead and ask them for further help.

Ask them for blanket permission for either you or your tenants to enter their yard whenever one of you notices that they have forgotten to turn off the sprinklers. You don't want to be found trespassing in their yard even if you are there on a worthy mission.

Ask them to let you buy them as many timers as they need to program the watering times for their sprinklers. There are all kinds of timers available today for both garden hoses and complete sprinkler systems. They are all inexpensive. The neighbors probably know nothing about these timers because they have cheap water available to them and aren't concerned about waste. You could buy them a quarter bushel of timers for less than the price of a bushel of fresh tomatoes.

Cooperation from the neighbors will help only so much in solving the problem. They can help control the amount of water which flows from their yard into yours, but they can't help you move the water off your property. You have to do that.

To do that, you could work your way up from inexpensive solutions like digging a shallow swale to expensive solutions like putting in a French drain, but you might want to hire an engineer to do a "quick and dirty" analysis and give you an educated opinion about what you should do. You don't need a detailed written report. All you need are ideas. All you need is for the engineer to tell you what he would do if the house were his.

For inside the house, all you need is an accurate hygrometer (available from hardware stores) to monitor the relative humidity and some fans to exhaust the humid, stagnant indoor air to the great outdoors. The relative humidity inside the house ought to be 30-50%. Likely you will find that your dank house will be above 50%. That's a perfect environment for mold spores and dust mite allergens.

Once you have confirmed that the relative humidity inside the house is higher than normal, educate yourself and your tenants in the various methods available for reducing it. Keeping certain interior doors open and others closed helps. Using exhaust fans in the kitchen, bathroom, laundry, and basement, the rooms where humidity tends to be the highest, helps. Insulating around exterior doors and windows helps. Using an air conditioner (during hot days only, of course) to reduce both the indoor air's temperature and humidity helps. Using a space fan to keep the inside air from becoming stagnant helps.

Try one method, try them all.

Monitor the ground moisture outside the house and the relative humidity inside the house yourself, and do what you can in cooperation with the tenants and the neighbors to keep water from saturating the soil, the structure, and the indoor air, and you will be going a long way towards keeping trouble at bay.

7
Considering the Legalities

Tenants quote laws to confound landlord.

Q. I have had a couple of tenants quote me landlording laws for Georgia. Can you tell me where I can find these laws? Does your book have information for Georgia landlords?
—K.W., Georgia

A. Tenants love to quote laws favorable to themselves, but their quotations are seldom accurate. Don't assume that a tenant's rendition of a law is indeed the law.

All states now make their laws (codes) available over the internet on their legislatures' websites as a public service. Go to "legis.state.ga.us" and you will find Georgia's codes available there.

Every state's official website is at "state.[two-letter state abbreviation].us" where there's a link to the state legislature's website. To go directly to the laws for a particular state, you may also try "law.cornell.edu/states/listing.html" where there are links to laws by jurisdiction.

The *Landlording* book is specific to no state. It applies as much to Florida as it does to Georgia and Oregon and Massachusetts. The body of state laws governing rental properties in the United States is more generic than you might think. The *Landlording* book is generic as well.

Lawyer-tenant tells new landlord of law governing grace periods.

Q. I'm a new landlord, and I'm renting a condo in a seaside city to a lawyer. Yes, I know lawyers aren't known to be the best of tenants, but I took a chance on this one. In his lease, we agreed that the rent due date would be the first of every month, with a grace period extending to the fifth.

From the very beginning of his tenancy, he has never paid before the fifth. Once he even paid on the tenth. When I questioned him about his habitual delinquency, he said that there is a state law preventing me from assessing him a late fee until the rent is ten days delinquent. He refuses to pay before the fifth and would prefer to pay on the tenth.

Immediately upon hearing this, I questioned two independent property managers. They told me that they had never heard of such a law. When I asked my tenant to provide me with the specific legal reference, he ducked the question, stating that he was busy and would try to get to it some other time. That time has never come.

Is there such a law? If so, what is the specific legal reference?
—R.B., California

A. This tenant of yours is mistaken. There is no such law. No law in any state requires landlords to give a grace period for rent payments. The grace period is a matter addressed in the rental agreement, and it is freely given by the landlord to the tenant. It is not something forced upon the landlord by a law.

Some hard-nosed landlords give their tenants no grace period, none whatsoever. Their tenants must pay on the first or be prepared to face the landlord on their doorstep on the second. He gives them a pay-or-quit notice, and they must leave within the time specified in the notice or face certain eviction.

Laws in some parts of the country do specify that the rent due day must be a normal banking day, but that's all they specify. They say nothing about grace periods.

Because a rent due day may fall on the Saturday of a three-day weekend, in which case the tenant would automatically get three extra days to pay without penalty, I recommend that landlords give a grace period of four days every month, that they shouldn't consider a rent which is due on the first to be delinquent until the fifth.

You are being generous in giving your tenant

a grace period of five days. Your tenant's rent doesn't become delinquent until the sixth.

You might want to address your tenant's habitual delinquency with a letter stating that he has a choice. He may choose to leave things just as they are and pay on or before the fifth of the month without penalty, incurring the penalty stated in the rental agreement only if he chooses to pay after the fifth. Otherwise, he may choose to have his rent due date changed to the tenth of the month, in which case he would have until the fourteenth of the month to pay without penalty.

Should he choose to have his due date changed to the tenth, his rental period would be from the tenth of one month through the ninth of the next. Also, you would need to charge him for nine days extra upon changing to the new rental period. That one month only he would owe from the first of the month through the ninth of the following month.

In giving him this choice, you are reaffirming what the rental agreement says about the grace period and late payments, and you are saying that you are willing to accommodate him if he wishes to pay on the tenth and not incur a penalty. You are calling his bluff.

He may think he can bluff you because you're a novice landlord and don't know what you're doing. You need to call his bluff to prove to him that you do know what you're doing and that you expect him to follow the terms of the rental agreement or else.

Tenants claim there's a law about changing carpets.

Q. My tenants have told me that there's a state law requiring landlords to change the carpet in their rental properties every five years, even if the carpet isn't damaged, even if it shows no obvious or excessive wear. Is this true?
—N.D., California

A. Some jurisdictions have laws about how frequently landlords must paint their rental properties, but none that I'm aware of have laws about how frequently landlords must replace carpets.

Were there such a law, this country would be dotted with carpet mills, and they would be turning out carpet 24 hours a day.

Were there such a law, our landfills would be bulging with old carpet and carpet padding. There wouldn't be any room left for all the Pampers®.

Your tenants are pulling your leg. Laugh!

Landlord wants free legal help.

Q. I am being sued by a tenant who was cultivating a marijuana farm in my home. When the police were called to the home, the tenants fled the premises. I received a threatening letter from the city stating that I could be jailed and fined and have my property seized if this activity continued. I posted and sent a 30-day notice to the tenants to vacate the premises due to unlawful acts in the home, and now I am being sued for wrongful eviction. The problem is that I cannot afford an attorney. Do you know of a free legal service that can help?
—H.M., Utah

A. Attorneys do *pro bono* work for indigents, that is, for people who are homeless or hopeless, and you might qualify if you go to your nearest legal aid office and give them your particulars. Frankly, I doubt whether they'll hear you out once you mention that you're a landlord. Except for those New York City landlords who are owned by their rent-controlled apartments, landlords are considered meal tickets by attorneys.

Self-defense (*in pro per*) is the only way I know for you to defend yourself at no cost. If you feel game enough to try, do it. Go to your local law library, ask the librarian to help you select materials which might help you defend yourself, read them, gather every bit of evidence you can find, go into court, and be as plain and honest as you can be in your defense. You may succeed. People of average intelligence succeed in defending themselves in court every day.

If you don't want to represent yourself or you can't, you'll have to find the money somewhere to hire an attorney to represent you. You have no other choice.

Landlord wonders whether his agreement will stand up in court.

Q. I have been a landlord for ten years and am using a rental agreement I developed myself. My agreement charges tenants a late fee of $5 per day for every day they're late. I'm wondering whether this clause and others I originated myself will stand up in court so long as each tenant signs the agreement. Might a judge find anything in it illegal and rule against me even though it is clearly written and properly signed?
—T.N., Arkansas

A. The short answer to your question is a resounding YES. A judge might well rule against you on your hefty, unending late fee and on your other one-sided clauses, too. Just because an agreement is clearly written and properly signed doesn't mean that it's legal and enforceable.

Let's suppose that two people owe you money and you get them to sign an agreement stating that they will work off their debt at less than the minimum wage and that they will be responsible for any harm they do to themselves accidentally while on the job. You might get away with this arrangement so long as they aren't hurt on the job and so long as the agreement never sees the light of a fair employment office, but if they get hurt on the job or if the fair employment cops see the agreement, you'd better be prepared to give these former debtors of yours the PIN to your savings account. You're about to become a debtor of theirs. Making them work for less than the minimum wage and not covering them with workers' comp insurance is illegal, no matter how clear the agreement they sign to waive their rights.

Judges know that you as a landlord have the upper hand when you give tenants an agreement to sign. It's your agreement, not theirs, one written to protect you, not them. Tenants have little choice. They sign it or they don't get the keys to the dwelling they want to rent. So, whenever judges are deliberating over a dispute about a rental agreement, they tend to treat tenants as ignorant and landlords as informed. Tenants get the benefit of every doubt because they didn't write or select the agreement and aren't expected to know the law. Landlords write the agreements and are expected to know the law. They're in the landlording business, and they're held to a higher standard.

A single one-sided clause in an agreement will make a judge suspicious about the entire agreement and subject it to greater scrutiny. Keep your agreement as impartial as possible, starting with your prompt-payment policy.

You must have a prompt-payment policy in your agreement. That's a given. Even tenant-partial judges can understand the reasons why, but your policy must be fair. Charging tenants $5 per day for every day they're late is not a fair policy. At the end of a month, they could owe you a late fee of as much as $155. Try getting a judge to enforce that. Nope, it ain't gonna happen. If you charge a reasonable fixed-sum late fee, such as $50, or a percentage of the rent such as 5%, or a *per-diem* fee with a maximum of $50, the judge will likely consider it fair and help you enforce it. Late fees such as these bear some relation to the damages you suffer when the rent is late and ought to be so identified. Put something in your rental agreement stating that you and the tenant agree that because actual damages of late payment of rent are impracticable or extremely difficult to fix, both parties accept the late fee given in the agreement as liquidated damages.

No matter what's in your agreement, you'll never know for certain whether it will stand up in court until you go into court to find out. Even then, if one judge approves your entire agreement line by line, another one might pick it apart. Make it fair to begin with, and you won't have to wonder whether it will stand up in court. It will.

When reviewing your agreement, ask yourself this question, "Would I rent from a stranger who has this clause in the contract?" If the answer is yes, leave it. If the answer is no, change it. Make your agreement fair. You'll sleep better at night, and your golf game will improve.

Landlords want agreement to provide for inflation.

Q. We are getting ready to rent out a condominium we own and would like to include a clause in our rental agreement enabling us to adjust the rent automatically according to the change in the cost of living. Do you have any suggestions for verbiage we might use?
—C.T., Washington

A. If you want to include a clause in your rental agreement which will adjust the rent automatically without your intervention, you are asking for something you don't want, trouble.

If you want to include a clause in your rental agreement which will provide a guideline for adjusting the rent automatically with your intervention, you are asking for something you do want, support.

Trouble will arise if you expect a clause in your rental agreement to free you from having to do anything about adjusting the rent. The clause isn't going to remember to check the index you choose. The clause isn't going to apply the percentage of change in the index to the tenants' rent, and it isn't going to notify the tenants of the change. Somebody has to do these things, you or your tenants.

You can't expect your tenants to do them. They may forget. They may get something wrong.

You have to do these things yourselves, and because they're important to you, you won't forget. You'll get them right.

A sound rental agreement clause addressing rent adjustments and tying them to an external index will help ease you through the process of adjusting rent. It will support your decision to adjust the rent by a certain amount because it will show the tenants that the adjustment you decide upon is not arbitrary, not something you plucked out of the air. It's objective. It's based upon a perfectly reasonable and well recognized index.

There are two indexes you should consider for your index, the Cost-of-Living Adjustment (COLA) used by the Social Security Administration (SSA) and the Consumer Price Index (CPI) used by the Bureau of Labor Statistics (BLS). Both are good standards to use for measuring inflation.

The SSA bases its COLA on statistics gathered by the BLS, specifically the Consumer Price Index for Urban Wage Earners and Clerical Workers (CPI-W), and it publishes this figure during the fourth quarter of every year. As an index for your use, COLA has two advantages. It is widely known because it affects everybody who benefits from Social Security, and it has never gone down since the SSA began using it in 1975. It has risen steadily every year.

The CPI is actually not one number. It's many numbers. It might be called the Consumer Price Indexes rather than the Consumer Price Index. The BLS follows the prices of many different categories of goods and services and the wages of many different occupations region by region throughout the country, and it makes the findings available in printed form and on the internet (bls.gov). It follows the prices of everything from "navel oranges" to "rent of primary residence" and the wages of occupations from bartender to magistrate. You could identify a narrow category and a narrow region as your index, or you could identify a broader index based upon a basket of goods and services in a broad region. The statistics are there for you to use. They're all Consumer Price Indexes.

As an index for your use, a narrow CPI covering rents in your statistical area has the advantage and disadvantage of focus. It focuses on rents and nothing else, so it's representative of the market for rental housing in your part of the country, and that's good. It's measuring what you want it to measure, but it also has the disadvantage of focus. It's affected by areawide supply and demand. If new apartment complexes become available and there is no influx of people in the area, the index will go down. If new employers come into the area and generate a demand for rental housing, the index will go up.

Be prepared to raise or lower your rents if you adopt a narrow CPI as an index. It will swing both ways and be more volatile than a broader index.

Before you adopt any index, check its history. See how it has fluctuated in the past and consider whether you would have wanted to have adopted it as your index ten years ago. Do you want an index which goes up steadily year after year if only in small increments, or do you want an index which goes up in some years and down in others, sometimes in large increments? The choice is yours.

Once you select an index, identify it in the rental agreement and be consistent. Use it throughout the tenancy. Consistency is fair to you and fair to your tenant.

The actual verbiage you use in the rental agreement clause ought to be as specific as it can be. It ought to define the index you plan to use. It ought to identify who will check the index. It ought to include a time frame for checking the index. It ought to identify who will apply the index to the rent. It ought to specify the type of notice used, what will appear in the notice, and how and when it will be served. It also ought to mention whether the landlord has any "wiggle room" to raise the rent an additional amount for other reasons.

Here's my version of such a clause:
ANNUAL RENT ADJUSTMENT—Every year, two months and one week prior to the anniversary date of this rental agreement, Landlords will check the latest [cross out the alternative which does not apply and initial this paragraph] (Cost of Living Adjustment used the Social Security Administration) (Consumer Price Index produced by the Bureau of Labor Statistics covering "rent of shelter" in the dwelling's statistical area) and will adjust the monthly rent according to the percentage of change in this index. Landlords will inform Tenants of this percentage, of the result-

ing dollar change in their rent, and of their new rent in a sixty-day notice served in person or by first-class mail. This clause does not preclude Landlords from adjusting the rent at other times and for other reasons.

Previous owner's agreement is the question.

Q. When you buy an income property, must you honor the previous owner's rental agreement, or can you start fresh with your own?
—D.W., Ohio

A. Fixed-term and month-to-month rental agreements go with the property unless the current agreement provides otherwise.

Should you buy a rental house with the intention of making it your primary residence, for example, and should the tenants have a year's lease which still has five months to run, you would have to wait the five months before you could move in unless you were able to convince the tenants to move early of their own volition.

Rental property buyers should always review every current rental agreement before committing to buy.

The long-form rental agreement in the *Landlording* book contains the following provision: "Sale of the Dwelling–If Owners sell this dwelling or otherwise transfer its Ownership to another party, they shall have the right to terminate this Agreement by giving Tenants written notice of at least sixty days, notwithstanding any conflicting occupancy rights Tenants might have under a fixed-term agreement. Should Tenants have conflicting occupancy rights guaranteed them by law, however, those legal rights shall prevail."

That provision would enable a buyer to break the current fixed-term rental agreement upon giving sixty days' notice unless there were a state law to the contrary.

His parents have verbal agreement and want to evict.

Q. My parents live in Denver and own a home in Los Angeles which they rented to a family with only a verbal rental agreement. They have decided to evict the family because nobody there is abiding by the agreement.

Can they legally evict somebody under a verbal agreement?
—A.L., California

A. Verbal agreements aren't worth the paper they're written on, but they're legal agreements all the same and they don't preclude the landlord from pursuing an eviction. Because there are no signed documents to prove that there was agreement between the parties about dates, amounts, pets, people, and conditions, proving one's case in court is more difficult, though by no means impossible. Your parents should proceed with the eviction immediately if they have reason to evict. They should not let the verbal agreement delay or stop them.

Good son that you are, keep them from ever renting the home using a verbal agreement again.

She wants to evict tenant from illegal dwelling.

Q. I live in a house in Queens, New York City, and rent out the attic, the basement, and the second floor to tenants. Recently I became ill, and now my son wants to move back home to take care of me.

I just found out that the attic and basement are actually illegal dwellings since my house is registered as a two-family, rather than a four-family, house. The laws here are not particularly favorable to landlords who own such dwellings. I am trying to do the right thing by asking the tenants to leave so that I can legalize the dwellings or leave them unrented if legalization is too expensive. I also want my son to move into the attic.

The problem is that one of my tenants does not want to leave. He's really mad. He has a month-to-month, non-rent-stabilized tenancy, but even so, the laws say I can't evict him through housing court since he's living in an illegal multiple dwelling. Instead, I must seek an ejectment action through superior court. This could take six months, and in the interim the tenant does not have to pay any rent! I could also get assessed penalties from the department of buildings and housing if they come around to inspect the attic or basement because they will surely give me a violation notice which I will need to comply with.

What can do? I'm at a loss. I'm trying to conform to the law by getting rid of my illegal apartments, and now they make it unbelievably difficult for me to do just that. I'm trying to make this building safe, and it seems that I will have to pay a lot of money to make it so. Is there any

advice you can give me?
—B.N., New York

A. Yours is a "let sleeping dogs lie" situation. Wake the dog, and watch out for trouble!

The best thing you can do as far as your building is concerned is nothing. You are better off allowing your current tenants to stay put than you are trying to get them to leave against their will.

Landlords are always better off to stay clear of bureaucrats and courtrooms. You're going to be tied up with both of them, and you're going to be begging for mercy if you continue. You're also going to be paying out some big bucks to set everything straight.

As for your son's returning home to help you during your illness, you should find him some space in your own living quarters or find him a place to rent nearby. When one of your tenants leaves on his own accord, move your son into that unit.

Tell that tenant of yours who doesn't want to leave that you have changed your mind. He can stay. You don't want him waking the "sleeping dog," and he surely will if you force him to move.

Little by little, fix your two non-conforming units up so that they will comply with the housing codes, and then apply to put them on the official rolls as rental units.

Tenant may not vacate in thirty days.

Q. I've given a tenant a 30-day notice to terminate tenancy, and I'm thinking he's not going to move. What do I do if the tenant does not vacate and causes problems?
—H.B., Illinois

A. If the tenant does not vacate at the end of the thirty-day period, you may proceed directly to court with an eviction action if you want to. You do not need to serve another notice or wait any longer.

Make sure that you wait the entire thirty days. Some landlords think that the thirty days in 30-day notices equates to a month, and they get into trouble by filing their court papers prematurely. You can't get into trouble filing an eviction action late, but you can get into trouble filing one early. The thirty days in 30-day notices equates to thirty days, not to a month.

You may not want to go directly to court at the end of the thirty-day period, however, if you think you can deal with the tenant. Going into court will cost you money and time. Offer to give the tenant all or most of his deposit back if he vacates within three days, and get the agreement in writing. Such an agreement looks good in court to a judge should you eventually wind up in court because the judge will understand that you were trying to negotiate with the tenant in good faith.

Landlord wants tenants out in 60 days, but they want 75.

Q. Our tenants were given a 60-day notice to terminate tenancy. On the same day we gave them notice, they sent us notice that they would vacate in seventy-five days. We want them out. What are our legal rights?
—S.M., Wyoming

A. Even though you have given the tenants sixty days to move out and you could exercise your legal right to get rid of them in sixty days, you would be hard pressed to evict them on the basis of your sixty-day notice in less than seventy-five days. You'd have to file court papers, you'd have to get the papers served, you'd have to wait the required time, and you'd incur legal costs, too.

Wait the seventy-five days and see whether they move out. If they don't, you may go directly to court to file the papers to evict them.

Tenant wants to break lease four months early.

Q. We just bought a five-unit property about a month ago and inherited the tenants and their leases.

One of the tenants has told us that she wants to break her lease and move out four months early. We gave her verbal approval and asked that she fill out a notice of intention to vacate which we're going to give her in the next day or two. We don't expect her to pay rent for the next four months if the unit remains vacant. We'd probably have trouble collecting it anyway.

We think we could rent the apartment soon after she moves, but we want to renovate it (which may take four weeks) before we re-rent it. We feel we could get a higher rent if it's renovated.

What do we do in this case? Can we charge her a fee for breaking her lease? There's nothing in her current rental agreement about a fee. Is that something we need to write into our future rental agreements if we want to enforce that? Or is it illegal?

—M.P., California

A. The penalty tenants pay for breaking a lease is the rent they are supposed to pay for the balance of the lease, provided that the unit remains vacant. If the tenant moves before the end of the lease and pays for the balance of the lease period, you must make an effort to re-rent the unit to another tenant. If you do re-rent the unit, you must refund the money the first tenant paid for any overlapping period of the tenancies. You cannot charge double rent.

You needn't include in future agreements any special fee for breaking a lease, but you may want to clarify what the penalty is. Some tenants might not understand when signing a lease that they are obligated to pay rent for the entire lease period.

In your case, you might tell the tenant that she owes you four months' rent for breaking the lease but that you will charge her only a fourth of that amount, only one month's rent. She would likely feel relieved, and you could go ahead and do the renovations as quickly as possible while still making an effort to re-rent the unit during the renovations. You'd be doing her a favor and yourself a favor as well.

Tenant breaks lease and finds new tenant who fails to move in.

Q. I am a landlord's personal assistant and have begun handling some of the management of his apartment building. Two months ago, a woman moved into one of the nicer apartments and signed a year's lease. A month later, she let me know that she had found her dream job out West and was moving there as soon as possible. She wanted to know what her options were, and I told her that she needed to find a new tenant to take over the remaining ten months on her lease.

She and I both ran ads and took several calls, and she found someone named Emily who was interested. When I took Emily's application and deposit, she told me that she definitely wanted the apartment as of the first of the next month. Then she went out of town and didn't return until the sixth. She called that same day to say that she would like to meet with me to sign the lease, and so we did. That's when she told me that she wouldn't be able to move in until the middle of the month, and she wanted her rent to start then. I told her that she had earlier agreed

to take the apartment as of the first but that I would compromise with her and make her rent start on the sixth. She was agreeable to that, but she balked at signing a rider to her lease making her responsible for maintaining enough heat in the apartment to keep the pipes from freezing. She said that she would have to think it over and get back to me. Today she called to say that she did not want the apartment. I was taken aback after all we had been through with her.

Emily's decision not to take the apartment raises several questions. Can I legally deduct anything from her deposit? I haven't deposited her check yet, and I've thought about just returning it to her, but then I'm also thinking that she ought to pay us something for what we did for her. After all, we interviewed her, checked the references on her application, ran a credit check, and took the apartment off the market just for her. What do you think?

When I informed the former tenant that Emily had decided not to rent the apartment, she told me that she feels she has no further obligation to us and that she ought to get her security deposit back. Is she right?

—C.B., Illinois

A. Laws applicable to this situation vary. Generally, members of the armed services who are reassigned to an out-of-town base, as well as any employee who is transferred by an employer out of the area, may break a lease without penalty. Your former tenant left the area of her own volition, so she would remain bound by the lease terms, whatever they are.

Given that she left the place clean and undamaged, that she tried to find a replacement tenant, and that she did leave the area to get another job, however, I would be inclined to return half of her security deposit and half of her last month's rent, if any.

As for the replacement tenant, I would return her entire security deposit check and wish her well. She has probably stopped payment on the check already, and you'd be hard pressed to collect anything from her without a hassle.

In the future, whenever you come to terms with an applicant who wants to rent from you but doesn't want to move in right away, use an agreement to hold the dwelling off the market, such as the one in the *Landlording* book, and deposit the check immediately. Then you would be on firm ground in keeping some or all of the applicant's deposit.

Accuse me of being an old softy. I don't mind. I have learned that hassling tenants for every last nickel doesn't pay. Treat tenants fairly, and they will treat you fairly. Either the former tenant or the replacement tenant might come across somebody who is looking for just the apartment you have available and make a recommendation which results in your getting a good tenant.

Landlord wants to void tenant's lease and move back in.

Q. I have two questions.

First, I own a two-family house in Massachusetts, and I occupied half of it myself until several months ago when I decided to relocate. I leased my old apartment for fifteen months. Now I want to move back into the property, but there's still almost a year left on the lease. I was told that there's a state law here which allows an owner or family member to void a lease if they want to move in. Do you know anything about this?

Second, my tenant just emailed me last night that he had put a stop payment on this month's rent check because the sink started leaking on the first of the month. Although he had my home telephone number, my cellular number, my dad's cellular number, and my beeper number, he did not contact us on the night when this leakage supposedly began. Instead, he waited until the following evening to send me an email message which I did not receive until later that night. He said that he will not pay any rent until the problem is fixed. What should I do?
—A.E., Massachusetts

A. Frankly, I doubt whether even Massachusetts has a law allowing owners and their family members to break a lease in order to move in themselves. Such a law would be too easy to abuse and would make leases practically worthless.

Nonetheless, you should consult the actual laws yourself (do an internet search) or consult an attorney who handles landlord-tenant matters to learn what the laws say. If you can break the lease, do so. If not, approach the tenants with an offer to buy them out, or else find yourself a place to live for the next twelve months and exercise caution the next time you decide to use a lease rather than a month-to-month rental agreement.

As for the sink problem, I would fix it immediately myself or hire somebody else to do the job. Your tenant sounds as if he's playing games.

Good tenants do not do such things. I'd make special note of his behavior, and I would give him no slack in the future. I would treat him "strictly by the book."

Once the sink is fixed, I would demand the rent payment in person. If it isn't forthcoming, I would begin eviction proceedings for nonpayment of rent immediately.

Interpretation of "optional" is at issue.

Q. I'm a rental property manager. Among the properties I'm managing is a house which was leased for six months. Normally I wouldn't lease any property for less than twelve months, but these tenants were well qualified and I wanted to rent to them in spite of their insistence that they wanted only a six-month lease.

The lease we signed has a clause which gives them an "optional extension for six months at the current lease rate."

Here's the problem: The owner of this house is unexpectedly returning to the U.S. and wants to move back into the house when the original lease expires. The renters are now wanting to exercise their option to stay another six months. I've indicated to them that they have no option because the owner wants to reoccupy the house. I've told them that they must move out at the end of their six months. I interpret "optional" as meaning that both parties must agree to the option. In this case the option does not exist from my point of view.

If they don't move when the lease expires, what process do I use to go about evicting them in the state of Texas.
—M.M., Texas

A. When somebody grants an option to somebody else in a contract, that option cannot be withdrawn simply because the person who originally granted the option later changes his mind.

These tenants received an option to extend their lease for six months. They have every right to exercise that option. Don't even try to evict them. You'll lose the battle. Instead, help the owners of the house find other accommodations for six months until they can move back into their house at the end of the tenants' optional lease extension.

Owner wants tenants gone.

Q. Last week I ran the lease contract by a landlord-tenant attorney, and she disagreed with your interpretation. She said the contract doesn't indicate which party has the option so it is assumed either party would have the option. I think I may get another opinion just to be on the safe side.

On another note, the owner is now pursuing other clauses in the contract, such as the tenant's running a business out of the house and also their keeping a pet with no deposit, something clearly against the lease agreement. Basically, the owner wants these people out, and I'm stuck in the middle as the property manager being the bearer of bad news. Besides resigning, do you have any suggestions for me?

—M.M., Texas

A. I beg to differ with the attorney you consulted. Whenever there's an option and there's some doubt about who can exercise the option, the "consumer" will always win. I certainly wouldn't go to court in the case you described. The owner will lose. The attorney will make money.

As for your situation, I'd quit and tell the owner to handle the matter himself.

Tenant wants to rescind her notice to terminate tenancy.

Q. Eleven days after giving me a properly signed and dated tenant's notice of intention to vacate, which specified a 30-day move-out date, my tenant verbally informed me that she had changed her mind and was no longer intending to move. During those eleven days, I placed an ad for the expected vacancy, I showed the apartment in accordance with the rental agreement, and I accepted an application and deposit from new, prospective tenants. The current tenant was cooperative in allowing the apartment to be shown during this time and gave no indication of having changed her mind until now. This tenant insists she has a legal right to stay regardless of her prior written notice.

My question is this: Does the current tenant have any "obscure" legal right to retain her tenancy under these circumstances, that is, some legal "grace" period during which she may change her mind without consequence? The situation seems absurd, I know, but I've never encountered anything like this before.

—P.F., California

A. The tenant has as much legal right to rescind the notice of intention to vacate as a gambler has to switch bets from one horse to another when the race is half over. If the tenant isn't out by the time her notice expires, you may file a summons and complaint immediately to evict her. You do not have to serve her with a notice, nor do you have to wait even a single additional day before proceeding against her.

When all is said and done, however, if you want to keep this tenant and if you have no legal obligation to the prospective tenants, then you might want to approach her and tell her that you will let her stay provided that she reimburse you for your costs in trying to fill the vacancy.

You will find some information pertinent to your situation in the *Landlording* book in the section entitled "Two Tenants–One Rental Dwelling."

Husband alone signs agreement, and he alone moves out.

Q. My tenant just notified me that he is divorcing his wife and is now staying with his sister. He is the only one who signed the rental agreement, but the agreement does mention his wife and three children. Since he did not give me a 30-day notice, is he still responsible for the next thirty days? What if his family does not move out? Also, he informed me that another lady, who is eight months pregnant, has moved into the house. To make matters worse, the $600 rent was due seven days ago. Do I give a 3-day notice to him even though he's out, but his family is there with another lady? How do I legally get everyone out?

—D.G., Idaho

A. Whether the husband is occupying the dwelling himself, shacking up somewhere else with his own little Monica, or twiddling his thumbs alone in Timbuktu, he is still responsible for paying the rent. He's the one who signed the original rental agreement, and he's the one responsible. Furthermore, he's responsible for paying the rent until his wife and children move out, not just for the next thirty days. He simply cannot release himself from the agreement by moving out. Unless you release him from the agreement yourself, his having moved out of the house does nothing more than turn him into a kind of co-signer.

Do not release him from the agreement!

Serve him a notice to pay rent or quit, wherever he is. In addition, serve a notice on the two adults who are occupying the house. Waste no time! Do it today!

If somebody does come up with the rent, then you will have to decide what you want to do with the tenants who are remaining, but under no circumstances should you release the husband from his responsibilities under the agreement for as long as his wife and children reside there as your tenants.

He wants off lease after breakup.

Q. Some time ago I rented a house in Florida to a man and a woman. The man had good credit while the woman had poor credit. I have learned that the man is no longer living there and wants off the lease. The woman has someone else staying with her, but she is paying the rent on time. Can the man legally be let off the lease or am I obligated to keep him on? Does he need the written agreement from the woman to be let off the lease? He says that it is endangering his health to argue over this conflict of the lease with her. He says that he needs to get away from her and wants off the lease. Can I legally let him off, or is he obligated to stay on it? The woman cannot seem to get anyone else to sign the lease to take the man's place. What should I do? I feel bad for the man. He is basically a good guy done wrong.
—D.D., Florida

A. Only you may eliminate the man from the lease. The woman has no say in the matter. Even if she does come up with a substitute for the man, you do not have to accept the substitute. Consequently, there's no reason why the man needs to argue with the woman over his being eliminated from the lease. He doesn't need to communicate with her at all. Instead, he should be praying earnestly that she continues to comply with the terms of the lease so that he doesn't have to make up for her failure.

If you take pity on him and eliminate him from the lease, then you cannot force him to comply should she stop paying you the rent, damage the property, or leave prior to the end of the lease.

If I were you, I would tell the man that you do not intend to eliminate him from the lease but that you will contact him immediately if she ever puts him in jeopardy. He will then have time to rectify the situation. Tell him that she is currently paying on time and that he is in no jeopardy whatsoever. Tell him also that he will be eliminated automatically when the lease expires, whenever that is, and should you continue to rent to the woman after that, he would have nothing to worry about.

Divorcee wants former husband removed from rental agreement.

Q. We rented to a married couple who are now getting a divorce. The husband has moved out and has left his wife and children behind. She says she wants his name removed from the rental agreement.

If both of them agree to remove him from the agreement, do we need to draw up a new agreement or merely modify the existing one? Does he need to sign something saying he is agreeable to taking his name off the agreement? Is there a form I can obtain for this?
—M.W., Kentucky

A. Removing his name from the rental agreement is a simple matter, one you may handle in several ways.

You may modify the existing agreement by crossing out his name everywhere it appears and then getting every party to the agreement, including yourself, to initial the modifications. At the top of the agreement, put the words, "[Person's name] was removed from this agreement as of [date] and relinquishes all tenancy and deposit rights."

You may draw up a new agreement in the wife's name only and get the husband to sign and date a separate statement saying that he agrees to the termination of the old agreement, thereby relinquishing all tenancy and deposit rights, and is aware that a new agreement in her name only is now the controlling agreement. You don't need a form for this. Plain English on plain paper will do, perhaps something like the following, "I agree to the termination of the rental agreement I signed on [date] to rent the dwelling located at [address]. I understand that terminating this agreement terminates my tenancy rights and responsibilities and my rights to the security/cleaning deposit. I am aware of, and approve of, a new agreement governing the tenancy at this address."

Please note that removing the husband from the agreement releases him from all responsibility for paying the rent. The wife alone is then responsible. Make sure she has the wherewithal to pay the rent herself. Before you agree to make the change, have her complete a new rental application, so you'll have current information about her income sources, and discuss with her the ramifications of removing the husband from the rental agreement. She may be eager to have him removed from the agreement so she can have the locks changed and legally deny him access. She may not have thought about anything else. Enlighten her.

She doesn't want to rent to smokers.

Q. I am getting into the landlording business pretty soon and have a question. I know that you can't exclude children from rental housing, but what about excluding smokers? When I bought my townhouse, the ceilings were stained yellow and the place stank like a biker bar. I don't allow smoking in my home. Can I do the same with my rentals?
—C.N., Illinois

A. You may legally prohibit smoking in your rentals. You may specify that you rent only to non-smokers because smokers are not one of the legally protected groups against whom you may not discriminate.

They don't want to rent to Section 8 tenants.

Q. We have a clean, beautiful house that we're currently advertising for lease through a website. We've been getting inquiries asking if we accept Section 8 tenants. I understand that they are government-subsidized. I don't feel comfortable renting to Section 8 tenants because I have heard from other landlords about all the problems they have had. I was wondering whether turning these people down because they're Section 8 is against the law. If not, do you have any suggestions on how best to decline their offers?
—R.R., California

A. You don't have to rent to Section 8 tenants. Be straightforward and tell them that you don't rent to Section 8 tenants because you don't want to have to submit to housing authority inspections and you don't want to do things according to their timetable. That's all.

Keep polling landlords about their Section 8 experiences. You're much more likely to hear about the bad experiences than about the good ones. Landlords who have had good Section 8 experiences tend not to share their stories unless asked.

She wants occupancy guidelines.

Q. How many people can legally occupy a three-bedroom rental house?
—T.W., Oregon

A. The guidelines from the Department of Housing and Urban Development (HUD) are two people per bedroom. A three-bedroom rental house could accommodate up to six people. If the bedrooms are small or if they aren't really "bedrooms," that is, they lack a closet, then the number may be adjusted downward.

Certain jurisdictions make that HUD's guidelines even more restrictive. They say that you must allow up to two people per bedroom plus one additional person.

Other jurisdictions use the Building Officials and Code Administrators (BOCA) guidelines, which are more objective than the HUD guidelines. BOCA guidelines say the following: "Every dwelling unit must contain a minimum gross floor area not less than 150 square feet for the first occupant and 100 square feet for each additional occupant. Every room occupied for sleeping purposes by one occupant shall contain at least 70 square feet of floor area and every room occupied for sleeping purposes by more than one person shall contain at least 50 square feet of floor area for each occupant."

Other factors which come into play in determining how many people may occupy a rental house are "fire loading," which means the quantity and type of combustible material in a building (consult your fire department for numbers), and on-site wastewater treatment capacity (consult your septic tank service company for particulars). They take precedence over HUD guidelines.

Please note that "people" includes adults and children. You must not differentiate between them at any time, either during the tenant selection process or during the tenancy.

Manager asks about age and sex of children sharing bedrooms.

Q. I manage several apartment complexes and have come across prospective tenants who want to put a boy and a girl in the same bedroom.

I heard somewhere that children over a certain age are not permitted to share a bedroom with another child of the opposite sex. Is that correct? Also, if a couple wishes to occupy a bedroom with a child, what are the age restrictions for that child?
—H.N., California

A. The age and sex of tenants' children ought to matter to the bureaucrats who come up with rental housing occupancy guidelines, but they don't. Bodies are all that matter. Federal occupancy guidelines say that you must allow up to two people per bedroom in your rentals.

Nowhere do guidelines say anything about the ages of those people or their sex other than to say that you must not discriminate according to age or sex.

Prospective
tenant asks about safety.

Q. How would you respond to an inquiry from a prospective tenant about safety? I don't think anyone can guarantee safety other than to describe precautionary measures. What answer would you give if you were asked the question, "Are these apartments safe?"
—P.J., District of Columbia

A. This question is a loaded gun, a loaded shotgun, because any misconception you create with your answer will be used against you if the prospective tenant becomes your tenant and later becomes a crime victim on the premises. You'll be sued, and the rosy picture you created about safety will blast you and your insurer backward.

The question is certainly a valid one. Good tenants want to know such things about their prospective home. When they ask the question, you should be ready with a straightforward, unflinching answer.

The answer might go something like this:

"Because of the liability involved in my giving you the wrong impression about the safety of these apartments, I have to be careful about what I say. I can tell you that I live [or work] here myself without fear for my safety, but you must understand that I'm biased. For an unbiased opinion of criminal activity in this neighborhood, contact the local police department and ask them your questions about safety. They'll tell you what you want to know.

"We are concerned about safety, and we take every reasonable precaution to deter crime here. We have good outside lighting. We have deadbolts on the outside doors. We have closet safes. We have screens on the lower floor windows. We have stops on the windows to keep outsiders from opening them all the way.

"We respond to tenants' maintenance requests promptly when they report a malfunctioning lock or a burned-out bulb or a missing screen. Moreover, we listen to tenants' suggestions for improving our operations.

"We also encourage and participate in the 'Neighborhood Watch' program. We do what we can to thwart criminal activity, and we expect our tenants to help in this effort.

"That's all I can tell you on the subject."

Changing locks
between tenants is the question.

Q. Are landlords required to change locks between tenants? I am in a situation where I know the tenants have been trustworthy and returned all the keys, but I wonder if there's a legal obligation to change the locks anyway. Can new tenants request this service upon their occupancy? I am in the state of Washington, and our landlord-tenant laws do not mention a thing about changing locks.
—K.N., Washington

A. Whether there's a law in your jurisdiction about changing locks between tenancies or not, I recommend that you change them every time there's a change in tenancy, no matter what. Your former tenants may be wonderful people and think that they have returned every key to you, but what about their good-for-nothing, cocaine snorting nephew who stayed with them for a time? Might he still have a key?

Landlords have enough worries. You shouldn't be worrying about whether there might be an unauthorized key circulating somewhere, and you won't be if you simply change the locks whenever a tenant moves. Not only is changing locks cheap insurance against one more landlording worry, it shows your new tenants that you know what you're doing as a landlord and that you care about their security.

Fumigating for termites
causes tenant problems.

Q. My question concerns fumigating for termites. My tenant informed me one day that his garage was infested with termites. I inspected the property and verified that there was indeed a severe infestation. I asked the tenant to call three termite companies to obtain bids for treating the infestation, and he did.

I then met with the tenant to make arrangements for tenting the entire structure and for him to vacate the house for two days. The tenant agreed to bag his food, remove his aquarium and plants, and do everything else he was supposed to do. He did all that and went off on a camping trip early Monday morning. The termite company was supposed to arrive and tent by noon Monday. The previous Friday somebody from the company stopped by to pick up the key and the agreement which I signed authorizing the work. The tenant told the guy that the key would require some jiggling in the front door lock and would not open the back door at all.

Monday the termite company arrived on schedule, but they were unable to open the door, so they didn't do the tenting or the fumigation. When the tenant returned the following Friday, he was upset to learn that the 6-8 hours of his time spent preparing for tenting had been a waste.

Now he is asking whether he will have to vacate the house and repeat all the required pretenting preparations again. He is unhappy about having to stay in a motel, even at my expense, and he is refusing to prepare the house a second time. He says that the house has no termites and I ought to have only the garage treated.

Are you aware of any laws relating to fumigating for termites?
—A.C., California

A. There are no laws relating to rental properties and fumigating for termites just as there are no laws relating to rental properties and baiting for snails. Although they do cover many aspects of landlord-tenant relationships, laws cannot cover every possible circumstance. In the absence of specific laws, landlords and tenants are charged with the responsibility of acting like reasonable people in their dealings with one another.

In the circumstance you outlined, I can understand why the tenant is unwilling to spend 6-8 hours preparing for tenting after having done so once already.

You as the landlord bore some responsibility for making sure that the tenting and fumigation proceeded as planned. After all, the procedure was to benefit the building, your building, more than it was to benefit the tenant. The tenant cooperated and arranged his affairs to assure the success of the procedure, but you failed to monitor everything to insure that it proceeded as planned.

You should be grateful that the tenant was so cooperative the first time. Now you need to be all the more cooperative yourself to get the build-ing treated as soon as possible. Offer the tenant some assistance and some compensation to prepare for a second attempt, and then make sure that you monitor everything closely this time to make sure that the work proceeds according to plan.

Owners of old building face up to lead-based paint liability.

Q. Friends of mine own a two-family property which was built in the early 1900's and renovated by various owners over the years. My friends, the current owners, moved into the first-floor apartment two years ago, and because they had small children, they encapsulated some of the paint they suspected might be lead-based. They did not test the paint, nor did they treat the entire apartment. They couldn't afford to. They treated only the trim around the windows.

Until recently, a single adult lived on the second floor, and they were not concerned about the paint there. Now that he's gone, they would like to make his old apartment available for rent to tenants of all ages, including tenants who have small children, but they do not want to be responsible for any lead poisoning that could occur as a result of the old paint. I should say that the paint is in good shape. It's not peeling, cracking or flaking, at least not visibly, but it is old, and the presence of lead in the paint is a virtual certainty.

Is there a legal form new tenants could sign prior to occupancy in which they would agree not to hold the owners liable if their children were to show signs of elevated lead levels while living there? Although one hopes that this never happens, it is a concern to my friends. Have you ever heard of a lawsuit being filed because of a situation such as this?
—L.G., Massachusetts

A. Lead poisoning is a silent menace in older dwellings, and your friends are right to be concerned about it, but they are wrong to think that they ought to get their tenants to sign a form absolving them as owners of any responsibility for whatever increase in lead levels the tenants' children might experience while living there.

According to federal law, landlords must prepare a disclosure form and provide an informative booklet on lead-based paint whenever they rent a dwelling built prior to 1978. The form and booklet are meant to inform prospective tenants that the dwelling may contain lead-based paint and to suggest ways for them to live with it.

The form is called "Disclosure of Information on Lead-Based Paint and/or Lead-Based Paint Hazards." The landlord must sign it and get the tenants to sign it as well. The landlord must also provide the tenants with a pamphlet called "Protect Your Family from Lead in Your Home." Both the form and the pamphlet are available on the Environmental Protection Agency's website (epa.gov). Look for them there, or go to a search engine and search for them by name.

So long as your friends comply with the disclosure laws and monitor and maintain the paint in the apartment, they should have nothing to worry about. After all, people of all ages lived with lead-based paint in their homes for centuries before the federal government decided that it was enough of a hazard to warrant special treatment. People have never suffered health problems as a result of living with lead-based paint.

The mere presence of lead-based paint is not a hazard. It's a potential hazard. It becomes a hazard when it deteriorates and becomes dust or chips, and it becomes a hazard when it is actively interfered with, that is, when it is being gnawed on, sanded, scraped, heated, or removed. In any case, it has to be taken in through the mouth, skin, or nose to elevate a person's lead level.

Little children put just about anything into their mouths, and they are the ones who are particularly susceptible to medical problems associated with lead-level increases in their bodies because their neurological systems are still forming. By notifying parents of the possible presence and potential dangers of lead based paint and by keeping the paint in good condition, landlords are doing all they can do to protect their tenants, old and young, from the hazards.

Landlords are never immune from lawsuits, even if their tenants do sign an agreement holding them harmless, but tenants seldom win lawsuits against their landlords unless they can prove that the landlord was negligent. The cautious, concerned landlord has nothing to fear. Your friends sound as if they are cautious and concerned about the hazards of lead-based paint. So long as they follow the relevant laws and maintain their property to reasonable standards, they should feel comfortable renting an old apartment in good condition to tenants with children.

Tenant wants to take certain cosmetic improvements with her.

Q. We are in the process of purchasing a home which is occupied by a tenant. During the time the tenant has lived there, she has made certain cosmetic changes, changes such as crown molding, ceiling fans, etc. She says she is taking the molding and the ceiling fans when she leaves. Is that legal? I'm sure she does not still have the preexisting light fixtures. What do we tell the seller?
—J.H., Ohio

A. Consider yourself fortunate that you know the tenant's intentions before you take possession of the house.

At this point, the problem you mention, the tenant's removal of certain cosmetic improvements she has made, is really the seller's problem and not yours. Lacking an agreement to the contrary, the seller has an obligation to deliver the house to you just as you viewed it, and you should not accept it otherwise.

State laws and the controlling rental agreement determine how landlords and tenants handle move-out details. According to most such laws and agreements, tenants must restore the property to the same condition it was in when they rented it. If tenants replaced a light fixture with a ceiling fan, then they may leave the ceiling fan in place if it truly is an improvement over the fixture or they may reinstall the original light fixture. They cannot remove the fan and leave some wires dangling from the ceiling, nor can they replace the ceiling fan with a light fixture inferior to the original.

As for the crown molding, removing it would seem to be an act of spite because it had to be custom fitted when installed and wouldn't fit easily anywhere else. If the tenant were insistent on removing it and neither laws nor rental agreement prevented her from doing so, then she is responsible for restoring the affected areas to their original condition minus "normal wear and tear." Leaving holes in the walls where the molding had been installed is not normal wear and tear. It's "damage," and the tenant must pay for any and all damage.

Were I the owner of this house, I would work out some arrangement to compensate the tenant for her improvements so I could deliver the house to my buyer without any hitches.

Were I the buyer of this house, I would insist that the seller deliver the house to me in the same condition it was in when I agreed to buy it, or else I would expect some compensation for its deficiencies.

Stand your ground!

Tenants pay utility bills to landlord.

Q. I have a rental agreement which obligates my tenants to pay me their utility bills directly because the utility services are in my name. When they fail to pay, can the 3-day notice to pay rent or quit include the utility charges that have not been paid?
—D.G., California

A. You may include nothing except rent in a notice to pay rent or quit.

So long as you mention the utility charges in your rental agreement, you may ask for the utility charges in a separate notice, known as a notice to perform covenant or quit, delivered at the same time as the notice to pay rent or quit.

This situation is very similar to what mobilehome park owners face, many of whom charge their tenants separately for utilities. To see how they ask for utility charges in an eviction, see the chapter entitled "Handling Nonpayment & Noncompliance in a Mobilehome or RV Park" in my book, *The Eviction Book for California*. The complaint in such cases should ask for the utilities owed in what is known as the "prayer," under "other."

Landlord wonders whether he is liable for car stealing by tenant.

Q. I have a tenant in a rural area who is a mechanic. Last week the police raided the property searching for stolen vehicles and found one. They arrested my tenant and took him off to jail. He was later released on bail. As a landlord, am I liable for crimes committed on my property if I am unaware of the crimes? How do I evict him now as soon as possible?
—J.A., California

A. Depending upon the circumstances involved, you *may* be held liable for certain crimes committed on your property, including illegal drug activities, muggings, beatings, and sexual assaults. A tenant's car stealing is another matter. It should not involve you as well as your tenant, especially if you knew nothing about it.

Since you now do know something about your tenant's possible illegal activities, however, you should make a move to evict him. Serve him with a 30-day notice to terminate tenancy and hope he moves within the thirty days. If he doesn't, file an unlawful detainer action against him and force him out.

Act *now*.

Section 8 tenant's body bakes a week in his apartment.

Q. Last October I rented an apartment to a man on Section 8, and I busted my butt to get it ready for a strict housing department inspection. It passed, but then they demanded that my ex-husband's name be dropped from the deed, and they wouldn't pay me anything until I took care of this technicality.

Months later I finally got the grant deed in my name only, and I sent copies to the housing department and the county recorder. One week after that, the tenant overdosed on drugs and was found dead in the apartment. When found, he had actually been dead for seven days. He was in the bathroom with the heater on high and the door closed. Imagine the stench! His body might as well have been baking in an oven!

Making the place habitable again is going to cost me at least $1,000. Even the linoleum needs to be replaced because the odor has been baked into it. I have contacted an attorney about this matter, but he won't touch it. What can I do to get restitution for seven months of rent plus all the damages?
—B.W., California

A. Whether you are entitled to any restitution will depend upon the timing and the wording of the two contracts you should have signed before the tenant moved in. You and the tenant should have signed a rental contract, and you and the housing department should have signed a Housing Assistance Payments Contract. If you signed these contracts before the tenant moved in, then they apply to the full duration of the tenancy, and you should approach the man's heirs and the housing department to demand payment.

Even if you didn't sign any contracts, you should still press your case because you were attempting to satisfy a technical requirement while providing the man with housing. You were operating under the assumption that you would be paid.

Since the man had to prove that he was too poor to afford to pay for housing on his own, he likely won't have an estate, and your only recourse may be the housing department. Tally up what they owe you. Go to them. Explain the situation as best you can, and tell them that you expect payment. If they refuse to pay, take them to small claims court.

Prepare your case thoroughly before going to court and rehearse what you're going to say there. Remember that you'll be arguing in front of an impartial third party who doesn't know you from Eve. You need to convince that judge that you have a good case. If you lose in small claims court, sell the screenplay.

Landlord wants to protect assets.

Q. I hire workers to do repairs on my properties, but I do not always know whether they have active workers compensation coverage. If they hurt themselves or tenants while they're on my properties, I am liable and can be sued for substantial amounts.

I fear that my insurance may not pay in these circumstances. Some people have suggested that I put the properties in a corporate name, a family limited partnership, or a limited liability company to protect my assets.

What's your opinion?
—E.R., Utah

A. Legal entities designed strictly for asset protection cost some bucks to create and maintain. They give extra work to attorneys and accountants.

Rather than complicate your life with them, be vigilant in your operations and seek out and buy insurance which will protect you at your comfort level from asset-robbing lawsuits. In addition to the ordinary liability insurance you buy for your properties, carry an umbrella policy which increases the limits to three times your net worth, and you will sleep well at night.

Incorporation looks attractive to landlord.

Q. Are there any rules of thumb about when a small landlord should incorporate? I'm thinking about forming an S corporation since it is just for myself right now. I'm not interested in tax benefits. I'm interested in personal liability protection, especially in my area, which is so unfriendly to landlords.

Currently I own five units, three houses and a duplex, and I will be closing on another 24 units in the next two to three months. I plan on continuing to grow and expect to hire help as needed, either subcontractors or actual employees. Do you have any thoughts on incorporation?
—J.C., New York

A. The disadvantages of holding rental properties as a corporation seem to me to outweigh the advantages.

The disadvantages are these: When you are a corporation, you have to file an extra tax return; you cannot represent yourself in court, not even for the easiest of do-it-yourself evictions; you need separate accounts for monies; you have to complete state-mandated paperwork whenever required; and you probably won't be protected personally from lawsuits because limited ownership corporations are easy to pierce in this day and age.

Compared to these disadvantages, what are the advantages worth to you?

She thinks relatives hired to manage get special treatment.

Q. My sister and her husband will soon be managing a seven-unit apartment building for me in Montana. I've been told by a real estate agent friend of mine that since they're relatives, I don't have to count them as my employees and don't have to get workers' compensation insurance or take anything out of their paychecks. Is this information correct?
—B.L., Arizona

A. Who would be called upon to pay the medical bills if your sister or her husband were to break an arm or suffer a spinal injury while looking after your rental property? You would. All fingers would be pointing directly at you.

Much as you love your sister and her husband and want to believe that they would never sue you for any reason, neither you nor they can know how they would act were they forced to find a way to pay their mounting medical bills for some debilitating injury they sustained while working for you. You don't want to know. Cover them, cover you, get workers comp insurance.

Much the same applies to the way you handle the reporting of their pay. Do it correctly, reporting it to the IRS on all the proper forms, and you'll stay out of trouble.

You have assets to protect. Protect them.

Tenants give notice shortly after paying rent and ask for refund.

Q. I own a building in Boston divided into two flats. I live on the second floor and have rented the first floor to the same tenants for the past two-and-a-half years. They have been good tenants, and I have had no complaints about them whatsoever.

Every year they self-renewed the previous year's lease. The last time their lease came up for renewal, I raised their rent $50 (still far below market) in order to meet rising costs. They agreed to pay the increase and stay on for another year. Unfortunately I did not put anything in writing, nor did I have them sign a new lease. I figured I could take them at their word, but now I know that they became month-to-month tenants, also known here as "tenants at will," and that not getting something from them in writing was a big mistake.

On the third of the month, one of the tenants left a message on my answering machine asking me to call her at work. When I called, she informed me that she and her roommate had found another apartment thirty miles north of Boston and would be moving there by the first of the next month. She said that it was an opportunity they "just couldn't pass up."

That same evening she called me again and wanted to know if I would give them back the last month's rent they had prepaid when they moved in. I told her that she was not entitled to get a refund because she did not give thirty days' notice.

I'd like to know whether I have to refund any or all of her last month's rent. She claims that to be "fair" I should pro-rate it for the time that they were late in giving me notice.

What do you think is fair in this situation?
—J.H., Massachusetts

A. When a tenant who pays rent under a month-to-month agreement gives a 30-day notice of intention to vacate, she may give it on the day the rent is due and she may not. If she gives it on the day the rent is due and she has prepaid her last month's rent, she owes her landlord nothing. If she gives notice on another day, no matter what day it is, she owes rent for thirty days from that day, and you take all of her prepaid rent into account, her current prepaid rent and her last

month's prepaid rent, when you calculate who owes whom what.

In your case, the tenant gave notice on the third that she was planning to move by the first of the following month. She owed rent through the third of the following month. If we assume that she had already paid her rent for the current month on the first, she would be obligated to pay rent for three extra days and no more.

You should charge her rent for three days at the new rate, of course, and refund her the balance. That's fair. That's proper. That's legal.

Do not refund the balance until after she moves out because she may stay an extra few days, and you want to make sure that she pays for every last day she occupies the flat.

Do not chastise yourself for having done something wrong here. You haven't. Consider the results of this little experience. The first result is neutral. You lost no rental income whatsoever, nor did you have to incur any additional expenses for hiring an attorney and going to court. The second result is good. You learned that you should always commit an agreement to writing, and you won't forget that landlording lesson because you learned it from experience. The third result is very good. You can raise the rent on the flat to market and get more income from it than you were getting.

Tenant fails to buy renters insurance as agreed.

Q. According to his lease, my renter was supposed to obtain renters insurance and provide me with a copy of the policy thirty days after he signed the lease. Ninety days have passed, and he still hasn't shown me any evidence that he has insurance. During this time I have given him a verbal reminder and sent him a letter to remind him of his obligation.

Now I'm beginning to wonder whether I'm sitting on a powder keg. Can he sue me if he suffers any losses due to fire or theft? Is his inaction grounds for eviction? He has accumulated a few other lease infractions, like making minor alterations without written permission, but they're not enough to make me want to go to the trouble of evicting him.
—J.P., Pennsylvania

A. Even if you are sitting on a keg labeled "DANGER! HERCULES DYNAMITE!" don't worry. The keg has nothing in it. It's not going to blow up under your posterior. You are in no danger of being sued just because your tenant failed to heed your requirement to secure renters insurance. His failure is more his problem than it is yours.

You might be in some danger of being sued if you had several tenants and if you strictly enforced the insurance requirement upon all of them except this one. The tenants who obeyed might sue you for discriminating against them or for failing to be consistent in enforcing the leases. Other than that, your chances of being sued by this uncooperative tenant of yours are no greater than they usually are in this business. Stop worrying about being sued and concentrate on what you might do to achieve your objective.

From my vantage point sitting atop my own landlording powder keg, I'd say that you have four choices for dealing with this tenant.

1) You could ignore the matter and cross your fingers that the tenant won't lose his belongings in a fire or a burglary and won't need renters insurance to compensate him for his loss.

2) You could send him a letter stating that you do have insurance to cover the building against calamities but that you have no insurance to cover his possessions against calamities. You could have him sign a statement at the bottom of the letter acknowledging that he understands he is responsible for any loss to his possessions and for any damage to the building caused by his negligence.

3) You could press him further to get renters insurance, giving him the name of an insurance agent who sells renters insurance and giving him some idea what he can expect to pay for it.

4) You could buy a renters insurance policy for the tenant and send him a notice that you are increasing his rent a certain amount in order to pay for it.

Those are your choices, none of which should cause you lasting grief.

As for evicting the tenant over this infraction and others like it, I wouldn't. I would definitely make note of his infractions. I'd state what he did or didn't do and what I did as a result. I'd date the notes and keep them in his file just in case he became more uncooperative later and gave me greater cause to evict him. The notes would help prove to a judge that he had been uncooperative for quite some time and had been treated with forbearance all along until his behavior worsened and led to his being evicted.

8
Tackling the Tenant Challenges

Tenants expect to be spoiled after landlord spoils them twice.

Q. The people who rent a single-family home from me have clogged the plumbing twice. As a courtesy, I paid to have the clogs cleared even though their excess waste was what caused the clogs each time. Now the plumbing is clogged again, and they are insisting that I pay. According to their lease, they must make all repairs to the plumbing whenever it is the result of their misuse, waste, or neglect. They have been renting this house for a year and a half and have six months left on their lease. They say it's my house and it's my problem and are refusing to pay. Who should pay?
—R.W., Florida

A. You have witnessed what can happen when you are too good to some tenants. Because you paid the first two plumbing bills, which the tenants should have paid according to their lease, you trained them to expect that you would pay every plumbing bill, no matter who ought to be paying it. You spoiled your tenants, and now you have to "pay the piper" for having spoiled them.

You have several options now, each beginning with your paying the bill so that it gets paid and so that the plumber will provide you with service in the future. Plumbers don't care who pays their bills, but if a bill isn't paid and you have anything to do with it, then the plumber will ding your credit and refuse to respond to future service calls from you. Go ahead and pay the bill to keep the plumber happy.

Next, decide whether you want to let the tenants win this round or not. If you do, say nothing more to the tenants about the bill, and let that be an end to the matter until they clog the drains the next time and you have to decide once more what to do.

If you don't want to let them win this round,

charge them for the plumber's bill by putting it on every rent statement and receipt you give them in the future. Reminding them monthly that they owe you for this bill effectively puts them on notice that the matter is not settled, that you intend to enforce the agreement, and that you expect them to pay. They may or may not pay you while they continue to live there. If they don't pay, take the money out of their security deposit when they vacate, but don't tell them what you plan to do until you do it. If you tell them, they'll lessen their efforts to leave the place clean and undamaged. Let them holler and threaten you all they want when you do take it from their security deposit. You're within your rights.

If you really want to fight with them, serve them with a notice to pay the bill or face eviction proceedings. Then follow through if they don't pay. You may win in court. You may not. You're taking a calculated risk with this option. It could backfire and cost you dearly in court costs and fees and lost rent if the tenants decide to stop paying you their rent while the case is pending. Take this option only if you have the stomach for a knock-down fight and a pocketbook to back you up should things go wrong.

Husband and children leave wife and her boyfriend behind.

Q. My husband and I rented a single-family home to a single family with two children. Now the husband has moved out and taken one child, and the first husband has taken custody of the other child. This leaves the wife and her boyfriend-of-the-week. Since the husband signed the lease with his wife, isn't he still legally responsible for a portion of the rent?

Also, these tenants have paid their rent in cash from the very beginning. They pay weekly. The wife used to show up at my husband's office to pay the rent or ask him to stop by and pick it up.

Well, we had to put a stop to that. It took too much of our time.

We opened a separate savings account at our bank, and with the approval of the bank, we made up some rent coupons for them to present to the bank with their money. They get a receipt on the spot. She was not happy with this arrangement but she did it anyway every Monday. One Monday was a holiday, and since the bank was closed, she did not make that week's payment, and she still has not paid it. We have sent her a statement recapping her payments and all the late fees applicable to the one payment she missed, but she ignores us. She continues to make payments every Monday, but she's still a week behind. Her late fees are starting to add up and soon will surpass her deposit amount. What can we do?
—DS, Indiana

A. The husband who signed the lease is responsible for paying the entire rent, not merely a portion of it. He may have moved out, but he's still on the lease, and he retains his obligation to make sure that the rent is paid until the lease expires or until he convinces you to remove him from the lease.

As for the bothersome weekly cash payments, you deserve a commendation for having come up with a good solution to accepting them. It solves two problems, the cash payment problem and the personal contact problem. You don't have to worry about handling cash, nor do you have to worry about arranging to meet the tenant every Monday to accept the payments and then put them in the bank yourself. Arranging for the tenant to go directly to the bank to pay her rent there in cash is a very good idea!

Your late fees, on the other hand, are a bad idea. Apparently they accumulate if they're not paid promptly. When the tenant is late with a payment and refuses to pay the late fee, the late fees begin to accumulate, perhaps $1 per day for every day the rent and/or the late fees are late.

While such an arrangement may sound like a good idea to begin with, it works poorly in real-life landlording, and you wind up looking foolish because you can't enforce it easily. You're much better off with a one-time late fee based upon the amount of rent due, say, 5% of the rent due or a flat $50. If the tenant refuses to pay, then you merely keep track of it and deduct it from the security deposit when she moves out.

There's another matter you're neglecting when you're assessing the late fee. You're allowing no grace period, not even when one is legally mandated. You see, you cannot charge a late fee when a rent due day falls on a weekend or a holiday. If your tenant's rent due day is Monday, and Monday is a holiday, she has until Tuesday, when the bank is open, to pay her rent without incurring a penalty, regardless of what your rental agreement says.

Finally, consider this when you're devising a late-fee policy—courts frown on late fees, especially late fees which accumulate until doomsday. You cannot include late fees in the notice to pay rent or quit which you give a tenant to begin eviction proceedings. You have to ask for them separately, and you have to argue in court that they are not arbitrary, but rather that they reflect your reasonable damages.

Don't run afoul of the courts over your late-fee policy. Revise it!

Obnoxious girlfriend moves in and claims to be a tenant.

Q. I own a fourplex, all one-bedroom apartments. If I rent to a single person, how can I be certain he won't bring someone else in? I have this tenant who moved his girlfriend in a few weeks ago. She now states she lives there. She's loud, obnoxious, belligerent, and unemployed.

Is there a clause I can add to my rental agreements in the future about how many hours a guest can stay? Is there a clause in the Occupancy Law of Arizona (which I have heard about but cannot find)?

Also, I live near Phoenix. How can I find a local rental property owners association?
—LK, Arizona

A. Your rental agreement should identify the occupants of the dwelling and include a clause limiting guests to a reasonable length of stay. The long-form rental agreement in the *Landlording* book says this about guests: "Tenants may house any single guest for a maximum period of fourteen days every six months or for whatever other period of time the law allows. Provided that they maintain a separate residence, nurses or maids required to care for Tenants during an illness are excepted from this provision."

To review your state's landlord-tenant laws, go to your state legislature's website (azleg.state.az.us). Once you get to the site, look for the words, "laws," "codes," or "statutes," and go to those listings. Landlord-tenant laws are in the property category.

As for a rental property owners association in your area, contact the Arizona Multihousing Association at 602.224.1035.

Too many creatures are living in the apartment.

Q. My tenants have broken their agreement in regard to how many people are living in their apartment. The lease specifically states two people and one dog may live there. I am certain there is one extra person, possibly more. There is also a new dog on the property.

Is there a form available to give notice that the extra tenants must vacate? I need correct language. Do you have any suggestions how I might word it so that if there is more than one tenant, the notice would apply to them also?
—C.W., Montana

A. Your letter to the tenants who have violated the lease with the extra dog, and perhaps with an extra person, might read as follows:

"I am sending you this letter to remind you what your rental agreement says regarding the people and pets who may live in your apartment. It says specifically [insert here the exact language found in your agreement] 'TWO persons and ONE pet are to live in the dwelling. Without Owners' prior written permission, no other persons may live there, and no other pets may stay there, even temporarily...'

"These are the terms of occupancy we agreed upon before you moved in, and they haven't changed since then. Just as you expect me to live up to the terms of our agreement, I expect you to live up to the terms of our agreement so long as you live in the apartment.

"If you choose not to live up to the terms of our agreement, you must move.

"You have three days to decide. Should you choose to ignore the terms of our agreement and ignore this letter as well, I will have no choice after three days but to take legal action to evict you."

Although it does not begin legal proceedings, this letter is strong enough to show that you mean business. If the tenants do not comply within three days, you should begin the legal proceedings specified in your state to evict a tenant for breach of contract. The "Notice to Perform Covenant" form in the back of the *Landlording* book should be sufficient to begin those proceedings.

Tenants have too many vehicles.

Q. A handful of my tenants have more than their allotted number of vehicles. Many aren't registered, and many aren't even operational. I don't want to pay to have the vehicles towed, but I want them gone. Threats to the offending tenants have gotten me nowhere. How should I handle this problem?
—S.K., Connecticut

A. Stop threatening. Start acting. You're running an apartment house, not a storage yard for inoperable, unlicensed, and surplus vehicles.

To make certain you're legally correct, contact the local authorities to determine what you need to do to have vehicles towed from private property.

To make certain you can provide your tenants with the particulars they'll be most concerned about after their vehicle has been towed, contact a towing company to inquire about their requirements, forms, charges, and storage yard locations.

Send your tenants a letter outlining exactly what you plan to do about their excess vehicles. If your rental agreement already has a clause stating your excess vehicle policy, let the letter be a reminder. If your rental agreement has no such clause, let the letter be a thirty-day notice of a "change in terms of tenancy." Include in the letter the towing company's particulars. They show that you mean business.

Prepare or procure a parking violation sticker which says something like this: "WARNING! This vehicle (LICENSE NUMBER) is parked here illegally. Please move it immediately to avoid towing and storage at your expense. This vehicle will be towed on (DAY, DATE). You may make arrangements to retrieve the vehicle by calling (TELEPHONE NUMBER). Once retrieved, the vehicle must be kept elsewhere." The sticker should be on red or "day-glo" paper and be at least eight inches wide by five inches high.

Glue or tape the parking violation sticker on the driver's side of the windshield where it can't be missed, and arrange for the towing company to tow the vehicle on the appointed date. If the company wants prepayment for the towing charges, pay them yourself. Then present the bill to the tenant with the next rent statement.

If you want your tenants to toe the line, tow one or two of their excess vehicles. They'll come to realize that you mean business, and they will begin to toe the line on your vehicle restrictions.

New renters claim additional children keep them from moving.

Q. After going through the entire application process, convincing me in an interview that they would be good renters, getting their brother who owns a business and has good credit to be a co-signer, and paying their security deposit and first month's rent with a cashier's check, my new renters just told me that they couldn't move in because they have more children than they admitted to. On their application they said they had three children. Now they tell me they have seven. They signed a six-month lease and want me to release them from it.

Their story sounds a little far-fetched to me. I think they found a better place and came up with their extra-children excuse so I'd take pity on them and return all their money. How should I handle this?
—L.F., Idaho

A. Just as buyers sometimes get the "blues" over their decision to buy a property, renters sometimes get the "regrets" over their decision to rent a property. Each is making a major commitment, and they sometimes want to get out of that commitment as quickly as they got into it.

I thought I'd heard every excuse renters could concoct for getting out of a lease commitment. This extra-children excuse is a new one on me. Apparently, these would-be renters of yours think you should overlook the fact that they lied to you on their application and should return all their money.

Were they lying then about having only three children or are they lying now about having seven?

Then again, perhaps they weren't lying then and they aren't lying now. Perhaps they're one of those households with children from previous marriages. Perhaps a former spouse who had custody of four children decided to relinquish custody and give the children over to the other spouse, and this change occurred just after your renters made their commitment to you.

You could find out, but you needn't bother. Accept the fact that they don't want to live in the place you leased to them, and treat them the same way you'd treat others who change their minds for reasons good or bad after they make the commitment to lease from you.

Whatever the circumstances, you should not return all their money, nor should you keep it all. You did your part to qualify these people as renters, and you took the property off the market for them. You committed the property to them for six months, and they committed themselves to paying you rent on the property for six months. You could be uncompromising and hold them to the agreement, even to the point of requiring them to pay you five more months of rent, but they could retaliate against you for being so uncompromising. They could move in as a family of nine rather than as a family of five. They could demolish the place and leave you with all kinds of damage to repair.

Be businesslike, and be fair to them and fair to you as you calculate how much to deduct from the monies they have paid you. Total your out-of-pocket expenses for advertising and for processing their application, add something to compensate you for your time, multiply the per-diem rent by the number of days you held the property off the market for these people, and you'll have a justifiable figure. Deduct it from what they paid you, write them a check for the difference, prepare an accounting, and tear up their lease.

Depending upon their expectations, they may or may not be satisfied. Don't worry about their reaction. You are treating them fairly.

They planned to marry, but now they can't get along.

Q. I just leased a four-bedroom house to a nice couple who were planning to get married soon. Because of the size of the house, her adult sons are living with them and were included in the lease.

It's been only three weeks, and he called this morning to say they're not getting along. Because of arguments, illegal drug activities, and other things I don't want to know about, he wants her and the sons out of the house.

She then called with her version of the situation. She said that he goes on drinking binges and that she had to call the police because she thought he was going to hit her.

Without getting in the middle of their tug-of-war, I immediately spoke with neighbors, and they said they were unaware of any disturbances.

Both tenants signed my five-page lease agreement. How do I decide if anyone should move out and how do I go about evicting one or both

of them? I just want my monthly rent of $800.
—L.N., New Mexico

A. So far you have acted prudently in this matter. Good for you!

Your tenants' domestic disputes are not your problem. Your problem is keeping your house rented to good tenants who will have consideration for the neighbors, keep the place clean and undamaged, and pay the rent on time.

At this point, you should arrange a meeting of the three of you as soon as possible and tell them exactly what the financial requirements (income and credit rating) are for renting the house. If one of them cannot meet the financial requirements for renting the house, then that person cannot stay there without getting an acceptable co-signer. If each of them meets those requirements, then they must decide themselves who is going to remain in the house and who is going to move. Tell them that you cannot and you will not make that decision for them. If they cannot make that decision themselves, tell them that they both will have to move.

Tell them that you'd like to hear back from them as soon as they make their decision and that you'd like the person who is remaining in the house to complete another rental application and another lease (unless each of them has already completed a separate application, bring a blank application with you to the meeting). Tell them that the new lease will benefit both the person who moves (that person will no longer be responsible for the house), and it will benefit the person who remains (that person will accumulate a good tenancy recommendation for himself or herself alone).

Make yourself available to hear of their decision. If they don't contact you within two days, contact them.

Landlord doesn't want tenant to paint new fence.

Q. A tree branch knocked down a fence at my rental property. Because of its location, I submitted a claim to the city and will have to wait nine months while they evaluate my claim. In the meantime, I have replaced the knocked down portion of the old solid white fence with a new cedar fence and have left it unpainted. I plan to replace the whole fence in the future, and I want to keep all the wood natural. My tenant wants me to paint the fence. He has told me that he'll paint it himself and deduct $50 from his rent if I don't paint it. How should I handle this?
—J.H., California

A. Tell the tenant of your plans to replace the entire fence and keep it looking natural. Tell him that even though the new portion doesn't match the old one now, it will match everything as soon as the new fence is in place. Tell him that you do not want him to paint the fence. Tell him that if he does paint the fence you will not allow him to deduct $50 from his rent and that you will charge him whatever it costs you to remove the paint. Give him a letter to this effect and let him make the next move.

Tenant gets rid of mice, charges landlord for traps and rice.

Q. A tenant of ours had mice in his apartment and never told us about them until he presented us with a bill for all kinds of traps he'd used to get rid of them. We're willing to pay for the traps, but we're not so willing to pay for the forty-eight pounds of rice he claimed the mice ate. Do mice eat rice? Are we responsible for the loss of the rice?
—J.K., Idaho

A. If the tenant never told you about the mice so that you would have a chance to exterminate them using your own sound methods, then you are not liable to pay for his mouse traps or his mice's meals. If you want to keep the tenant reasonably happy, though, pay him for the mouse traps and for half of the rice the mice consumed.

Mice are omnivorous. They will eat practically anything.

Tenants put backyard off limits and claim to have legal counsel.

Q. Our tenants have put a padlock on the gate leading into the backyard. We need access to the backyard to mow and edge and do general cleanup. We do all the yard work at the house. Do they have a right to lock us out of the backyard?

Also, if they have a third party involved in this matter, somebody they are calling their "legal counsel," don't we have a right to know who this person is? They have been saying for three weeks now that their legal counsel is doing some research work and will be in contact with us when he is finished. They told us that he is holding the rent payment and the utility money until this

matter is cleared up. We have never been through anything like this before, so maybe you can answer these questions for us.
—S.J., California

A. In order to save yourself possible grief later, treat the tenants' locking you out of the backyard the same way you would treat their locking you out of the rental house itself.

Some tenants get a perverse thrill out of changing their locks so the landlord no longer has a key and can't get in. They think they're within their rights of tenancy by denying their landlord access. They're not.

You as landlord may enter their house in the following circumstances: 1) with their permission, 2) with twenty-four hours notice, or 3) in an emergency without either their permission or notice.

Consider your entering their backyard the same as your entering their house. Remember, they are renting both the house and the yard from you, and they do have the right to "quiet enjoyment" of both, but they have no right to exclude you.

Since they have locked you out of the backyard and since you have good reason to enter this yard in order to maintain the landscaping, you should give them a 24-hour notice whenever you intend to enter. Tell them that you expect them to give you access with a key or by removing the padlock, but if you have no access, you will remove the padlock from the gate.

If they haven't come to their senses and enabled you to enter the backyard, you should come prepared to cut the lock off with a bolt cutter and then go about your business.

Whereas you do have the right to enter after giving them notice, you do not have the right to enter at any hour of the day or night. Go there during normal business hours only, and you will stay out of trouble. They may be harassing you with their various shenanigans, but you have no right to harass them by mowing their back yard lawn in the wee hours, and you shouldn't.

As for their "legal counsel's" holding their rent payment until matters are settled, don't be fooled. They have no right to pay their rent to anyone other than to you or your agent. Give them a "3-Day Notice to Pay Rent or Quit" to smoke out their supposed legal counsel. You know and I know that there is no legal counsel. They're just playing games with you to avoid paying their rent.

Tenant claims rental period begins the day he moves in.

Q. My tenant thinks I owe him prorated rent. I checked his credit and accepted his application about a week before the end of April. We arranged for his wife to come from afar so we could all meet and sign the lease. His wife came and we signed the lease for a year beginning on that day, May 2nd, with the rent due on the first. The lease will end on May 1st next year.

A month after moving in, the tenant says that he really began his tenancy on the 4th of May because that's the day when he chose to occupy. I told him he could occupy sooner even though he didn't have his furniture yet. I told him that the place was his because he had paid for it and he could bring his sleeping bag if he wanted to sleep there. He did occupy on the 4th and wants me to start his rent then even though he took the keys on the 2nd. His kids and wife are living elsewhere for a little while longer because the kids are still in school. His family is coming after school lets out in the middle of June.

I can sympathize with his having to pay double rent for a while, but that's life, and that's their choice. Now he's threatening to sue me for three days of lost rent monies. I think he felt that we were still finishing up the house we had just bought, e.g., putting in improvements like a ceiling fan and new doorknobs, piddly stuff. He gave us permission to work on the third to finish up and we encouraged him to feel free to come on in.

I have looked for laws about prorating rents, but I can't find any.

Also, our lease agreement states that he must pay for all utilities. A local ordinance requires that anyone within the city limits who refuses garbage service must pay for it anyway. I asked him to place all the utilities in his name on lease signing day, May 2nd. It's June 8th today and he has failed to put the garbage in his name. He says that he's not going to do it until his family gets here on June 15th. This amounts to a breach of his contract and a violation of a city ordinance.

I know I could evict him over this, but I decided to write him a letter about the ordinance and remind him of his lease obligations instead. In the letter I said that I would help him with the garbage bill by paying all of May and half of June because I realized that he was paying rent on a property elsewhere.

This whole mess is irritating to me. I'm trying to get along with the guy, but he seems to be difficult to get along with. He's a grump.
—T.A., California

A. Proration of rent is not the issue here. The issue is what constitutes the start-date of this tenant's fixed-term lease. Leases generally state the start-date and ending-date, and if there is a start-date stated in the lease the tenant signed, that's the date when the rental period starts. End of controversy!

Lacking a start-date in the lease, the rent starts when you turn over possession to the tenant, that is, unless the two of you agree that it should start at some other time. Since you didn't agree to another start-date, your testy tenant's rent started on the second of the month. That's when everybody signed the lease and you gave him the keys.

There's no need to prorate the rent in this situation unless you want his rent period to be from the first day of every month through the last day of every month. In that case, he would pay you rent, one time and one time only, for twenty-nine days rather than thirty. Proration of rents in eviction paperwork is calculated using a thirty-day month. That's considered reasonable for evictions and ordinary rent prorations as well.

They want to get rid of tenant with mental problem.

Q. We have a tenant who lives in an apartment of ours which hasn't been cleaned in over twenty years. That's how long she's lived there, and I don't think she has ever cleaned it. We have never had any trouble with her. She's always paid her rent on time by leaving it in an envelope on her doorstep for us to pick up, and we have never had any complaints from her or about her.

We have always thought she was a little strange, but we never knew how strange. Now we know.

Because of a heating problem in the building, my wife and I had to enter her apartment the other day. That was when we discovered the mess she has been living in. It was so bad that my wife gagged and threw up as soon as we got outside. There were empty food cans everywhere, and there was every kind of garbage imaginable piled four inches deep wherever we walked.

The woman had even shut off the water supply valve to the toilet. We figured that it must have been leaking and that she shut it off so she wouldn't have to let anybody in to fix it. She must have flushed the toilet by pouring water from the sink into the toilet bowl whenever she felt like it, which wasn't often.

What troubled us most was the junk she had piled all around the baseboard heaters. We're lucky that there hasn't been a fire in her place. It would have gone up in flames in a hurry.

As you might imagine, the stench in the apartment was terrible. Even in your worst landlording nightmare, you couldn't image how bad it was. I don't know how any human being could live like this.

After what we saw, we want her to move. Even though I'll be doing all the cleaning and painting myself, we know that we'll have to spend an arm and a leg to fix everything and prepare the apartment so that somebody else can live there. We know that the rugs and floors will have to be torn up and replaced and who knows what else.

Her apartment is both a fire hazard and a health hazard, and we want to get rid of her as quickly as possible. How do we go about getting rid of her quickly before she burns the place down?
—W.L., Massachusetts

A. This poor woman is a mental case and needs help. She's a hazard to herself and to others living in the building. Contact both your county health department and your local fire department immediately, and tell them what you learned about this tenant of yours. They will be very interested and will help you get her out of the apartment as soon as possible.

Getting her out is only the first step to regaining possession of the apartment. Once she's gone, you may have to serve her with a notice of termination of tenancy to begin legal eviction proceedings, and you may actually have to evict her through the courts, depending upon whether she wants to stay or will agree to leave voluntarily.

Work with the public agencies who take this woman under their care. While helping the woman, they may help you regain possession of the apartment.

Until you have possession, you may enter the apartment only if you have the woman's permission or if you believe there is a hazard inside needing immediate attention. Even without her permission, you could make a good case that the space around the baseboard heaters needs immediate attention, and you could go in and clear the space to lessen the fire danger. Otherwise, stay out of the apartment until you have possession.

Tenant comes with his own rental agreement.

Q. I have been landlording for eleven years and thought I'd heard of everything. I thought wrong. Because my properties are in a college town, I have to rent to students and have learned to live with their sometimes silly ways. Last week a student pulled a new one on me. He said he would rent from me only if I would sign the agreement he had brought with him.

I was tempted to tell him that every tenant of mine has to sign my rental agreement, but I decided to look at his agreement anyway because the apartment I had for rent was going begging. The previous tenant had become homesick and had moved back home to be with his family only a month after classes started, and there weren't any other applicants looking to rent an apartment with school already in session. This fellow was looking for a place because he had decided he couldn't live in a fraternity house with all the commotion going on there.

His agreement turned out to be better than I expected although there were some things I found objectionable about it. It required me as landlord to provide him with an accounting of what I did with the previous tenant's security deposit. It required me as landlord to take at least two photographs of every room and to describe the condition of everything in every room before he moved in. Each of us was supposed to approve, sign, and date the photographs and the description, and each of us was supposed to get copies for our files. It further required me as landlord to put his security deposit into an interest bearing account which I would have to identify to him, and then I would have to give him the interest on his deposit as a credit on his rent every six months.

I asked him why he was so concerned about his security deposit, and he told me that he'd had a bad experience with a previous landlord who kept all of his deposit for no reason at all.

I know that some landlords do keep deposits when they shouldn't, and I could understand his concern, but I was reluctant to sign an agreement which wasn't my own, especially when the tenant was dictating the terms to me. I kept thinking that I would be opening myself up to other situations where he might try to take the upper hand and dictate something to me.

My pride was telling me that I shouldn't rent to a student who comes with his own agreement. My good business sense was telling me that I should rent to a student who is the only one interested in renting a vacant apartment which would likely remain vacant for a few months unless I do rent to him.

In the end, I agreed to his terms and rented to him. So far I haven't regretted my decision. Do you think I did the right thing?
—J.B., Nebraska

A. You did the right thing all right. You used good business sense to rent an apartment which would otherwise still be sitting vacant and generating no income. Rather than reject the applicant impulsively just because he wanted you to use his rental agreement instead of yours, you took the time to read and analyze his agreement, you determined how it was different from yours, you asked him why he wanted to use his agreement, you listened to him and understood what he was saying, you determined that you could live with his agreement, you signed it, and you followed it. You were flexible. You did not let your pride get in the way of making a good business decision.

Flexibility is an attribute of the successful landlord. Successful landlords know that theirs is a people business and that the people who are their customers have different needs. Satisfying those different needs requires flexibility.

Just as the successful landlord will stoop to bribing a troublesome tenant to vacate when faced with a costly eviction, the successful landlord will stoop to signing a tenant's rental agreement to fill a unit when faced with a costly vacancy.

You did the right thing, and you will benefit as a result.

New tenants want apartment cleaner than they found it.

Q. My 23-year-old daughter and I own a small one-bedroom condominium apartment where she lived until last week. When she moved out, she rented it to a couple for six months. She told me she cleaned it thoroughly before she left, but the new tenants claimed that it wasn't clean enough for them, and they phoned her to complain about the "mess." They refused to move in, hired a cleaning lady, and checked into a hotel for a night. Then they demanded to be reimbursed for their cleaning costs and hotel bill, and they wanted us to give them a two-day rent credit.

I can't believe that they're making such a big fuss over such little things, but they are. They claim that they took more than fifty photos of the mess they found. I did not see it myself, but I know it couldn't possibly have been as bad as they claim. A neighbor there, who is also the condominium association president and a friend of ours, witnessed the commotion they made when they were taking the photos and told me that they're turning a molehill into a mountain.

Not only are they being extremely picky, but they're beginning to sound litigious. The husband is an attorney and is threatening legal action if we don't pay them. We are not experienced at being landlords, and we feel that we are being taken advantage of. I suppose they think they can take advantage of us pretty easily because neither my daughter nor I can be there to face them. My daughter has moved 500 miles away, and I live out of state.

Can they do this? I mean, is what they're trying to do even legal? Is there such a thing as a standard for cleanliness?

I have already agreed to pay for the cleaning service and the carpet cleaning if they will send me the bills, but do I really have to pay for their hotel bill and deduct two days off the rent, too? How should we handle this?
—C.W., Utah

A. Consider yourselves fortunate on three counts. Your daughter found the tenants herself, so you didn't have to pay anybody a commission. The tenants were ready to move in as soon as your daughter moved out, so you didn't lose any rent while the place sat vacant. The tenants wanted the place to be even cleaner than your daughter left it, so you shouldn't have to worry about cleanliness while they are there.

Yes, this lawyer and his wife are trying to take advantage of you. Even a tenant advocate would admit that. They know that you live far away and that you're not going to make a special trip to see them and sort this matter out. They're asking for all they can get out of you and shaking their fists and briefcases at you as if to say they'll go into battle to get what they want.

Give them what they want. Pay their cleaning bills and their hotel bill, and give them two days credit on their rent. Tell them you're happy they had the place cleaned to their satisfaction. Tell them that you want them to take fifty photos of it now that it's clean and send them to you along with the fifty photos they took of it earlier to show what a mess it was. Tell them that the photos will help you understand what their cleanliness standards are and help you know in what condition they will leave the place when they vacate.

Then ask your friend to visit the tenants with a condition and inventory checksheet, such as the one in the *Landlording* book, to record in writing the condition of the apartment as of their move-in date. This checksheet will be the yardstick used when they move out to determine whether they left the apartment as clean as they found it, that is, after you paid for them to have it cleaned.

By the way, the word "clean" is a relative term. It means one thing to a surgeon preparing to remove a patient's appendix. It means another thing to that same surgeon when he's out camping and preparing a meal of fresh trout to eat on the trail, and it means still another thing to that surgeon when he's lost in the woods and eating grubs to survive. Likewise, it means one thing to a landlord who's preparing an apartment to show prospective tenants, and it means another thing to tenants who are moving out of an apartment they've occupied for five years.

Because "clean" is so relative, you as a landlord want to agree upon a definition every time you rent to new tenants so that when they move out, you will have a better chance of agreeing upon how clean you want them to leave it. You and the tenants should agree upon a definition when you do a walk-through inspection before they move in. Using a form as a guide, you should walk through every room together, you should indicate whether the room is clean or not, you should inventory its contents, and you should both sign the form.

Your new tenants and your daughter must never have done a walk-through inspection after she moved out and cleaned the apartment to her satisfaction. If they had, the new tenants would have had an opportunity to express their dissatisfaction with the cleanliness, and your daughter could have cleaned it or had it cleaned more to their satisfaction.

As for the legality of what these new tenants are trying to do, it depends upon whether they and your daughter agreed upon an actual move-in date and whether the tenants paid rent from that date forward. If so, you would owe them rent for the days the apartment was not ready for occupancy. If there was a written agreement which included a clause about a tenant inspection, and it stated that the tenants had inspected the apartment and its contents and found everything to their satisfaction, whether they did or did not actually inspect it, then you wouldn't have to pay them anything for further cleaning or give them any rent credit.

If I were you, though, I wouldn't argue legality with these tenants. I'd accommodate them. You're embarking upon a six-month relationship with them. You could make their lives miserable for six months, and they could make your life and your daughter's life miserable for six months. Avoid all this misery if you can, especially when the cost is reasonable. Give them what they want and move on.

Rude tenant sparks questions.

Q. My husband and I own a three-unit apartment house. We live on the ground floor and rent out the two upstairs units. One of our tenants, who has always paid her rent early, has become rude to us lately. We have only a verbal agreement with her, but we plan to give her a standard written month-to-month rental agreement with additional rules pertaining to her specific apartment. We hope that this agreement will help curb her bad attitude. She has been loud when entering the building and has made comments under her breath about my husband when she is with guests. If her behavior and attitude don't improve, can we give her a notice to terminate tenancy? Would we need some proof of her violation of the rules if we have to go to court? Since we have only a verbal agreement with her, can we just serve her a notice? We would give her more than thirty days. We do not want to resort to evicting her, but since we are taking good care of the property and also live there, we feel that she should at least show us some respect, whether she likes us or not. I have also thought about increasing her rent to make her think twice about whether she wants to continue living in our building. What would you advise us to do?
—M.G., Michigan

A. You won't change this woman's attitude for the better by giving her a written agreement to sign. You may change it for the better by asking her why she's being so rude to you. You'll never know unless you ask. Perhaps she feels she was slighted by you or your husband and is responding in kind. Perhaps she ran out of the medication which curbed a personality disorder. Perhaps she's jealous because you have a happy marriage and a little rental property and she doesn't. Perhaps she just doesn't feel herself for some reason or other.

Approach the subject by saying that you're worried about her and want to know if there's anything you can do to help.

If she's forthcoming, let her talk. Sympathize with her, listen to her carefully, and think about what you might say or do to help her change her attitude toward you.

If she's not forthcoming, tell her simply that you and your husband are upset by the way she has been treating you, and you would like her to be more considerate since you are neighbors after all.

No matter how she reacts to your conciliatory efforts, you should still go ahead with your intention to give her a written rental agreement. A verbal agreement is legal all right, but it's too vague, too subject to different interpretations and memory lapses. Every residential tenancy needs an understandable written agreement to define it in specific terms.

Understandably, any tenant who pays her rent early is worth salvaging, but if you feel you can't salvage this woman after making the effort, raise her rent high enough for her to conclude that she would be better off financially to find another place to live.

Only after you have tried everything else and the situation still remains intolerable should you resort to giving her a notice to vacate. Giving her sixty days would be reasonable and most generous. Unless required by local law, you don't have to specify the reasons behind the notice. You do have to follow the same procedure for tenants under verbal contracts as you do for tenants under written contracts.

Fret no more about how this woman is treating you. Take steps to change her attitude or else take steps to get her out of your life.

Nurse fails to live up to her good recommendations.

Q. My tenant included her four children's names on her rental application but no man's name. I assumed that she was either separated or divorced and was moving into the area from another state because she had found a new job here. She told me that one of her four children was away at college and a second one might be going away to college, too.

I contacted her supervisor at the clinic where she had worked for four years as a registered nurse and also the landlord of the place where she had lived for twelve years. The supervisor gave her a good reference, and the landlord gave her an outstanding reference. Then I called the supervisor of the local hospital where she had been employed for only two months. Her supervisor gave her a good reference and said that her job was permanent. None of these references said anything negative about her, so I decided to rent to her.

She signed a year's lease and gave me the first month's rent. She called at the beginning of the second month and told me that her rent would be about ten days late. I told her the rent is due on the first of the month, and according to her lease, there would be a late charge if she paid after the fourth. I handed her a notice on the fifth of the month, and she gave me half the rent.

She paid the other half with a post-dated check. She paid the next month right on the first, but she didn't pay the late fee she owed from the previous month. Her next month's rent check arrived late on the fifth. When I delivered a notice requesting that she pay the late fee for two months, a man answered the door and took the notice without identifying himself.

I called her later and asked if her husband was now living with her. She said he was. I told her I thought she was divorced, and she said that she had never said she was. I asked why she hadn't put his name on the application, and she said that she wasn't sure when he'd be finished working on a job some distance away, and she didn't know when they would be back living together.

Her lease reads as follows, "The premises leased herein shall be used as a residence establishment only, and except for births, restricted to the number of occupants shown on the rental application."

I have three questions.

Do I have the right to inform her that her spouse can't live with her because she didn't put him on the application?

What can I do about her not paying a late fee when she's late?

How can I get her to keep a cleaner house? She didn't have a vacuum cleaner when I asked her to clean the smoke detector after it tripped twice and they reported it to me. I'm especially concerned about cleanliness because I just spent $8,100 to replace some carpets, appliances, windows, and doors before renting to her.

—S.G., Virginia

A. Your somewhat irresponsible tenant appears to be a responsible employee and appears to be worth molding into a responsible tenant. You did all the right things when you checked her out before renting to her, and you shouldn't blame her or yourself for not finding out about the husband.

Assume that she's telling the truth about him, and accept him as an additional tenant. You accepted her and the four children initially, so you were willing to accept five people when you rented to her. With the four children coming and going all the time, the husband amounts to no real increase in the number of people living there on a permanent basis. Exclude him only if you want to be uncompromising and are willing to put up a fight to enforce the agreement, but understand that you will be losing the whole family if you exclude him. They aren't going to stay on as your tenants if you tell them that the husband has to live elsewhere.

If you want them all to stay on, accept the husband as an additional tenant. Have him fill out a rental application, add him to the rental agreement, and get him to sign it. He'll then be just as responsible for fulfilling the terms of the agreement as everybody else.

He'll even be responsible for paying whatever late fees they incur. To collect the late fees she already owes, send her a statement ten days before her rent due date, and show both the late fees she owes and her upcoming rent on the statement. Keep sending her a statement every month, and keep showing the late fees until she pays them. She needs to be reminded, so remind her, and keep reminding her. If she hasn't paid the late fees by the time she eventually moves, take them out of her deposit.

You do have to give her credit for calling you when she knew that she would be late with her rent. Bad tenants wait for you to call them after they are late. Good tenants call you before they are late to let you know when they will have the money to pay.

Good tenants are generally good housekeepers, and this nurse may be a good housekeeper, too, most of the time. Perhaps the smoke detector incident caught her when her vacuum cleaner was broken or being used by one of her children at some other place. Talk to her about cleanliness. She's a nurse. She understands cleanliness. Tell her about your concerns. Tell her how much you just spent to fix up the place, and ask her specifically about her vacuum cleaner. If she says that she doesn't have one, ask her how she intends to keep a clean house. She'll tell you.

Remember that this locally employed nurse lived in her previous dwelling for twelve years and came with excellent references. Sort out the little concerns you have about her now in a reasonable fashion, and she will turn out to be a good stable tenant for you as well.

Tenants refuse to vacate and refuse to allow inspection.

Q. I'm looking after a rental property for my landlord because he resides out of state. Last month I delivered a notice to terminate tenancy to the current tenants. They do not pay their rent or

their utility bills on time, and they have a dog which has done some damage to the property.

A week ago they informed me that even though their thirty days is up, they aren't moving until next month and they aren't going to pay any more rent. Do I still have the right to serve them with a 24-hour notice to inspect the property?
—R.C., Iowa

A. Whether these tenants are current in their rent or not, they still have tenancy rights. They retain those rights until they move voluntarily or until they're evicted. Likewise, you as agent for the owner have landlord rights, one of which is the right to inspect the property upon giving the tenants proper notice. Observe the correct procedures for serving them with a notice that you intend to inspect the property, and then go ahead. They have no legal right to keep you out.

Chronic complainer calls about phantom problems.

Q. We have a tenant who seems to be unhappy with the apartment he rents from us in an eight-plex that is relatively new and in very good condition. He calls us at least once every few weeks with a request that we fix something for him. He complained that the air conditioning wasn't working, so we hired a service technician to check it out. The technician said that everything was working fine and charged us $75. Several weeks later he called to say the washing machine stopped working. We checked and found that it was unplugged. Less than a week after that, he called about the dishwasher. We could find nothing wrong with it, but because he kept complaining, we called a repairman and paid $50 to learn that it was okay. We have stopped calling repairmen to check into whatever this tenant complains about because we have to pay the bills, and we don't like to pay bills for verification that there's nothing wrong with something.

Although we have stopped calling repairmen, the tenant has not stopped complaining about this or that. I could list at least ten more of his complaints about phantom problems, but I'm sure you get the point. When he complained that the refrigerator door wasn't closing tightly anymore, we called and told him that none of these problems existed when he moved in and that he's responsible for the repairs if any are required.

We're fed up with this guy. We'd like to terminate his lease early, but we're not sure we can. It still has five months left to run. We thought about evicting him because he's been late with his rent for the past four months, always making a different excuse each time. We have at least started charging him a late fee as prescribed in the lease.

We are sending him a letter offering to let him out of the lease at his earliest convenience. We told him that because he seems extremely unhappy, he might want to move to a place that better fits his needs. Do you have any other suggestions?

—J.D., Wisconsin

A. Your tenant is a difficult person of the "chronic complainer" variety. He wants to play his fiddle and watch you dance to his tune. You could take up a fiddle yourself and play your own tune, calling him every few days to say that you want to make a visit to his apartment to check on one thing or another, but that would likely turn into a cacophony and may not yield good results. You need to stop the music altogether.

Write him a letter stating that you will respond promptly to every one of his complaints. If you find no problem at all or you find a problem he caused negligently or deliberately, you will charge him a minimum of $60 for the visit plus $1 for every minute after the first thirty minutes spent fixing the problem, and you will charge him for any parts or professional help required to fix the problem at your cost plus 10%. If you find a problem and it is not of his making, you will take care of it yourself or hire somebody else to take care of it at no charge to him.

Send him the letter by certified mail, return receipt requested, just to show him you mean business.

He may care about money and stop calling you with his pesky complaints. He may not care about money and keep calling you with his pesky complaints, paying for the privilege. In either case, you can celebrate because you're no longer playing second fiddle to this chronic complainer.

Tenant wants to have her devil's food cake and eat it, too.

Q. I have been renting a house to a woman and her grown son for six years, and we've always been on cordial terms. Recently I had to replace her refrigerator. When I supplied her with a fairly new one in perfect condition which I retrieved from

storage, she complained that it had an odor which was making her sick. If I have to buy her a new one, I'll need to raise her rent, and she knows it, so she's playing games trying to get me to buy her a new refrigerator and not raise her rent, which, incidentally, is $100 below market. She sent me a certified letter with some demands and sent a copy of the letter to a local housing rights group. If I meet her demands and still raise her rent as a result of my increased operational expenses, am I legal in doing so? There's no rent control here.

Also, she has known all along that I plan one day to sell the house, and I know that she is interested in buying it except that I don't think she qualifies. Am I legal in giving her notice because I intend to rehabilitate the house or get out of the rental business in that area? I sense trouble no matter how I proceed. Do you have any advice?

—E.R., California

A. Consider yourself fortunate. Many landlords would love to have your troubles. At least you have a tenant who is paying her rent on time and isn't wrecking the house or bothering the neighbors. You have a tenant who merely feels threatened that you're going to raise her below-market rent, and she's doing everything she can to keep her rent low while also getting you to buy her a new refrigerator. Her actions are understandable but misguided. She's aggravating you when she should be appeasing you. If she wants to stay in your good graces and keep her rent low, she should be offering to buy the refrigerator herself. After all, she could easily buy a brand-new one for what she's saving in below-market rent over a three-to-four month period, and she could easily buy it on credit, too. By not doing so and by sending you a certified letter with demands, she wants to have her devil's food cake and eat it, too.

You have been too nice to this greedy tenant too long. She doesn't deserve what you've done for her in keeping her rent below market for six years. In effect, you have given this woman $7,200, and it's been money wasted. Go ahead now and buy her a new refrigerator if you must, but at the same time, give her notice that you are raising her rent $100 per month. She has given you every excuse for raising her rent. Do it! Let her look around for herself and see how much houses are renting for in her area today.

You are completely within your rights to raise her rent to market whenever you want, so long as you give her proper notice. You don't have to buy her a new refrigerator to justify a rent increase, but buying her one is a good excuse which even she can understand.

If you want her to move so you can rehab the house or sell it, do not give her notice now. She could be building a case that you are retaliating against her because she complained about her refrigerator and other problems, and you could encounter trouble if she stopped paying her rent when you give her notice and you had to evict her. Wait six months before you give her a notice to vacate.

Should you decide to sell the house, get a reasonable appraisal first. Then give the tenant the opportunity to buy it from you at a 3% discount before you put it on the market. You might be surprised by how much money your tightwad tenant has accumulated.

Cunning tenant tries to push landlord around.

Q. I have a rental property in a planned unit development. The homeowners association fined my tenant a whopping $400 for two egregious parking violations. The bill came to me as the unit owner, and I paid the fine right away to keep the association happy. Now I need to collect the money from the tenant.

When I informed him that he owed me for the fine this month in addition to his rent, he said, "I'll pay the rent but not the fine because someone told me that the landlord is the one responsible for such fines, not me." He did just as he said he would. He paid the rent in full but not the fine.

He's wrong about his responsibility. I know he is, but how can I collect the money if he refuses to pay. I don't think I can use a notice to pay rent or quit because it's restricted to past-due rent only. What other notice should I use?

By the way, there is a clause in this tenant's rental agreement stating that he agrees to comply with all covenants, conditions, and restrictions (CC&Rs), all bylaws, all reasonable rules and regulations, and all decisions of the homeowners association which are posted on the premises or delivered to the tenant. There's another clause in the agreement stating that he is liable for any fines or charges levied due to violations.

The rental agreement also states that he is allowed to keep one small dog. I have discovered that he now has three small dogs. I told him that he has to get rid of two of them, but he said that he cannot send two dogs to the animal shelter only to be killed. Since he won't get rid of the dogs, I'm thinking about raising his rent. In the notice, I would state the following: "In your month to-month rental agreement, we agreed that you would keep one small dog. Since you are keeping more than one small dog, there will be an additional rental charge of $50." Does this sound like a notice of change in terms of tenancy to you, and is it legal and enforceable?

What if later on, before the increase even takes effect, he decides to get rid of the other two dogs? Do I then need to lower the rent back to where it was? This tenant is a cunning fellow, and he just might hide the other two dogs somewhere until I lower the rent to where it was. When it's lower, I'm afraid he'll bring back the two dogs. Then what should I do? Do I need to raise the rent back and forth just to keep up with him? Am I making a big mistake by charging him additional rent to compensate for his having the extra dogs? I'm really puzzled.

There are just two more things that puzzle me. How many times can a landlord raise rent in a year, and how much of a late fee can I charge tenants?
—L.H., California

A. You have a cunning tenant all right and a dishonest one as well. If you let him, he'll take advantage of you in any way he can. Don't let him.

Decide first whether you want to let him keep the extra two dogs. If you do, give him a notice of change in terms of tenancy stating that he is allowed to keep as many as three small dogs. This notice effectively changes his agreement.

Then decide whether you want to charge him higher rent for the privilege of keeping the extra dogs. If you do, give him another notice of change in terms of tenancy raising his rent, but do not mention that the rent increase is related to the number of dogs he chooses to keep. It's nothing more and nothing less than an ordinary rent increase. You know and he knows why his rent is going up, but you don't want to tie the two together because you don't want to have to be concerned about whether he's keeping one, two, or three dogs. His rent is what it is, dogs or no dogs.

Next, deal with the fine he refuses to pay or the fine and the extra dogs, depending upon how you choose to handle his having the extra dogs.

This time you prepare a notice to perform covenant. You may list both covenants he broke or only the one related to fines. Include on the notice the relevant parts of the covenants verbatim. You may want to mention the amount of the fine as well, but you don't have to.

Give him seven days (you could give him as few as three) to respond. If he doesn't respond positively, prepare a summons and complaint and go to court to evict him.

As for the frequency of rent increases, you may raise rents every month if you want to so long as a tenant is on a month-to month agreement. I recommend annual increases because they alienate tenants less than more frequent increases.

As for the proper amount of late fees, they should be "reasonable" and should represent the damages you incur as a result of the late payment. A set fee of $50 or five percent of the amount of the rent owed, whichever is smaller, would be reasonable.

This tenant of yours is trying to push you around. You need to push back.

Tenant delaying sale wants more than free rent.

Q. I'm selling a rental property which includes a garden apartment. The prospective buyers want this particular apartment vacated when they take possession. I gave verbal notice to the tenant over a month ago and told her I'd let her live there free for a month so she could save enough money to pay the required move-in costs someplace else. Now she claims she doesn't have enough money to pay for the move. What are my rights under these conditions?
—P.A., Pennsylvania

A. You have become this tenant's sugar daddy. You have already given her more than you needed to, and now she's waiting for you to give her more. You may want to. You may not.

Whenever you want a month-to-month tenant to vacate, ordinarily you give the tenant a notice to terminate tenancy in writing, and if the tenant doesn't move, you begin legal eviction proceedings without delay.

You wanted to be kind to your tenant, and you were. You gave her a month's free rent. You certainly didn't have to, but you did. You did

have to give her a notice to terminate tenancy in writing, but you didn't. That's your big problem now.

You could give her the notice in writing now, but it cannot require her to move for another thirty or sixty days (period depends upon your state's laws), and that may delay your sale.

This tenant who accepted your kindness is not being kind to you in asking you to pay her moving costs, but she has you stymied. Either you pay, or she'll delay your sale.

You may want to pay her moving costs to get her out quickly. They're probably less than you'd expect anyway, perhaps just the cost of a rental truck and a couple of casual laborers for half a day at fifteen bucks an hour.

If you ever face similar circumstances in the future and you feel generous, give the tenant a notice to terminate in writing and tell her that as soon as she moves out, you'll give her a rent rebate which she may apply to her move-in costs elsewhere.

Tenant imperils cold house by refusing to pay her utility bill.

Q. A tenant of mine makes me hound her repeatedly to pay her rent on time, and she lets her utility bill go until the company sends her a shut-off notice. A clause I put into her rental agreement states clearly that she will get a 3-day eviction notice if her power is ever shut off.

We are now experiencing frigid weather, and the power company has informed me that her power will be shut off in three days because she hasn't paid her bill. They said that if I agreed, they would put the account in my name so I could keep the heater going and avoid freezing the water lines inside the house. I am not happy about putting the account in my name because she still has possession and could run up a big bill if she wanted to.

She claims that she is no longer living there and that she should not have to pay the utility bill. She says she is merely storing some of her things there until she relocates across the country within the next thirty days. She acknowledges that she owes rent until she removes her things, and she says she will pay whatever rent she owes. She just doesn't want to pay for the utilities.

If I do have the utilities put into my name, can I get her to reimburse me for the bill she should have paid while she had possession? If I don't have the utilities put into my name, can I get her to reimburse me for any damage resulting from a lack of heat?

Was I right to include a clause in her rental agreement that she would get an eviction notice in case she causes the power to be shut off? If the power is shut off and she still has possession, can I evict her on the basis of this clause?

Enough about that subject! There's another question I have about this tenant. When she rented the house, it had a washer and a dryer that were in good working order. In fact, they were practically new. I just found out that she moved them onto the patio, and that's where they've been sitting these past few months, out there in the freezing weather exposed to the elements. She bought new laundry machines, and instead of putting mine in the garage or asking me to pick them up, she just removed them from the house. I still can't believe that anybody would do such a stupid thing. If there is any damage to the appliances, can I also claim compensation for them?

I would really like to get her out immediately. How do I evict her legally in a timely manner? —C.F., Washington

A. You can imagine how loudly your tenant would be screaming if her rent had included utilities and you had decided to shut off the heat because she was no longer living there. She'd be calling you colorful names and threatening to sue you for any damage the lack of heat might cause the things she had stored there.

Since she's paying for the utilities, she's screaming out of the other side of her mouth. She's refusing to pay for something which won't benefit her, or so she thinks. Your property be damned!

You need to respond swiftly to the property danger and slowly to her shenanigans.

There are three responses you might make to the property danger. Put the utilities in your name. Prepare the house for severe cold. Do nothing.

The first response is simple enough. Pick up the phone, call the power company, thank them for alerting you as the property owner to the imminent shut off, and tell them to put the utilities in your name. Then enter the house, set the thermostat to at least forty degrees Fahrenheit (four Celsius), and monitor the house periodically to see that the heater is maintaining a high enough temperature to keep the pipes from freezing.

The second response is a more active one, but it's less expensive than the first response, and it's just as effective. It prepares the house to survive severe cold weather without heat. Owners of summer cottages in cold climates know what to do. At the end of every summer season, they get out their checklists and get busy. They drain the water pipes back to the water source. They open all faucets. They drain the water heater. They force water out of sink traps with a plunger and add antifreeze to what's left. They drain the hoses and sumps in the dishwasher and clothes washer. They empty the toilet tanks and add antifreeze to the water in the bowl. They drain the flexible hoses in showers and sinks. They disconnect and store the garden hoses, and they blow out the sprinkler system.

The third response is for gamblers. Don't choose it. Don't choose to do nothing. You know that you can't rely upon the weather to turn warm, and you know that severe cold is bad for water pipes. You learned in elementary school science class what happens to water when it freezes. It expands. Gambling that the water in your pipes won't expand when it freezes and won't burst the pipes is a bad bet. You might as well bet that a frozen chicken thrown out of a second-story window will defy science and fly up to the heavens and not fall down to the ground. Even if you did decide to do nothing now, you'd soon be facing the time-consuming tasks of repairing the damage and convincing your tenant or your insurance company to pay for the repair.

You might want to consider a combination of the first and second responses because there's a definite advantage to having the utilities in your name whenever there's a change in tenancy, and you wouldn't have to keep the temperature high or even turn on the heater unless you wanted to while this irresponsible tenant still retains possession because you would have prepared the house for severe cold. The advantage is that you'd have enough heat to make the house ready for occupancy after the tenant moves out, and you'd have enough heat to show the house to prospective tenants. You certainly don't want to work in a cold, cold house, nor do you want to show a cold, cold house, and if you refuse to let the power company put the utilities in your name while the tenant retains possession, you'll likely have to put them in your name later, when you regain possession, and then you'll have to pay the power company a personal visit, submit an application, pay a connection fee, and wait for their personnel to reconnect service.

Do note that if you intend to enter the house while the tenant retains possession, you must secure the tenant's permission before entering or give the tenant proper notice (usually twenty four hours), although you could argue convincingly, I believe, that you needn't give any notice whatsoever because you were entering in an emergency to protect the house from damage.

With damage control in place, you can turn your attention to your irresponsible tenant.

Much as you may want to evict her immediately, you should not. Evictions take time, from weeks to months, and since your tenant has already moved herself out and told you that she would be moving all of her things out within thirty days, you should be patient and let the scenario play out, although you should still serve her with a notice to pay rent when the time comes that she's late. She has said that she intends to pay her rent, but she may not. She may be thinking that she will use her security deposit to cover the rent she owes, and you don't want to let her do that. You will need her deposit to cover what she owes you for the utility bill she should have paid and for whatever damage she caused to the house and the laundry machines.

She is most definitely responsible for paying the utility bill so long as she retains possession. Though not entirely necessary, the clause you included in her agreement about paying for the utilities emphasized how important they are to maintaining the integrity of the house, and she assumed that responsibility when she signed the agreement and took possession.

She also owes you for any damage she caused to the house and to your laundry machines which she so thoughtlessly moved outside and left to deteriorate.

Were the weather not so foul right now, you might offer to help her move the rest of her things into a self-storage unit and even pay for a month's rent there, just so you could regain possession of the house and rent it to someone else. Because the weather is so foul, you might as well be patient with her and trust that she will be moving everything out in thirty days. Likely she will.

Ask the neighbors to keep a close eye on the house and let you know when they notice any activity there. You want to keep track so you can meet with her before she leaves and moves across the country. She may not be eager to settle up with you, but you should be eager to settle up with her because once she's moved that far away, you might as well forget about ever getting another penny out of her. She owes you. See that you get what she owes you.

Garbage problem is about to drive this landlord crazy.

Q. My tenants are driving me crazy. More specifically, the garbage problem my tenants have created is driving me crazy. I have an eight-unit apartment building, and the tenants are supposed to put their household garbage into the dumpster I provide for them. You would think that anybody could put garbage into a dumpster. Nope. They can't. They send their children out with the garbage, and the children set it near the dumpster rather than in it. As you might imagine, that's nothing but an invitation for every neighborhood dog to break open the garbage bag and paw through it looking for something edible or interesting. I have to clean up the resulting mess, and I do mean "mess." If the first dog doesn't scatter it everywhere, the second dog will.

We don't have a rat problem there yet, but I'm sure that one of these days some tenants will call me in a rage to tell me they saw a rat as big as an elephant rummaging through the dumpster and that if I don't kill that rat and every rat within the city, they're going to report me to the health department and close down the building and sue me for endangering the lives of their children and themselves. Arrgh! I'm at a loss as to what to do.

So far I've sent them three letters. I've asked them to take the garbage out themselves rather than send their children out with it. I've asked them to be more careful about making sure that the garbage gets put into the dumpster rather than around it or onto the closed lid. I've appealed to their pride and told them that they certainly don't want to contribute to the garbage problem and make their apartment complex look like a garbage dump.

My letters must have gone straight into the garbage because the problem continues.

Every time I visit the property, I'm left with the task of cleaning up the mess. I have to gather the garbage from around the dumpster, put it into the dumpster, climb on top of the garbage, and tromp it down so the lid will close and the garbage men will take it away. Our garbage company won't take any garbage which isn't in the dumpster, and they won't empty the dumpster at all unless they can close the lid. I've had to pay extra for them to come out a second time because they couldn't empty it the first time, when they came by on their appointed rounds and found that it was full to overflowing.

The other problem I'm having with the dumpster is people putting things in it which the garbage company won't take away or which fill it up so completely that nothing else can fit inside. The dumpster is for household garbage only. It's not for junk furniture, old car batteries, bald tires, broken bicycles, discarded TV sets, obsolete computers, or urine-stained mattresses, and yet that's the kind of stuff I find in the dumpster every now and then.

What can I do to solve this garbage problem? I'm going nuts.
—C.S., Florida

A. There are "dumpster divers," and there are "dumpster dancers." You're a dumpster dancer. Every hands-on landlord is a dumpster dancer. Every hands-on landlord knows the "garbage dance," performed to no music in particular on top of heaped garbage cans or dumpsters and preferably performed solo without an audience. It consists of jumping up and down in place and results in compaction sufficient for the garbage company to take the garbage away completely and without protest.

Landlords need to know the garbage dance, but they should not need to perform it often. You are performing it far too often. You have already tried writing your tenants about the garbage problem without success. Now is the time for you to try any number of other approaches until you hit upon something that works.

Below are six suggestions, some simple, some less so. Each suggestion begins with your giving your tenants garbage guidelines written to inform them what they can and cannot put into the dumpster, how they should bundle their garbage, where they should put their garbage, and when the garbage collector will come. If you haven't already given your tenants that information, get busy. They need it, no matter what you do to solve the garbage problem.

All right, here's the first suggestion.

You have been sending letters to your tenants. They're impersonal, and they got you nowhere. Switch gears. Get personal. Get in their face about the problem. Call a meeting of your tenants at the dumpster to demonstrate what happens when garbage misses its mark. Be as amusing as you can be at the same time you're being instructive. Demonstrate what happens when a child puts a garbage bag down on the ground and a dog tears the bag apart and scatters it all over the place. Scatter the garbage, and then ask the tenants to help you clean it up. They'll balk. Let them. Tell them you'll clean it up yourself just as you have been all along. They can watch. Tell them you're used to doing it, but you're also tired of doing it, and they're not paying you enough in rent to do it. Ask for their cooperation in solving the problem, and produce a little agreement for them to sign in duplicate saying that they promise to put their household garbage into the dumpster as instructed and refrain from putting any forbidden items in the dumpster in the future. Give them a copy and keep one for your files. Repeat the demonstration for every tenant who fails to show up for the first demonstration.

Here's the second suggestion.

Ask your neatest, strictest, or most agreeable tenant to be your garbage supervisor. Say that you need somebody who lives on the premises to keep the dumpster and the area around it tidy. Say that you need somebody who isn't afraid to touch other people's garbage when necessary and isn't afraid to approach offending tenants to get them to clean up their own messes when necessary. Say that you will give the garbage supervisor some compensation (a twenty-dollar bill, movie theater tickets, a restaurant gift certificate, ball game tickets, or whatever else seems attractive and appropriate) every month for taking on this responsibility, and say that either you or the tenant may decide after a few months to terminate the arrangement. In other words, it's temporary.

Here's the third suggestion.

Send the tenants a 60-day notice of change in terms of tenancy stating that you are raising their monthly rent by twenty dollars. That's a total of $160 for the eight units. In the notice, say that you have been cleaning up the garbage area yourself long enough, and you have decided at last to hire somebody to do it. Say that you are increasing their rent in order to pay for this custodial service. Say that you will give them a full forty-five days to show you that they can keep the garbage area clean themselves, and if they do, you will send them another notice rescinding the increase in their rent. Should they regress after that, you will send them a notice increasing their rent, and you will give them no further opportunity to prove themselves.

Here's the fourth suggestion.

Compare the garbage company's charges for the dumpster and for eight separate garbage cans. If the costs are comparable and if you can place a can near each tenant's back door where only that tenant can readily get to it, replace the dumpster with eight garbage cans, each one stenciled on its lid and side with an apartment number. Avoid placing all the cans together somewhere if possible because tenants too frequently disregard the markings on the cans and put their garbage into any available can. Conscientious tenants whose can has been violated may become annoyed enough to remove any garbage not their own, set it on the ground, and cause a mess. Tenants will respect one another's garbage can when it's located by itself adjacent to the apartment, and they will look after their own cans more responsibly, too, when the cans are isolated. If they don't look after their own cans responsibly, you know exactly which tenant to reproach.

Here's the fifth suggestion.

Talk with each tenant separately face to face rather than by telephone. Say something like this to each of them, "You know we have a garbage problem here. It's really gotten out of hand, and we have to do something about it right away. If we don't, we're going to have insect and rodent problems, and I'm going to have to raise the rent to hire a custodian and an exterminator and to bring in an extra dumpster. I know you well enough to know that you wouldn't put your garbage on the ground by the dumpster and that you wouldn't put something like an old sofa or TV set into the dumpster, but somebody is, and we can't let them do it anymore. I'd like you to help me eliminate the garbage problem. If you see anybody breaking the garbage rules, say something to them. That's all I ask." You know, of course, that one of them is part of the problem. Maybe several of them are parts. As they listen to you, they may see themselves that way and decide to mend their ways.

Here's the sixth suggestion.

Identify the culprits who are creating the garbage messes by keeping a close eye on the dumpster yourself, asking a willing tenant to keep a close eye on it, or installing an inexpensive wireless security camera and recorder. Once you know who's responsible for the messes, talk with them about changing their bad habits. Tell them that you really need their cooperation. Tell them that if they don't cooperate, you'll be forced to do some things you really don't want to do. You'll be forced to increase their rent or else give them a notice to move out.

There you have them, six suggestions. One of them should suffice to solve the garbage problem at your apartment building and save your sanity. If none of them does, keep looking for other ideas, and keep trying to solve the problem until you do find something which works. You will.

Unmarried couple want house; only one has good credit.

Q. An unmarried couple want to rent my house, but only the man has a job and good credit. The woman has no credit to speak of and she doesn't work. How should I handle this situation? Should I put him alone on the lease and stipulate that when he vacates the premises, she must vacate also?
—L.F., California

A. You can never predict what will happen when you rent to two adults, whether they're married or unmarried, whether they're two guys, two gals, or one of each. Their relationship may last and last, or it may last only until they've spent their first night together under one roof.

You are right to be concerned about what to do should this unmarried couple break up, especially when only one of them is working and has good credit. Should they break up, you can hope that the one with no job and no credit will vacate and that the one with the job and the good credit will remain. You can hope and hope some more. It won't happen.

Should they break up, the one who moves out will be the one with the job and the credit. You'll be stuck with the other one, the one who has neither. That's a landlording law, number thirty-six, I believe.

OK, so what do you do about it?

Before you let them move in, tell them both

that the rental agreement they sign binds the two of them to every responsibility of the tenancy so long as either of them occupies the dwelling. If one of them vacates, both of them are still responsible for the full rent. What's more, the deposit they pay when they move in will remain in your hands until both of them vacate.

Make sure that they understand and agree to this policy. If they do, rent to them. If they don't, don't rent to them.

9 Coping with Pets and Pet People

Insurer won't renew policy because of dangerous dog.

Q. I manage a six-unit family apartment complex which has very little turnover. We have good people living harmoniously together here with their children and pets. Several weeks ago, when an inspector from the company that insures the property paid us a visit, she saw a tenant outside exercising his two dogs. One of his dogs is a Staffordshire Bull Terrier, which is often taken for a pit bull by those who don't know dogs. The other dog is a cute, long-haired mongrel which looks like a Border Collie. Both dogs are family pets. They're always around children, and they're very well-behaved.

Well, the next thing we knew, the owner called to inform me that the insurance company had refused to renew her million-dollar liability policy because of the dogs. Is this legal?

We're at a loss as to know what we should do now. Should we plead our case to the insurance company? Should we make the tenants get rid of their dogs? Should we look around for another insurance company? Should we tell the tenants to buy a pet liability insurance policy?
—S.M., California

A. Some insurance companies have been so badly bitten by lawsuits involving dangerous dogs that they're trying to control their exposure however they can. You can't blame them. They have felt the pain from dog bite lawsuits. Such lawsuits are expensive to defend and expensive to settle, all the more so because the hardest hit victims of dog bites are children who are bitten on the face. Juries will award large sums to compensate innocent children facing reconstructive surgery, perhaps even a lifelong deformity, and insurance companies have to pay those large sums.

Some insurance companies have identified what they consider to be dangerous breeds and simply refuse to write policies covering those breeds. In the absence of any breed discrimination laws, they break no law when they refuse to cover what they consider dangerous breeds.

They have identified eleven breeds as dangerous: Akita, Alaskan Malamute, American Pit Bull, Chow Chow, Doberman Pinscher, German Shepherd, Presa Canario, Rottweiler, Siberian Husky, Staffordshire Bull Terrier, and wolf hybrid.

According to a twenty-year study conducted by the Centers for Disease Control and Prevention and published in 2000, two of the eleven, the American Pit Bull and the Rottweiler, account for more than half of all dog bite fatalities in the United States.

Even though your tenant's dog is not a pit bull and is a family dog used to being around children, it is on the list of dangerous dogs. That inspector may have been more knowledgeable about dogs than you suspected and may have recognized it for the Staffordshire Bull Terrier that it is.

One thing is sure. The owner of your apartment complex can no more go without providing liability insurance than she can go without providing a roof over the heads of her tenants. Liability insurance is a must. It's available from some company somewhere, and you, the tenants who own the dog perceived to be dangerous, the owner of the complex, and the owner's insurance agent who wrote the policy need to work together to find it.

Begin your groundwork by asking the property owner straightaway when the present insurance policy expires, so you know how much time there is to secure another satisfactory policy.

Then talk with the dog's owners and tell them what has happened. Tell them that you need their help in order for the property owner to get an affordable liability insurance policy to cover mishaps occurring on the property. Ask them to help you by documenting whatever they can about their dog's good characteristics and background. Their dog may not be a guide dog for the blind as some German Shepherds are, but it may have been to obedience school, it may have been neutered or fixed, it may have been in the family for a long time and never given any cause for alarm, it may be too old to be aggressive, it may be a favorite at the vet's, and it may have fans in the neighborhood. Evidence of these things may help convince somebody who doesn't know the dog that it is as safe to be around as any dog.

Also, ask the dog's owners whether they have their own liability policy covering the dog. If they don't have one, ask them to look into getting one because they have no liability coverage once the dog leaves the apartment complex. The property owner's liability policy covers mishaps on the property, not those off the property. A dog owner's liability policy covers mishaps wherever the dog happens to be. At the very least, they should know the cost of such a policy.

Asking the dog's owners to help document their dog's good points may yield enough positive information to make the insurance company relent, but even if it doesn't, the dog's owners' efforts and inquiries will prepare them for whatever you may have to require of them because of their dog, including requiring that they pay higher rent or a surcharge to cover the increased cost of another insurance policy or else requesting that they get rid of the dog or move.

While you and the dog's owners are doing your parts to help, the property owner should call the insurance agent to protest the insurance company's refusal to renew and should ask for suggestions. The agent must have faced similar situations in the past and should have some suggestions. The property owner should say that the inspector mistook a perfectly harmless family dog for a dangerous dog. She should say that the tenants have children whose safety they would never jeopardize by keeping a dangerous dog. She should say that the tenants will provide evidence to show that their particular dog is no threat to anybody.

The agent will know whether the insurance company would respond favorably to a logical, well-documented plea, and if not, what other course you should follow. Perhaps it won't budge.

Perhaps it will. The agent will know. Insurance companies are as different from one another as are the breeds on the list of dangerous dogs.

An independent insurance agent who represents a number of insurance companies will steer the property owner to a company which continues to write policies without regard to dog breeds or to one which judges dogs on a case-by-case basis.

As the on-site property manager, you are the one person who knows both the people affected by this problem and the dog. You know the property owner and want to do a good job for her. You live with the tenants and the dog and want to see them treated fairly. You know what kind of people the dog's owners are. You know how they treat dogs and how considerate they are of other people, and you know what kind of a dog this particular Staffordshire Bull Terrier is. You can put faces and names on those involved, whereas the insurance company is looking at statistics only. The more information you can provide the insurance company about these good people and this good dog, the better. The more you can do to coordinate everybody's efforts to solve this problem, the better.

You can be a big help to everybody by working to solve this problem in a timely manner to everybody's benefit.

Son and girlfriend defy parent landlords with dangerous pit bull.

Q. Our son has been living in our second home for two years under a lease-option which has now expired. He'd like to buy the house, but he can't get the financing. We have continued to let him live there as long as he pays the rent, and he's been paying it promptly right along. We have no complaints about that.

We do have complaints about some other things. They're things related to his girlfriends and their dogs. One girlfriend moved in with him, and her dogs destroyed the landscaping in the back yard. He said he would fix it, but he hasn't done anything about it yet. We haven't pushed him. In fact, we told him we'd help him fix it in the spring.

When he and that girlfriend split up, she and her dogs moved out. They were replaced by another girlfriend who has a pit bull. We used to have nothing against pit bulls. As far as we were concerned, they were just dogs. Then, a few weeks ago, we changed our minds. Our son was playing tug of war with the pit bull when it attacked him and bit his throat. He might have been seriously hurt, even killed, if he hadn't been strong enough to pull the dog away. As it was, he had to go to the hospital to have his throat sewed up.

The hospital reported the incident to the humane society, and they came to interview the girlfriend. She told them two lies. She told them that she was only visiting our son, and she told them that the dog did not live there. They believed her and left without doing anything.

Our son did not make her get rid of the dog because he was afraid of "losing her." He says he loves her and wants to marry her.

She won't talk to us at all now because we're insisting that the dog has to go. She thinks we're being ridiculous. We think we're being realistic. Already our insurance has been canceled because there's a vicious dog on the property. We have tried, but we cannot get rental property liability insurance that will cover the dog.

Our son has said that he will never speak to us again if we throw her out, and we don't want to alienate him for life, but we cannot afford to lose everything we've worked for during our lifetimes, including the home we occupy, if the dog bites someone and we get sued. We cannot even list the property for sale because the real estate agent won't go near the house with the dog there. We can't blame him. He knows what the dog did to our son.

We care about this girl and don't want to interfere with the relationship, but the dog has got to go. She says that her parents have a house they will rent to her four months from now, but until then she says she does not have the $2,000 required to buy dog-owner liability insurance on the dog.

We have thought about selling the house to our son using a contract-for-deed purchase agreement so that he could get liability insurance in his own name. We have thought about looking for some legal way to evict the dog and only the dog. We have thought about other ways to handle this situation, too, but we haven't come up with a good one yet. They all seem to have disadvantages.

What do you suggest we do?

—T.M., Washington

A. Pit bull owners are a breed apart. They know what their dogs were bred to do. They know how

temperamental, vicious, tenacious, and uncontrollable their dogs can be, and still they believe that their own little "Terminator" would never hurt anybody. Your son found out otherwise. His girlfriend's dog is a menace, and everybody knows it, everybody except the two of them.

You know it. You know that the dog nearly killed your son. The real estate agent knows it. He won't go near the house while the dog's there. Your insurance company knows it. They canceled your policy. The dog-owner liability insurance company knows it. They want $2,000 as a liability insurance premium just in case the dog bites somebody. That's a higher premium than it would be if the dog were another breed and had never bitten anybody.

Even though your son, blinded by love, believes that the dog is no menace, and even though your son's girlfriend, blinded by love for her dog, believes that the dog is no menace, you know that it is, and you know that you must do something quickly because you know from personal experience that the dog is dangerous and because you as landlords have no insurance to cover you in case the dog causes further injury.

Unfortunately, you cannot simply pluck the dog out of the lovebirds' household, at least not legally, and even if you could, another one would soon take its place. You have no choice but to deal with the people responsible for the dog's being there, your son and the girlfriend.

She has already alienated herself from you by refusing to speak to you because you have insisted that the dog must go. Such behavior is additional evidence of the bad judgment she showed when she decided to get a pit bull in the first place. You have to wonder whether she would continue showing bad judgment by keeping a pit bull in the same house where she is raising your grandchildren. The girlfriend is wrong in keeping the dog, wrong in giving you the silent treatment, and wrong in lying to the humane society. Your son is wrong in supporting a girlfriend who is acting so childishly and so selfishly.

She may be likeable in some ways and you may want to please her and your son by doing nothing about the dog, but you know that you have to do something. You must use sound judgment even if they refuse to use sound judgment themselves.

If you had rented the house to a stranger and the stranger had moved in a girlfriend with a pit bull, you would not have thought twice about giving them a notice to perform covenant, citing the dog as the reason for the notice. They could choose to get rid of the dog or move. That's the way the system works.

You must deal with your son and his girlfriend in the same way, just as you would if they were strangers, even though they say they will shun you if you try. You have to take that risk.

I would take that risk because I would have enough confidence in my son that he would come to his senses in due course and realize that the girlfriend is more of a girl than a friend. At some time in the future, she will treat him just as she is treating you now. She will want to get her way and she will tell him that he'd better do what she wants or she'll shun him. When that happens, and it will, he will return to his parents much the wiser and ask for forgiveness.

Do not bend to these children's demands. They are wrong. You are right. Use your good judgment. Be as tenacious in getting rid of this dangerous dog as it is tenacious when it attacks.

Tenants use rental agreement oversight to justify vicious dog.

Q. I have had a certain tenant for seventeen years. Six months ago she signed a month-to-month rental agreement which I asked her to sign. In it, I wrote "dogs o.k." She'd had the same docile dog for years, and I foresaw no problem about including that phrase in her agreement. I was mistaken.

A big problem arose when her live-in boyfriend acquired the most vicious dog I've ever encountered, a full-grown pit bull. When they're home, they leave the dog in the front yard all the time, and when they go out, they chain it to a thick steel cable suspended between two trees. Its fran-

tic pacing has destroyed the yard between the trees. What used to be green grass is now a dirt brown trench.

This dog is so terrifying that neighbors no longer allow their children outside. No one can get near the property without the dog's growling and baring its teeth.

I'm afraid that it will maul somebody if it gets loose. I informed the tenant that the dog had to go. She told me she has a right to keep it because her agreement states that dogs (plural) are o.k. I'm just as mad at myself now for putting "dogs" in her agreement as I am at her for citing my oversight as authorization for keeping the beast.

I called the police about it, and they said that they can't do anything unless the dog is running free.

I'm desperate. What can I do?
—D.C., California

A. You need to act immediately. As a landlord, you cannot allow a tenant to have a vicious dog, no matter what the breed. That dog in your tenant's yard is a land mine set to explode, and it will surely hurt somebody when circumstances set it off.

By "act immediately," I don't mean dispatching the dog with a firearm or poison. That kind of action is illegal. You want to stay completely within the law. You want to give the tenant proper notice that the dog must go or else.

Since the tenant has not breached the agreement or broken any law, you cannot serve her with a three-day notice to perform covenant or a three-day notice to quit for unlawful acts, but you can serve her with a three-day notice to quit for nuisance. After all, this dog she has allowed to stay at her rented home is a loathsome nuisance to everyone except her and her live-in boyfriend.

That's your first choice, a three-day notice to quit for nuisance. You have two others as well, each of them requiring a notice period longer than three days.

Your second choice is to serve the tenant with a thirty-day notice of change in terms of tenancy which specifically excludes the vicious dog. It would rescind the right your rental agreement gave the tenant to have more than one dog. It might say something like this: "This thirty-day notice changes the month-to-month rental agreement dated MMDDYYYY between tenant XXX and owner YYY. 'Dogs o.k.' is hereby changed to 'dog o.k.,' and the following wording is hereby added to the agreement, 'Tenant may house no pet of any kind on the premises, even temporarily, without first obtaining owner's written permission and executing a pet agreement. Permission is hereby granted for XXX to keep Fido, and only Fido, as a pet, provided that XXX execute a pet agreement for Fido.'"

Your third choice is to serve the tenant with a notice to terminate tenancy. It would inform the tenant that she and her live-in boyfriend and their dogs must move out. State law determines the length of the notice period for termination notices. Generally, it's thirty days, although California law requires that landlords give sixty days to tenants who have lived somewhere for a year or more. Since your tenant has been with you for sixteen years, you'd have to give her sixty days.

The first and third choices give the tenant no opportunity to remain as a tenant upon getting rid of the vicious dog. The first one cancels the existing rental agreement, and the third one terminates it, no matter what. The second one is more obliging, allowing the tenant to remain upon getting rid of the dog.

You must decide which approach would work best with this particular tenant in this particular situation. You may not want to give her only three days to get out because you feel that it could trigger an altercation. You may not want this long-term tenant of yours to vacate because you know that she's otherwise agreeable and basically a good tenant.

Weigh the pros and cons of each approach and then decide. No matter which one you decide upon, it should be the one least likely to compel you to go to court to evict the tenant. You don't want to go to court because it will take time, cost money, introduce uncertainty, and alienate the tenant.

Knowing nothing about your tenant, I would tend to choose the second approach for most of my tenants in similar circumstances. This approach is almost like saying, "Oops, I made a mistake in writing the new agreement to allow you to have more than one dog. I want to correct that mistake now, and I'm going to give you a whole month to comply." If the tenant wants to keep the dog, she'll have time to look around for another place to rent. If she wants to keep the rental dwelling, she'll have time to find another place for the dog. She's not so rushed, and she's less likely to feel she's being wronged and ought to stand her ground, forcing you to evict her through the courts.

Departing husband refuses to take responsibility for his dog.

Q. Last year I rented a house to a newly married couple. The wife has been a friend of mine for years. Now, a year later, they are divorcing, and he's moving out. My problem is the husband's dog. It has dug holes and done its business all over the yard. The husband was supposed to keep the yard clean and mow the grass, but he's done neither. I've been paying a guy to maintain the yard and have had to pay him extra because of the dog mess. When I asked the husband to pay something to offset my extra expenses related to his dog, he refused. He told me he'd be leaving shortly and didn't care what happened. Isn't he responsible? Should I pursue a judgment for damages against him if he moves without taking care of the damage?
—L.W., Virginia

A. Just as a husband and wife are jointly responsible for one another's debts during a marriage, they're jointly responsible for the damage done by one another's dogs, cats, pythons, and pigs. In this case, be grateful that only the husband had a troublesome dog. He's 100% responsible for it, but then so is she. If he tries to leave without paying for the damage, you have several avenues to pursue.

Whatever you do, assess the damage caused by the husband's dog and assess your additional costs in maintaining the property because of the dog. As soon as possible, present him with a bill for the total, and tell him you expect payment before he moves out. If he doesn't pay, you could deduct the amount of the bill from the security deposit and tell the wife, if she intends to remain as your tenant, that she will need to bring the deposit back up to its original level within three months. Since he "owned" half of the original deposit, he would be paying for half of the damage.

If you prefer, you may go after the two of them in small claims court and let the judge sort out who's liable for what. You could go after him alone, but if the judge were to decide that each of them ought to pay half, you might wind up getting a judgment for only half of your expenses.

Friend or no friend, the wife needs to accept some responsibility for the damage. She allowed it to occur. She could have cleaned up after the dog herself. She didn't.

They want to have the same number of cats as their landlord.

Q. We are tenants and hope you might help us with a problem we're having with our landlords. A few months ago we moved into a building owned by some friends of our family. Before we agreed to rent the apartment, my fiance and I asked whether we could have a cat. Both the landlord, who lives in the building, and her son, co-owner of the building and also living in an apartment here, have two cats each. We were told that we could have cats but no dogs. We moved in without signing a lease, so we have nothing other than a verbal agreement on any of this. When we went to adopt another cat from our local humane society a few days ago, our landlords refused to allow us to have another cat in our apartment. We pointed out that they each had two cats, but we were told that they were the owners of the building and were entitled to do as they please. Since they are friends of the family, I am reluctant to do anything about this matter, but now they are saying that we never had permission to bring our cat here to begin with. I am wondering what, if any, rights we have in a matter such as this?
—J.V., Iowa

A. Your rights hinge upon the verbal agreement you had with your landlords when you moved in, but you'd be hard pressed to prove exactly what that verbal agreement was. Lacking a written agreement, but relying upon your own interpretation of your verbal agreement, you ought to keep the cat you have had since you moved in and just not make an issue of it, but don't press your case for a second cat, even though your landlords have second cats and even though you origi-

nally thought you could have two cats.

Your landlords are entitled to have as many cats as the law allows them to have. You are entitled to have as many cats as your landlords allow you to have. They are well within their rights to ban cats from the building. They are even within their rights to ban cats from the building after first having given permission for their tenants to have cats, but they would have to give their tenants proper notice of a change in terms of tenancy and they would have to expect a mutiny.

Because you have had the one cat for some time, because your landlords must have known that you had it, and because your landlords are "cat people" themselves, you have reason to expect that they will allow you to keep the cat you already have if the issue comes to a head. Do not expect them to allow you to keep a second cat.

Your situation illustrates the importance of written agreements. Tenants need them. Landlords need them. Cats need them.

Tenant wants to replace grandfathered dog that died.

Q. When my landlord bought the apartment building where I live, he decided to implement a no-pets policy. I had two dogs at the time, and he told me that they would be grandfathered in so that I wouldn't have to get rid of them.

Just recently, one of my dogs died under mysterious circumstances. I have reason to suspect that somebody poisoned him. I can't say for sure who is the guilty party, and I'll probably never know for sure.

My remaining dog is a social animal and is having a hard time adjusting now that she has lost her playmate. I would like to replace the dog that died, but I'm afraid that my landlord won't let me.

Am I entitled to have two dogs once more or not? What does "grandfathering" really mean?
—D.F., California

A. "Grandfathering" is a concession designed to placate those who have been enjoying a certain privilege while living under an old, more liberal, set of rules. Grandfathering extends that privilege to existing tenants even though new rules eliminate it for new arrivals. It's meant to be a temporary concession, easing the way to conformity with the new rules. It lasts as long as its elements remain in place unchanged.

In your case, the elements are you and your two dogs, all three of you. You are the key element, and your dogs are key dependent elements. You are grandfathered together. So long as nothing changes, you and the dogs have nothing to worry about, and you may enjoy one another's company with impunity so long as you all shall live.

If you should die, the dogs must go because you as the key element no longer reside there, and nobody else in the apartment building could take the dogs because nobody else there was grandfathered with them. Nobody else may substitute for you as the key element, and without the key element, the key-dependent dogs lose their standing as grandfathered pets.

If one of the dogs should die or disappear, you may not replace it because it was one of the three originally grandfathered elements, and no other dog may substitute for an originally grandfathered element. No replacement dog could possibly become a newly grandfathered element, for grandfathering occurs only once, not repeatedly, and the time for grandfathering has come and gone.

You may not replace the dead dog. You must content yourself with the one remaining grandfathered dog, and when she dies, you may not replace her.

If you want to have two dogs once more, you'll have to move to an apartment building where the owners welcome pets.

Applicants with pets clamor to rent houses with lots of land.

Q. For the past three years, we have been managing five houses on my husband's grandfather's seven-acre property. Grandfather is ill and lives in one of the houses. The others are rentals.

Right now we're looking for new tenants to fill a vacancy, and we're finding that most of the applicants have a pet or two. None of our current tenants have pets, and we feel strongly about sticking with our no-pets policy.

Are we doing the right thing in being firm about this policy?
—E.H., California

A. Since you feel strongly about your no-pets policy, continue with it. Do not waver. You do not have to rent to pet owners other than to those who have service animals. Don't.

You may be getting more than the usual number of inquiries from pet owners because they tend to look for houses to rent rather than apartments and especially houses on large plots of land. If you give them any indication in your advertising that you have a house for rent on an acre of land, pet owners will be clamoring to rent it. To keep them from bothering you, put "no pets" in your advertising.

There are more good reasons not to rent to pet owners than there are good reasons to rent to them, and so long as you are successful in renting to people without pets, keep doing what you're doing.

Tenants think "no agreement" means they can have a dog.

Q. I bought a triplex some nine months ago and live in one of the units. When I bought the building, there were no written rental agreements, and the tenants were renting their units on a month-to-month basis.

The tenants were described to me as good people who behaved themselves and were never late with their rent. That description fits the tenants in one of the units but not those in the other.

Between the time when I agreed to buy the building and the time when I took possession, the tenants in one of the units got a dog. They told me about it two days after I became their landlord. Their misconduct didn't stop there, and as a result, I have had to keep a close eye on them all the time just as if they were naughty children.

So far, I have had to notify them in writing twice that they needed to clean up after the dog, I have had to give them three notices about their rent being late every month for the past three months, I have had to confront them about giving the other tenants permission to use my personal washer and dryer, and I have had to get after them several times to remove a car they were storing for a friend of theirs in our residents' parking area.

The same day their friend's car left, leaving behind an oil stain in the driveway, they showed up with another vehicle, which has now been here two nights. I'm fed up with these people doing whatever they please just because they have no rental agreement, and I'm planning to have a heart-to-heart talk with them and lay down the law.

I plan to talk with them about our miscommunications in the past and to tell them that they need to ask permission when they're thinking about doing something questionable rather than do it first and ask for forgiveness later. I plan to talk with them about having a second vehicle and explain to them that I will have to charge them extra for a second parking place if they plan to keep the vehicle. I plan to give them a month-to-month agreement along with rules and regulations covering things like parking and pets.

I'm wondering whether there's anything else I should do. Should I ask them for a non-refundable pet deposit? Their dog has already scratched up the wooden floors, and I know that I'll have to refinish them when the tenants move. What's reasonable for me to do?
—S.J.S., New Jersey

A. You have tenants who think they have rights they don't have, and you are correct in spelling out in writing what rights and responsibilities they do have. You are also correct in talking with them about their past as someone else's tenants and their future as your tenants.

You are not correct in asking them to pay a non-refundable pet deposit. Instead, ask them to add a reasonable sum, such as $150, to their refundable security deposit to cover any damage done by their dog.

Not only is the phrase "non-refundable pet deposit" an oxymoron (a deposit must be refundable), it will most certainly spark an argument with these naughty tenants of yours. They will resist you, maybe even defy you. They will assume that you are punishing them, charging them an extra sum just because they decided to get a dog, when there never were any guidelines about their having pets.

You want them to respond positively to your request, not negatively. You want them to understand that the additional deposit you are asking them to put up is nothing more than a reasonable request, something asked of every tenant who ever brings a dog into a rental unit. It's refundable so long as their dog leaves no damage behind when they move out.

Increasing their security deposit is better than asking them for a pet deposit because you may use security deposit monies to pay for any damages or charges they owe you when they move out. Pet deposits are limited to damages related to the pet. For example, a landlord may not use a pet deposit to apply to a rent arrearage when a tenant vacates.

As for pet rules and procedures, check the section about pets in the *Landlording* book under "Should You Allow Pets?" There you will find several pet policies and a pet agreement which you may want to use or modify for your use. Be sure the tenants understand that whatever terms you agree upon regarding their pet dog cover only this one dog and no other. The tenants may not substitute a German Shepherd for Ned, their Cocker Spaniel.

By introducing a written rental agreement, along with rules and regulations, and asking your dog-owning tenants to sign a pet agreement and increase their security deposit, you are acting quite reasonably to turn disorder into order.

You need do nothing else other than convince your tenants that order is better than disorder and that you will do your best to maintain order. Tell them that if they want to live in disorder according to their own rules, they had better start packing.

10
Collecting the Rent

They want to change previous landlord's lax rent policy.

Q. For seven months now we've been landlords. My wife and I bought a fourteen-unit apartment building with the money we inherited from her mother. We didn't know what else to do with it. A friend of ours was selling his only two rental properties when we were looking around for an investment, and he gave us a good price on the one we were interested in, so we bought it.

We haven't regretted that decision.

There's just one thing we're having trouble with, and that's collecting the rents on time. Malcolm, our friend who sold us the building, is a nice guy. He reminds us of the "What me worry?" character in *MAD* magazine. He should never have been a landlord because he was too lenient. He let the tenants walk all over him. They would pay their rent whenever they felt like paying it, sometimes even a month or two late. He told us he never worried about payment because he knew everybody there and he knew they would pay eventually. They were long-term tenants, and he trusted them.

As if to prove that he was doing the right thing, he told us that he never had to evict anybody as long as he was a landlord and he never lost any rent. Of course, he never mentioned how long he had to wait for the rent sometimes.

We are trusting people ourselves, but we are also more aware than Malcolm was that there are bills to be paid and they have to be paid on time. We can't pay the water bill late and the loan payment late without incurring some sort of penalty, and we can't pay the bills at all if we don't have the rent money to pay them with. We used our entire inheritance and then some to buy the building, and we don't have the money to be carrying tenants who want us to wait a month or two for their rent.

Because we were new to the business when we took over and didn't want to upset the tenants too much, we decided to continue with Malcolm's policy for collecting rents, but we'd like to change it now. Out of our fourteen tenants, five of them are delinquent, two of them by fifteen days, two of them by thirty days, and one by a full two months.

Malcolm also never charged a late fee, and we want to change that, too. We think that tenants who are late ought to pay something extra.

How should we go about making these changes without upsetting the tenants too much? —J.M., Florida

A. The only tenants you'll upset are the ones who have been taking advantage of you and paying late. The tenants who are current with their rents will probably applaud your decision to tighten up on rent collection. Just as you don't like to see speeders flouting the law by driving 90 m.p.h. in a 55 m.p.h. zone when you're observing the speed limit yourself, people who pay their bills on time don't like to see other people paying late without being penalized.

To make the change to a stricter rent collection policy, you may prepare a notice of change in terms of tenancy and serve every tenant with a copy. The notice ought to give them thirty days to comply, and it ought to say that all rents are due on the first of the month and late on the fifth. If Malcolm included a late fee in his rental agreements and wasn't enforcing it, the notice ought to restate the amount of the late fee and say that you will enforce it religiously as soon as the notice takes effect. If Malcolm did not include a late fee in his rental agreements and you want to start charging a late fee now, you may state your late payment policy in the same notice.

Your late fee ought to be reasonable, say $50

or less, and you ought to introduce it using verbiage something like this: "Tenants who pay their rent after the due date incur a late fee of $XX. Because the actual damages for late rent payments are difficult or impossible to determine, landlord and tenants agree to the stated late fee as liquidated damages."

Better still than serving your tenants a notice that you are changing Malcolm's lax rent collection policy would be preparing entirely new rental agreements and including your new rent collection policy in them.

Surely the old rental agreements need updating anyway, and you might as well take this opportunity to update them.

Once you come up with a new rental agreement, sit down with your tenants to discuss it with them and get them to sign it. Give them a copy and keep one for your files.

As soon as the notice or the new rental agreement takes effect, begin collecting your rents according to the policy you outlined. Enforce the policy when tenants are late, and you'll be sending these spoiled tenants of yours the message that Malcolm is no longer in charge. You are, and you mean business when you're collecting rents.

He blames landlord for blown fuse and stops rent check.

Q. I have a tenant who gave me a post-dated check for his rent, and I'm not happy about it.

Here's what happened.

Last month there was a long holiday weekend at the end of the month, and I was away from home spending time with friends and relatives. When I returned Sunday evening, I found an angry message from the tenant on my answering machine informing me that a fuse had burned out in his apartment, and as a consequence, he had no lights in his bathroom. He said he was going to put a stop payment on the check he had mailed me earlier and leave it there until I fixed the fuse. I replaced the fuse the following day. When I went to cash his check the very next day, the teller informed me that the check was still marked "STOPPED." I contacted the tenant, and he replaced it with another check, but his new check was post-dated until the end of the month.

Apparently, when I did not return his call to fix the fuse right away, he was so angry that he went right out and found another apartment, and he used the rent as a deposit on this other apartment. He has informed me that he has decided to stay where he is, but the other landlord will not return his money until the end of the month.

I am not a rich landlord. When my mortgage payment was due, my account had insufficient funds in it because this tenant's check wasn't there. The bank penalized me $25 for being late and tacked on another month's interest charge of approximately $800. His refusal to pay his rent on time cost me a lot, and I'm sure it affected my credit, too.

After all I've suffered, what penalties can I impose on the tenant?
—K.J., Ontario, Canada

A. Your tenant sounds as if he's pretty thin-skinned, and he's going to keep blaming you for little things and withholding rent and giving you postdated checks whenever he can. Too bad he didn't move to that other apartment! I'd urge him to do so now.

If you have a clause in your rental agreement about late payment and another about bad checks, and you should have, then you should enforce those clauses with this tenant.

If a check is no good when you try to cash it, then payment has not been made. He was late with his rent, and he gave you a bum check. Force him to pay the consequences of both actions, and give him notice that you will no longer accept his checks for payment. Paying by check is a privilege. Tell him that he must pay his rent with a cashier's check or a money order from now on. (Check with your attorney or your rental property owners association to make sure that you *can* make this demand of your tenant before you make it.)

Unfortunately, you cannot force him to pay all the additional costs which you incurred as a result of his giving you a bum check. All you can do is charge him for what he owes you according to the agreement you have with him.

I would strongly suggest that you approach your mortgage company, explain what happened, and ask them for leniency in paying the penalties. Mortgage companies have been known to be human and to give their good customers some slack especially if your records show that you have consistently made your payments on time.

I would also strongly suggest that in the future you leave enough of a balance in your own checking account so that no check you write, especially one which carries a huge penalty if it's late, would bounce if a tenant were to give you a bum check.

Tenant can't seem to pay her rent on time.

Q. My husband and I own a beautiful two-family house in Massachusetts. One of our tenants who lives there with her seven-year-old son is always late with her rent. Many times she gives us two checks, one to cash right away and one to hold for two weeks. I've been nice about the matter and have told her at least a week before the rent is due that she should let me know in advance when she can't pay her entire rent and not wait until the last minute to say something.

She says that she doesn't know what to do, that she's having problems paying her bills.

This past year she asked whether she could take in a lodger to help her out with the rent. I let her, and she found a wonderful woman to move in with her, but she says she still can't afford the rent.

I told her that maybe she should look for something cheaper. I said that we need to pay our mortgage and that her being late all the time is not helping any. I told her that she needs to pay the rent on time or I'll have to give her a 30-day notice. What do you think we should do about her?

—M.S., Massachusetts

A. Some people simply cannot handle money. The more they have, the more they spend. You essentially gave this tenant more money to pay her rent with when you allowed her to have a lodger to help out. That should have improved her situation, but it didn't. Too bad! You tried.

Because the woman is no problem otherwise and because you don't have many tenants to deal with, you might want to try one last resort with her before giving her a 30-day notice and sending her packing.

Sit down with her and ask her when she gets paid. It'll be weekly, biweekly, or semimonthly. It won't be monthly, that's for sure. Tell her that you'll change her rent due date so that it coincides with the date when she gets paid. With her rent due on the same day she gets paid or the day after, she won't have to worry about setting the money aside to accumulate for the one day a month when her rent is due. She can pay what she owes on time every time. In exchange for this accommodation, you should charge her a little extra, say, five dollars per payment, because it is, after all, more work for you to keep track of the amounts owed and to write the receipts.

If you and the tenant agree to handle the rent payments this way, make sure that you keep a good accounting of the period each payment covers. In the case of weekly or biweekly payments, you should calculate the rent by the day. Multiply the current monthly rent by twelve and divide by 365 to get the daily rent. Each weekly payment should be seven times the daily rent plus $5 for the accommodation charge. Each biweekly payment should be fourteen times the daily rent plus $5 for the accommodation charge. Each semimonthly payment should be half the monthly rent plus $5 for the accommodation charge. Identify the period covered by each payment directly on the receipt.

Accommodating your tenant in this way may prove to be good for your tenant, enabling her to keep living in a beautiful home, and good for you, enabling you to keep a good tenant.

Long-term tenant always pays late but never pays the late fee.

Q. We have a tenant who has been with us for over twenty years. He always pays his rent on the last day of the month or as late as five days into the next month. I have told him several times that the rent is due by the fifth day of the current month and that a late fee must accompany any later payment. He continues to ignore us by paying late, and he never pays the late fee. What can I do? I told him again last month and he said, "Well, you never complained before," and he walked away.

I want to write him a very forceful letter telling him to pay on time or face serious consequences.

—N.V., California

A. This tenant needs to be retrained, but before you retrain him, you must examine his rental agreement. It must state that the rent is payable in advance. Otherwise, he may pay in arrears, just as he has been doing all along.

There's another wrinkle in this case which you should know about. Your having accepted his rent late so many times is tantamount to your having given him permission to pay late, and you would lose your case in court if he used the "estoppel defense," arguing that your conduct in accepting the late payments contradicts whatever the rental agreement says. Those verbal warnings you gave him don't count. Accepting the payments late month after month is what counts.

As of now, don't even try to take him to court over his habitual late payments, no matter what your rental agreement says, because you would lose if he or his attorney knows the estoppel defense, and you have to assume that they do.

Instead, send him a notice which establishes your new ground rules for paying on time.

The notice should be labeled a "notice of change in terms of tenancy," and it should provide for advance notice of thirty days or more.. It might be worded something like this:

"You are hereby notified that the terms of tenancy under which you occupy the premises known as [address of the unit] are to be changed. Effective XX/XX/XXXX, there will be the following changes:

"'Rent is payable in advance on or before the first of the calendar month for which the rent is due. The late date is four days later. In other words, tenant may pay the rent on or before the due date, or he may pay it on any of the three days following the due date without penalty. The very next day, the fifth, is the rent late date. This is the first day when owners will consider the rent late. Owners expect to have received the rent before this date.

"'Owners expect tenant to pay the rent promptly. Should exceptional circumstances prevent prompt payment, tenant will pay a late fee of $XX.'"

Deliver this notice to the tenant and tell him what it says so there is no misunderstanding. He cannot ignore the notice as he has ignored your verbal warnings. It becomes a part of his rental agreement, and it establishes new ground rules regardless of what his original agreement says and regardless of what your conduct has been in accepting late payments.

Thirty days following service of the notice, you must be prepared to enforce the new ground rules. If he doesn't pay by the fourth, be there on his doorstep on the fifth with a notice to pay rent or quit.

Tenant tells landlord to beg for the rent.

Q. I have a house and a garage apartment on the same lot. I occupy the garage apartment and rent out the house. I have been renting to the same tenant for many years, and up until now, there have been no problems. We have gotten along just fine as landlord and tenant and as neighbors.

My tenant recently invited the son of a friend to stay with her "until he got on his feet." Five days after he moved in, he lost his job. He has been there now for five months, and from what I can see, he's pretty much worthless.

Since he moved in, my tenant has undergone an attitude change. She complains constantly about his habits and once went so far as to have the locks changed, but upon his return, she immediately gave him a new key. His latest exploit was to leave his wrecked automobile on my front lawn, where it has sat for two weeks. My tenant is now five days late with her rent, and she says that if I want the rent, I can "beg her for it."

My problem is this: I have only a verbal agreement with her, and I'm not sure that it would hold up in court. If I get her to sign a lease, should I get her subtenant to sign it as well? If I do get him to sign and she moves out, I'm stuck with him, aren't I? Is there any way to evict her, being that her agreement is verbal only?
—T.M., Alabama

A. Don't bother with a new lease. You don't need no stinkin' lease to evict a deadbeat tenant and her worthless guest.

Whereas a verbal agreement isn't the best kind of agreement to have for any rental property, it's still a valid agreement. Since yours with this tenant has been long-term, a judge will look upon it as something akin to a common-law marriage arrangement, valid but subject to a little extra questioning.

The two basics of any rental agreement, verbal or written, are the habitable dwelling and the rent. Since you are providing the tenant with a habitable dwelling and the tenant is not providing you with the rent, there's a just cause for eviction, and you should begin eviction proceedings immediately.

Serve the tenant with a notice to pay rent or quit, and get things moving. Tell her that you are not playing games with her and that you are not going to beg her for the rent. Tell her that she has an obligation to pay you the rent, just as you have an obligation to provide her with a habitable dwelling. Tell her that if she doesn't pay you within the state-mandated time-frame given in your notice, you are going to evict her and smudge both her credit and her good name so that henceforth she will have a more difficult time renting from anybody.

At the same time you serve her with the notice to pay rent or quit, serve her with a notice to get that wreck of a car off the front lawn. The notice should give her ten days to make it disappear before you have it towed away at her expense.

Do name the worthless guest in your paperwork, just in case he should claim that he has certain tenancy rights based upon the length of time he has lived in the house.

Since your tenant has changed her attitude, you need to do the same. You need to get tough with her. Otherwise, she'll continue treating you like a laughing stock.

Rent is overdue and tenants have disappeared.

Q. The last time I saw my tenants was just after Christmas. They notified me that they would be traveling during the month of January and would return the second week of February. They pre-paid January's rent, but now that we're into March, their rent is overdue for February and

for March as well. There is no sign of anyone in the rental house. I have left answering-machine messages and a note on the door, but there's been no reply. What should I do? What can I do?
—N.C., Nebraska

A. Something must have happened to your tenants while they were out traveling for five weeks, or else they would have contacted you by now to arrange to pay their rent. They acted responsibly by pre-paying their January rent and would be paying you their current rent now if they could. For some reason they can't, and you need to find out why they can't, so you can make plans.

Look at their rental application first. If you're using the application from the *Landlording* book, you'll find a "person to contact in case of emergency" listed there. Call that person first. No luck? Call the personal references on the application. No luck again? Call the employer.

If all of your calls turn up nothing, try searching for them on the internet as missing persons. The internet has all kinds of resources available.

While you are searching for the tenants, begin abandonment proceedings in order to retrieve possession of the property as soon as possible. The proceedings require waiting periods, and you might as well do the waiting while you're actively searching for the tenants rather than begin the proceedings after you fail to find the tenants and have to do the waiting later. If the tenants turn up, you can always abort the abandonment proceedings. They're non-judicial and require no outlay of funds.

Learn the proper abandonment procedure for the jurisdiction governing your rental property and follow it.

Get moving. You're losing money every day the place sits there abandoned.

Tenant asks for change in rent due date.

Q. I have a renter who has asked that the due date for his rent be moved from the first to the tenth of every month. The contract states that his rent is due on the first. Should I switch the date?
—S.R., Texas

A. Rents ought to be due on the first of the month because they're easier for a landlord to track and they're easier for a tenant to remember.

When a tenant asks specifically for another rent due date, he must have a compelling reason for requesting the change, most likely so that his pay date will coincide with the rent due date. Accommodate him. You want to make his rent paying to be as painless as possible. You don't want to give him any excuse for not paying his rent on time.

Whenever you change a rent due date, however, you and the tenant should sign an agreement which states that the rent due date has been changed from such and such day of the month to such and such day of the month, beginning on such and such date. This agreement should also state exactly what the rent proration will be for the first month when the change takes effect.

If you are changing rent due dates from the first to the tenth, then the rent for the first month the date is changed should equal one month's rent plus nine days, and the rent receipt should indicate that the rent has been paid through the ninth of the following month. After that, the rent receipt should indicate that the rent period covered is the tenth of one month through the ninth of the next.

Landlord wants to seize deadbeat tenant's horses.

Q. My tenant owes me $1,100. He has no property, no money, no car worth anything, and no job. The only things he has of value are a mare and a colt worth about $3,500. He has moved out of my house and lives with his sister because she lets him live with her for nothing. The horses are still boarded on my property.

When he moved in, he signed one agreement for renting the house and another agreement for boarding the horses. He owes me back rent on the house and back board on the horses. The boarding agreement states that if he does not pay the board, I can seize the horses and sell them to pay what he owes me for board and expenses. The outstanding board is now $125. The rest of the money he owes me is the outstanding rent due on the house.

I've rejected going to small claims court because even with a judgment in my favor, I couldn't collect it because he has no money and no assets and does not plan to get a job anytime soon.

How can I legally get a lien on the horses so I can get my money out of him?
—J.T., Ohio

A. You cannot get a lien on a tenant's property without going to court, but in your case you don't

need a lien. You have an agreement signed by this deadbeat tenant which gives you the right to seize the horses and sell them to collect the cost of the boarding. What's keeping you? Hire somebody to seize the horses and move them someplace where the tenant cannot get to them.

Notify him in writing that you have seized the horses according to the agreement and that you will return them only when he pays all that he owes you, provided that he does so within thirty days. Tell him that if he does not pay, you will sell the horses for whatever you can get for them, deduct the monies he owes you plus your expenses, and give him the balance, if any.

Strictly speaking, you cannot, according to the boarding agreement, keep the money he owes you for back rent on the house, but let him take you to small claims court over that. If he dares to take you to small claims court, file a counterclaim against him for the rent, and tell your story to the judge.

My guess is that his sister will lend him the money to pay you. Accept nothing less than everything he owes, and do not allow him to bring the horses back onto your property.

Tenant misinterprets meaning of "last month's rent."

Q. We have a family living in our house while we are living out of the area. In the original lease agreement, we charged first month's rent, last month's rent, and a security deposit. The agreement was for one year.

We have just signed another one-year agreement with the tenant and did not include a charge for the last month's rent. I was under the impression that it would roll over to the next term, so I left it out. The tenant signed and returned the agreement but did not send his rent for the last month of the original lease period, stating that he had already paid his last month's rent.

I told him that he had to pay rent for the last month of the original lease period or he'd have to move out by the end of the month. Am I correct?
—J.W., California

A. Your question underscores the danger of making assumptions whenever you're dealing with tenants. You assumed that "last month's rent" in the original lease agreement referred to the last month of possession, whereas your tenant assumed that it referred to the last month of the original lease period. A reasonable person would say that you are correct, that "last month's rent" always means the last month of possession, that is, the last month before the tenant moves out, but your tenant assumed differently.

In the absence of clear language to the contrary and even knowing that you would likely win against the tenant in court, you should roll over on this one. Living out of the area as you do, you are in no position to contest the matter yourself. Doing so would create ill will and cause you grief.

Tell the tenant that you can understand the confusion and will go along with his interpretation of "last month's rent." Give him a receipt stating that you have applied his last month's rent to the last month of the original lease period, that you no longer hold a last month's rent for him, and that he owes you rent, due and payable in advance, for his last month of occupancy, when it arrives. End the matter there for now.

Tell yourself that you have learned a useful lesson, that you will assume nothing in the future when you make agreements with tenants, and that you will repeat certain things if you have to, in order to make yourself clearly understood.

Tenant disappears owing landlord money.

Q. My tenant has not yet paid her rent for this month. What's more, she has paid her rent late seven times so far over the past twelve months without ever once paying the late fee. Plus, she paid $20 less than the full rent one month, and she paid $40 less than the full rent last month.

I called last week and left a message on her answering machine that I needed this month's rent pronto. Since I still hadn't received it, I called again today and learned that her phone had been disconnected. I tried her employer and learned that she no longer works there, so I went by the apartment.

I knocked on the door and got no answer. Knowing that sometimes people who live alone can die and not be found until their bodies start to stink, I decided to declare an emergency and use my passkey right then and there to enter her apartment. I didn't find a body. I found a mess. Most of her furniture and clothes were gone, and there were bags of trash in every room. The place looked as if she were well along in the process of moving out even though her lease doesn't run out for another month.

What is my best approach for getting the last two months' rents, the outstanding late fees, and hopefully even the $20 and $40 rent shortages owed?
—F.R., Virginia

A. Your situation is a perfect example of why you should always do two things whenever you rent to a tenant:

1) Collect a hefty security deposit, and
2) Use a rental application which asks for the name and telephone number of a person to call in case of an emergency.

If you have a hefty security deposit, you may take enough out of it to pay yourself for what the tenant owes you upon moving out.

If you don't have a hefty security deposit to cover what the tenant owes you upon moving out, you will have to use small claims court to get a judgment and collect.

If you have the name and telephone number of a person to call in case of an emergency, you may call that person now and find out what's going on. Is the tenant moving out? If not, then what's happening?

If you don't have a person to call, contact the tenant's neighbors and ask them what they know about the tenant's intentions and whereabouts. If they know nothing, ask them to call you immediately when they notice the tenant on the premises. Go there and confront the tenant. Find out what's happening.

Right now, you should be more concerned about regaining possession of the apartment than collecting what is owed to you. You can always pursue the tenant for money after you have possession of the apartment. You want to get possession as soon as possible so you can prepare the place for new tenants who pay their rent on time.

Even though you have already determined that your tenant has mostly moved out, you cannot be certain that she has, in fact, moved out unless she *either* tells you in no uncertain terms that she has moved *or* arranges to return the keys to you. If she has done neither of these things, then she hasn't moved out, and you must resort to establishing that she has abandoned the premises.

Your state has a procedure to follow for establishing abandonment. In California, it takes 29 days in all and does not involve going to court. Check into your own state's laws regarding abandonment and follow them if you have to.

Tenant skips out eighteen months before lease expires.

Q. One of my tenants skipped out at night without saying boo to me or paying her rent for the current month. She signed a two-year lease and stayed only six months. Her lease states that she is responsible for all rent payments through the end of her lease period or until I find another qualified tenant. I have tried to find a replacement for her, so far unsuccessfully, and she now owes me rent for two months.

I'm wondering what I need to do to take legal action against her for the amount she owes. I'm also wondering what I need to do to report her to the credit bureaus.

—L.N., Dallas, TX

A. When this tenant rented from you, she must have paid you her last month's rent and a security deposit. Take what she owes you now for cleaning, damages, and rent out of those monies. If there's anything left over, keep it until you know whether she owes you any more, that is, until you find a qualified replacement tenant. You are entitled to charge her for rent to cover the period when the unit is vacant. If there's anything left over after her security deposit and last month's rent have paid you for all that she owes, including the rent to cover the duration of the vacancy between tenants, return the balance to her. If there isn't enough money to compensate you for what she owes you, you may take her to small claims court.

Be aware that taking her to small claims court is a hassle, and it's not worth your time unless she winds up owing you a thousand dollars or more. Even then, after you've spent the time and money to take her to small claims court and you've been successful in getting a judgment against her, you still may be unable to collect anything at all from her because she may be what attorneys call "judgment proof," lacking in attachable income or assets.

By all means, report your experience with this tenant to a credit bureau so that it will appear on her credit report the next time she applies for credit. Report her to the same credit bureau you use for credit checks, or if you have no relationship with a credit bureau, make one now and report her. Local credit agencies, local rental property owners associations, local tenant screening services, or their internet equivalents (go to google.com and search on the words "report bad tenants") can help you.

11
Keeping the Peace

They have broken nearly every rule in the rental agreement.

Q. I'm a tenant myself, but I'm also an on-site property manager. For the past eleven years I've been managing five houses and an apartment building for my landlord.

Recently I rented an upstairs apartment to a couple who have a nineteen-month-old child. The understanding was that they would move into a house when one became available. When one did become available, they said they couldn't afford it, so they're still in the apartment.

They asked if they could bring their dog when they moved in, and I told them that the rental agreement says "absolutely no pets allowed." Five days after they moved in, when I was installing a new screen door handle for them, I saw that they had a cat. They said it was an exotic cat and they couldn't live without it. I asked the landlord what he wanted to do, and he said I should have them sign a pet agreement stating they would be responsible for any and all damage done by the cat. They signed.

On the fourteenth day after they moved in, they brought their yellow lab dog to live in the apartment which, by the way, has no yard. I immediately gave them a 30-day notice to vacate the premises. That was a month ago, and they are still in the apartment.

They have broken just about every rule in the rental agreement. Besides that, they call the sheriff's office every day and tell whoever will listen to them that either I or one of the neighbors is picking on them or calling them names. I can't go out in my back yard without hearing him yell dirty names at me from upstairs.

The lady in our rental house next door has taken a liking to these people. She parties with them, lets them use her washing machine, babysits the child, and invites them over for dinner. She

had a party last night at her house, and I was amazed at the scruffy looking people who came.

Now she's telling everyone that when she first moved in, the landlord or I went into her house when the back door was open. That is simply untrue. The landlord never comes over unless I call him, and I definitely know better than to go into a tenant's residence without first giving a 24-hour notice or declaring an emergency.

I'm at my wit's end. The landlord and I are going to the attorney tomorrow to file an unlawful detainer against the couple. Are we doing everything we should be?
—S.H., California

A. You have heard how one rotten apple spoils the whole barrel. Now you have witnessed how one rotten tenant will cause another tenant to go bad.

The one tenant who has come under the influence of your rotten tenants may have been lonely and in need of friendship and acceptance, so she invented the story about you and the landlord to gain these people's friendship and acceptance. She likely thought that it would never get back to you anyway. Don't worry about her and her lie, at least not now. She should change for the better after the rotten tenants move.

You did the right thing by serving the rotten tenants a notice immediately upon learning about their dog, and you did the right thing by serving them with a 30-day notice to vacate because an eviction initiated with this kind of a notice is the hardest to defend. In fact, there is no defense against it other than that you are discriminating or retaliating against the tenants for some reason, and the burden of proof is on them to prove that you are.

You should still be gathering as much evidence as you can to show the court just in case you get a judge who wants to know why you are evicting

131

this young couple and their little baby. The evidence might consist of things such as a tape recording of the tenant yelling obscenities at you, sheriffs' reports showing that the complaints about your behavior are bogus, a photograph of the dog on the premises, and statements from other tenants about you and these tenants.

You will prevail in the eviction. Have faith. Also, because you have acted quickly, you may have enough left from the tenants' security deposit to pay the cost of the eviction and the cost to repair the damage which the tenants will invariably cause when they vacate.

Incidentally, whenever you discover that applicants have a pet while you're checking their application, you must assume that they will be bringing it with them to their new dwelling whether it's forbidden or not.

Loud music and loud swearing alienate the older generation.

Q. I have a four-unit apartment house with all older people except for one tenant who's in her thirties. We told her when she moved in that this was a quiet complex and we expected her to be quiet. After she moved in, we had to warn her first for playing loud music and later for loud swearing. The very next night she played her music loud again. We wrote her a letter telling her that we were going to evict her and that we wanted her out right away. She agreed to go, saying that she had decided to leave anyway. That was twenty-four days ago. Last weekend, she said she was leaving, but she didn't. She also has not paid any rent since we sent her the eviction letter. We have a $300 deposit, but the rent is $455 a month. I wrote her a letter telling her that I'm coming there this weekend to move her stuff out and change the locks. That was four days ago, and she's still there. Can I move her out this weekend and not get into any trouble?
—J.J., Illinois

A. You will get into a heap of trouble if you throw her and her things out on the street this weekend or any other day of the week. Every state has judicial proceedings which you must follow to evict a tenant, and Illinois is no exception. Serve her with the notice required to evict her for nonpayment of rent since she's delinquent now and since nonpayment of rent is the easiest to prove of all the grounds for eviction.

Begin judicial proceedings immediately by

serving the notice, but also begin trying to convince her that she ought to move out immediately for her own good. Tell her something about the consequences of being evicted. Nowadays they're worse than they used to be because eviction records are easier for landlords to check through tenant qualification services. Once she's evicted, she will be branded as an undesirable tenant, and the doors to the best rentals available will be closed to her.

Let this tenant be a lesson to you that you never accept an uncooperative tenant's word about moving out. Push and shove the eviction paperwork and the psychological campaign to get the tenant out legally, but do not push and shove the tenant's possessions out the door unless you want her to be dragging you into court instead of your dragging her into court.

They want to keep older children away from younger children.

Q. My husband and I have owned a triplex for three years. We live in the front unit and rent out the back two. We have a large play yard for kids and a swing set with a slide and monkey bars.

We have custody of our three grandchildren, a nine-year-old girl, a seven-year-old boy, and a four-year-old girl. Tenants in one of the other units have a four-year-old girl and a new baby girl. A single mother in the other unit has an eight-year-old boy.

The whole street is full of apartments, all triplexes and fourplexes except for a fifty-unit complex across the street. Several of the kids from this large complex, who are older than any of our kids, are coming over to play with the single mother's eight-year-old boy. They sometimes use bad language and never clean up the messes they make. They have never destroyed anything, but we're concerned about the bad language they use and the influence they might have on our kids.

My husband and the single mother have argued several times about this, but nothing has changed. We are wondering if we can refuse to allow these kids to come into our yard and play. I know that our tenants have a right to have visitors, but when their visitors are disrespectful kids, I think we should have the right to exclude them.

This woman has always been a good tenant. She never causes any problems and always pays her rent on time. She just allows her son to play with older kids, kids we don't want around our grandchildren.

What should we do about this problem?
—J.L., Missouri

A. Tell the single mother that you have decided after much thought to exclude all visitors from the play yard.

She'll say that you're being unfair, and you can agree with her. You aren't being fair. You're being unfair, but you're being unfair to all of the children who reside in the triplex, not just to her son. None of them may have friends over to play in the yard. If they want to have friends over to play, they and their friends will have to play together inside. They can't play together outside.

As the property owner, you have every right to make the play yard rules, but those rules must apply to everybody equally. You can't slight anybody.

After making new rules, you must "sell" them to the people they affect, your tenants. They will only "buy" into the rules if they can see that everybody is being treated in exactly the same way. In this case, they are.

You could make a rule restricting the play yard to younger children, but you'd be hard pressed to sell that rule to the single mother and you'd be harder pressed to enforce it. Don't bother. Exclude all visitors from the play yard. Enforcement will be simple, and you'll be able to defend the rule on reasonable grounds. You might say that outsiders are less responsible when using the equipment and you don't want to risk a lawsuit. That sounds reasonable enough, doesn't it?

Be sure that you contact the other tenants to explain the new rule. They need to hear about it from you, not from the single mother.

Tenants are always calling the police on one another.

Q. I own a duplex and am having some problems with my tenants. They're always calling the police on one another. They call when there's no adult around to watch the children next door. They call when a neighbor kid sprays bug killer though the fence, and some of it gets into the eyes of their kid who was standing by the fence looking at what was happening on the other side. They call when a neighbor kid yells at their kid. They call when the neighbor kids start bouncing balls at 8 a.m.

One of them told me that the police are tired of coming out and finding nothing of any conse-

quence for them to take care of. She said that the police told her that the tenants should take this stuff up with the landlord.

What should I do as a landlord to stop this?
—S.R., New Jersey

A. Your tenants are all kids, and you have to treat them like kids. Arrange a meeting with both sets of parents and tell them that the police can't discipline their kids, and you can't discipline their kids. They are the only ones who can discipline their kids. Tell them that if they don't discipline their kids and put an end to this squabbling themselves, you will evict them all and find some new tenants who know how to get along with one another.

Tenants bicker about noise and cigarette smoke.

Q. My husband and I have been landlords for twenty-two years. By now we ought to know what to do about every problem we face as landlords, but this one has us stumped. We haven't faced it before.

We have a young single man living in a downstairs apartment in our fourplex and a middle-aged single woman living above him. The woman moved in six months ago and is a grandmother. Her daughters come over to see her with their children once or twice a week and make enough noise to disturb the man downstairs. He calls me about the noise above him, and she calls me about his smoking underneath her window. They have had some cross words with one another.

I am not happy about the grandmother's many visitors, even if they are her grandchildren, but I know that I must be careful not to say something that will trigger a lawsuit accusing me of discriminating against children. We have house rules which say that the noise level must be minimal between 10 p.m. and 8 a.m. and that because footsteps can be heard distinctly throughout the building, everybody must tread lightly at all times. The rules also say that tenants are to keep visitors under control at all times.

Usually our tenants are young, single people, and our problems have never involved noisy children. We've been able to solve our problems somehow every time, but this one is different, and I'm not sure exactly what to do about it. My husband keeps telling me to "let them deal with it." I'd like to, but I don't know how to stop them from calling me whenever one of them does something to aggravate the other, and I'm the one who has to take the phone calls, not my husband. I need to find a solution.

Are we as landlords responsible for the noise? Are we the ones to deal with it? I have told them to solve it between themselves, but they haven't done anything other than yell at one another and then call me.

My husband's niece lives in a neighboring state and is married to a policeman. She says that noise at an apartment complex is a police matter in their state. I'd like to tell our tenants to call the police whenever they have a noise complaint instead of calling me, but I haven't told them to do that yet. I wanted to ask you first how you would deal with this kind of problem.

In a nutshell, the problem is that the kids make too much noise upstairs and on the stairs when they're visiting, sometimes even as late as 11 p.m. They're active kids and they like to jump around. Anybody downstairs couldn't help but hear them and be bothered. The woman upstairs complains that she can hear her neighbor downstairs talking loudly on the phone and that she can smell the smoke from his cigarettes in her apartment because he smokes right under her window.

I am a somewhat desperate and tired "landlord," and I sure could use some advice. What advice can you give me?
—I.H., Utah

A. Don't rely upon the police to solve your "bickering tenants" problem. When called upon for help, they may come out to your fourplex, listen to both tenants for a few minutes, tell them to respect one another's right of quiet enjoyment, get back in their patrol car, write a report on their laptop, and leave shaking their heads. Keeping the peace to police officers means keeping noise down to a reasonable level in a whole neighborhood, not in a single apartment house. It doesn't mean enforcing house rules about noise. A grandmother who is letting her grandkids be rambunctious and disturb a neighbor now and then is not committing a crime. She's violating house rules, and police don't much care. Calls from tenants or landlords for police help in settling a petty dispute about noise from another apartment rank as low as calls for help in getting a cat down from a tree.

Call the police only if the trouble between the neighbors escalates to a level where you believe they might do harm to one another. Otherwise,

try to solve the problem yourself. You alone are responsible for enforcing your house rules. You shouldn't call the police to enforce rules which you ought to be enforcing because you'll be undermining your authority among your tenants and tarnishing your building's good reputation in the neighborhood. You don't want police and police cars associated with your property.

By now you're weary of your downstairs tenant's phone calls. You dread getting them. You've heard his complaints many times over, and you've repeatedly called the offending grandmother to talk with her. Still the problem persists. It persists because it's a problem you can't solve over the phone. You have to visit the tenants and try to work out a solution together.

Resist the temptation to go to the grandmother and tell her that you've had it with the complaints about her unruly grandchildren and the noise they make and that you're going to evict her if she doesn't control them when they come to visit her. Yes, her rental agreement does require that she control her visitors and keep the noise down, especially after 10 p.m. She's being inconsiderate and she's violating the agreement and she ought to control her grandchildren or move. With her out of there, you know you could find a younger single tenant who wouldn't have any noisy grandchildren. That approach might seem to be straightforward and productive. It is, sometimes, but you can't count on it. As frequently as it works, it fails. Use it as a last resort.

Try some other approaches first. Here's one.

Make an appointment to see both tenants at the same time when the grandmother knows that the grandchildren will be visiting. Arrange to meet the two tenants in the downstairs apartment at an appointed time so you can demonstrate to the upstairs tenant just how bothersome is the noise coming from her apartment. Leave the mothers and children upstairs, and call them on the phone to tell them that you'd like them to "act up" a little. Once the grandmother has heard for herself what the downstairs tenant hears when the children are playing, go upstairs with both tenants and greet the mothers and children. Tell everybody that the noise has become intolerable and that something has to be done about it. If either mother doubts how bad the noise sounds downstairs, give her a demonstration. Then go back upstairs and ask them all for some solutions to the noise problem. More than likely, the grandmother will say that she hadn't realized how bad the noise was downstairs and that she will see that everybody is quieter in the future. She may mention something about the downstairs tenant's smoking under her window and about his loud voice on the telephone, and he will say that he will take care of those concerns now that he knows how much they trouble her. Smile broadly and tell them all that you are happy that they know one another's concerns better and that you know they will try hard to be good neighbors. Shake hands with everybody, and go home and tell your husband that he owes you a dinner at your favorite restaurant.

That approach is one of the best because it brings the tenants together to witness the problem first-hand and talk about a solution. They feel obligated to fulfill whatever commitment they make to one another because they made the commitment themselves. It wasn't imposed upon them. She may never bake him cookies, and he may never bring her flowers, but at least they will think about how their actions affect their neighbor in the future.

Here's another somewhat similar approach.

Arrange to take the two bickering tenants out to a meal at a modest restaurant, just the three of you. Tell them that you're buying and that you want to discuss what's bothering them. While you're waiting for your food, ask them various questions about themselves, where they went to high school, what their first job was, and what they like about the area where they live now. While you're eating, moderate a discussion between the two of them about their problems. Let them do the talking. Listen, and try to direct the conversation so that it doesn't bog down into too many trivial details. While you're having dessert, tell them that you'd like to leave the table with some sort of verbal commitment they feel comfortable making to one another so that they can live together as neighbors in greater peace and harmony. If they can't think of anything to agree upon, suggest something reasonable, and see what happens. Before you go your separate ways, summarize what was said and agreed upon, tell them you appreciate their help, shake hands, and tell them that the next time you break bread together, you'll expect them to split the bill with you, but this time you don't mind paying because you're so happy that they have agreed upon a way to settle their differences.

Here's a third approach along the same lines.

Arrange to meet with the bickering tenants in either tenant's apartment. Tell them you have an idea you'd like to discuss with them which just might help them get along better. When the three of you get together, tell them you've been thinking a lot about them lately. You know that they're unhappy with one another and that they'd like the other one to move. The downstairs tenant wants to enjoy his peace and quiet, and the upstairs tenant wants to enjoy her daughters' and grandchildren's company. They seem to have mutually exclusive objectives, and they're both frustrated because they haven't found a way to enjoy what they want to enjoy without irritating their neighbor. Tell them that their plight is similar to what they encounter whenever they're out driving and want to cross a busy intersection. Everybody would try to cross at the same time, and there would be crash after crash except for the order imposed on the traffic at the intersection by a signal or stop sign, the sole purpose of which is to keep people from crashing into one another. Tell them that they have been "crashing into one another" repeatedly and indiscriminately and that you have been wracking your brain trying to come up with some way to put an end to it. One day the lightbulb came on in your head and you thought that you might have come up with an answer. "Scheduling" is what you came up with. Say that you thought scheduling the grandchildren's visits might be a good way to take care of the problem. The grandmother would schedule her grandchildren's visits no more frequently than once a week and for no longer than three hours. She would advise the downstairs tenant of the schedule at least five days in advance, and having been advised of the visits, he could arrange to leave his apartment during that time or stay and bear the noise. Ask them for their ideas. They may think your idea is ridiculous and would never work, but at least they'll know that you are trying to help. If you fail to interest them in this idea, tell them to think more themselves about what they ought to do and arrange to meet in the other tenant's apartment a week later to talk some more. Go there a week later and see what ideas they come up with. If their ideas are ridiculous and the three of you cannot agree upon a solution, tell them that you will impose one of your own on them and begin enforcing your house rules to the letter.

Whereas the three approaches above rely upon the tenants' getting to know one another better so they will treat one another more kindly as people who have faces and names and needs and habits and thoughts and histories and families, these other approaches are less personal. They handle the problem with physical interventions to reduce the noise level to the downstairs tenant.

The physical interventions are ear plugs, a white-noise radio, and sound-deadening carpet. You would have to buy the first two and give them to the downstairs tenant to use whenever the grandchildren visit. You would have to buy the carpet and have it installed in the upstairs tenant's apartment. Each of these physical interventions requires you to spend some money and in the case of the carpet, a fair amount of money. What's more, you'd have to keep your fingers crossed that they would work. They may not.

When you have exhausted every idea you can think of and find that none of them works, you'll have to resort to the final solution, an eviction. You'll just have to evict the grandmother who cannot control her grandchildren sufficiently to abide by the house rules and please her downstairs neighbor.

Tenant babysits two little girls and lets them run amok.

Q. My husband and I own a duplex and live in one of the units ourselves. Last night our tenant brought two little girls home with him who are about three and five years old. He was babysitting them for a friend. From the time they arrived, around 7 o'clock, he let them run amok, screaming and carrying on. Because my husband and I own a bakery business and get up very early, we are in bed by 8 o'clock, so they irritated us at night, and they irritated us again early the next morning when their behavior continued unchecked. He simply was not looking after these children.

We tolerated the noise this time, but we want to see that it doesn't happen again, and we want to see that the children's parents don't blame us if the girls hurt themselves while playing on our property.

Should we have the tenant and the parents sign a waiver releasing us of any and all injuries and/or responsibilities while these children are in his care? Should we have him sign a statement that he will keep the children quiet whenever he babysits them in the future?
—S.H., Hawaii

A. Apparently, your tenant doesn't know how to look after young children, and these children don't know how to behave when they're out from under their parents' thumbs. Tell the tenant that he must either babysit these children elsewhere or else keep them quiet and well behaved when they are visiting him. Remind him that he and his guests, no matter what their age, must observe quiet hours from 8 in the evening until 8 in the morning so that everybody living there can be accommodated and get their sleep. Remind him of the serious consequences should he choose to ignore your request. One of those consequences is eviction. Another is reporting him to the authorities for child endangerment.

Don't bother introducing more paperwork into your landlord-tenant relationship by having the tenant sign a statement and the tenant and the parents sign a waiver, that is, not unless you currently have neither a written rental agreement nor written rules which spell out quiet hours, guest restrictions, and guest responsibilities. Such things do need to be spelled out so you can enforce them without question.

By the way, your tenant may be just as bothered by these unruly children as you are and may seize upon your chat with him as a reason he can cite to his friend for why he cannot babysit the children again.

Tenant goes berserk when challenged about his mother.

Q. A tenant I inherited when I bought a duplex has violated his month-to-month agreement by letting his mother move in with him. She has been there for over a month now. I sent him a letter telling him that he has violated his rental agreement and should find an alternative residence for his mother within a week. He responded by berating me over the phone and threatening to beat me up. I have since filed a police report about his threat and have given him a 45-day notice to terminate tenancy (his agreement calls for thirty days). I am thinking about sending him another notice imposing a charge of $5 per day for the extra unauthorized person living in the apartment. Would I be doing the right thing by charging him extra for his guest after serving him a termination notice?

His rental agreement calls for him to secure his landlord's authorization for guests staying over five days.

—M.Y., Florida

A. Don't aggravate the situation by charging him an extra $5 per day. He's trying to provide for his mother, one of the most cherished people in his life. When you challenged his desire to help her, he went berserk. Don't challenge him still more. You don't know how he'll react. Be businesslike even though he is being childish. Get him out of your life without jeopardizing your life.

College boys turn apartment into high school hangout.

Q. We have been landlording for a little over a year now and live in the apartment building we own.

Three college boys rented an apartment from us and have been trying our patience ever since. For one thing, they always seem to have visitors.

After observing their comings and goings first-hand, we have reason to believe that more than the three boys are living in the apartment and even more young people have keys. Because the apartment is an hour's drive from their school and because their parents' homes are close to their school, they frequently stay with their parents during the week and spend weekends at the apartment. They are not always around the apartment, but somebody is. One of their girlfriends is definitely living there. The girlfriends are mostly high school seniors, and the boys are college freshmen and sophomores. We have come to believe that the apartment has become a place for high school seniors to hang out, a place where they can go to get away from their parents, and we're not quite sure what to do about it.

Obviously, we can't prevent the boys from having friends over, but they're doing more than that. They're letting friends live there. They're taking advantage of us. We rented to three boys, not to a whole frat house. Our rental agreement states that they may have guests stay for as many as fourteen consecutive days without our written permission. The one girlfriend has already been there three months, and she's not the only one who's exceeded the fourteen-day limit.

How should we approach this problem? Should we confront the boys in their apartment? Should we set up a meeting in our apartment where we normally do business? Should we contact their parents? We're not sure what to do.

This excess of occupants has created a second problem, and that is parking. It's just as big a problem as the excess of occupants because it affects our other tenants.

Every apartment has two assigned parking spaces in our tenant parking lot behind the building. There is ample parking on the street for guests. We want our tenants to park in our lot so we can keep track of who's at home and who's not and so our tenants will always know that they have a space reserved for them close to their apartment door. We don't want them to have to park on the street and lug their groceries a block because a visitor has parked in their reserved space. They're paying for a reserved space, and it's our responsibility to see that they get it.

We have told the boys that the only vehicles they may park in our lot are the ones listed on their rental application, and they seemed to understand us when we told them why. We did tell them that their one friend who has an expensive Porsche may park his car in one of their two spaces, so long as they exchange parking spaces with the friend who has the Porsche and so long as other friends don't park there, but we keep noticing other cars back there, sometimes in other tenants' spaces. We can't let them take other tenants' parking spaces.

Do we have the right to allow only our tenants to park on our property? What can we do to enforce this? Are we allowed to tow violators at their expense?

—C.B., Massachusetts

A. Ah, college kids! How brave you are to rent to them! Like puppies, most of them have to be trained. You as their first landlords have to train them to behave the way adult tenants are supposed to behave.

Consider yourselves fortunate that you're having only two problems with them, excess occupants and parking. You could be having rent problems, noise problems, pet problems, cleanliness problems, breakage problems, maintenance problems, insubordination problems, drinking problems, and drug problems. Those can be very serious problems. Yours are serious enough, but they're manageable.

Before you decide how to handle the two problems, ask yourselves one basic question. Do you want to continue renting to these boys? They are using their apartment less as a domicile than as a party house and teen shelter. Since they go home on school nights, you wouldn't be depriving them of essential housing if you decided to evict them. You wouldn't be making them homeless, and you wouldn't need to feel that you're being heartless. You'd simply be making a business decision based upon what's good for you and your other tenants. Do you want to shape them up, or do you want to send them home to mommy and daddy?

If you decide to evict them, arrange for the three of them to come to your apartment. Tell them how disappointed you are that they haven't lived up to your expectations as tenants. Be specific in your remarks about how they have violated their rental agreement and made life miserable for you and the other tenants, and tell them that you have decided to give them a notice to vacate for cause. Tell them that you don't want to humiliate them by contacting their parents. You simply want them to move out within thirty days and take all of their friends with them.

If you decide to shape them up instead, arrange the same kind of meeting, but tell them what you have observed with your own eyes, that they have turned the apartment into a commune with people coming and going at all hours. Tell them that the apartment house is home to you as well as to the other people living there. Say that you rented the apartment to them so they would have a home of their own where they could live independently of their parents for the first time in their lives. You did not rent it to them so they could invite all of their friends to come and live with them. Tell them that you cannot tolerate what they are doing with the apartment, and give them a list of what you want them to change if they want to continue renting from you. Tell them that you know many of their friends have keys and that you want to change the locks and issue new keys to the three of them. Tell them that they can label you as the bad guys when they tell their friends about the changes. They don't have to take their friends' condemnation which is sure to come. You'll take it upon yourselves. You'll take the heat.

You do have the right to reserve parking on your property for your tenants alone. Contact a towing company and ask them what kind of signage you need to display and where you need to display it in order for them to tow vehicles parked on private property where they're not supposed to be. Put the signage in place, identify every space clearly with a name or number, advise your tenants in writing about the procedure you plan to follow for towing vehicles, and follow the procedure to the letter. The very first time you have a vehicle towed, you will make believers out of your tenants.

Whereas your college-age tenants may think that they can do whatever they want with their apartment so long as they pay the rent, you have to teach them differently. You have to teach them what they can and cannot do with it, and the sooner you start teaching them, the better.

Tenants defy landlord and smoke in non-smoking apartment.

Q. My husband and I rented out a duplex apartment and stipulated verbally that nobody was supposed to smoke in it. The tenants have lived there for a month now and smoke daily in the apartment. We know because we live in the other half of the duplex. We can smell it. We sent them a letter stating that we find their smoking unacceptable and if they continue, they will be served with a 30-day notice to vacate. They signed a rental agreement with the standard clauses about maintaining the property, keeping a pet, paying their rent on time, etc. Unfortunately, we mistakenly omitted any mention of smoking from the agreement, and we're kicking ourselves now about this omission. What is the best way to handle this situation?
—C.P., North Carolina

A. Your inconsiderate tenants are playing games with you. They're defiantly blowing smoke in your face. They know that you told them about your no-smoking policy. They also know that you neglected to include a no-smoking provision in their rental agreement. Now they're betting that you can't, or won't, evict them just for smoking.

Don't play games with them. Make them understand that you mean business.

You have two choices, depending upon whether you can evict a tenant for any reason at all with a 30-day notice to vacate. If you can, then continue what you have already started with your letter, that is, serve them with a 30-day notice to vacate after giving them a week to stop their smoking.

If you cannot use a 30-day notice to vacate, serve them with a 30-day notice of change in terms of tenancy stating that no smoking is allowed on the premises. In thirty days, if they haven't either moved or stopped smoking on the premises, begin eviction proceedings for breach of contract.

Pot smoke bothers downstairs tenant.

Q. Two of my tenants have been bickering about pot smoke. The upstairs tenant, who has lived in her apartment for over ten years, has a grandson who is living with her. He smokes pot regularly. His grandmother is fine with that so long as he smokes it only in his bedroom. The downstairs tenant's living room is directly beneath the grandson's bedroom, and she can't stand the smell of the smoke. So long as he keeps his windows closed, the downstairs tenant can't smell it, but when the weather turns warm and he opens his windows, she really smells the smoke because she opens her windows, too.

The downstairs tenant complained first to the upstairs tenant, but nothing changed as a result. Then she complained to me. I guess I didn't respond fast enough because she complained to the police department the same day she complained to me. The cops came out and talked with the tenants and the pot smoker and concluded that there was nothing they could do. They said that his pot smoking wasn't illegal, that it was on private property, and that they couldn't be of any help in settling the dispute.

Now the downstairs tenant is complaining again to me, expecting me to find a way to get this fellow to stop letting pot smoke get into her apartment. What can I do?
—J.S., Ohio

A. No matter what you do, this pothead will continue smoking his dope. He's addicted. Don't even try to talk with him. Strictly speaking, he's not your tenant anyway.

Your efforts to end the neighbors' dispute must center upon arranging a meeting of the tenants to discuss solutions, getting the grandson to smoke elsewhere, installing fans to dissipate the smoke, penalizing the upstairs tenant and compensating the downstairs tenant, or moving one household or the other elsewhere.

Arrange a meeting with both of the tenants at some neutral location and explore solutions with them. Open the discussion by telling them that the problem is important to you and that you want to solve it because you want them to be happy and stay in their apartments for a long time. Then listen to what they have to say, moderating the discussion so that each of them has a chance to say something. Avoid making suggestions of your own if you can. Let this be their meeting. Let them come up with their own solutions. If they do come up with a workable solution, try it. If not, try your own.

You could try convincing the grandmother that she ought to tell her grandson to smoke elsewhere, that is, if she is dominant and forceful enough to lay down the law for him.

You could try installing fans, either ceiling or window exhaust, in one or both of the apartments to dissipate the smoke. Try installing one in the downstairs tenant's apartment first and see whether that is enough to keep the air there from becoming contaminated.

You could try raising the upstairs tenant's monthly rent by a hundred dollars and lowering the downstairs tenant's monthly rent by fifty dollars. Unless asked, give no explanation for the rent increase to the upstairs tenant. Do give an explanation to the downstairs tenant.

If nothing works to satisfy the downstairs tenant, as a last resort, you'll have to give one of the tenants a notice to vacate. Because the one causing the stink is the upstairs tenant, even though she has lived where she is for a long time, she should be the one to go.

Smell of curry nauseates tenants.

Q. The ethnic composition of my apartment building has changed over the years. I used to have mostly white tenants. After them, I had mostly blacks. Then Spanish-speaking tenants replaced the blacks. Now I have a real mix. I have "everything." I have so many immigrants that you'd think my building were on Ellis Island. I don't care what my tenants look like, what language they speak, where they came from, or how long they've been in this country, so long as they follow the rules and pay their rent on time.

As you might imagine, my tenants don't all cook alike. When I'm there at the property, I never know what cooking odors I'm going to smell. It might be garlic, butter, fish, greasy burgers, bacon, cabbage, onions, curry, popcorn, coffee, fried chicken, hot cookies, basil, oregano, or something else equally distinctive.

Recently I rented to some East Indians. They're good people, family oriented and friendly, but the problem is that they seem to prepare their every meal with curry, much to the chagrin of my other tenants. I've never had complaints over cooking odors before, but I'm having them now. The curry odor enters other tenants' apartments as no other cooking odor does and it lingers. Some tenants have told me that the curry odor nauseates them.

I'm at a loss as to what to do. I don't want to tell my Indian tenants how to cook, and I don't think they would listen to me anyway. Besides, that would smack of discrimination, wouldn't it? Got any suggestions? -P.H., Pennsylvania

A. The smell of curry and exotic spices starts the salivary glands working in some people and the nausea response working in others. When the curry lovers and the curry despisers live in close proximity to one another, there's bound to be trouble, just as there's trouble when a cigar smoker lights up in a restaurant filled with non-smokers or when somebody wearing strong perfume sits down next to you in a theater. People don't want their space contaminated by other people's odors.

There are at least five possible solutions which a landlord confronted with the curry odor problem might try:

1) Reduce the source by asking the curry users to limit their use of the offensive spice;

2) Move one or the other of the tenants elsewhere;

3) Give sway to curry lovers and become a "curry-welcome" apartment complex;

4) Treat the odor with a deodorizer; or

5) Reduce the odor through purification.

Try the easiest one first. Talk. Find out whether the neighbors have complained directly to the Indians about the offensive odor. If they haven't, approach the Indians yourself and tell them that the smell of their curry is bothering the neighbors so much that they have complained to you. Ask the Indians to be more aware of their neighbors and to use curry more sparingly from now on. After using curry all their lives, they become so desensitized to the smell that they cannot imagine how it could be offensive to others. Tell them that it is offensive to others, and you would like them to be aware that it is and to think about how they might enjoy their native dishes while containing the smell of their food within the confines of their own apartment so their neighbors wouldn't smell it.

If the neighbors have complained directly to the Indians already, approach the Indians and emphasize that you want everybody to get along. Say that everybody has rights and everybody has responsibilities. They have the right to eat what they want in peace and not be bothered by their neighbors, but they have the responsibility to get along with their neighbors and not bother them with disagreeable odors. Ask them to be understanding and to try various ways to keep the curry odors from bothering their neighbors.

Talking with the Indians and with the complaining neighbors may be enough to solve the problem. Pray that it is.

If talk doesn't work, offer to move one or the other of the tenants to another unit where they wouldn't bother one another, and look for odor-tolerant tenants to live next to the curry lovers. Odor-tolerant people tend to have insensitive noses, and they will tolerate odors which would nauseate other people. They're the ideal tenants to live around curry lovers.

I remember one vacant apartment I had with a persistent cat odor in it. The odor was so bad that I wouldn't even show it to anybody for fear that they would turn up their noses at the entire building ever afterward. At the time, the rental market was so tight that people were out banging on doors looking for apartments. When they discovered that I had a vacancy, they kept asking to see it. I kept turning them away because I was trying everything I could think of to get rid of the odor. Finally, just as I was about to replace the carpet, along came a former fighter pilot who told me he didn't care about a cat odor. He said he'd been breathing pure oxygen so long in the cockpit that he had no sense of smell left. He asked to see the apartment, and he rented it without hesitation. He lived there for quite some time and never complained about the odor. He couldn't smell it, and gradually it dissipated so that I couldn't smell it either.

If moving tenants around isn't an option for you and neither is replacing odor-sensitive tenants with odor tolerant tenants, you could turn your building into a "curry welcome" apartment complex and tell your existing tenants that you plan to do nothing at all about the odor other than ask everybody to get used to it because you want to make curry lovers welcome in the complex. That will make some tenants so happy that they'll stay and others so unhappy that they'll move.

If none of these three options appeals to you, consider the two options intended to deal with the curry odor itself, masking it or reducing it.

To mask it, you'll need to experiment with various home remedies and proprietary products. Some say that simmering white vinegar in a pan works. Some say that dampening cotton balls with pure vanilla and putting them around the house works. Some say that simmering cinnamon and cloves in a pan of water works. Some say that baking soda in small pie tins works. Some say that certain aerosol air fresheners work. Try these remedies in cooperation with the Indians and the odor intolerant neighbors and smell what happens.

When you've exhausted these possibilities, try reducing the odors or eliminating them altogether using any number of the "odor-eliminator" products on the market, from sprays like PureAyre Odor Eliminator® and Petrotech Odor Eliminator® to stand-alone activated carbon filter systems like the Hamilton Beach TrueAir Odor Eliminator® and the Honeywell Enviracaire Air Purifier®. Ask your most cooperative tenants to help you test these products, whether they're the source of the offensive odors, that is, the Indians, or those who are offended, the neighbors.

Don't bother trying High-Efficiency Particulate Accumulator (HEPA) air cleaners or electronic air cleaners (electrostatic precipitators, ionizers, or ozone generators). Either they're ineffective in reducing cooking odors or they pollute the air.

Do try air purifiers which use activated carbon. Activated carbon is charcoal treated with oxygen to open up the many pores between the charcoal's carbon atoms. This treatment results in a highly adsorbent material.

It works so well in eliminating odors that people prone to flatulence who wear a special undergarment layered with activated charcoal needn't worry that the gas they pass will be an embarrassment. The activated charcoal in the undergarment adsorbs the foul odor. A pad in the undergarment muffles the telltale sound.

One or more activated charcoal filters placed in strategic locations should reduce the curry odor outside of the Indians' dwelling significantly, perhaps even eliminate it entirely.

Do not ignore the problem. It will not go away without your intervention, and do keep your tenants informed about what you have decided to do about it.

Just as we are what we eat, we are what we breathe, and we are so used to clean air and good sanitation today that we don't want to settle for anything else. Your tenants shouldn't have to.

"Boomerang" children add up to more noise and wear and tear.

Q. My husband and I have two flats in Chicago. We live in the downstairs flat ourselves and have rented the upstairs, a large three-bedroom, to a single mother with three children. During the seven years she's been there, the children have all grown up and moved away.

Recently, two of the grown children have moved back. A few days ago, the daughter returned with a baby and announced that she will be staying "temporarily" for four to six months, maybe more. The 27-year-old son moved back several months ago, and two of his children visit and stay over approximately three days a week. So that makes three adults, all smokers, and sometimes three children in the one apartment.

I do not consider her two grown children to be very responsible people and would have turned them down as applicants had I screened them and had they not been related to our tenant.

I have to say that I really don't like the situation. There are too many people, and there's too much noise up there.

We've given her an extremely reasonable rent and have always made repairs quickly. The rent has been $525 per month, with the tenant paying for heat and electricity. I would like to raise it to $650 or $700 per month and have them all sign a month-to-month agreement since the grown children cannot give me a specific move out date.

My husband and I just bought a brand-new $3,000 furnace for that apartment and put in new carpeting in the living and dining rooms. We had professional painters come in and paint the inside because the apartment was due for an upgrade. We have to wonder what their smoking is doing to everything.

We've always maintained good relations with the tenant, but there is definitely some tension between us now. Sometimes I think it would be a good idea to ask her and this extended family of hers to leave. What is the best way to go about this? I dread the thought of living in an atmosphere of hostility for the two months or so it

will take them to find another apartment.
—M.D., Illinois

A. If your three-bedroom apartment upstairs were vacant, you would have to follow HUD's (Department of Housing and Urban Development) occupancy guidelines when renting it. The guidelines say that you must give equal consideration to anybody interested in renting it so long as they have no more than six people in their family, that is, two people per bedroom. This long-term tenant of yours and her family total six people at most.

They may be frustrating you now with their excessive numbers and their tromping around upstairs and their cigarette smoke seeping through the walls and floors, but apparently they aren't giving you any of the many other problems you might encounter with replacement tenants. Before you give them the boot, take a reasonable step-by-step approach to resolving the problems. If you can't resolve the problems, then give them the boot and take your chances with new tenants.

The approach you might want to take is one which would compensate you adequately for the frustrations these tenants are expecting you to endure on their behalf.

Step 1: Research the rents for apartments similar to yours by checking the classified ads and the internet and by walking the neighborhood. Take a look at the actual places for rent and talk with the landlords. They know the market better than you do because they are in the market now. You haven't been in the market with your apartment for seven years. You might be surprised by how much you could get for your apartment if it were on the market today.

Step 2: Come up with a current market rent for your apartment, and set its new rent slightly below market to give your long-term tenant a little break. Don't shy away from doubling the rent if that's what the market indicates the rent should be. You should not be subsidizing the rent of a tenant who is frustrating you.

Step 3: Complete a rent increase notice which shows the new rent becoming effective in sixty days. Put together a forms packet consisting of a blank month-to-month rental agreement and rental applications for each of the adult children living in the second floor apartment.

Step 4: Treat the mother of this extended family to lunch at a nearby cafe and talk with her about the situation. Tell her you know that so-called "boomerang" children, who leave their parents' homes to live on their own and then return to the nest, are common nowadays but that any increase in the number of people living in the apartment puts a strain on it. Tell her that her grown children living with her are tenants, not guests, if they stay longer than fourteen days in any six-month period and that they must each submit a rental application if they want to continue living there. The applications are necessary, tell her, because she may die or decide to move out, and the grown children may be staying on as the principal tenants who are themselves responsible for paying the rent. They must be on the contract, and you must have their information on file should that happen. Then give her the rent-increase notice, and tell her that you have checked around and found what the current market rent is for the apartment. Tell her that you are giving her a discount off the current market rent because she's been a good long-term tenant. Tell her also that you are giving her sixty days notice of the rent increase so that she can have some extra time to look around for herself and decide whether to remain. Tell her that if she decides to move, she need give only thirty days notice. Finally, show her the new rental agreement, and tell her that she and each of her grown children must sign it in order for them to stay.

Step 5: Wait thirty days and contact the tenant if she doesn't contact you first. If she decides to stay, ask her for her grown children's rental applications and complete the rental agreement with everybody's names and particulars on it. Indicate that the new rent starts thirty days hence. If she decides to vacate, give her a blank notice of intention to Vacate and ask her to complete it then and there.

So much for the steps you might want to take to resolve the problem.

By following these steps rather than booting her out with a 30-day notice, you are giving her a choice. She decides whether she stays or moves, not you. Consequently, she shouldn't feel so antagonistic toward you. You, in turn, needn't feel that she is taking advantage of you if she stays. She will be paying you what she should be paying you for the services you provide, especially when she chooses to stretch those services to the limit.

12
Resolving
Maintenance Concerns

Frequent toilet
clogs stump landlord.

Q. Don't ask me why I enjoy maintaining the three apartment buildings my wife and I own. I just do. Our buildings have forty-eight units in all, and they keep me busy much of the time. I don't mind. I like to fix things and help people.

I handle the turnovers, the remodeling, the regular maintenance, and the emergencies. I know how to do electrical, plumbing, carpentry, painting, glazing, roofing, concrete finishing, ceramic tile installation, carpet installation, and cleaning. I do it all.

Every so often a problem arises which stumps me for a while, but eventually I find the solution and am overjoyed when I do.

Right now I'm facing a problem which has had me stumped for more than a month. Maybe you can help me with it. It's a plumbing problem.

One of our tenants is a single mom with two preschool kids. Actually she's a widow. Her husband died in the Iraq war. She works hard at an office job to make ends meet, and she works hard at raising her kids. I do more for her than I do for other tenants because I know her hard-luck story. Besides, she's a good tenant.

Well, I never used to hear from her about anything. I'd have to ask her whether anything needed attention in her apartment, and I'd even suggest things.

Within this past month, she has called me three times to report that her toilet is clogged up. She doesn't know why it clogs so frequently, and neither do I. She says it clogs every day, and she unclogs it herself with a plunger. She calls me only when the plunger doesn't work. I attack the clog with my trusty closet auger and clear the clog every time. The next thing I know, though, she's on the phone again to report another clog.

Do you have any idea why her toilet clogs so frequently?
—P.B., Utah

A. As a matter of fact, I do have an idea why your tenant's toilet clogs so frequently. I encountered the same problem myself, not once, but twice. Unclogging the toilet with a plunger or a closet auger was only a partial fix. For a complete fix, I had to remove the toilet altogether and root around in the trap from both directions, top and bottom. I didn't want to remove the toilet, but I had to. Nothing else worked, and if that hadn't worked, I'd have had to replace the toilet.

The problem I encountered and the problem you have encountered is this—something is lodged in the trap of your tenant's toilet. It could be anything from a toy to a sponge to a Popsicle® stick. You can't see it, but you know it's there because it hangs up the solid waste again and again. A plunger will sometimes force the waste by the obstruction and make the toilet usable again. A closet auger will always force its way by the obstruction, take the waste with it, and make the toilet usable again. Water will flow through the toilet all right, and so will some solid waste, but the trap is still obstructed, and that obstruction will soon snag enough solid waste to clog the toilet again.

Here's the fix. Remove the toilet, take it outside where you have access to a garden hose, where you have plenty of room to work, and where you can splash water about. Straddle the toilet across a wooden or plastic box and test it. Fill the tank with water from the hose and trip the flush lever. You'll see the toilet appear to work normally. The bowl empties and water gushes out the bottom. Fill the tank again and put a small wad of paper towels in the bowl. Flush again and watch the water in the bowl rise as soon as the wad catches on the obstruction and impedes the

143

flow. Some water will flow out the bottom, but it won't gush out.

Congratulations! You have successfully clogged the toilet.

Use your closet auger to clear the clog and check what comes out the bottom. If you see something besides the wad, you may have successfully unclogged the toilet and dislodged the obstruction. If you see only the wad, try again with a larger wad, increasing its size with every attempt until you finally dislodge the obstruction. Even if you fail to notice a foreign object in the bottom of the box, you'll know you have dislodged the obstruction when you try flushing a wad and it comes gushing out the bottom of the toilet right away.

For especially unyielding obstructions, you may have to do what pipeline operators do when they want to clean their pipelines of debris or prepare their pipelines for a change of liquids. They insert a "pig," a flexible plug in contact with all sides of the pipe, and force it through. A pig for your toilet could be a spongy rubber ball roughly equal in size to the diameter of the trap. You push it through with the closet auger to sweep the trap clean.

Jack of all trades that you are, you will find a way to clear the obstruction and restore the toilet to reliable working condition, but if you can't, go ahead and install a new toilet. It'll solve the problem.

Wobbly toilet causes subfloor damage.

Q. A bathroom in one of my apartments has an uneven floor, and no matter what I do, I can't seem to keep the toilet from wobbling. I tightened one toilet down so hard that the base broke and had to be replaced. Even when that toilet was bolted down tight and hadn't yet broken, it would still wobble a bit. I've been using plastic shims, and they seem to work pretty well, but tenants are careless with toilets, as every landlord knows, and my tenants are overweight anyway, so the shims tend to shift when the tenants push the toilet this way and that while getting on or off.

That's only one of my toilet problems. The other problem I'm having comes from the wax ring. It loses its seal when the toilet wobbles, and then waste water leaks out at the base and rots the floor. I've had to cut out dry-rot in this floor once already, and I don't want to have to do it again. Is there any solution to this problem?
—I.R., Montana

A. What plumber hasn't cranked toilet nuts down so hard that the toilet broke? You're not alone! Though toilets are made tough, they will break when you crank the nuts down too tight, and you're always tempted to tighten them a little bit more if the toilet moves even slightly.

When you tighten the nuts, make sure that you alternate the tightening so you distribute the pressure evenly around the base. That helps keep the base from cracking and helps the wax seal make good contact.

You're on the right track in using plastic shims under a toilet to compensate for an uneven floor. Water won't shrink or soften them as it will wood or cardboard shims. To keep them from shifting, determine where you need to put them before you set the toilet on the wax ring and fill its tank with water. Set the toilet over the waste line without the wax ring and finger-tighten the nuts. Fit the shims where needed to eliminate the wobbling, and remove the toilet. The shims will remain in position, and you can glue them in place to the floor with caulk. Put the wax ring on top of the waste line, set the toilet, and tighten the nuts with a few pounds of pressure. The toilet shouldn't wobble or twist, and the shims shouldn't move even when your heavy tenants use the toilet.

The wax ring you install, if you install a wax ring at all, should be a urethane wax ring with a plastic horn attached. The urethane is nothing more than a sponge inside the wax. It gives the wax resiliency, helping it retain the seal by expanding and contracting as necessary when the toilet moves. The horn extends down into the waste line to help direct the water into the pipe rather than onto the floor.

While a wax ring used to be the only toilet seal available, now there are others that are completely waxless. They're less messy, and they seal better under variable conditions.

My favorite is the Fernco seal (fernco.com) because it's simple and foolproof, and it flexes enough to hold its seal no matter how much rocking the toilet does. It consists of a flexible rubberlike pipe about five inches long with a flange and adhesive on one end and ribs on the other. To install it, you clean the area around the horn on the bottom of the toilet, remove the protective paper from the adhesive on the flange, press the flange with its exposed adhesive over the horn, and set the toilet in place. The ribbed end of the rubberlike pipe fits down into the waste line and makes a good watertight seal, come what may. The Fernco seal comes in two sizes, one for three-inch waste lines and one for four-inch waste lines.

The other waxless seal you might try is the Fluidmaster (fluidmaster.com). It's a Rube Goldberg contraption of sorts consisting of sliding plastic sleeves and rubber gaskets. Just by looking at it, you wouldn't think that it would work, but it does. You assemble the pieces for either a three- or four-inch waste line, and push its lower end down into the waste line to where the two make good contact. Put the provided spacer under its flange to hold up the top sleeve while you set the toilet so that the rubber gasket built into the flange can form a seal with the horn on the bottom of the toilet. Somehow the whole thing works.

What makes me prefer the Fernco seal over the Fluidmaster are its telltale signs of good contact. You know the seal has good contact with the toilet itself before you ever set the toilet, and when you set the toilet, you can feel the ribs on the flexible pipe making contact with the waste line. Since you can't see under the toilet after you set it, you have to rely on other clues to tell you whether the seal has done its job. The Fernco seal gives you tactile clues. The Fluidmaster gives you no clues whatsoever.

When deciding which seal to use, check three things carefully to see whether the one you want to use will actually fit your particular application. Check the diameter of the waste line, the straightness of the waste line, and the position of the floor flange relative to the finished floor. Observe and measure these things and visualize your seal of choice in its final position making a watertight seal between toilet and waste line. Sometimes these three things will dictate which seal you have to use, and sometimes they won't. Check them carefully before you make your final seal decision.

Whatever you do, don't caulk around the base of the toilet once it's in place. The caulk will trap any wetness underneath the toilet and cause the underlayment and subfloor to rot. You want that wetness to escape from under the toilet and show up on the floor covering around the toilet, where the tenant may notice it and alert you to the leaky seal in time for you to repair it before there's major damage. If you think you must caulk around the base of the toilet to keep it from dancing around the bathroom, leave inch-long gaps in the caulking so the water can escape.

Because you can't monitor tenant toilets as you can your own, you must take great pains to install them correctly every time or you will be wasting your time later making bothersome maintenance calls.

Raccoons pose problem, but whose problem are they?

Q. Tenants at my rental house have complained that raccoons are active in the backyard and are leaving "calling cards" here and there. They want me to get rid of the raccoons. Should I? Am I responsible?
—D.W., California

A. Whenever unwanted critters invade one of my rental properties, I consider them my responsibility. Some tenants will take charge and not even bother me with such problems, while others will call me straightaway at the first sighting and ask for help.

When asked, I always help for two reasons: 1) Landlords are responsible for making their rental properties habitable, and unwanted critters can quickly make a property uninhabitable. 2) Tenants who ask for help generally need it. If they don't get it, they may botch the job of getting rid of the unwanted critters themselves and cause me to spend more time and more money later to remedy the problem.

When evicting raccoons from your rental property, you must secure the cooperation of your tenants first. Tell them that raccoons will not leave an area if they have good reason to stay, and the ready availability of food is a very good reason for them to stay. Tell the tenants not to leave food outside for either domestic or feral animals. Tell them to secure their garbage can and compost bin with lids held in place by a bungee cord or a heavy weight, so the raccoons cannot get to the goodies inside.

Tell them that raccoons dislike strong odors, bright lights, and loud noises and that you are going to have to use one or more of these three repellents to evict the raccoons from the property.

Of the three repellents, you should try the one which is least objectionable to ordinary humans first. That would be strong odors. Different choices of strong odors include ammonia-soaked cotton rags, naphtha flakes, predator urine, RO-PEL® (a proprietary product available at pet stores), ground-up red pepper (cayenne pepper), and a solution of Tabasco® pepper sauce (three parts sauce per hundred parts water).

Leave liberal amounts of your choice of these strong odors around the area the raccoons frequent, and tell the tenants to monitor the raccoon activity over the next week. If the activity continues unabated, try another one of the strong odors until the raccoons decide to seek sweeter-smelling backyards elsewhere.

The two other repellents, bright lights and loud noises (hard rock, heavy metal, and rap music played at high volume definitely qualify), are so much more objectionable to ordinary humans that you shouldn't try them unless you have no other choice.

Tiny bugs infest condominium apartment. Who pays?

Q. I own a two-room condominium in Jersey City. I used to live there myself, but I haven't been able to sell it, so I'm renting it out. I've been using your *Landlording* book for years and have taught experienced real estate agents a trick or two with it. However, I've finally encountered a problem your book doesn't help me with.

My tenant, who has been paying his rent on time for over a year now, is not the handiest guy in the world. He called last night to tell me that his apartment has an insect problem. He referred to them as termites, but the description he gave me sounds more like fleas, "tiny bugs leaving lots of eggs around." I advised him to have an exterminator come in, determine the problem, and give him an estimate.

Still hanging in the air is the question of who is going to pay for the work.

My first thought is that the tenant is responsible for payment under his obligation to keep the apartment clean, but because there is no specific language in the lease about bugs, I don't know for sure.

The tenant may be a nut about cleanliness and still have a bug problem because they may have migrated from another apartment or are infesting the building in general. In that case, it's probably the condominium association's responsibility.

What do you say?
—B.T., New Jersey

A. The responsibility for paying to exterminate bugs in rental properties rests with those who cause them. Determining who caused them is always the problem.

If dog-owning tenants vacate, and fleas attack my wife or me while we're cleaning the apartment, we charge the tenants for the extermination. The responsibility is clear.

If roaches or ants appear in any rental we own, we have them exterminated, pay the bill, educate our tenants in the ways of good housekeeping, and take preventative measures such as boric acid for cockroaches and ant stakes for ants. The responsibility is not clear, especially because these bugs do not respect the walls between tenants' units. Roaches and ants in any dwelling have migrated from somewhere, whether inside or outside, or they will.

Because the bugs your tenant has discovered, whatever they are, may have migrated from another unit and because the complex is a condominium, you should contact the association to learn what they do in such situations. They likely have a policy already in place. Perhaps they have a contract with an exterminator to provide regular service and will service your unit at no charge to you.

If they won't service your unit, direct your unhandy tenant to get two estimates and call you to discuss them. Then have the work done and pay the bill.

Tenant claims to have fleas and no pets.

Q. To relieve myself of the many problems associated with pets, I enforce a strict "no pets" policy at my rental properties. As you might imagine, I was surprised when a tenant called me about a flea problem. I associate flea problems with pets. I know that fleas can live outdoors on their own, but I also know that they're parasites and are always looking for a host. A knowledgeable clerk at a pet store once told me that a pet is a far more likely host than a human, assuming, of course, that the human practices good hygiene.

My tenant told me that she has seen an opossum, a raccoon, and a cat underneath her house, and she thinks that they could be the reason why the fleas have appeared. She has told me she's allergic to fleas and has tried to get rid of them herself without success.

I did have her unit treated two months ago for pests, though not specifically for fleas. She said nothing about fleas then.

I'm wondering whether she might have a pet or be looking after a pet for someone else. I was told confidentially that her niece asked her own landlord if she could have a cat, and that triggered my suspicions.

Do you have any advice?
—R.S., North Carolina

A. Tell the tenant of your suspicions. Tell her that fleas don't just invade a dwelling if there are no pets around. Ask her point blank whether a cat is ever in her dwelling, even for a few minutes. Tell her that pets are not allowed in her dwelling at all, period. Tell her that you will have her dwelling sprayed for fleas at your expense if the pest control person finds no evidence of the presence of an animal inside the house or at her expense if the pest control person finds evidence of the presence of an animal inside the house. Tell her that you will have the pest control person look for evidence of small animals living anywhere underneath the house and that you will approve and pay for any work necessary to get rid of them.

Be frank and firm with her, but give her the benefit of the doubt. Those fleas could have arrived on a human.

Landlord refuses management company's pest control bill.

Q. Last month the property management company looking after my rental property submitted a pest control bill to me. I didn't know anything about it before I saw it and don't see why I should be the one to pay it.

A small claims court judge once told me that as a landlord all I had to do was keep my property in compliance with the county building code. He said that any messes and filth that attracted insects and rodents to a tenants' unit were the tenants' responsibility to take care of.

The bill I received was to spray for ants. Are ants my responsibility or are they the tenants' responsibility?
—G.W., California

A. Let's assume that the ants exterminated for bothering your tenants were the most common household ant invader, the sugar-feeding ant.

There are lots of others, but they're not nearly so common. Some common names for the others are acrobat ants, Argentine ants, black ants, carpenter ants, crazy ants, fire ants, ghost ants, odorous house ants, pavement ants, pharaoh ants, thief ants, and white footed ants. Some of these ants will invade a dwelling which is as clean as a never-lived-in model home just to find water or to nibble on the wooden substructure. Such invasions would never be the tenants' responsibility. They're always yours.

The pesky sugar-feeding ants likely invading your rental property are your responsibility as well as your tenants'. Your tenants are responsible for keeping their dwellings clean enough so that ant scouts won't find any food available as they wander about looking for something for them and their pals to devour, and you as landlord are responsible for keeping ants of all varieties generally at bay.

Sugar-feeding ants will enter a dwelling seeking food or shelter or both, and the dwelling needn't be filthy or messy for them to arrive in numbers. They may even use part of a dwelling as a trail from their nest to a food source somewhere else.

You might say that if ants appear in a tenants' dwelling to feast on food scraps left lying about, the tenants are responsible for the invasion, and if they appear in a tenants' dwelling to seek shelter, the landlord is responsible. You might say that, but you can't always prove exactly why ants materialize somewhere.

Trying to assign responsibility for any particular infestation is more trouble than it's worth. Instead of trying, landlord and tenants ought to unite in combating the infestation and should treat it as a do-it-yourself project they can undertake together. The landlord should give the tenants some guidance in food handling and cleanup and should provide an effective do-it-yourself aerosol insecticide for the tenants to use. The tenants should follow the landlord's guidance and apply the insecticide, that is, if they insist upon immediate results and care little about the environmental health drawbacks of insecticides formulated to kill ants.

You ought to discuss the three drawbacks with your tenants before handing them a spray can.

The first drawback is the insecticides' toxicity. Aerosol insecticides are toxic and may harm lungs, skin, and nervous systems. Read the label carefully to yourself before buying a product, and tell the tenants to read it carefully before deciding whether to use the product. Tell them that they may want to try a less toxic solution if they wish, especially if any of them are chemically sensitive or have ecological concerns.

A less toxic solution would involve cleaning up every crumb and food scrap, sealing everything edible, wiping up the live ants with a moist sponge, cleaning their trails with a soapy sponge, and sprinkling chili powder around where the ants enter. These measures will keep them out of the house at least temporarily.

The insecticides' second drawback is the residue which results from the inevitable overspraying. You cannot pinpoint-spray every ant separately with an insecticide. You spray an infested area. When you do, you spray far more insecticide than needed to kill the ants, and you pollute the whole area with the excess. This residue contaminates food and leaves an oily film on everything it touches. For the sake of health, safety, and cleanliness, it must be cleaned up immediately.

The third drawback is temporary effectiveness. Insecticides will kill roaming ants on contact, but they won't wipe out the nests. Other ants from the same nest will keep coming to the same dwelling later to seek food and shelter.

For lasting effectiveness, try setting out baits. Ants feed on them and take them back to their nests to spread the delicious poison to the queen and her entire empire. Baits come in gel, liquid, granular, and solid forms. Experiment with different ones until you find one which works well for you. Ant stakes, which come filled with a gel and a tiny amount of arsenic, work best for me. Placed around the foundation of a building, they keep ants at bay for months and months.

In your case, you can't know whose responsibility the ants were, that is, whether they appeared spontaneously or as a result of the tenants' poor housekeeping. You didn't witness the infestation and the property manager likely didn't witness it either. The tenants must have called the manager to report the ants, and the manager called the pest control company without considering alternatives. Property managers tend to solve problems the easiest way they know how without regard to cost because they don't pay the bills.

Pay the bill this time and tell the property manager to find out whether the pest control company guarantees its work for any length of time. If so, make sure the manager is well aware of the guarantee and takes advantage of it should the need arise.

If you don't want to pay any more such bills in the future, tell the manager not to call a pest control company whenever tenants complain about ants. Tell the manager to supply the tenants with an aerosol insecticide instead. An aerosol insecticide will cost a tenth as much as a visit from a pest control company.

In addition, tell the manager to research ant baiting and then have a maintenance person bait the perimeter of the property on a regular basis. Baiting costs little and keeps the ants at bay forever so long as it's part of a property's regularly scheduled maintenance.

Follow these suggestions and you won't have to argue with anybody about unexpected bills from pest control companies. There won't be any.

Washing machine floods house.

Q. My husband and I rented a house out to a couple with three children. We left a washer and dryer there for them to use and let them move in a week early. We even let them make time payments on the deposit.

About two weeks after they moved in, they put towels in the washer and left for two hours. While they were gone, a large grommet in the bottom of the washer's outer tub broke loose and water went everywhere. The carpet and padding are still wet, and the walls already have mold growing on them. A water-damage repair service wants a thousand dollars to clean the house. Are the tenants responsible at all for the damage?
—P.M., Virginia

A. You are the kind of people who give landlords a good name. You bent over backwards to help your new tenants by letting them use the laundry machines, letting them move in early, and letting them pay their deposit in installments. The tenants, for their part, were living up to their agreement with you and enjoying their new home.

Unfortunately, the washer did not do its part. It tried to wash the whole house when it should have been washing only a load of towels. The tenants probably feel as bad as you do about what happened, but they're not to blame. They did nothing negligent, nothing stupid, nothing malicious, nothing wrong. They simply loaded the washer, your washer, expecting it to do its job, and returned to find it flooding the house. You can't blame them. You can't charge them.

You should check your insurance policy to see whether such damage might be covered. Likely it is. Lacking coverage, you're stuck with the bill, I'm afraid. Bad things sometimes do happen to good people.

Consider reducing the chances that there will be another flood in the future by taking one or all of these three preventative measures:

1) Place a drain pan (with drain hole) under the washer. Building codes in some areas require drain pans under washing machines. They work. They trap any water coming from the washer and let it flow out through a hole to the outside or underside of the house.

2) Change the water supply hoses every five years or replace ordinary hoses with reinforced hoses guaranteed for twenty years. New hoses or better hoses won't burst unexpectedly before their life expectancy is up. Burst hoses are the primary cause of laundry machine flooding.

3) Install solenoid cutoff valves (Flood Stop™) between the laundry hose bibs and the water supply hoses. Solenoid cutoffs turn off the water supply when a hose breaks and nobody is there to turn off the valves manually.

Irrigation water outside beach apartments causes problems.

Q. We have a 50-unit apartment complex which is near an ocean beach. We keep water hoses at the bases of the staircases for the staff to use to water plants and hose down the walkways. Tenants have been using these hoses to wash their cars, water their plants, wash their dogs, and wash their feet when they arrive home from the beach. The water, soap, mud, and oil all end up on the stairs and landing. A lady fell there recently because it was so slippery. Fortunately for her and for us, she was not hurt.

Are there any resources, standards, printed materials, etc. that address the responsibilities of a landlord to limit the use of water or even forbid it?
—D.A., California

A. You have no responsibility to provide outside water for your tenants to use to wash themselves, their animals, their plants, or their cars, and because the area they have been using for these purposes has become hazardous, you should stop

allowing them to use the water there immediately. If you don't, somebody will surely fall there again, break a bone, bring a burdensome slip-and-fall lawsuit against you, and cast terrible aspersions in your direction because you were aware of the hazard and did nothing about it, you dirty dog.

To keep tenants from using the water, you have two choices: Replace the existing hose bibs with hose bibs requiring a special key (readily available at hardware stores), or use a hose bib locking system (lockpeople.com) which essentially padlocks the hose threads of the existing hose bib. Like any doorlock, these lockout measures can be foiled by anybody bent on foiling them, but they will certainly foil the casual water user.

In addition to locking out the hose bibs, put the hoses on hose reels which staff can take with them, and post signs directly above the hose bibs stating that the water is for staff use only.

Shower water from third floor floods second-floor tenants.

Q. We are first-time landlords who recently purchased a 6-unit apartment building. Right away we have had to face a distressing problem, and we're not quite sure how to handle it.

The second-floor tenants complained that the third-floor tenants, when showering, were flooding the second-floor bathroom. We checked and found that they were correct. They can't use their bathroom when the upstairs tenants are showering because the water drips down on their heads. We also checked the bathroom in the third-floor apartment and found that the floor was indeed flooded. The third-floor tenants obviously cause this mess because they don't use the shower curtain properly. We have told them twice now that they must stop flooding the floor, but talking to them hasn't stopped the flooding.

There is considerable visible water damage to the second floor, and I'm sure that there's more to be found within the walls. We're thinking about installing a shower enclosure with sliding doors in the third-floor apartment to help stop further damage.

Can we request immediate reimbursement from the tenants for the shower enclosure, given that it has to be installed because of their negligence?

If we can't request reimbursement, can we take our costs for repair of the water damage, includ-

ing the shower enclosure, out of their security deposit? What if the total costs amount to more than the security deposit? Should we document this problem in writing and present it to the tenants? In general, what responsibilities do these tenants have for damage that they cause to another apartment? Do you have any other suggestions for how we should handle the situation?
—K.M., Illinois

A. First of all, I'm surprised that this problem wasn't remedied before you took possession. It should have been. It's the stuff of termite reports and building inspections which are designed to inform buyers about such problems. Once the problems are identified, the buyer can require the seller to fix them or at least negotiate how they will be handled. Now that you have acquired the building, you have no choice but to wrestle with the problem yourself and then determine who's going to pay for the fix.

You're definitely on the right track in considering an improved physical barrier to keep the water inside the tub. A bypass tub door is a definite improvement over a shower curtain. A perfectly adequate door will cost less than a hundred dollars and shouldn't take more than an hour for a do-it-yourselfer to install. Prior to installing the door, inspect the walls around the tub. Decide whether you ought to install one of the five-piece wall surrounds or just caulk thoroughly. You do not want any water penetrating the walls inside the tub enclosure.

When you install the door, install a water-saving shower head as well. It will cut down on the volume of water, so that if all else fails, at least you'll have minimized the water which might somehow make its way to the floor below.

Educate the third-floor tenants in the proper use of the tub door. If they don't heed what you say and use it properly, closing the panels all the way at each end, screw the one panel closed which is nearer the shower head. They'll groan and complain that you have limited their access to the tub when all you have done really is limit the access position. You haven't reduced the size of the opening one inch.

Monitor the situation closely. When you are confident that the leakage has stopped, repair the damage to the walls and floors in both apartments and the damage to the ceiling in the lower apartment.

With the leakage stopped and the damage re-paired, you'll know the cost of everything, and you can try to get the third-floor tenants, who were primarily responsible for the damage, to be responsible for the payment, too. Itemize the cost, divide it in half just to be fair, and tell them that you'll split the cost with them. They may pay you on the spot. They may not. At least they'll have some idea how much the repairs cost.

If they aren't forthcoming, offer to divide their half of the bill in six parts and let them pay it over a six-month period along with their rent. If they refuse to pay anything at all, don't waste time arguing with them or taking them to small claims court. Put the bill in their file, and jot down some relevant notes. Then deduct it from their security deposit when they vacate. If their security deposit isn't large enough to pay what they owe you and they refuse to pay, then take them to small claims court, but only if you think you have a good chance to win a judgment and a good chance to collect it.

Tenants botch painting job.

Q. My renters recently moved out, but before they did, they tried to repair some damage they did to the walls and used paint they found in the basement to repaint those areas. They used a roller and painted large areas but not an entire wall. Needless to say, the walls look terrible. I sent them a certified letter describing the damage they caused. Their contract specifically states that they are not to paint without securing written permission, which they did not get. Repainting the whole interior is going to cost me a bundle.

Even though I'm sure they did not mean to cause this damage, they did. When they moved in two years ago, the walls were in good condition. Some had just been painted.

What's a fair price to charge them for the damage?
—L.Y., North Carolina

A. Take some photos of the damage before you do anything else. You may have to prove to a judge just how bad the damage was in order to justify whatever you decide to charge the tenants.

As for what you ought to charge them, it should be based upon the cost of the repair, the extent of the damage they caused, and the length of time they occupied the dwelling.

Get several estimates for the painting. Divide the lowest estimate by the number of walls and ceilings to be painted to get the cost per wall or ceiling. Decide which walls and ceilings the tenants damaged. Multiply the "cost per" times the number of damaged walls and ceilings to arrive at a cost figure attributable to the damage caused by the tenants. Because the tenants stayed for two-thirds of the minimum life-span of interior paint in rental properties, you should charge them one-third of the cost figure attributable to the paint damage they caused.

Remember, tenants shouldn't be charged more than the prevailing price for interior painting.

Remember, tenants who cause damage to walls in two rooms shouldn't be charged for repainting six rooms.

Remember, tenants who vacate a dwelling after three or more years shouldn't be charged anything if the place needs repainting on the inside. Tenants who vacate after two years should never be charged more than one-third of the cost of whatever painting is necessary.

Stove malfunction prompts tenant to ask for meal allowance.

Q. A tenant called to say that his stove wasn't working. I called a repair service and they said that they wouldn't be able to fix it for two days. The tenant said that he would have to go out to eat and he wanted me to pay for all of his meals while the stove was being repaired. The unit is rented with a stove.

Do I have to reimburse him for his expenses and what would be considered reasonable?
—G.R., California

A. Almost never does a stove stop working completely. A burner goes out or the oven goes out but not the entire stove, unless, maybe, somebody somehow shut off the stove's gas or electricity. Ask the tenant exactly which part of the stove has stopped working, and tell him to use the rest of the stove to cook with until the repair service can put it back into good working order.

If the entire stove has indeed stopped working, get him a hotplate and a microwave oven to use temporarily. A single-burner hotplate and a microwave oven will cost you less than a hundred dollars and are good things for you to have around for just such situations anyway.

Do not reimburse him for meals. If you do, you may find that other kitchen appliances mysteriously stop working and you're paying for more of his meals. He is being inconvenienced, that's true, but he's not being kept from eating at home altogether. He doesn't have to go out to eat. If you can't supply him right away with some means of cooking or heating his food, tell him to eat sandwiches or cereal for a few meals. He can even eat cake, for all you care, so long as you aren't paying for it. You're doing all you can. You're responding to the situation in a timely manner. You shouldn't be paying his food bills on top of the stove's repair bills.

Landlord refuses to pay for food spoiled during refrigerator repair.

Q. A refrigerator in a rental unit of mine wasn't cold enough for my tenants. The freezer would freeze ice rock hard, but it wouldn't freeze ice cream. They notified me on a Friday night, and I checked it the next day, Saturday. They were telling the truth all right. Their ice cream was mush.

Monday I got hold of a repairman, and he told me to unplug the refrigerator for several hours and then restart it to see whether that would fix the problem. The tenants unplugged it and called me Wednesday to say that it was better but not completely fixed.

I called the repairman to give him a status report and met him at the rental unit the next morning. He found that a small fan had stopped working and replaced it.

Now the tenants are happy to have hard ice cream once more, but they want me to pay them $200 for their food that spoiled during the period when their refrigerator was acting up.

Because I have refused to pay, they are taking me to small claims court. Am I doing the right thing in refusing to pay? Is their claim valid?
—D.M., Oregon

A. Ice cream must be mighty expensive in Oregon these days! The way you describe the situation, they needn't have lost anything other than their ice cream because there was only a two-hour period when the refrigerator had to be unplugged. Even then, the tenants were the ones who unplugged it, so they controlled when it stopped working and could easily have made arrangements for their most perishable food to be stored elsewhere. Besides, the contents didn't have to be exposed to warm air. That's not what the repairman wanted. He merely wanted somebody to unplug the refrigerator, so its coolant would have time enough to settle.

You don't owe them even a pint of their favorite flavor, which must be rocky road, I'd wager, because they're putting rocks in your road, these tenants of yours.

Don't get upset. Don't give in. Let them take you to small claims court. Prepare yourself with dates and times and bills. Tell the judge that you took care of the matter in a timely manner, and there was no reason why any of their food should have spoiled except for their own carelessness.

The next time you rent their unit, tell the new tenants that you're renting it without a refrigerator but that you'll lend them the existing refrigerator for a while until they get their own. They'll be so grateful to have the use of something capable of keeping their milk cold that they won't trouble you if it won't keep their ice cream as hard as a hockey puck in Antarctica.

Tenant asks for rent credit while gas was shut off.

Q. My tenant smelled gas and called the utility company to investigate. They found a leak, turned off the gas at the meter, and locked it. To have the lock removed, I had to have the gas lines replaced and have them checked by the city. The work took six days. The tenant is asking me to give her a rent credit for the six days, saying that she couldn't inhabit the premises when her gas was shut off. Should I go along with her?
—S.Y., California

A. Give the tenant a credit for the six days when she was without heat and hot water. That's the least you should do for her. Be happy that she's not asking you to give her the credit and compensate her for staying in a motel, too.

Tenant blames repairmen for breakage they never caused.

Q. I'm a new landlord who has inherited tenants from a previous owner. Two of the tenants told me that another tenant is always blaming things on repairmen. She blamed a broken glass patio door on one repairman when there was no way he could have broken it. She had to have broken it herself.

I'm now hiring a roofer to replace the roof, and I'm worried that she'll say the roofer broke something of hers while doing the job. I sent her a letter stating that we have confidence in this man's work and that we expected him to do the work without incident and without bothering the tenants any more than absolutely necessary. I

mentioned that we will keep in contact with the roofer as the job progresses.

Is there anything else I might do to prevent her from blaming the repairman for something already broken in her apartment?
—S.R., Kansas

A. Prior to commencement of the roofing job, you might ask everybody in the building to give you a list of the things which are broken or in need of repair in their dwelling. You want this information anyway so you can schedule the work to be done.

If the tenant then claims that the roofer broke something, at least the breakage would have to show signs that it occurred recently in order to be considered "roofer-caused."

Remember that some tenants are liars and some are cheats, and some are both liars and cheats. No matter how much you prepare or how hard you try, you aren't going to thwart their every incidence of lying and cheating.

Tenant has phone jack repaired at cost of $126.

Q. One of my tenants has informed me that she had a telephone jack repaired at a cost of $126. She has been in the apartment about a year, and she says that the jack, located in the kitchen, has never worked. Am I responsible for the cost of this repair?
—B.M., California

A. Tenants must notify their landlord about the things which don't work around their dwelling and must give their landlord an opportunity to make the repair. If the landlord doesn't investigate and make the repair within a reasonable period of time, then the tenants have to take matters into their own hands and may deduct the reasonable cost of the repair from their rent.

As a landlord, you are under no obligation to pay for a repair, especially one which involved no emergency, unless you authorized the tenant to hire the work done and agreed to pay for it.

In any case, $126 to repair a telephone jack in a kitchen is outrageous. Had the tenant told you about the problem, you likely could have fixed it for less than $10 yourself or hired an independent telephone repair service company to fix it for less than $70. If you want to compromise with the tenant, offer to pay half the bill, and tell the tenant to inform you in the future whenever something needs to be repaired so you can get it fixed yourself and pay the entire bill.

Tenant takes repair matter into his own hands.

Q. What should a landlord do when a tenant takes matters into his own hands, hires someone to do a repair, and deducts the cost from his rent?
—B.B., California

A. Your response as a landlord ought to depend upon the responsibility for the repair, the magnitude of the repair, the immediate need for the repair, and the amount of notice the tenant gives you before taking the matter into his own hands. It should not depend upon your relationship with this particular tenant.

I say that it should not depend upon your relationship with this particular tenant because you must make every effort to treat your tenants alike so that you won't be accused of discriminating against tenants who are in one of the protected classes. If, for example, you dislike a particular tenant who's always difficult to deal with and you go after her when she does a "repair and deduct," but you don't go after another tenant who does a similar "repair and deduct" but is easy to deal with and just happens to be a man, you might be accused of discrimination by the woman. Treat all your tenants as "alike" as you possibly can.

That said, I would say your response should take the responsibility for the repair into account. If, for example, the tenant hired somebody to replace a broken window and he expected you to pay for it, you ought to make sure he understands what your policy is regarding broken windows. My rental agreements state specifically that the tenant is responsible for broken windows regardless of who breaks the window. In the case of a "repair and deduct" for a broken window or anything else he is responsible for, I would send the tenant a strongly worded letter telling him that he is responsible to pay for the repair and that he will not be allowed to deduct the cost from his rent.

Always respond to "repair and deduct" matters in writing because they may wind up in a courtroom tussle, and you want to be able to document your case to a judge.

The magnitude of the repair comes into play, too. If the "repair and deduct" matter is a toss-up as to whether you think the tenant handled it properly, but it involves only a small amount of money, say, less than a hundred dollars, then I would tend to go along with the tenant in the matter. I would write him a letter and explain my position regarding "repair and deduct" matters in general and tell him how I would want him to handle such things in the future.

The immediate need for the repair is an important aspect in "repair and deduct" matters. You want your tenants to understand what constitutes an emergency and what doesn't. Let's say that they decide to have their air conditioner repaired in November and charge you for the repair when they're not going to need air conditioning for six months. That's not a repair I would allow. I might pay for part of it, but I wouldn't pay for the entire repair. You would need to impress upon the tenant in writing that "repair and deduct" matters must be pressing in nature.

Lastly, there's the amount of notice a tenant gives you before resorting to "repair and deduct." If a tenant gives you no notice at all before hiring somebody to do something like trim a tree which may or may not be a safety hazard, then you should tell him in no uncertain terms that he must approach you first and give you enough time to take care of the matter. Otherwise, he's going to have to pay for the work himself because you never authorized it. If he gave you several weeks' notice and you didn't get around to taking care of it because you were too busy doing other things, then you probably ought to pay for it, especially if it were a safety hazard.

All in all, in dealing with "repair and deduct" matters, you must understand your role and the tenant's role. You have a legal obligation to make the rental dwelling habitable, and there are very detailed laws outlining what constitutes a habitable dwelling. You also have an obligation to take care of repairs promptly. If you are going to keep your good tenants and charge them market rents, then you have to provide them with habitable dwellings and you should want to make repairs promptly. That's just how the business works.

Your tenant, on the other hand, should understand that some things take time and that you must authorize work to be done in order for you to be responsible for payment. The tenant must alert you to the problem and must give you an adequate amount of time to take care of it before resorting to "repair and deduct."

One of the things included in the *Landlording* book is something called a timely maintenance guarantee. It's a guarantee you make to your tenants that you will handle repairs within certain time limits or else the tenant is relieved of the obligation to pay rent until the matter is taken care of. Ever since I've been using this guarantee, I have never had a tenant try a "repair and deduct."

You might want to look into adopting the timely maintenance guarantee yourself.

Tenant calls plumber to do work landlord could have done.

Q. We had a tenant who installed a new washing machine in our rental house and then called a plumber out to change the drain pipes so they could handle the new washer. Apparently, it pumped too fast for the existing pipes. The tenant did not tell us anything about the problem before he called the plumber. Had he said something, my husband, who is a plumber by trade, would have done any necessary work himself. When the tenant next paid his rent, he withheld $400 to pay the plumber's bill. Rather than argue about the matter, we let it slide.

Several months later, the tenant moved somewhere out of state, and we got a call from the plumbing contractor who did the work saying that we were responsible for paying the bill. The tenant hadn't paid it with the money he withheld from the rent. The bill was originally in the tenant's name. Now the contractor has changed it to our name. Are we responsible for this bill?
—D.K., Montana

A. First the tenant took advantage of you, and now the plumbing contractor is trying to take advantage of you. You are not responsible for this bill. Don't pay it.

Write a letter to the contractor explaining what happened. Include a copy of the original bill which shows the tenant's name and which the tenant must have given you when he deducted the charge from his rent. Include copies of any correspondence you had with the tenant about the bill. In addition, include any information you have in your files which might help the contractor collect the bill from your cheat of a tenant.

If the contractor takes you to small claims court or puts a lien on your house, fight back with all the evidence you have at your disposal to prove your case.

Looking backward with perfect hindsight, I can identify mistakes the tenant made, mistakes you made, and mistakes the contractor made.

The tenant made the mistake of not calling you about the problem in the first place, and then he compounded that mistake by cheating you and cheating the contractor.

You made your first mistake by letting the tenant deduct the bill from his rent payment without putting up a fight. You made your second mistake by not deducting the money from his security deposit when he moved out.

The contractor made numerous mistakes. He did the work without first determining who owned the house. He did the work without getting the authorization of the owner. He did the work without getting the owner to agree to pay for it. He didn't collect for the work on the spot. He let the bill become stale, and then he changed the party responsible for the bill to someone who had nothing to do with ordering the work in the first place.

See that you don't make your same mistakes again, and if you ever do allow a tenant to deduct a bill from his rent, make him prove that he paid the bill.

Tenant hires unlicensed plumber, and both try to scam landlord.

Q. My tenant hired a fix-it man to do some work in the house he's renting from me. He contacted this person himself. When the time came for him to pay rent the following month, he deducted the amount of the fix-it bill from his rent. I was very upset by the fact that I was not contacted regarding any maintenance problem and was not given a choice as to who would do the work.

Now, two months later, the fix-it man contacts me and wants to be paid. Apparently, the tenant never paid him as he said he had. Since I did not give my permission for this worker to come onto my property to do any repair, am I legally responsible for his bill? By the way, this fix-it person calls himself a "plumber," but he's not licensed. He also seems to be one of my tenant's friends.

My tenant has cheated me before, and I let him get away with it. This appears to me to be another one of his cheating schemes.
—D.W., Colorado

A. Your tenant and his "plumber" pal are scam artists. Look back at the tenant's application. Isn't that a one-jump-ahead-of-the-law boilerroom brokerage firm he works for? He's likely telemarketing penny stocks to widows and orphans during the week and peddling aluminum siding on weekends. For laughs, he and his buddy scam their landlords whenever they can. They're certainly trying to scam you.

You are not obligated to pay a handyman hired by your tenant without your knowledge. Your tenant should have come to you with his maintenance request, so you could have decided how you were going to handle it. If you had chosen to ignore the request and it was something affecting the habitability of the dwelling, then the tenant could have hired the repair, paid the worker, and deducted the cost from his rent.

Tell the scam-artist handyman that you did not hire him to do any work for you. Therefore, you owe him nothing. Tell him to collect from the person who hired him. Tell him that you will report him to the state building trades licensing board if he harasses you.

Tell the scam-artist tenant that he cannot deduct any repair bill from his rent without first contacting you and giving you a chance to do the work yourself or hire your own worker to do it. Tell the tenant he still owes you for whatever he deducted from his rent payment two months ago. Had he just this month tried to get away with deducting the bill from his rent, he'd be deserving of a no-nonsense notice to pay rent or quit. Since he deducted it two months ago, you'd be late in giving him the notice now.

Instead, give him a statement showing what he owes you for the amount of the handyman's bill he fraudulently deducted. Every month from now on, make a note on every rent receipt you give him that he is in arrears by this amount. When he finally moves out, deduct the amount from his deposit.

Three can play their game. Go ahead and beat them at it!

Owner refuses to provide window screens.

Q. I have managed apartments before, but I'm new here. I'm managing seventeen apartments in a three-story building located in the city of Chicago.

I have asked the owner of the building to supply window screens for the entire building, but he says they're too expensive.

We accept Section 8 tenants, and I'd hoped that the Section 8 requirements would say some-thing about window screens. They don't. They say only that the windows must be workable. In other words, they must open and close. They cannot be nailed or painted shut.

My concerns are safety and liability. I don't want to see some child hurt or killed after falling through an open window which lacked a screen, and I don't want the owner sued for failing to provide screens.

How can I get the owner to provide screens?
—B.A., Illinois

A. Legally required or not, window screens serve at least five functions. They keep bugs out. They keep children from falling out of open windows. They keep adults from jumping out of open windows. They keep criminals from entering easily. They keep attorneys from arguing that the penny-pinching landlord who refused to install window screens on his client's apartment is liable for the mayhem caused there by men wearing pantyhose over their heads who gained entry through an open, unscreened window.

Tell your penny-pinching owner that he should pinch pennies on other things. He needs to put screens on the building's windows.

Landlord fails to keep promise to refinish bathtub.

Q. I have a tenant who's complaining about the condition of her bathtub. Six months ago I told her that I was going to redo her tub with a new acrylic liner, and now she's griping that I'm taking too long to get around to the job. She says that her tub is peeling and has moldy caulking. I don't really have enough money at this point to do the job now. What are my responsibilities?
—C.B., Ohio

A. Your tenant has reason to gripe. She's been waiting half a year for you to fix her bathtub. That's long enough.

Whenever you make a promise to a tenant, you should try your best to keep it. Tenants hold you to a higher standard because they feel dependent upon you for the place where they live, their home. Since you don't have the money right now to fix the tub permanently, fix it temporarily. Take a close look at the tub and determine exactly what needs to be fixed. Visit your local hardware store to ask questions and buy materials. Then, spend the time to clean the tub thoroughly and make it waterproof and attractive.

Your making this effort will please the tenant for a time and won't cost you much, but don't expect it to please her for long. Do the job right as soon as you can. As a landlord, you should be maintaining your rental property at a level high enough to please the people you want to attract as tenants. Bad maintenance will get you bad tenants.

Maintenance man reports finding Ms Piggy's apartment.

Q. I manage an apartment complex in western New York state with more than a hundred units. Recently I received a phone call from a tenant asking for service from our maintenance department. I asked the tenant if she would be home later that day, and when she replied that she wouldn't, I asked her if we could enter her apartment and do the work while she was gone. She said we could, so that afternoon one of our maintenance men went into her apartment to do the work.

After entering and seeing how messy and dirty it was, he called me in to take a look. I was shocked. The apartment looked absolutely disgusting. There were piles of clothes scattered around every room. There were dirty dishes piled not only in the kitchen sink but also here and there all over the apartment. Toys and garbage were everywhere. An empty fast-food restaurant bag sat in the hallway outside the door. You get the picture. She's dirtier than a pig.

Besides the fact that she is the mother of two small children and is endangering their health, I worry that she may be attracting rodents and other pests to the apartment. Is there any way for me to tell this tenant to clean up her apartment without making her defensive? Can she be evicted because of her terrible housekeeping?
—A.R., New York

A. Let the tenant know that you want to see her in your office as soon as possible. When she comes to see you, put her at ease. Don't open the conversation with an attack on her for her lousy housekeeping. Open it with an account of the maintenance man's work that day in her apartment. Since she initiated the work order, she'll want to know what he did there. Tell her. Say that your maintenance man fixed whatever it was that she wanted to have fixed, and give her as many details about the work as you can, perhaps even showing her the parts he replaced.

Then say something like this, using neutral words to describe the condition of her apartment and neutral words to describe your reaction to it, "By the way, the maintenance man happened to notice that your apartment was kind of messy when he was there, and he thought I should take a look at it. I did take a look at it, and I had to agree with him. It was kind of messy. I told him that you must have been in a hurry when you left it because I was sure that you were a good housekeeper, but I told him that I would talk to you about it anyway. Of course, you have the right to leave your beds unmade and throw your clothes on the floor if you want to live that way. You have the right to leave dirty dishes in the sink and let your children leave their toys wherever they want to leave them inside your apartment. We can't tell you what to do about those things. That's your business, but we have to tell you that we are concerned about the dirty dishes and the food scraps we saw lying around because they can become a health hazard for you and your family. The food spoils and causes foul odors, and it attracts the kinds of pests nobody wants to see inside their homes. We're concerned that these pests, the ants, the cockroaches, the rats, and the mice, will invade not only your home but those of your neighbors as well. That's when a messy apartment becomes our business. If there should be a pest invasion, we will have to spray and set traps to get rid of the critters, and at the same time we will begin looking for a reason why they invaded the building. If we find that your messy apartment was the reason, we will charge you for the remedies we had to use to exterminate the invaders, and we will consider giving you a notice to terminate tenancy. As you know, we keep the outside of our apartment complex as clean as we can because we want everybody to know that we are concerned about cleanliness. We cannot afford to have our complex's reputation tarnished by pest invasions. We want to keep you and your children as tenants, and we hope you'll do whatever you can to help us keep everything clean here."

When you finish, let her speak her mind. Maybe she really was in a hurry when she left her apartment in such a mess. Maybe she has been wrestling with some big problem in her life or many little problems which caused her to put cleanliness lower on her list of priorities. Listen and respond appropriately in a non-confrontational way.

Monitor her cleanliness as best you can without being too obvious or too nosey. If her messiness becomes a problem for other tenants, you would have cause to evict her, just as you would if you had a clause in your rental contract specifically requiring her to maintain certain cleanliness standards in her apartment and requiring her to submit to periodic inspections. Otherwise, you would have to evict her using a notice to terminate tenancy. The notice period is generally thirty or sixty days, but you don't have to show cause when you evict a tenant with this kind of notice.

Weight of pool table weighs upon landlord's mind.

Q. We recently renewed a six-month lease with the tenants who are renting our two-story house. During the walk-through, we discovered that they have placed a pool table in the living room on the second floor. I didn't think about it then, but lately it's been bothering me. I'm concerned about how heavy the pool table is and whether it could cause any structural damage due to its weight. How might I ask them to remove this pool table?
—R.Y., California

A. Asking your tenants to get rid of an installed pool table would be like asking a tenant to get rid of a cherished pet. Unless you relish confrontations and squabbles, you don't want to do either. The pool table is there. Leave it there.

To ease your anxiety, however, there is one thing you ought to do and another thing you might want to do. The one thing you ought to do is insist that the tenants obtain a renters' insurance policy which would cover, among many other things, any damage done to the house by the pool table. The other thing you might want to do is consult an engineering firm to determine the house's floor loading limits and then see how they match up to the weight of the table spread over the floorspace it occupies.

Mold holds big worries for this landlord.

Q. Mold has become a big issue for landlords. I can't pick up a newspaper without reading something about it. My husband tells me I shouldn't worry so much. He says that the sensational stories I'm reading about serious health problems caused by mold and high dollar settlements awarded to mold victims are written to sell newspapers. I'm still worried that one of our tenants might be especially sensitive to mold and get sick and sue us into bankruptcy.

I'm wondering how worried I ought to be about it and what we should do when a tenant complains to us about it.
—D.S., California

A. Mold is indeed the "threat of the hour" for landlords. It has taken over from asbestos, lead-based paint, and radon. Remember them?

Molds have always been with us. They're everywhere. Who hasn't seen a moldy piece of bread in a spotless kitchen? They're nature at work.

Depending upon where they appear, molds can be helpful or harmful. The drug penicillin, which has saved countless lives and is still the most widely used antibiotic today, is derived from mold. Molds play a key part in the breakdown of plant debris. Without them, we would be buried under mountains of tree leaves.

Yet, certain molds, such as *stachybotrys chartarum*, can cause all kinds of health problems in those who are especially at risk—young people, elderly people, mothers-to-be, and people with allergies, asthma, respiratory problems, or immune system deficiencies.

Thirty-five years ago, when I was a novice landlord, I remember battling black mold on one wall in one apartment of an eight-plex I owned and attributing the invasion entirely to the tenants' poor housekeeping. Every few months they would call me to report that the mold was back. They could see it spreading along the wall behind a dresser in the spare bedroom where they stored their seldom used stuff. I would go over there, move the dresser away from the wall, vacuum up the dust balls, scrub the wall with soap and water, dry it good with a terry cloth towel and a hair dryer, lecture them about good housekeeping, and go about my business. Their poor housekeeping definitely contributed to the growth of the mold, but a tiny water leak I discovered later was the bigger cause. I repaired that leak, cleaned and treated the wall, and never saw evidence of mold there again.

Thinking back on that experience today, I realize that I was lucky then, lucky that neither the tenants nor I ever became sick from exposure to the mold, lucky that I found the cause, lucky that I could repair the cause and the effect myself at no great cost, lucky that I didn't have to tear the apartment apart to cure the problem permanently, and lucky that I didn't have to give any concessions to the tenants.

Today I would approach a mold invasion in one of my rentals quite differently. We all should. The stakes are higher for us because insurance companies are excluding mold from their rental property package policies. They cannot afford to pay huge sums to settle the escalating number claims being made, so more and more of us landlords are becoming self-insured, whether we want to be or not, and we could wind up signing our rental properties over to our tenants who suffer serious medical problems as a result of the mold we refused to acknowledge and eliminate.

Face the facts. Some molds will make some people sick and some people very sick. We need to maintain our rental properties as if every one of our tenants were sensitive to molds and could become very sick if exposed. We need to remember that molds grow best wherever they find moisture and warmth together, and we need to do our best to eliminate this environment in our rental properties as a matter of routine.

According to the Centers for Disease Control, routine tests for molds are a waste of money. They're expensive, and their results are unreliable for judging what is an acceptable quantity of mold. You don't need to know the identity or quantity of a mold in order to know that it's present and proliferating. You'll see it and smell it. If your tenants want to test for molds when there are none to be seen or smelled and if they agree to pay for the tests themselves, let them. If they interpret the test results as evidence that there is enough mold present in their dwelling for them to become ill, take their assessment seriously, and act immediately.

Examine their dwelling yourself looking for telltale signs. If you find any, eliminate them. Then look for the causes and eliminate them. If you find no signs of active mold growth, tell the tenants that you will try to deal with the two conditions necessary for molds to flourish but that you cannot guarantee success. Tell them that they must do what is best for themselves, that is, if they believe mold has contaminated their dwelling and is causing them health problems, they may want to move, and you will help them. You will release them from whatever fixed-term lease obligations they are under, and you will return their deposits. You may even want to offer to pay for their moving truck and supply some muscle.

You have to make them understand that they have to take care of themselves. You cannot.

You can be responsive to their concerns. You can check the humidity in their dwelling with a hygrometer and take measures to reduce it. You can increase the flow of clean air throughout their dwelling with well-placed fans. You can check everywhere for water intrusion. You can talk with them about their housekeeping. You can educate yourself about mold and pass along to them what you learn. You can cooperate fully with them in finding solutions. You must.

You must also keep a level head about mold. Websites abound with shocking information about "toxic mold." The people behind such websites want you to mistrust the experts and trust them instead because they "really know the truth." Be skeptical about them. They have something to sell—a product, a book, a seminar, equipment, or a service. Trust the experts who have nothing to sell. Here are some websites you can trust to provide you with the truth about mold: epa.gov.iaq (Environmental Protection Agency); cmhc-schl.gc.ca/en/index.cfm (Canada Mortgage and Housing Corporation); healthhouse.org (American Lung Association); and cdc.gov (Centers for Disease Control). Visit them and read what they have to say about mold.

More than anything else, regular maintenance will keep your rental properties from becoming sick with mold and keep your tenants from becoming sick with any number of health problems caused by mold. Practice good maintenance and you needn't worry yourself sick over sensational newspaper articles about mold and its dangers.

13
Dealing with
Diverse Issues

Wolves in sheep's clothing nearly fool expert in fraud prevention.

Q. A short time ago I had an applicant for my rental unit outside Philadelphia show up with his wife and family and ooh and aah over the unit's immaculate condition and improvements. We spent almost an hour talking about the unit and the surrounding area. These people were so outgoing and so neat in their appearance that they aroused no doubt in my mind that they would make excellent tenants. I felt certain about them.

Since I manage a fraud prevention unit for a large mail-order company, I truly did not believe that anyone could con me by their appearance or their conversation.

In any event, I spoke with their current landlord (the previous one had "moved to Florida") who could not say enough positive things about them. She answered all of my questions to my satisfaction and even empathized with my previous negative tenant experience which had been handled by a local real estate agent.

I was preparing to have these people sign the two-year lease they requested when my mother, who's a landlord herself, convinced me to pull a credit report on them. I can't tell you how shocked I was when I learned that they had been evicted legally from their past four or five apartments, that they had been sued and had judgments filed against them any number of times, that they had multiple auto repossessions, and that they almost never paid a bill on time in their entire lives!

Obviously, I did not rent to them.

Is there any way to press charges against them for lying on their application? They flatly denied that they had ever been evicted. They said that they had never refused or been unable to pay rent, and they made other gross fabrications on their application.

I do not want to take them to court over their lying, but I do feel compelled to notify somebody about them. I want to keep other unsuspecting landlords from being hoodwinked by these smooth talkers. Any ideas?
—C.S., Pennsylvania

A. No punishment is too terrible for these deadbeats who have left so much misery in their wake. They're thieves and should be treated like thieves. Because they have duped their previous landlords and others repeatedly, they aren't mere amateurs who have fallen on hard times and need a helping hand. They're professionals. Duping others is a way of life for them, and they're not going to change unless they absolutely must.

The trouble is that they know exactly how "the system" works. They know how to get away without paying their bills and still not be jailed. They know that they won't be locked away in a debtors' prison for their crimes. They know that they won't be put in stocks on public display in the town square. They know that the law isn't going to touch them.

After all, what's a little lying on a rental application when even the people who perjure themselves in court under oath never do any jail time? What's a little landlord-cheating when scalawags cheat investors out of their life's savings every day and never wind up in jail?

Be glad that you as a landlord discovered before you ever rented to them that these people were not what they appeared to be and that they would have cheated you out of your rent money just as they had cheated their previous landlords.

Short of following these deadbeats around and warning anybody who might consider renting or extending credit to them about their appalling credit history, there's nothing you can do to protect the public from these menaces.

These are the people we landlords are warned

about. These are the people credit bureaus exist to provide us information about.

The records on these people speak for themselves. All a landlord has to do is check the records just as you did.

Take comfort in knowing that with the proliferation of information available over the internet, hiding previous evictions and bad credit is becoming increasingly difficult. Because the information is available and inexpensive to secure, more and more landlords are checking every applicant thoroughly before committing to rent to them. That's the best defense there is against deadbeats.

He questions need for credit card information.

Q. As a new landlord, I'm wondering about the reasoning behind, and advisability of, asking applicants to supply credit card information on their rental applications. Aren't people leery about giving that information to a landlord? I would be. I know that anybody can use a credit card number, expiration date, and cardholder's name to make fraudulent charges to a card over the phone or the internet. That's frightening!

Even if an applicant isn't concerned about fraudulent use of the information and supplies it willingly, I don't know what I would do with it as a landlord after I obtained it. Can you clue me in?

—J.K., Maryland

A. As a seasoned landlord, I want to get as much information as I can about an applicant to help me determine whether the applicant will be a good tenant and pay the rent on time.

Before identity theft and credit card fraud became such an issue, landlords didn't think twice about asking for credit card information on rental applications, and applicants didn't think twice about providing it. Now that identity theft and credit card fraud are an issue, a big issue, landlords should think twice about asking for the information, and applicants should think twice about providing it.

We landlords don't really need all the credit card information we have been requesting on rental applications unless we're letting tenants charge their rent every month to their credit cards. Then we need it. Otherwise we don't, and we shouldn't be asking for it, because once we have it, we become responsible for keeping it from falling into the wrong hands.

We need credit card information which will help us determine whether an applicant will pay the rent on time, nothing more. We need to know how many credit cards the applicant has, and for each one, we need to know the card brand, the last four digits of the card number, the card balance, and the monthly payment. This is not the information an identity thief can use to make fraudulent charges.

If we run a credit report on the tenant, this information will help us determine whether the applicant is telling the truth on the application and is capable of paying the rent.

If we don't run a credit report, we can still use this information in our calculations to determine whether the applicant is capable of paying the rent.

You're right to be thinking about the reasoning behind, and advisability of, asking applicants to supply credit card information on their rental applications. Times have changed, and we landlords must change. We should be asking only for the financial information we need and not for information, especially sensitive information, we don't need.

Check the rental application you're using to see what credit card information it requests, and change it as necessary to request only that information you need to complete your tenant qualification procedure.

Owner living downstairs wants to limit tenants above her.

Q. I live downstairs in a triplex I own and rent out the upstairs studio units. I want to listen to only one person in each unit walking around and making noise above me. Besides, I pay all the utility bills, and if there are more people living in these units, then obviously my monthly bills will be higher. These units have only one room other than the kitchen and bathroom, so I don't want any children living in them either, but according to your *Landlording* book that would be discriminating. Would I be discriminating if I told them they couldn't have children living with them since the child would not have a separate bedroom?

—G.H., Arkansas

A. You may limit your studios to two people but not to one, and you must definitely not advertise "no children" or "adults only."

You may, of course, rent to a single person.

You simply may not advertise that you will accept only a single person, and in the selection process, you may not discriminate against applicants who have two people living in their household.

You can, and you should, check out every application thoroughly, and you should ask the applicant's current and previous landlords about noise when you're checking the applications. If the people are noisy, don't rent to them. You may be discriminating about that.

He wants to exclude children without seeming to discriminate.

Q. Is there any way to advertise an apartment for rent and say "no children" without really showing that you are discriminating against them? If not, do you have any suggestions?
—K.F., Iowa

A. Do not even hint in your advertising that you want to exclude children. Like it or not, you must rent to people with children if they apply to rent from you and qualify. That's the law, and you must comply or face the expensive consequences.

Death in apartment scares off prospective tenants.

Q. A woman recently passed away in one of my apartments. She did not die of AIDS or of any deadly infectious disease, nor was she murdered. She died of natural causes. When I show the apartment and tell prospective tenants that someone died there, they suddenly lose all interest in it. I remember reading somewhere that I am supposed to tell prospective tenants if there was a death in an apartment they want to rent. Is this true? If so, is this rule set in stone or is it sort of a gray area? If someone moves into the unit and then later learns about the death and wishes to break their lease, what should I do?
—H.F., Iowa

A. This death in one of your apartments was entirely incidental to the property. It had nothing to do with the location of the apartment or with any dangerous condition there. You don't have to say anything about it unless you want to. Health and safety are not the concerns here. If they were, you should say something about the death and give details. The concern here really is superstition, and you have no obligation to awaken and assuage anybody's superstitions about the apartment and this death. Just because somebody happened to die in the apartment, that doesn't make it an apartment of death. Many people die in hospitals. That doesn't make them places of death. Death is altogether natural, and a death of natural causes in an ordinary, habitable apartment is nothing worth mentioning.

Should tenants occupying the apartment later learn that a death occurred prior to their occupancy and should they wish to move out as a result, let them break their lease and extend them every courtesy.

They wonder about disclosing baby's murder.

Q. We rented our condo to a young couple last year. The woman was a few months pregnant at the time. She had the baby, and four months later the baby died in the condo. We assumed that the baby died of Sudden Infant Death Syndrome (SIDS), but we just found out through reading the newspaper that the father beat the baby when he was alone with the child and it died as a result. The wife just gave us her 30-day notice to move. Now we are looking to rent out the condo. Must we disclose what we know about the child's death to prospective tenants?
—Z.D., California

A. Disclose what you know about the child's death if you want to. I wouldn't. After all, you know so little about what actually happened there from reading a newspaper article that whatever you'd disclose would likely be wrong anyway. You don't know the facts.

Even if you did know the facts, they're incidental to your condo. This kind of crime has nothing to do with this particular neighborhood or this particular condo. It's a crime of passion. It may have happened in your condo, but it means nothing as a predictor that a similar crime will occur there again.

Parents apply to rent apartment for disabled son.

Q. I am not naturally suspicious, but I am suspicious about a family who are applying to rent an apartment from me for their disabled son. They have told me that they are only trying to help their son, who has always lived with them, set up house on his own. The parents came to look at the apartment without the son. They liked it and returned the next day with a completed application. I told them that the son would have to see the apartment for himself and appear for an interview before I could rent to him, and I would need to check the references on the application.

They have been calling me every day to say that they definitely do want the apartment for their son and that they want me to approve him as soon as possible. Every time they call, I tell them that I have to meet their son and talk with him before I will approve him. You'd think that they would understand by now what they have to do to get the apartment. Produce their son, and let me see what he's like. They always have some excuse why their son is unavailable, and they have never told me what his disability is. I've asked them. They just say that he's disabled, whatever that means nowadays.

The last time they called, they mentioned "lawsuit." They accused me of giving them the runaround because their son is disabled. They said that they needed me to approve their son by the end of the week or they would go talk with the housing agency about my discriminating against him because he's disabled.

I'm not discriminating against anybody. I know better than that. I just want to see this son of theirs and check him out to see whether he fits my tenant standards. There's nothing wrong with that, is there?

What is wrong with these people? They want me to rent to their son without ever meeting him. I don't do that with anybody. I don't care whether he has two left hands and an eye in the middle of his head. I want to see him. I want to know the people I'm renting to. I want to look them in the eye, tell them what my rules are, and get an impression about whether they're going to be cooperative tenants or stinkers.

How do I know what kind of a disability this son of theirs has if they won't tell me? They might be saying that their son is disabled when he's got an alcohol problem and he's a devil-may-care biker. He could be a registered sex offender who just got out of prison. He could be a peeping Tom who likes to wander around the neighborhood at night in the nude. He could be a paraplegic who has a service animal and is the nicest person you'd ever meet. I don't know. I'd like to know so I can make a good decision. I owe it to the other tenants in my apartment building to find them good neighbors.

I don't like people being so secretive and then telling me that they're going to sue me if I don't dance to their tune. Something's fishy here. I don't know what it is, and I don't know what I ought to do about it. Any suggestions?
—D.R., Texas

A. You have reason to be suspicious. Any time somebody wants to rent an apartment for somebody else and keeps making excuses for the absence of the prospective tenant, you have to be suspicious. Horror stories abound in these circumstances.

For all you know, these parents may be telling you the truth. Then again, they may not be. Some well-meaning parents will go to great lengths to help their good-for-nothing children move along in life, forever hoping that the children will do right this time.

Because these people have mentioned the "L" word, you need to be extra careful and document every contact you have with them so you can prove to a third party you were not discriminating against a disabled person. Those who enforce our fair housing laws are tough on landlords who cannot prove that they were acting fairly in selecting tenants.

If you don't already have written standards for selecting tenants, now is the time to write them. Your standards must be legal and universally applied to everybody who applies to rent from you. For example, you could state in your standards that you rent only to non-smokers, only to people without pets, only to good credit risks with FICO scores above 620, only to those who have never been evicted, only to those who have a verifiable income exceeding $1,500 per month, and only to those who will submit to an interview in the place where they are currently living. Anybody who falls outside of those standards is automatically rejected.

In your case, you know nothing about this disabled son other than what the parents are willing to tell you, and that is nothing except that he's disabled. You haven't seen the son. You don't even know whether he is truly disabled or whether he is being touted as disabled by parents who want to shirk their responsibility for having created a monster they now want to get out of their house.

When they call the next time, tell the parents that you are continuing to look for tenants who meet your standards and that if they want their son to be considered for the apartment, they must set up an interview for him before somebody else comes along who qualifies to rent it, and you rent it to that person. The parents are the ones who need to move quickly, not you.

Be firm. Be patient. This, too, will pass.

Applicant's credit is much better than it once was.

Q. I am considering an applicant who is in her mid-20's and messed up her credit when she was a teenager. Since her irresponsible days, she tells me she has had credit counselling and is making all her payments on time. She has a letter of reference from her current landlord, to whom she has paid rent on time for the past two years. Also, her parents are willing to co-sign the lease. After verifying all of this information and her income, should I rent to her?
—M.N., Missouri

A. I would. She appears to be trying hard to overcome her youthful mistakes, but even so, don't you make the big mistake of failing to check her out carefully. She might be deluding herself and trying to delude you. Before renting to her, order up a current credit report on her, verify the information she provided about her landlord and her credit counselor, and then check out her parents.

Applicant asks about aerobics exercise.

Q. I was all set to rent a room in my house to a young woman, but then she asked if she could exercise while playing her aerobics videos in her upstairs bedroom. Originally I said yes, but people have been telling me that jumping up and down could cause cracks in the downstairs walls of my house. Do you know anything about this? Is it okay for me to tell this young woman that I've changed my mind about her exercising to aerobics videos in my house?
—J.B., Louisiana

A. Rent to this girl. Your house is built to take much, much more impact than whatever she can create while exercising to her aerobics videos, that is, unless she is big enough to qualify as the fat lady in a circus.

More important, though, is her approach to you. She asked you in advance whether you would object to her exercising. Most tenants wouldn't bother bringing up the subject before they move in. She should turn out to be a good tenant.

They want definition of "overnight stay."

Q. There is a nice, responsible single woman renting the first floor apartment in my duplex. She has been there almost five years. In all that time, she has given me no trouble, and she always gives me her rent check on the first of the month. Because she is such a good tenant and only a single person, I have been renting to her on a month-to-month basis at an extremely reasonable rent.

Last summer she met a guy who has been visiting her constantly ever since. I know only his first name and have never been formally introduced to him. He is not the quiet, silent type. He slams doors and flicks cigarette butts all over the front yard. He is never there when she is not, so I suspect that she hasn't given him a key, at least not yet, but he's there so much that he might as well have moved in with her.

Her rental agreement states that she alone may occupy the apartment. That's what I wanted, and that's what we agreed upon. The agreement doesn't say anything about guests.

Because of this thoughtless guy she has let into her life and her apartment, I'd like to raise her rent and add a clause to her rental agreement limiting overnight guest stays. I've been advised that I have a legal right to do so.

What is the definition of an "overnight stay," and how do I legally write this into the agreement?
—B.T., Massachusetts

A. There is no legal definition for "overnight stay." You might come up with your own definition to put in your agreement if you feel you must, but any definition would invite trouble.

Let's say that you base your definition upon one or more of the following conditions—whether a guest stayed on the premises ten or more hours during a 24-hour day, whether a guest stayed on the premises four or more hours between 11 p.m. and 7 a.m., whether a guest was on the premises at three o'clock in the morning, whether a guest ate two meals a day on the premises, or whether a guest kept three changes of clothes on the premises and bathed there.

These definitions aren't bad, but they aren't good either. They invite trouble because they're too precise and hence too easy to circumvent. The tenant and guest might decide to circumvent the first one by making sure that the guest stayed only nine and a half hours during a 24-hour day. What would you do then, change your definition to nine hours in a 24-hour day?

Circumvention is only one of the troubles you face when you define "overnight stay" precisely. Measurement is another. No matter what your definition says, its measurement must rely upon the honesty of your tenant to determine whether a particular visit constitutes an overnight stay within the definition. You can't very well stop by the duplex every morning to check whether a guest stayed there overnight according to your definition. You have to rely upon the tenant to make that determination, and you will always be wondering whether the tenant is making the correct determination, especially if she will suffer adverse consequences as a result.

Rather than puzzle over the definition of "overnight stay" right now, go talk to the tenant about your concerns. She has shown herself to be responsible as a tenant even if she hasn't shown herself to be discriminating in her choice of boyfriends. Tell her what your concerns are and find out what her intentions are. You may find that she doesn't have a clue how concerned you are about her boyfriend. You may even find that she's been looking for an excuse to get rid of the guy, and she may relish the thought of using you as her excuse.

If she wants to continue allowing this guy to stay with her, tell her that you want her to stop him from slamming doors and flicking cigarette butts. That behavior bothers you. Tell her that you will shortly give her a written 30-day notice of change in terms of tenancy, changing her rent to market and limiting any one guest's overnight stays to fourteen every six months. Then go home, draft the notice, and give it to her within a day or two. Don't define "overnight stay" in your notice. Say something like this, "Tenants may share their home with any single guest for a maximum period of fourteen days every six months or for whatever period of time the law allows." Trust her to determine what constitutes a guest day, and trust her to tally them. She'll be fair.

Upon giving proper notice, you have a legal right to change a month-to-month agreement. Go ahead and change the agreement so that it reflects your position and so that you can stop being frustrated by this inconsiderate guy who has all but moved in with your model tenant.

She wants to add 18-year-old son to mother's rental agreement.

Q. I rent an apartment to an adult woman and her high-school-aged son. When they moved in two years ago, she signed the rental agreement. When the son turns eighteen, should I have him sign a rental agreement, too? I really don't expect her to move and leave him behind, but I'd feel like an idiot if that were to happen and I didn't "cover my bases."
—D.W., Kentucky

A. Whether the son signs a rental agreement or not, he'd still be bound by the agreement which his mother signed if she moved and he stayed. I wouldn't bother getting him to sign an agreement when he turns eighteen, so long as he and his mother continue living there together, but I would get him to sign an agreement if he became the sole tenant.

Getting him to sign a rental agreement while he's still living there with his mother just puts them on edge, and it doesn't do you any good. Getting him to sign an agreement if she does move out, however, makes him understand that you expect him to be more responsible.

Tenants want month-to-month tenancy after lease expires.

Q. I have good tenants who have paid their rent on time pretty consistently for almost a year now. Their lease is expiring, and they want to continue as tenants on a month-to-month basis. They like the house they're renting from me and do not want to leave it. When they are ready to leave, they say they will give me a thirty-day written notice. They say they do not know what is going to happen in the future and cannot commit to a twelve-month or even a six-month lease.

The property is a three-hour drive for me. Going there to do all the work I'd need to do to prepare it for another renter would be tough for me right now. I'm inclined to let them stay there without a lease.

Should I let them become month-to-month tenants? If I do, do we need to sign a new agreement or an addendum? Can I increase their rent, and if so, how would I determine how much to increase it?
—T.J., Arizona

A. Lacking any wording in a lease to the contrary, when a lease ends, it automatically becomes a month-to-month agreement if you accept rent beyond the end of the lease period. Typically, leases include wording something like this: "Upon expiration, this fixed-term agreement shall become a month-to-month agreement automatically, unless either tenants or owners notify the other party in writing at least thirty days prior to expiration that they do not wish the agreement to continue on any basis."

A lease doesn't have to include any wording about its becoming a month-to-month agreement automatically. The wording merely clarifies the circumstances. What triggers the transformation of a lease from a fixed-term agreement to a month-to-month agreement is the acceptance of rent. If you don't accept any rent beyond the end of the agreement, then it doesn't become a month-to-month agreement, and you should be ready to deal with a vacancy or with tenants who have an agenda different from yours.

If you want the tenants to stay on a month-to-month basis, and you don't mind their staying under the same terms as their original lease, then accept rent from them. You don't need to draw up a new agreement or even an addendum. Everything other than the lease period remains the same.

Once tenants are on a month-to-month basis, you may increase their rent at any time with proper notice, generally thirty days, although some states now require sixty days for long-term tenants who have lived in a dwelling for a year or longer.

To find out how much to increase the rent, check the local newspaper's classified ads for similar houses in a similar neighborhood. Call the phone numbers in the ads and ask questions landlord to landlord.

Once you know how much rent you could charge if the house were vacant, come up with a rent which fits the good tenants who currently occupy the house, one which will make them feel they dodged a bullet rather than got hit in the heart. Keep the increase close to the annual cost of living increase in the area, and you'll have happy tenants.

In my experience, a landlord is almost always better off keeping good tenants as long as possible, lease or no lease.

You have the opportunity to keep good tenants who will save you from having to make a long trip, from having to prepare the property for rent to new tenants, from having to advertise the property for rent, from having to interview and check applicants, and from having to risk that your new tenant selection will be a deadbeat and cause you grief.

Keep these good tenants of yours.

Subletting tenant wants to stay.

Q. I rented a 2-bedroom semi-detached home to a couple. The basement was previously a separate bachelor apartment with a separate entrance. When I rented the house to this couple, they stated that their intention was to rent the basement to their sister. They did, but after six months the sister left, and they re-rented the apartment to someone else. The couple have experienced marital difficulties and have given notice that they are vacating. However, the basement tenant has refused to leave. What obligation do I as the owner have to the basement tenant? I have no lease, no post-dated checks, and I have never received rental payments of any kind from him directly. Currently, I understand that what he paid to the couple for rent was $150 under market value. What can I do to get this guy out?
—K.J., Ontario, Canada

A. I cannot tell you exactly what you CAN do in Ontario, Canada. I can tell you only what I WOULD do were I facing a similar situation here in the States.

I would take a very practical approach to keeping the guy and making him a tenant of mine. I wouldn't try to force my departing tenants to deal with the subtenant. Were push to come to shove and involve a legal case, you know that you as the owner would ultimately be held responsible for the subtenant, but even if you weren't, you know that you wouldn't be able to force your tenants to be financially responsible for the subtenant because they are unlikely to have sufficient assets.

First, determine exactly what value the rental market places on the bachelor apartment. Then, draw up a rental agreement reflecting the terms explained below. Next, visit the subtenant and tell him that you want to make him legitimate. You want to give him a proper rental agreement with you, the owner of the property, as his landlord. Tell him that you have looked around at other similar properties and have determined that the market rent for his bachelor apartment is XX. Tell him that you will give him two months at his old rent to look around himself and determine whether what you have found to be a fair market rent is, in fact, correct. If he thinks it's too high, he may move out. If he thinks it's fair and he wants to stay on as a tenant, he has that option. Whatever he decides to do, he should complete a tenant information form (see *Landlording* book) and sign a rental agreement with you (you should have one with you when you visit him, and it should reflect exactly what you are telling him).

If he's unreasonable about your terms or if you don't want him to stay, you may always give him written notice that you want him to leave and then evict him through your courts if necessary. You don't need a written agreement with someone in order to evict him. You do need to prove that you own the property, and you do need to give the tenant proper notice.

By the way, yours is a situation which illustrates perfectly why you should have a rental agreement prohibiting subletting. Because you allowed subletting, you were left with a rental unit occupied by somebody who had never had anything to do with you before. You own the property. You must have control of the property. You cannot have control of the property if you allow your tenants to act as landlords for others.

Husband and bimbo remain after wife and kids move.

Q. When my tenants moved in, they were a nice family of four, but now the wife and kids have moved out, and the husband is living there with some bimbo. What should I do?
—P.W., California

A. Separated spouses and bimbos can make good tenants, too, even though you didn't rent to them originally.

As soon as you determine that there has been a change in the tenants occupying your rental, approach the primary tenant and ask that the new tenants complete a rental application (one for each adult). Then put everybody on a new rental agreement and get it signed.

Husband's income alone isn't enough to pay the rent.

Q. I rented a three-bedroom house to a nice couple on the basis of their combined incomes. The wife has now left, and the husband is living there alone. Based on his income alone, he can-

not afford the house. How do I renegotiate the lease which the two of them signed as equals, and how do I handle the security deposit?
—D.S., Illinois

A. In your situation, you MUST pay the husband a visit and ask him what he's planning to do. Tell him you know that he cannot afford the rent on the house all by himself, and you don't want his continued tenancy to lead to an eviction for nonpayment of rent. That would be terrible for his credit.

Tell him that you sympathize with him in his changed circumstances, and you want to help. Tell him that you will either help him find another place to live, or you will help him accommodate a roommate (see the roommate agreement in the current *Landlording* book and the information there about dealing with roommates).

As for the security deposit which the two of them put up when they rented the house, tell him that half of the deposit belongs to the spouse who moved out, and you cannot return all of it to him upon his moving out unless he can come up with a verifiable agreement signed by the spouse waiving all rights to it. Without an agreement, it belongs to the two of them, fifty-fifty. Also, tell him that you will not return any of the deposit so long as he continues to occupy the house.

Tenant is conducting business in her apartment.

Q. I'm a novice landlord in New York City and have a tenant who is conducting business in her apartment even though the rental agreement clearly states that the residence is to be used as living quarters only. The tenant acts as a consultant and doesn't disturb my other tenants, but I'm not sure if I will get into trouble if something happens to one of her clients on my property. Is this a breach of contract on her part? The lease is for one year in a subsidized multi-unit building. Should I just leave the tenant alone?
—J.W., New York

A. With more and more people working out of their homes, the distinction between living quarters and working quarters is becoming fuzzier every day, and you'd be hard pressed to evict your tenant for violating the lease just because she is working at home as a consultant and seeing a client there now and then.

Although she is in technical violation of the lease, she isn't causing you, the other tenants, or the building any problems. Leave her alone.

When you next revise your lease, consider changing the clause prohibiting all business activities. Give yourself some wiggle room so that you can approve innocuous business activities and deny all others. Consider using a clause something like this: "Before the tenant can engage in any business activities on the premises, the landlord must approve those business activities. The landlord shall be the sole arbiter in determining whether any business activities will be allowed, and then the landlord must give approval in writing. In general, businesses likely to cause noise problems, parking problems, traffic problems, or building problems will be denied, as will unlawful businesses. The landlord's approval of a particular business activity for a particular tenant may be withdrawn at any time upon five days' notice when the landlord determines that the conduct of an approved business activity is causing problems."

Late fees become issue for tenants behind in their rent.

Q. I have a couple who are behind in their rent. The question I have is whether I ought to charge them for being late on their current rent payments and also charge them a penalty for the past due amounts? Right now they are trying to catch up, but they don't think they should pay the added late fee since they are paying the current month on time, along with payments on the past due amount.

They also have stated that they believe it is not legal for me to charge them all the extra late fees and that it may not be legal for me to treat their current month's payment as merely their past due amount. They think that it is called "revolving credit with late fees that can be considered interest payments" or something like that, and that I am supposed to be licensed as a financial institution in order to charge them interest. Is this true?

—J.D., Washington

A. If your tenants are honestly trying to become current on their rent payments, I would try to help them out by not piling on the late penalties even if their rental agreement entitles you to extra penalties. Charge the tenants the one late penalty which you assessed them when they first became late, and don't charge them any more beyond that.

Remember, though, that you should always post their payments first to the past-due amounts and then to the current rent. Posting their payments the other way around tends to confuse judges into thinking that the tenants are current in their rent payments.

Remember also that you want to be reasonable rather than greedy. Your business is renting out places to live. Your business is not gathering all the late fees you can gather.

Refrigerator disappears.

Q. We have rented our condo here in southern California to an unmarried couple for almost a year and a half. The rental agreement includes a washer, dryer, and refrigerator. During an annual inspection of the property a few months ago, I learned that the tenant was using his own refrigerator and did not need mine. He said it was stored in the garage. I let him know that I may want to collect the refrigerator from him since he had no need for it.

Two weeks later I contacted the tenant to arrange for pickup of the refrigerator. He said an emergency came up and he needed the garage for other storage. He said he moved the refrigerator to a storage unit about sixty miles south of the condo. I asked him to return it, and he said he would bring it to our residence. He has yet to return it although we made the arrangements twice. During one attempt, he asked whether I would like to sell it. I refused. I sent a letter to the tenants two weeks ago informing them that they must return the refrigerator to the condo or to our residence within fifteen days or we would consider it stolen and report it as such. I still have not heard from the tenants about it. The refrigerator is worth somewhere between $400 and $500.

Is this considered stealing property? Should I report it to the police? What should I do or can I do next?

—N.A., California

A. Like it or not, you are in a business which can't always be run by the book. You have made various attempts to retrieve your refrigerator without success, and you could continue with more attempts to retrieve it, but if you do, you should expect more frustration.

More than likely, the tenant has let somebody else use the refrigerator or has actually sold it.

Don't expect any help from the police. Your situation is akin to somebody's owing you money rather than their having stolen your belongings. It's a civil matter rather than a criminal matter.

At this point, I would take the tenant up on his offer to buy the refrigerator from you. Tell him you want $500 (the high range of your estimate of its value) for it, and see what happens. If he doesn't pay up, then I would take him to small claims court.

She disappears, and they want to collect what she owes.

Q. My wife and I rented a condo to a young widow on a year's lease. The lease states that she is responsible for all rents and expenses if she breaks the lease and moves.

After just three weeks, she called and told us that the nursing home where she was working was "losing money," and she was moving to California (we're in Ohio). She stated that she would pay the next month's rent and all of our advertising bills, so we could find a new tenant.

When the next month's rent came due, she paid us for three weeks, saying she was "short of money" because of the move and couldn't pay us the full amount. I called and asked her to meet me to discuss the situation, and she stood me up. I then taped a letter on her door, along with a copy of several advertising bills, and asked her to pay the next month's rent and the bills. She paid the rest of the month's rent but nothing for the advertising.

She moved out a week earlier than planned and gave us her sister's address in Toledo as a temporary forwarding address. She said she would send us a forwarding address in California as soon as she got one. This was three weeks ago, and we haven't heard a peep out of her since.

Her lease states that she is responsible for the entire year's rent if the condo remains vacant, and it's still vacant. She now owes another month's rent, electric bills to the end of the month, and the advertising bills she never paid. I applied her security deposit to what she owes, and she still owes us $750.

My question is this: How far should I go to pursue her? I suspect that we will never hear from her again, although her credit was good when we checked it, and her previous landlord indi-

cated she was a good tenant. We called her job and learned that there was no emergency. Her move was totally voluntary. How should I proceed? All I have is an address in Toledo, where her mail is being forwarded. Should I initiate a court case if the rent continues for a few more months and the amount owed escalates to several thousand dollars?
—R.M., Ohio

A. If you want to go to all the trouble of pursuing your departed tenant, go ahead, but I can assure you that it will be an exercise in futility. You won't get another dime out of her.

Put all your efforts into preparing the condo so that it will attract a new tenant. Then find that new tenant and get on with your life.

You have just learned the lesson that leases don't mean much to tenants. You might think that tenants are tied down by a lease. They are only if they want to be.

Tenant wants landlord to reimburse him for redecorating.

Q. I'm a happy landlord with great tenants who never give me any trouble, but I must admit that I have one tenant who has given me pause for thought. He has redone his apartment with my permission and has done a good job of it. For some reason, he thinks that when he moves out, I ought to reimburse him for his alterations and improvements.

I have always been under the impression that if a tenant changes a ceiling light fixture or adds closet shelving or replaces a towel rack or anything else attached to the walls, floors, ceilings, or cabinetry that it automatically becomes the property of the owner and that the owner does not have to pay the tenant for these things.

I have looked everywhere and cannot find an answer. Can you tell me?

I'd also like to know who is responsible for replacing burned out light bulbs, who is responsible for replacing a malfunctioning kitchen light fixture, and who is responsible for replacing a broken toilet seat which has seen five years of duty. Is the tenant responsible or the landlord?
—S.D, Maine

A. You have a tenant who wants to put his own stamp on his home. Lucky you! Such tenants are to be prized because they tend to stay longer than tenants who do nothing but hang a few pictures on the walls.

Good as this tenant is for you, he is still obligated to return the dwelling to you in the same condition it was in when he took possession, minus ordinary wear and tear. That's the law.

If a tenant alters a property in such a way that the alteration cannot be removed without damaging the property, then the alteration must remain when the tenant vacates, and the landlord is not obligated to pay for it unless he agreed in advance to pay for it.

If a tenant alters a property in such a way that the alteration can be removed without damaging the property, then the tenant may remove the alteration provided that he restores the property to its original condition.

Let's say that your tenant replaces an ordinary light fixture with an extraordinary fixture. He replaces the thirty-dollar ceiling fixture you installed in the dining room with the twelve thousand-dollar Baccarat chandelier he inherited from his mother. When he vacates, the tenant does not have to leave his extraordinary fixture behind so long as he puts the ordinary fixture back where it was and leaves no trace of the swap for you to deal with.

Let's say that your tenant installs a closet organizer which costs him three hundred dollars. It's screwed to the walls in dozens of places, and he doesn't want to remove it when he vacates. He considers it an improvement, and he wants you to pay him for it when he vacates. You may consider it an improvement, too, but you don't have to pay him for it. If he wants to leave it behind when he vacates, he may, and you owe him nothing unless you want to pay him something for it. If he wants to take it with him, he may, but he'll have to restore the closet to the same condition it was in before he installed the organizer. He'll have to patch the dozens of holes he put in the walls after he removes it, and he'll have to paint the patched walls as well.

When your tenant-decorator ultimately vacates, you may want to negotiate with him about leaving certain alterations and removing others. You may want to offer to pay him something for those alterations which will help you command more rent from the next tenant. After all, whether you like his alterations or not, they have no value to you unless they can help you attract a new tenant who values them enough to pay more in rent because of them or unless they add to the useful life of whatever the tenant "improved."

Your tenant is thinking "redecoration" and "compensation." You should be thinking "restoration" and "value."

As for who's responsible for replacing burned-out light bulbs, who's responsible for replacing a malfunctioning kitchen light fixture, and who's responsible for replacing a broken toilet seat, those questions revolve around each item's useful life. Light bulbs have short useful lives. They're consumables. You provide working light bulbs in all the fixtures when the tenant moves in, and the tenant replaces them as needed during his tenancy. He is supposed to leave working light bulbs in all the fixtures when he vacates, or he pays for replacements out of his deposit.

Light fixtures and toilet seats, on the other hand, are not consumables. They have long useful lives or should have. When they malfunction or break during ordinary usage, you are responsible for replacing them. When they malfunction or break because the tenant is abusing them, the tenant is responsible for replacing them.

If a tenant reports that his kitchen light fixture is malfunctioning, fix or change it immediately at no cost to the tenant. You don't want it to short out and cause a fire. If he calls you a week later to report that it's malfunctioning again, find out why. He may be tampering with it or abusing it. If he is, charge him. He has shortened the useful life of the fixture.

If a tenant reports that his toilet seat has broken after five years of service, fix or replace it at your expense. That toilet seat's useful life is spent. If a tenant reports that his toilet seat has broken after six months of service, determine whether it broke because it was poorly made or because the tenant abused it. If it was poorly made, replace it with a better one and apologize to the tenant for the inconvenience. If the tenant abused it, charge him for the replacement.

Good tenants such as yours will listen to your explanations and come to understand your point of view.

He feels hard-hearted for displacing long-term tenant.

Q. We have a tenant who has been with us for eight years. Although she hasn't maintained the property very well, she has been a good tenant overall, and we have kept her rent low in return.

We now find that we need the house for a fam-

ily member to occupy and we must ask her to vacate. We can give her two months' notice and will help her in any way we can, but we're feeling hard-hearted nonetheless. Do you have any advice for us? Is there a form we should use to advise her of our intentions?
—F.W., California

A. Unless the property is in a rent-controlled area, in which case you will need to consult the rent-control laws about terminating a tenancy to make room for a family member, you need to give this tenant only a standard notice to terminate tenancy. Since she has lived there for longer than a year, California requires that you give her a 60-day notice. That's a generous amount of time in any case, and you're generous in agreeing to help her in any way you can.

You needn't feel hard-hearted. You're not. Besides, you've been giving her below-market rent for eight years. Consider how that has benefitted her. At $25 per month for 96 months, that's $2,400! You're mighty generous to be giving that kind of money to any tenant!

Were the shoe on the other foot, that is, were the tenant giving you a notice of intention to vacate, do you think she would feel she were being hard-hearted in moving out and leaving you with an empty house? She wouldn't.

Fill out a notice for termination of tenancy, give it to her in person, tell her you're sorry about needing the house for a relative, and tell her that you'll do what you can to help her relocate. Be specific about what you're prepared to do. Are you prepared to call around to other landlords for her? Are you prepared to pay for a van? Are you prepared to help her move her stuff? Are you prepared to pay for self-storage for a few months?

Be sympathetic with the tenant, help her if you must to ease your conscience, but proceed with the business at hand. You need the house for the family member, and you're entitled to it. Don't let the tenant or your feelings of guilt stand in your way.

They want to cheat landlords when they move.

Q. We gave our tenants notice telling them that we were not going to renew their lease at the end of the latest term. They in turn sent us notice of their intention to move at the end of the lease term. Their lease is up on the 28th of the month. The monthly rent is $700. They moved

in three years ago on the 29th of the month and gave us a check that day for $700. Since then, they have paid their rent on the first of every month. In their letter, they informed us that they were going to "prorate" their last month's rent ($700 divided by 31 days = $22.58 x 28 days = $632.24). Their rental agreement clearly states that they are required to make monthly payments of $700 beginning on the 29th. We weren't picky about not charging them for three days at the front end of the lease. Can we now charge them for those three days? Ordinarily we wouldn't make a big deal out of this, but they have been horrible tenants. We bent over backwards to help them out on many occasions and bit our tongues on many more occasions just to keep peace.

Also, in regard to the final water bill, the water company is charging a $10 certification fee for the final water reading. Can I bill the tenants for this fee?
—C.C., Pennsylvania

A. Write the tenants a note informing them that their rental period has always been from the 29th day of every month through the 28th day of every month. It has never been from the first day of the month through the last day of the month because they never paid a rent proration for the last three days of the month when they moved in.

If they had paid a month's rent when they moved in plus a sum to cover three days' rent, then their rental period would have been from the first through the last day of every month. Since they never paid for those three days when they moved in, they cannot deduct them from their rent payment when they move out. Tell them that if they wish to hold over for some additional days, then you will charge them $22.58 for each day they hold over.

As for the water certification fee, you should charge them for it so long as you have been paying the water bills on their behalf and then charging them a like amount. It's a pass-through charge.

These move-out misunderstandings are two good reasons why you need to charge tenants a deposit before they move in. When they move out, you are in a position to deduct such things from their deposit. A security deposit may be used to pay for damages, cleaning, rent, or anything else associated with the tenancy which the tenants owe you when they move out.

Condo tenants won't cooperate with owner who wants to sell.

Q. After putting our condo up for sale and notifying the tenants who live there that we are selling, we discovered that one of the tenants was telling a lie to prospective buyers when they walked through. He was informing them that we cannot evict him because he's disabled.

The condo has been on the market for a month now. According to the condo association secretary, it would have sold within three days if this tenant hadn't been scaring buyers away.

My husband recently had a talk with the tenant and told him that if he continued telling this lie, he would get a notice to vacate. My husband also notified the real estate agent that he wants to come along the next time the agent shows the property.

I have three questions. What can we do to expedite the eviction of these tenants? Would the fact that the one tenant is disabled cause any eviction delay? Can we as owners give the tenants a three-day notice advising them that we want to inspect the condo inside and out due to the pending sale?
—A.G., California

A. Unless there's an emergency or you have the tenants' permission, you must give them at least twenty-four hours' notice that you plan to enter. The notice may be verbal, but it should be written if you and the tenants aren't on speaking terms. It should be as specific as you can make it, that is, it should specify who's going to enter, when, and why.

As for evicting the tenants, you might want to consider "greasing their palms" with a promise of at least a hundred dollars for their cooperation during the showing of the place. You have already learned that you need their cooperation or their absence if you're going to find a buyer. Once you find a buyer and consummate the sale, you definitely need their absence. Whatever you promise to pay them is money well spent. Most of all, it's payment for the inconvenience of having strangers parade through their home, but it's also payment for their assistance in facilitating the sale.

Remember this: Cooperative tenants who agree to keep the place looking good and agree to say a few good words about the building and the neighborhood can make the sale happen more quickly and get you more money for the property.

Of course, you may evict the tenants if you prefer. Everything may go smoothly, and than again it may not. They could try to make a case revolving around the husband's disability and could run up your legal bills, but they'd lose eventually. A disability has nothing to do with an eviction unless it involves discrimination, and that's not an issue here. What you could lose by evicting them would be time, aggravation, and money. In addition, once you'd evicted the tenants, you'd have to spend the money to clean, paint, and repair the vacant unit so that it would show well.

All in all, I'd say that "greasing their palms" in exchange for their cooperation would serve you better than strong-arming them to vacate.

He wants to use one checking account for two rental properties.

Q. I feel like a proud father for the second time. I have just purchased a second multi-family rental property after having had the first one for about a year and a half. I love this landlording business, but I do have a question.

My first rental property has an established name, and my checking account uses that property's name. I would like to know whether I should come up with another name for my second rental property or should I just carry the name from the first property over to it? I realize that I need to keep separate records for each property's income and expenses, but I really don't want to open another checking account for the second property.
—B.S., Maine

A. Don't open another checking account for the second property. Use the same account for both properties. When you next run out of checks, have them imprinted with a name which reflects your combined rental property operations. Your surname with the word "properties" after it is one good possibility.

Mark every deposit and every check with some identifier so you can keep the monies separate for each property within the one checking account. Your computer check-writing program will then be able to create income and expense reports which combine or separate the properties, according to your direction.

The name you use for your checking account and the names you use for your properties are different matters, and you should know how they are different.

The name you use for your checking account is a simple bookkeeping identifier which has no legal standing. You could use one account for any number of properties, even those which have registered fictitious names. The bank doesn't care how the account is identified, but it does care whether you are legally entitled to deposit checks made out to the various entities listed for that account. The entities could be one or more of the following: yourself, that is, your own name; a business name which has your own name in it, as in "[Your Surname] Properties" (needn't be registered as a fictitious name); or a business name which does not have your own name in it (must be registered as a fictitious name).

If you own one rental property with thirty units called "Palms Apartments" and you own another property with twenty units called "Sunset Manor Apartments" and you want to use those names on your rental documents, you should register them as your fictitious business names. Your tenants could then make their rent checks payable to those names, and you could deposit the checks into one account set up to receive checks in both of those names.

If you have two properties with well established names, but you don't want to use their names on your rental documents, you need not register them as your fictitious business names. You could use "[Your Surname] Properties" instead, and you could have your tenants make their checks out to that name.

You do have some choices.

Whatever you do, do not use a fictitious name on your rental documents and require your tenants to make their checks out to that same fictitious name without first filing a fictitious name statement. Without having filed a fictitious name statement, you could run afoul of the bank should somebody else start using that same fictitious name you've been using. What's more, you could lose whatever legal action you file against your tenants merely because you failed to file the statement.

They want to write off big travel expenses for little rental property.

Q. My husband and I are planning to rent out a small trailer located on some country property we own. The monthly rent will be low, probably less than $200 a month. Can we deduct the cost of trips to visit the property, which is 175 miles from our home, to the point where the cost of the trips might exceed the rental income? In other words, for tax purposes, do we have to show a profit or can our "rental expenses" exceed our "rental income?"
—J.R., Washington

A. Rental property does not have to show a profit on one's tax return. Because of depreciation tax write-offs, some properties never show a profit. Nonetheless, you should be cautious about attributing travel expenses to rental property ownership when you are dealing with a small property which is quite a distance from your home.

I would not write off more than two trips a year to the property even if I had to make more. You should easily be able to justify expenses for two trips. Under no circumstances would I run up the expenses for trips to the property. I would keep very good records of my expenses just as if I knew for sure that I were going to be audited every year.

Whatever you do, don't let this little rental sideline jeopardize the integrity of the rest of your tax return.

Landlord wants to start business providing services for landlords.

Q. I've been a landlord for thirteen years and am thinking about starting a business on the side to provide services to landlords. I'm thinking about services like typing legal paperwork for evictions, bookkeeping, screening tenants, and arranging for maintenance work. What do you think about this idea? Is there anything I should watch out for?
—R.C., Idaho

A. Lucky you to have time on your hands after having been a landlord for thirteen years! Personally, I'd rather buy more rental property to keep me busy than start a business providing services to other landlords. There's more money in the landlording business than there is in providing services to landlords.

If you do start such a business, be mindful of your state's licensing laws. They may require you to have a special license to offer managerial and secretarial services to the public.

Remember that some people in the landlording business are notoriously cheap. They don't want to pay for anything. Charge enough for your services and get as much payment up-front as you can. You might want to give your clients a choice of whether to pay you by the job or by the hour.

Referral service takes fee up-front.

Q. We used a rental referral service to obtain a tenant. Their fee was half of one month's rent. When we agreed to accept a particular tenant, they took a money deposit from him and then mailed us a check with their fee already deducted. My spouse and I disagree on how the service took their fee. He feels that they should have sent us a check for the full amount and then waited for us to mail them our check. I told him that the way they did it is normal. Is their procedure normal or is my husband correct?

—M.K., California

A. The next time you use any rental referral service, ask them in advance how they expect you to pay them when they find you an acceptable tenant, and you will avoid any surprises or family disagreements.

The company you used resorted to the most common collection method used by anybody who provides a service for a fee. They deducted it from the money they received on your behalf and then paid you the balance. Attorneys, collection agencies, and real estate agents all collect their fees in pretty much this same way because they can't trust their clients to pay in a timely manner.

Management company quits business, keeps owner's funds.

Q. About a year ago I hired a property management company to manage my one and only rental house. Last month they found a new tenant to replace a tenant who moved out. They received a security deposit and the first month's rent from this new tenant and have given me none of it. They also have a $200 petty-cash repair fund and some rent money from the previous tenant. A week ago I received a letter from the company saying that they were quitting the property management business. Upon receiving their letter, I made several phone calls and sent several letters asking them to settle their accounts with me, but they have yet to do so. The tenant they selected sent me a check for this month's rent, but it bounced. He has said that he will replace the check with a money order. Today is the fifth day since we talked on the phone, and I still have not received his money order. What should I do?

—P.D., Vermont

A. Your situation calls for drastic action.

Make personal visits to both the property management company and to the tenant. Tell each of them in no uncertain terms that you are not leaving until they pay you all or most of the money they owe you.

Find out whether there is a government agency responsible for licensing and controlling property management companies in your area. If there is one, tell the property management company that you are going to "turn them in." If there isn't one, tell the property management company that you are going to take them to small claims court to force them to settle up unless they pay you NOW!

Give the tenant a "Notice to Pay Rent or Quit" TODAY unless he pays you all that he owes you.

Owners want to replace their property manager.

Q. We hired a property manager to look after our rental house, and we are thinking about replacing her because she doesn't communicate well with us. She has all the keys to the house. She also holds the tenants' security deposit and the money we keep for emergencies. Do you have any recommendations for how we might go about replacing this property manager?

—A.J., California

A. In California, professional property managers must be licensed real estate agents. They tend to take their fiduciary responsibility seriously when handling other people's money, but they don't make enough money from managing one rental house to pay close attention to the other management responsibilities involved. They prefer to list and sell properties. That's how they make their money.

Your property manager would likely rejoice if you replaced her. She sounds as if she has neither enough interest nor enough commitment to do a good job for you. Don't worry about getting the keys and the monies from her. She'll turn them over to you when you ask for them.

Finding a good property manager to look after one rental house, on the other hand, is something to worry about. Because it's chancy, take few chances as you search for the right one.

Your search might include any or all of the following:

1) Contacting the local rental property owners association and asking them for a list of their members who manage rental properties for others;

2) Checking the Yellow Pages under "Real Estate Management";

3) Using an internet search engine to find the property management companies in the area where your rental house is located; and

4) Calling telephone numbers in the classified ads for rental houses and asking for help in finding a property manager who manages rental houses for others.

You'll want to check their references, of course, and you'll want to meet them in person to compare their attitudes, their services, their contracts, and their charges.

If you can't find the right manager or if you'd like to try another approach to managing that rental house of yours, consider this alternative. Separate the job into two parts. Do the off-site management yourself, that is, things like checking the applications, collecting the rent, keeping the books, writing the checks, fielding the tenant calls, and coordinating the repair work. Pick a neighbor who lives near the house and seems to be concerned about the neighborhood to do the on-site management. Pay that neighbor by the hour to do things like showing the house to prospective tenants, eyeballing the property for potential problems, handling minor maintenance requests, overseeing repair work, and maintaining the yard.

There are some things you just can't do if you live miles away from your rental house, but there are many things you can do no matter where you happen to live. Consider doing those things yourself and hiring the others out.

Involving yourself in the management of your rental house affects the tenants' attitude toward the property. They know that the owner cares about it and will treat it better themselves.

Owner must move far away from duplex but still wants to keep it.

Q. We own a duplex and live in half of it. Due to a job transfer we will be leaving the state soon, but we would like to keep the duplex until there is no longer a prepayment penalty on our loan.

We have three questions:

1) What is the average percentage property management companies charge?

2) Does it make any sense to go this route (as opposed to selling and swallowing the penalty) since after paying the management fee and the other expenses, we will actually be losing $100-$200 a month?

3) What should we be looking for in a property management company?
—S.B., Kentucky

A. A property management company generally charges fees ranging from 3-10% of the gross. The higher figure applies to houses and duplexes. The lower figure applies to large complexes.

Your decision to keep or sell the property depends upon how large the prepayment penalty is, how long you'd have to keep property to avoid the penalty, how much negative cash flow you'd be enduring, and whether the property is appreciating.

Rather than hiring a property management company, consider approaching the people who live in the other half of the duplex, or else the next-door neighbors, whether they would be interested in looking after the property. They would have a greater interest in the property than would a rental property management company. That interest and some good common sense would go a long ways toward their managing the property well for you.

Insurer wants premiums but will not pay another claim for 3 years.

Q. After a break-in and a rather spectacular vandalization of our property, we filed a claim with our insurance company. They responded quickly and were easy to work with, but they told us that we couldn't file another claim with them on any of our properties for three years. That being the case, would it make sense for us to insure each of our properties with a different company should we have the misfortune to have to file more claims in a short time?
—D.C., North Carolina

A. Why should you pay the premium for any insurance which won't pay off when you have a claim? Start shopping for other insurance immediately and be frank about why you're shopping. Tell the insurance agents that you want coverage which won't stop for a minute should you have a claim. Avoid placing your insurance with different companies unless they all tell you the same story about time restrictions following claims. Insuring all of your properties with the same company entitles you to better rates and simplifies your business.

They disagree about charging for his labor.

Q. My wife and I have been landlording together for years. We agree on almost everything, but we have come to a disagreement about something and would like you to help us settle it.

If tenants move out and leave behind minor damage as well as a cleanup job and if I go in and clean and repair the unit myself, can we deduct my labor from their deposit along with supplies and parts?

My wife says, "No, we can't deduct anything for my labor. We can deduct only our actual expenses and nothing more."

I say, "Yes, we can deduct a reasonable amount for my time. My time is worth something. If I work an entire day getting a unit back up to rentable condition, then we should be able to deduct more than the mere cost of cleaning supplies, furnace filter, caulking, paint, lightbulbs, etc."

Can you help settle our disagreement?
—T.N., Arkansas

A. That wife of yours is a good landlording partner. She's conservative when she's not sure about something. She wants to keep you out of trouble.

She has also lived with you long enough to know that your time is valuable, and she wants more of it for herself. She doesn't want you to spend all of your time working on your rental properties, not when she has things for you to do around the house, not when she wants to enjoy your company on a trip to the big city or a cruise around the Mediterranean. Can you blame her?

Perhaps her wanting to have more of your time for herself has prompted her to assume that you cannot deduct anything for your time from a security deposit when you have to do cleaning and repair work, whereas you can deduct the actual cost of labor performed by somebody else.

This assumption is incorrect.

The truth is that you are entitled to charge tenants for work which must be done to make a unit rentable again after a tenant moves out, whether you hire it done or do it yourself. You must, of course, document it and itemize it as a deduction from the security deposit. If you hire somebody else to do the work, you must document it with a description of the work performed and a completed work order or a receipt. If you do the work yourself, you must document it with a description of the work performed, an accounting of the time spent doing the work, and a statement of the hourly rate you're charging for your time.

Problems arise when you charge tenants for work you shouldn't be charging them for, when you spend too much time doing a job, and when you charge a high hourly rate for your time.

To stay out of trouble with your tenants, be reasonable when you determine these things. Do not charge them for work to repair deficiencies resulting from ordinary wear and tear. Do not inflate the time spent doing a job. Do not charge any more for your time than what you would have to pay somebody else to do the job.

To stay out of trouble with your wife, downplay her incorrect assumption about charging tenants for your time. Hire more and more work done. Do things for her around the house. Remodel her kitchen. Buy her fresh flowers every week. Do things with her. Take her to the places where she's always wanted to go.

Spoil her.

After all, this love of your life, this landlady in your life, is half the reason for your landlording success.

He wonders how rental income would affect child support.

Q. I'm thinking about buying a duplex townhouse. I would live in half and rent out the other half. I am recently divorced and am obligated to pay 14% of my income to my former wife for child support.

Is the rent that I would collect from the rental unit considered income?

If so, how is it reported on my tax returns?
—D.K., Wisconsin

A. The entire amount of the rent you receive from a rental property is its gross income, and gross income from a business is not what your child support is based upon. It may be based upon your gross pay from a job, but it's based upon your net income from a business.

Deduct from the gross rental income the various expenses you must pay to own the property, expenses such as property taxes, utilities, insurance, maintenance, interest, etc., and you get the net income. If you're occupying half the property, then only half of the expenses could be deducted from the gross income. The other half of the expenses would be treated like expenses for an owner-occupied primary residence.

For child-support calculations based upon your income, the net income from your rental property would be treated the same way as the net income you'd receive from any other business, whether it's a restaurant or an auto repair shop. You needn't worry about having to pay more child support as a result of owning one duplex and renting half of it out. Chances are good that you would have little, if any, net income from it.

Rental income and expenses appear on Schedule E of your tax return. That's the schedule which lists supplemental income and loss.

Vacancy rates are the question.

Q. What are the worst vacancy rates you have ever experienced in one month and over the course of a year? What are your average monthly and yearly vacancy rates?
—J.N., Alabama

A. The worst vacancy rate I've ever experienced for a single month was 50%. That was when I was remodeling a small apartment building. For a year the worst vacancy rate I've ever experienced was 25%. That was in an area which lost a major employer.

My average monthly vacancy rate is 5%, which is the same as it is on an annual basis.

Remember, your vacancy rate is only part of the mix. Set your rents low and you'll have a 0% vacancy rate. Set them high and you'll have a 100% vacancy rate.

14
Handling Deposits

Applicant backs out and wants holding deposit back.

Q. My husband and I have been landlords for nine years. We own four buildings with a total of sixty apartment units. We have never run across this particular problem before and are hoping you might be able to help.

Last month we had an applicant for an efficiency unit who checked out all right, so we accepted him. Because he wasn't prepared to move in right away, we asked for a deposit to hold the unit for him until the first of the month, and we verbally explained the purpose of the deposit. He gave us a deposit, and we canceled our ads in the paper, assuming that he would show up on the first to sign a month-to-month agreement and pay the next month's rent. He finally showed up on the third of the month and said he had found another place. He requested that we return his entire deposit and left an address where he wanted it sent.

We think that we should not have to return the entire deposit, that we may use at least a portion of it to compensate us for lost rent until we find another tenant. After all, we're losing rent because of this guy, and now we have to put another ad in the paper and go through the whole tenant selection process once more. If we do find another tenant during the month, then I would feel obligated to return what's left of the deposit for that portion of the month, beginning when the new tenant moves in.

My husband would like a second opinion. What do you say?
—A.A., Colorado

A. Your husband has an astute business partner. You are correct in assuming that the deposit should be used to compensate you for lost rent until you find another tenant to move in.

You took that deposit on a perishable commodity, the use of a rental dwelling over a period of time. Time is the key element here, and just as some people simply do not understand the time value of money, some people do not understand the time value of rental property. The applicant may think he's entitled to get his entire deposit back because he didn't actually use the unit, but he did reserve it and he did keep you from renting it to somebody else for a period of time. Neither he nor you can turn back the calendar and get that time back. Because the applicant reneged on his commitment to rent the unit from you after you reserved it for him alone, you have every right to use the deposit to offset whatever rent you lose during that period of time.

Send the fellow a letter explaining why you are keeping his deposit and tell him that you will return whatever remains of it should you find a new tenant to move in before the monies are completely exhausted.

When you next take a deposit from somebody to hold a rental unit off the market, formalize the arrangement with either the complete written rental agreement you plan to use or with an agreement which states the deposit arrangement as clearly as possible (the *Landlording* book has just such an agreement). Then there will be no doubt as to what happens to the deposit if the tenant fails to move in.

Tenants take possession and change their mind an hour later.

Q. We took a $900 deposit to hold an apartment off the market for nine days. When the tenants arrived on the move-in date, they signed the lease, received the keys, and took possession. An hour later, they went back to the manager, handed her the keys, and informed her that they had decided not to take the apartment. We kept the security deposit because the lease states that there is an early termination fee of two times the monthly

177

rent of $900, so technically they still owed $900. The apartment was not rented for another month. Is keeping the security deposit justified in this case?
—H.G.N., California

A. Keeping the security deposit is justified under the circumstances. These tenants, who took possession and then decided not to move in, cost you thirty-nine days of lost rent. For nine of those days you were holding the apartment off the market exclusively for them, and for thirty of those days you were actively seeking replacement tenants. The key factor here is their taking possession, even for just an hour. Had they not taken possession, they'd likely have been entitled to receive a portion of their deposit back, depending upon what you had agreed upon with them when they gave you the deposit to hold the apartment off the market in the first place.

Whenever you accept monies from applicants to hold a dwelling off the market, specify in writing exactly what you will do with the monies under every possible circumstance which might arise, and then deposit the monies into your bank account.

You were wise to deposit their monies immediately. You were not so wise to give them possession without requiring them to pay you rent for thirty-nine days, plus a security deposit. For a $900-per-month apartment, they should have paid you $270 for the nine days, $900 for one month's rent, and a minimum of $450 as a security deposit, for a total of $1,620. Then, if they had decided not to move in and you were unable to find replacement tenants for a month, you would have been obligated to return only their $450 security deposit. If you were making an active effort to find replacement tenants and found them within a week, you would have been obligated to return $1,140 to your "tenants for an hour." $690 of that would be a rent refund and $450 of it would be the security deposit refund. Remember, you may not collect rent from two tenants for the same period of time.

Tenants want deposit back when they decide not to move in.

Q. We recently rented to a young couple who couldn't move in until the first of the month, but they agreed to put up a $400 deposit for us to hold the place for them. We told them that this deposit was not refundable if they changed

their minds since we were taking it off the market and holding it for them. We also told this to their co-signer who actually put up the money for the deposit. We have a signed rental agreement and a signed co-signer agreement. Six days after giving us the deposit, they called to tell us that they had changed their minds and were staying where they were and they asked for the deposit back. We explained to them that they would be forfeiting the deposit if they didn't move in and that was the last we heard from them for a long time. Now they have sent us a certified letter which I haven't seen yet because I wasn't here to sign for it so I'm assuming that they are planning legal action. Where do we stand on this?
—V.J., Florida

A. The certified letter is likely a summons demanding that you appear in small claims court to explain why you have refused to return the deposit.

Go and tell the truth about what happened, but don't expect this young couple to tell the truth themselves and don't expect to win. Yours is a good case; it's not "open and shut." Lacking anything more than a verbal understanding that the deposit would be nonrefundable if the couple changed their minds, you will have to stress to the judge exactly what you told them and why. Your side of the case gains some strength because you have a signed rental agreement which entitled the couple to move in on the first of the month, some days following your acceptance of the deposit. It would gain more strength if you could prove conclusively that you suffered damages equal to or exceeding the $400 deposit. Your damages would amount to the rent you lost in taking the place off the market, the costs you incurred in restarting your advertising campaign, and the compensation you might expect for having to spend additional time to find new tenants—answering the phone, showing the place, interviewing the applicants, and checking applications. Put dollar values on those things. Outline them on paper for the judge to see.

Cross your fingers that you'll get a small claims judge with some street smarts and not one who's trying to be a Solomon and will award the young couple half their claim when they deserve none of it.

Next time use a deposit receipt which states the terms governing the payment of the deposit. The receipt should state that the deposit is non-refundable and why it is and should be signed by both tenants and landlord.

Landlord keeps entire holding deposit when tenants reconsider.

Q. I found an apartment to rent and put up a deposit in the amount of $350 so the landlord would hold it for me. Three days later I decided not to move there, and now the landlord is refusing to give me back my deposit because she said the apartment was empty for two weeks before I showed up and decided to rent it. What can I do to get my deposit back?

—J.W., Kansas

A. When you put up the deposit to hold the apartment, you made a commitment to rent it, and the landlord responded to that commitment by taking the property off the market. The landlord committed herself not to rent it to anybody else and was just waiting for you to sign the agreement, pay the upfront monies, and move in. Had she rented it to somebody else after taking your deposit, you would have been livid, and you would have had good cause to berate her verbally and expect compensation. She didn't rent it to somebody else. She remained committed to you, and she lost rent monies and incurred certain expenses as a result. She has every right to expect compensation from you for her having taken the property off the market for your benefit until you changed your mind three days later.

Whether she has the right to keep the entire $350 is the real question, and the real answer to that question depends upon the answers to two other questions. How much rent did she actually lose because of you and how much did she have to pay in various expenses, such as running a credit check and reinserting the classified ad, because of you?

She should not charge you anything because the apartment was vacant for two weeks before you showed up and decided to rent it. That had nothing to do with you. That's a bogus reason for keeping your deposit.

No matter how you feel about getting your deposit back, don't expect her to return the entire amount. She doesn't owe you the entire amount. She does owe you some of it, and she appears to need a little prodding before she'll do the right thing and return some of it to you.

Use some initiative here and do a little research to determine approximately how much she should withhold from your deposit. Include the three days' rent she lost. That's easy enough to determine. Divide the monthly rent by thirty and multiply by three. Then make a couple of phone calls. Call a local credit bureau and ask how much a credit check costs, the one most landlords order when they're checking applicants' credit. Call the local daily newspaper and ask how much a five-line classified ad costs for one week. Deduct these three figures from the $350, and you'll have an amount you have good reason to expect her to return to you. Send her your calculations along with a letter informing her that you expect to receive this very amount from her within seven days or else you'll take her to small claims court.

Maybe she'll respond to this approach. Maybe she won't. If she does respond, but she isn't being reasonable, or if she doesn't respond at all, take her to small claims court and make your best case before the judge using the figures you came up with.

Tenants promise to pay deposit with their second month's rent.

Q. I rented a house to some folks who were strapped for the security deposit. I agreed to wait until the second month's rent was due to collect the deposit along with the rent. They said they would give me small payments leading up to the second month's rent due date. We wrote this into the lease. I have received NO small payments of any kind from them yet, and the second month's rent due date is almost here. I have tried to call them and never get an answer (I've called at all times of the day and night). I even sent them a letter by certified mail stating my concern and have not received the certified mail confirmation from the postal service. When I drive by, there are no signs of life. What should I do next? I'm worried and need the money!

—D.M., Utah

A. Welcome to the real world of landlording!

Always, always, always get move-in monies from new tenants before you allow them to move in! Move-in monies include the first rent payment and all deposits. If new tenants don't have the money to pay you before they move in, chances are good that they won't have the money to pay you after they move in.

From what you have described about these tenants, they appear to have abandoned the place for some reason. Start calling the references given on their application, beginning with the person to call in case of emergency. Then call their employer and find out whether they're still working at the place you called when you checked out their application. You did check out their application, didn't you? Call the personal references, too, and don't forget the neighbors. Your new tenants have not vanished off the face of the earth. They're around somewhere, and they can't hide from you forever.

If nobody knows where the tenants are, find out what your state's abandonment procedures are and follow them. Whatever you do, don't delay.

Tenants hold over and want entire deposit back.

Q. Last month my renters gave me a 30-day notice that they would be moving by the end of the month. On the second day of this month they were still moving things out. On the tenth, when I had not received the keys back, I sent them a certified letter stating that since they had not returned the keys and still had some belongings on the property, I had to assume that they had not vacated. I said that I would be charging them a daily rental fee until I received the keys back and they had removed their belongings. On the fifteenth they finally removed the last of their belongings and turned in their keys, and when they did, they said they were going to take me to court unless I returned every penny of their deposit.

I want to send them a letter accounting for their deposit, but I need some help first because I don't know how many days I can charge them for. Can I charge them rent only for the first two days of the month when they removed most of their belongings or can I charge them through the fifteenth when they removed all their belongings and returned the keys?

Their contract states that they must pay a $25 late fee for rent not paid by the tenth. If I do charge them for rent through the fifteenth, should I charge them a late fee as well?

—L.Y., North Carolina

A. Tenants have not vacated until they have moved out all of their belongings and turned in their keys. Those are the physical and symbolic acts which return possession of a rental property to its owner. Your tenants "held over" for fifteen days after their tenancy ended, so they owe you fifteen days of "rental damages" equaling one-thirtieth of their current rent for every day they held over. Do not charge them a late fee.

They disagree over definitions of "damage" and "wear and tear."

Q. For the past fourteen years I have been renting out two bedrooms in my home to supplement my minimal Social Security income.

One of my tenants is vacating, and I'm thinking about withholding some money from his security deposit to repair damage he caused. His mother, who also signed the rental agreement, has stated that unless every penny is returned to him, she plans to file a case against me in small claims court. I sent her and her son a detailed letter indicating what they needed to do to get their entire deposit back.

The rental agreement signed by everyone clearly states: "Tenant will be responsible for damage caused by his/her negligence and that of his/her family, invitees, and guests. Tenant will not paint, paper, or otherwise redecorate or make alterations to the premises without the prior written consent of the Owner." Also: "Tenant will not commit any waste upon the premises…"

Without any authorization from me, the tenant proceeded to decorate his room with posters and cloth banners, using those plastic stick pins that often hold notes on cork bulletin boards. Some thirty-eight holes were noted during the final inspection. They didn't deny that the tenant had placed the holes in the walls. They just claimed that the holes were "normal wear and tear."

The second item of damage involves a large "hide-a-bed" couch in an adjacent "bonus" room. I own this couch and allow tenants to use it whenever they wish. Here the tenant watched television and listened to his music. Often he would sit on the couch and drink from a large plastic cup filled with ice and a beverage, and invariably he would place the cup directly on the wooden arms of the couch without using a coaster.

When I observed and commented on this practice, his response was that he kept a paper napkin under the cup. This, of course, only made the problem worse. The condensation removed the finish and left ring marks on the arms. Mother and tenant said they could see no damage whatsoever.

Several repair people have estimated that they would charge $60 to refinish the couch arms. I

calculate the total repairs to be $173. Should I deduct this sum from the tenant's deposit?
—D.S., California

A. No. I agree with the tenant that the holes left by push pins amount to normal wear and tear. You can't expect a tenant to live in a room without putting anything on the walls, and they have to mount their wall hangings with something. Be happy that your tenant used push pins rather than tenpenny nails.

The damage to the wooden couch arms is another matter. Because he caused the damage in spite of your warnings, I would charge him the $60 for refinishing the arms.

Take a photograph of the arms before you have them refinished and save the receipt you get for the work so you'll be well prepared should the tenant's pushy mother follow up on her threat to take you to small claims court.

Landlord returns deposit too soon.

Q. Is there anything I can do if I returned a renter's deposit to her on the day she moved out and later found problems which I should have charged her for?

Things seemed okay when I made a quick inspection, but when I went back to do some touchups, I found little messes here and there. She said she had cleaned behind the fridge and stove and under the vent registers, but she hadn't. Everywhere I looked, I found things to clean. I spent seven hours there cleaning the place to get it ready for the next renter. In addition, I had to spend $48 to have the carpets deodorized and disinfected because of the cat urine. I hadn't noticed the cat urine during my inspection in the cool of the morning. When I returned in the warmth of the afternoon, the odor was overwhelming.

I now realize why a landlord should hang onto the deposit for a few days and then send the refund.

This woman is on her way out of town now, and I'm not sure how to get in touch with her. I left a message with her previous co-worker who may talk to her in the future, but I know she has no address yet where can I write her a letter.

I suppose I have no legal recourse. Should I consider this just another lesson learned, or should I ask her if she would compensate me?
—C.L., Alberta, Canada

A. Don't even try to get the money back from the former tenant. You'll only frustrate yourself. You won't get it back. Besides, when you returned the deposit to her, you were essentially telling her that everything was okay and that she deserved to get the deposit back. Consider this experience just another lesson you learned in landlording at Hard Knocks College.

Lessees want to give enough notice to get their deposit back.

Q. We have been renting an apartment and have just now bought a house which should become legally ours on the twenty-fifth of the month. Our lease is up at the end of the month, but we are giving the owners our written thirty-day notice on the seventh. If we vacate the apartment on the last day of the month, do we still have to pay through the seventh just because the written notice expires then?
—B.M., Texas

A. When you're renting on a month-to-month basis, you owe rent for thirty days following the date when you submit your thirty-day notice, regardless of when you move out.

When you're renting on a fixed-term lease, you may or may not have to give notice. Check your lease to see what it says. If it mentions nothing about giving notice, then you may simply move out at the end of the lease, and you won't owe rent for any days beyond that, but you should give the landlord a courtesy notice as soon as you know that you will be moving at the end of the lease. You don't want any misunderstandings, and you want to get your deposit back.

Landlords discover that trash was tenants' treasure.

Q. When our tenants moved out after five years, they didn't turn in their keys. Now they're suing us in small claims court for the return of their deposit and for $1,000 to pay for valuable personal things they claim they left in the garage, things we thought were garbage and had to take to the dump.

Although they say they tried to clean the place, they did a lousy job of it. They left us with a lot of cleanup and repair work.

They changed the keyless locksets on the bedroom doors to keyed locksets and never gave us the keys to those locks nor did they give us the original keyless locksets. We had to replace the locksets they installed with new ones.

The carpet was almost brand new when they moved in. When they moved out, it was so stained with paint, ink, oil, dirt, and unidentified liquids that we couldn't clean it. We tried to steam-clean it, but it wouldn't come clean. We had to replace it.

The vinyl kitchen floor covering was in good shape when they moved in, too, but when they moved out, it was scratched, permanently stained, and torn. We tried to find a piece of vinyl in the same pattern to repair it, but we wound up replacing the whole floor with new vinyl.

The place needed paint and a good cleaning, but we figured that after five years, we should expect to paint and do some cleaning. We're more concerned about the carpet and the vinyl they ruined and the locks we had to replace. We know that we can't expect them to have to pay the entire cost of the carpet, vinyl, and locks, but we think they ought to pay part of the cost.

How much do you think they ought to pay?

Also, your *Landlording* book has a list of move-out charges. They're mostly lower than what we pay here in northern California for those same things. Do you have a more current list of charges?

—I.W., California

A. Whenever tenants move without either turning in their keys or leaving incontrovertible word that they have moved out, you must assume that they have not moved out completely, and you must try everything you can think of to get some word out of them and get their keys.

Only after they turn in their keys or give you their word that they have moved out do you obtain possession. Only then are you free to enter the dwelling, discard what they have left behind, and make it ready to rent again.

Your tenants did not turn in their keys, and apparently they never told you that they had moved out completely. Still, you assumed that their tenancy had ended and that they had no intention of returning. You assumed that you were free to take possession.

They assumed something different. They assumed that they had not returned possession to you and that they still had the right to go back for the things they left in the garage. They assumed that you would not remove those things and dispose of them.

They probably did not assume that they were continuing to incur the obligation to pay you rent for as long as they kept possession of the dwelling. They were. They became holdover tenants when they gave you a moveout date and kept possession beyond that date, and they owe you rent up until the time when possession returned to you, either through their actions or yours.

Make sure you tell the judge that they owe you rent for every day they held over. Determine exactly how much they owe, and give the judge that figure to include in your total when he calculates who owes what to whom.

Keep in mind that there is a procedure you should follow if your tenants move and leave any of their belongings behind. It begins with a "Notice of Right to Reclaim Abandoned Personal Property," which you send to the tenants at their last-known address, and ends with your becoming entitled to dispose of the belongings in one way or another if they aren't retrieved within a reasonable period of time. State law outlines the procedure.

Since you did not follow the procedure, you are at the mercy of a judge, and you will have to spend some time to prepare a good defense. Your best defense against the tenants' claim would be photographs of the stuff as it was and where it was when you first laid eyes on it. Lacking photographs, you might try to come up with an inventory of the stuff or testimony from a third party who actually saw it. At this point, that's the best you can do.

As for the things you had to replace because of the tenants' thievery and carelessness, you ought to charge them a sum prorated according to the useful life of the item and the remaining life it should have had when they took it or destroyed it.

Interior door locks should have a useful life of fifteen years. Let's say that the locks had already been in service for five years when the tenants moved in. Counting those five years and the five years the tenants lived in the dwelling, we get ten. That's two-thirds of the locks' useful life with one-third remaining. Consequently, you ought to charge them for one-third of the cost of the locks.

Ordinary vinyl flooring has an average useful life of ten years when installed in rental property. Let's say that it had been in service for a year when the tenants moved in. That year and the five the tenants lived in the dwelling make six, leaving a remaining useful life of four years. Four-tenths is forty percent, so you ought to charge them forty percent of the cost of the new vinyl flooring you installed.

Ordinary carpet, on the other hand, has a useful life of five to ten years. Its average life expectancy in a rental dwelling is seven years. Assuming that it was one year old and in good shape when the tenants moved in, there should have been one year of life left in it when they moved out. That year translates into fourteen percent, so you ought to charge them fourteen percent of the cost of the new carpet because you had to replace it one year prematurely.

Documentation is important whenever you're determining how much to charge a tenant for damages when the tenant vacates. It's especially important when the tenant is suing you in court to force you to return more of his deposit. You need to prove to the judge that you're being objective rather than arbitrary. Your receipts tell the tale. Save them. Copy them. Submit them.

Every state has regulations governing the handling, accounting, and return of rental deposits. Generally, they include a framework for the accounting and a timeframe for the return of the deposit. Find out what they are in your state, and follow them without fail.

As for the list of move-out charges in the *Landlording* book, I must say that each of them should be a range rather than an exact sum because they vary so much throughout the United States. In some parts of the country, a painter will charge ten dollars an hour, and in other parts, the going rate will be sixty dollars an hour. Repainting a room when you're paying six times more for labor will cost you more, even if the sixty-dollar-an-hour painter is three times faster than the ten-dollar-an-hour painter. In some areas with competitive merchants, you may pay thirty dollars for a thermostat, while in others where the local hardware store has no competition, the cost may be double.

You must come up with the appropriate costs for your area. The ones in the *Landlording* book are averages, and they're much like the average of the heights of a giant and a midget, pretty useless. You have a much better idea how much a shower curtain rod and a sliding door screen costs in your area. Put those numbers in the blanks of the "Move-Out Charges" form found in the back of the *Landlording* book.

Tenant tries to dictate terms for her moving out.

Q. My husband and I recently inherited a rental house in Seattle and have been having some difficulty with the tenant.

Several years ago the tenant convinced the relative who willed us the house to pay half the cost of installing a wood stove. Now the tenant is leaving and is asking us to pay her $850 if we want to keep the stove or else she is going to have it removed. This stove is a permanent fixture (a hole had to be cut in the ceiling for the flue, and a special marble base had to be laid). Do we have to pay her for the stove?

Also, her security deposit was $800. We received a letter from her today stating that she wants us to apply $700 of her deposit to her last month's rent. That leaves only a $100 balance as her deposit. I am certain that this is not legal, but I don't know what recourse to take.
—L.D., Washington

A. Check the original agreement which governs the tenancy and see what it says about tenant alterations. The long agreement in the *Landlording* book says the following about such alterations: "When approved by Owners, Tenants' plans for alterations and decorations shall bear a determination regarding ownership. If Tenants are able to convince Owners that Tenants can remove the alterations or decorations and restore that part of their dwelling to its original condition, then Owners may grant Tenants the right to remove them. Otherwise, any alterations or decorations made by Tenants become the property of Owners when Tenants vacate."

Lacking any agreement covering the installation and ownership of the wood stove and knowing as you do that the previous landlord originally paid half the cost, tell the tenant that she may remove it if she will pay you $850 (the same amount she asked you to pay her; remember, you have half an interest in the stove, too) and restore the premises to their original condition. If she says that $850 is too much, tell her to come up with a fair figure, so that each of you has the option of paying a fair figure and not one which she has just pulled out of the air.

Under no circumstances should you allow her to remove the stove without her compensating you for your half ownership and without her restoring the premises to their original condition.

Likewise, under no circumstances should you allow her to dictate a ransom figure for her to leave the stove. Negotiate. Tell her that you want to treat her fairly and that you want to be treated fairly.

Using a security deposit as last month's rent is one of those misguided tenant tricks which is both irresponsible and illegal. Tell her in no uncertain terms that she cannot use her security deposit as rent and that you will begin eviction proceedings against her immediately unless her rent is current. Tell her also that you will report her rent delinquency to a credit bureau immediately and that she will have to live with it on her credit report for a long time to come.

If she does not pay the rent she owes you, follow up on your statements. Serve her a notice to pay rent or quit, which will begin eviction proceedings, and find out what you need to do as a landlord in Seattle to ding her credit. You may have to subscribe to a credit bureau service or join a rental property owners association to ding her credit, and that may cost you something. Don't hesitate to pay the cost. You need to be able to ding tenants' credit when they do you wrong. You should not suffer in silence. You should tell the world what kind of a person this tenant is.

This tenant is playing hardball with you. You must play hardball with her.

Tenant tries to bully landlord into getting her deposit back.

Q. Our departing tenant wants all of her security deposit back and has submitted a $211 "bill" to us for certain expenses. They include carpet cleaning, a garbage disposal service charge (no receipt included), and "lawn service," even though we provide landscaping and she's ruined the lawn in several places.

This is sort of a no-brainer, I realize, since I know from reading your book that these are just normal expenses she voluntarily assumed, or in the case of the carpet cleaning, an expense associated with moving out. She should be clear on these expenses but isn't.

She's a bully and no real fun to deal with, and I'm not looking forward to arguing with her.

What recourse does she have since I am giving her no credit for these things and will be deducting from her security deposit the cost of repairing a hole she put in the wall of the garage? Does she have a leg to stand on in court? She's

going to be very upset with me because she has already told me she'd like to call her expenses and mine a "wash" and she expects to get her entire security deposit back.

—B.W., California

A. Your tenant's supposed expenses are her own to bear. You should not be paying for them because they're nothing more than her cleaning and preparation for moving out.

On the other hand, the hole in the garage wall is damage, and she ought to be paying for it.

Her recourse is a small claims court action against you, but I can't believe that she would be awarded anything even there for these expenses. Document everything just in case she does take you to court.

Stand firm against this bully, and be glad that you're rid of her.

Tenant wants to trade keys for deposit.

Q. A problem tenant of ours gave us a one-week notice that he was moving. When my husband went to retrieve the keys and the garage door opener on the first of the month, the tenant refused to turn them over until he got his deposit back. In our state, we have thirty days to check the property for damage and return the deposit. Our attorney said we should charge him rent until we get the keys back and that it should come out of the damage deposit. If we do that, how will we ever get our keys back?

I left a note on the door with a list of the charges for damages and the things not cleaned and indicated that he would be charged rent daily until the keys are returned and that per our attorney we have thirty days to settle up with him. I've heard nothing. What steps can I take now? Would a notice to pay rent serve any purpose at this stage? Can the police help?

—J.D., Ohio

A. Your attorney is correct in saying that the tenant hasn't vacated until he returns the keys, but that knowledge doesn't help much in a standoff which serves no purpose.

If the tenant has already moved out, change the locks and change the garage door opener's combination so that neither will work any longer. Replace the opener and add a charge for it to the tenant's bill when you're calculating all that he owes you. Don't charge him for rent beyond the day when you change the locks. Give him the reckoning within the thirty-day time frame and whatever you owe him out of his deposit, and rejoice that you're rid of this gem of a tenant!

If the tenant has not yet moved out, begin eviction proceedings by serving him a notice to pay rent or quit.

You can play tough, too.

Couple break lease and still want their deposit back.

Q. We rented a house to a couple on a two-year lease. We haven't returned their security deposit because they broke the lease. They moved out after only thirteen months. They have threatened to sue us stating that they said they might be transferred, that we raised the rent $25 and therefore no one would rent it, and that we turned away would-be renters. Nothing could be further from the truth. The reason the house sat vacant for a month was due to the Christmas holidays and the weather. Can we win in court? Also, should we send the tenants 5% interest on their security deposit?
—C.W., Ohio

A. If these former tenants take you to court to force you to return their deposit, you may win or you may lose. Judges determine such matters. Laws and common sense do not. If you believe you have good grounds for keeping the deposit, keep it, and wait for the tenants to sue you. Then do your explaining to the judge and hope for the best.

As for sending the tenants any interest on their deposit, do so only if applicable laws require you to or if you have agreed to. Otherwise, you owe them no interest on their deposit.

Landlord keeps deposit from tenants who broke agreement.

Q. A young couple with a child signed a month-to-month agreement to rent a mobilehome from me. The agreement said "no pets." I also told them "no pets."

They gave me proper notice and moved out after only four months because they bought a house. Three weeks later, they told me they wanted their deposit back. I told them that they broke the agreement by having a pet and that their cat had damaged one of the dining-room chairs.

There were some other concerns I had about them while they were renting. They didn't take

the trash out to the curb, and they kept an inoperable vehicle, an automobile transmission, and some old furniture in the driveway.

Do I have a right to keep their deposit since they broke the agreement and since they lived there only a short time and since I have been unable to re-rent the place?
—C.P., Wyoming

A. You cannot withhold money from a security deposit because your tenants weren't living up to the letter of their agreement. You can withhold money to pay for damage they caused or rent they're obligated to pay but haven't.

In this case, you may withhold a reasonable sum to pay for the damage the cat did to the chair but not merely because they had a cat and the agreement prohibited pets, nor can you withhold money because they kept a mess in the driveway, because they didn't take out the trash, or because you haven't been able to re-rent the place.

Many states require landlords to give tenants a written move-out accounting or deposit reckoning within a specific time period (two to three weeks). Even if your state does not require such a reckoning, you ought to prepare one anyway. It's good business. It finalizes your relationship with the tenant in explicit terms.

Tenant moves without notice leaving ten months on lease.

Q. My tenant of fourteen months moved without giving me any notice. When he moved in, he signed a two-year lease. Can I go after him to collect the remaining ten months' rent? Am I correct in assuming that I can keep his security deposit to help offset what he owes me?
—C.S., South Carolina

A. Provided that your tenant has returned the keys or given you some other valid indication that he has moved, provided that you put the dwelling on the market as soon as possible and try to rent it to someone else at a reasonable rent, and provided that the dwelling remains unoccupied, you have the right to charge the departing tenant for whatever rent you lose during the ten months left on his lease.

You may deduct that amount from the security deposit, and you may try to hound the tenant for whatever he owes you in addition, but you might as well be strapping cardboard wings onto your arms and trying to fly. Forget trying.

Don't forget that states have laws governing

security deposits. Comply with them.

Landlords want to collect double rent.

Q. My husband and I had the same tenants for three years. They were excellent, that is, they were excellent until they broke their lease and moved elsewhere without giving us any notice.

Fortunately, we lost no rent at all after they moved because other tenants wanted to move into the place right away. Are we obligated to return the tenants' security deposit even though we did not lose any rent for the following month?
—N.C., New York

A. You want to collect double rent, and you can't. If the tenants move without giving notice and you find another tenant to move in immediately so that you do not lose any rent, you are obligated to return the security deposit, so long as they leave the place clean and undamaged. Whatever rent you lose, from one day up to the end of the lease period, you may deduct from the deposit. If you lose no rent, then you may deduct nothing from the deposit for lost rent. You may deduct only the cost of repairing the damage they left behind.

Tenants take one of their improvements when they vacate.

Q. My last tenants attached, installed, and planted a number of things at the house they rented from me, and I wasn't quite sure what was supposed to become of these things when the tenants moved out.

When these tenants left, they took one of the things with them, a ceiling fan, and left the others. They left a retractable clothesline attached to the side of the garage, a 10 x 6-foot privacy fence, a basketball hoop on a pole cemented into the ground, and numerous plants. Did they have the right to take any of these things or were they supposed to leave all of them behind when they moved?
—J.B., Florida

A. Tenants are supposed to leave a rental property pretty much the way they found it when they moved in. If they want to make alterations, they are supposed to ask their landlord for permission in advance. When discussing permission, tenants and landlord are supposed to discuss what will happen to the alterations when the tenants move out, and they are supposed to put their mutual

understanding on the subject in writing.

Lacking any advance mutual understanding, tenants and landlord should discuss the matter of alterations when tenants give notice that they plan to move. The discussion should cover every alteration and what's to become of it when the tenants move.

The landlord has the right to require the tenants to restore the property to its original condition, minus ordinary wear and tear, of course. If the tenants fail to restore the property to its original condition, the landlord may use the security deposit to pay for any expenses incurred to do so.

In your case, the tenants should have replaced their ceiling fan with the original fixture or one at least as good. If they didn't, charge them for a fixture. If you have to remove the clothesline, the privacy fence, the basketball hoop, or the plants because they happen to be eyesores rather than improvements, charge the tenants for removal and restoration. Likewise, if the tenants had removed all their additions to the property and left a mess behind, you would have every right to charge them to restore the property to its original condition.

Sometimes tenants will make certain improvements to a property for their own satisfaction and then ask the landlord for reimbursement. Unless you're inclined to be generous, you needn't pay anything for them. As attachments to the property, they're yours anyway.

Tenants stick landlord with maintenance bills and chores.

Q. Several months ago, the city where I own a rental house did some sewer work which resulted in a backup inside my house and damage to the flooring and carpet. The tenants called a plumber to check the line. He charged $216. Then they called me and said that they were going to deduct the bill from their rent.

I met with them to explain what their lease says: "Tenant pays up to $135 for maintenance or repairs with Landlord's approval. Landlord pays everything above that." I told them that they should have called me or the home warranty company first rather than the plumber. The warranty company would have charged $35 to send someone out. They knew about the warranty company because they had used it before to repair a hot water heater.

Because I did not approve the call to the plumber, I don't think I should pay for his visit. I did hire a professional to clean the carpet and paid that entire bill myself.

Actually, the city is responsible for what happened and would have paid the bills if only I could have submitted them within thirty days. I tried to get the tenants to give me the plumbing bill and any other bill related to the incident, but they never did. Now that the thirty-day deadline has passed, the city won't reimburse us for any of the expenses.

The tenants' lease has just expired, and they have moved out. I know that I will have to replace the flooring and the carpet. Can I deduct the cost from their deposit?

This same couple decided to paint some personal items shortly after they moved in. They left overspray and blotches of paint on the front porch, in a workroom, on the back porch, and in the garage. The floors of the workroom and front porch were painted gray four years ago and looked quite good. I told the tenants they would have to repaint the floors and they agreed. So far, they have moved out and returned the keys, but they have yet to return to paint the floors even though we have made several appointments to meet at the house so I could let them in. They never showed.

I am tired of accommodating these people. They have had plenty of time and plenty of chances to repaint the floors, and they have done nothing. How would you handle this? Would you repaint the floors and deduct the costs from their deposit?

—P.H., Texas

A. Rejoice that you have enough of a security deposit to offset what your tenants owe you for these two mishaps.

As for the first mishap, I'm assuming that they deducted the $216 from their rent. I would then deduct from their security deposit the $135 they agreed in their contract to pay for maintenance or repairs, and I would swallow the $81 difference between what they agreed to pay and what the plumber charged. I would pay for the other work myself. Yes, I know that the tenants were supposed to have called you first and that they were supposed to have submitted the plumbing bill right away so you could get the city to reimburse you. They didn't. I still wouldn't force them to pay the entire bill because you could have done

a few things yourself within the thirty-day timeframe to get the city to pay. You could have contacted the plumber and asked for a copy of the bill, and you could have arranged to replace the flooring and carpet promptly. You didn't. If you're inclined to be hard-nosed, the most you should charge the tenants would be the $216. They bear no responsibility for the damage done to the flooring and carpet.

The city bears that responsibility, and you shouldn't let them off the hook, even though they have set an arbitrary thirty-day time limit for the presentation of bills.

Replace the flooring and carpet immediately. Then, gather all your bills related to the mishap, write a letter to the city requesting payment and explaining why you couldn't request payment sooner, and attach the bills to the letter. If the city fails to respond or refuses your request, file a claim in small claims court against the city and tell the judge how arbitrary the city was in handling its responsibility. Let the judge decide who should pay the bills.

As for the second mishap, I would hire a handyman to repaint the floors and deduct the cost from the tenants' security deposit. If you hire a handyman to do the work, you establish an irrefutable cost, whereas if you do the work yourself, the cost is questionable because you have to establish a fair charge for your labor and give some accounting of the time you spent doing the work. Tenants always expect their landlords to do such work for nothing. Hire the work done, and you avoid arguing over the cost. What you pay for the work is what you deduct from the deposit.

You are fortunate to have recourse available. Pursue it from the tenants and from the city.

Tenant's makeshift shower causes mold.

Q. I have several rental properties and have never come across this situation before. I'm not quite sure what to do about it.

I rented a four-bedroom house to a very nice family for a year. They did not renew their lease for another year because their jobs required them to move. The tenant saw the house before he rented it, so I never tried to conceal the fact that it has only one bathroom with a shower. The second bathroom has a bathtub. He asked me to convert the second bathroom's bathtub to a tub-shower combination, and I was willing until I found out how much the conversion would cost. He was so persistent about converting the bathroom and getting his shower that I finally had to write him a letter explaining that the expense was just too much for me.

When I was doing an early walk-through about two weeks before he was to move out, I noticed that he had rigged up a shower attached to the tub spout and had wired the shower head to the wall. The walls in this bathroom are drywall and were not meant to have shower water running down them. Luckily, his makeshift shower didn't damage the drywall, but it did cause some mold to form, just enough for me to have to hire a contractor to investigate and repair the damage. Again we were lucky. The contractor found that the mold was in its early stages of growth, and he was able to get rid of it and clean everything up without having to gut the whole bathroom.

These tenants were awesome. I wish all my tenants were as good. They were clean, quiet, and never late with their rent. The only problem I ever had with them was this makeshift shower. The man of the house was sorry for what he did, but I feel he should be held responsible for his decision.

The lease says that the tenant cannot alter the house in any way without written consent from the owner. Because I never gave my consent to change the plumbing, can I keep his $1,300 deposit? How much is considered fair?
—M.P., Montana

A. Keep only enough from the tenant's deposit to pay for the contractor's work to investigate and repair the damage caused by the tenant's makeshift shower. Do not keep anything as a penalty for the tenant's having broken the lease. You are not a public agency entitled to collect penalties from law breakers. You are a private entity entitled to collect rents, late fees, certain charges, and damages, and that's all.

Were you to keep the tenant's entire deposit as a penalty and were the tenant to take you to small claims court for being unfair, the tenant could argue that he did not actually violate the lease. The lease said he was not supposed to alter the house without first getting permission, and he could argue that he didn't alter the house when he simply attached a hose and a shower head to the tub spout any more than he did when he attached a garden hose and a spray nozzle to one of the outside spigots. Altering the house implies

something permanent. What he did was not something permanent. It was strictly temporary.

Don't give him cause to feel he's been treated unfairly. Deduct only what you had to pay the contractor to repair the damage caused by the makeshift shower. That's fair, and it won't provoke an argument. The tenant will understand that you treated him fairly. He caused some damage, and he had to pay to have it repaired.

Having encountered this one tenant who was so obsessed with getting a shower that he installed one on his own, you ought to think more seriously about converting the second bathroom's bathtub to a tub-shower combination permanently. Nowadays people want to take showers. They don't want to take baths. They don't have time for baths, and they don't think that baths are as sanitary as showers because they have to rinse themselves off with soapy water or else take the time to drain the soapy water and fill the tub with clean water for rinsing. Give them what they want. Give them a shower.

There are many ways to do the conversion, ranging from very inexpensive to very expensive. Your contractor must have quoted you a price for one of the expensive conversions, likely involving breaking into the walls to change the plumbing and then installing ceramic tiles over waterproof sheetrock. You needn't go to all that trouble to get the same results.

Early in my landlording career, I bought a seventy-five-year old building consisting of four one-bedroom apartments. It was appealing in every respect except for the bathrooms. They had tubs but no showers. When I bought it, two of the apartments were vacant, and they shouldn't have been because the market was good for such apartments. I did a number of things to make them more marketable, one being a conversion of every bathtub to a tub-shower combination. Those conversions cost practically nothing, not because I did them myself but because I decided to try something incredibly simple, and it worked.

Here's what I did—I cleaned the three walls surrounding every tub from its rim to five feet above it and made sure that the walls were thoroughly dry. I lined those walls with a solid-color Contact Paper®, making sure that there was at least a one-inch overlap at every vertical seam and that the paper spanned the juncture between the rim of the tub and the wall so that no water could seep through. Then I replaced the existing tub spout with a spout diverter, attached the diverter pipe and its brace to the wall, put up an inexpensive shower curtain rod, and hung an inexpensive shower curtain on the rod. That's all I did, and "presto chango," the bathtub became a tub-shower combination. I checked the bathrooms periodically for leaks over the years and found none during the five years I owned that building. I sold it that way, and for all I know, those bathrooms still have those cheapo tub-shower conversions made many years ago.

Because this particular conversion involves little labor and no opening and resealing of the walls, and because it uses what is essentially an inexpensive self-adhesive plastic membrane on the walls and some inexpensive and readily available parts, it is the least expensive of all the conversions. Other conversions using an external shower diverter and more conventional wall coverings are more expensive, to be sure, but not so expensive that you should avoid using them because of their cost.

Your tenants want showers, so give them showers. Don't force them to bathe in bathtubs. You'll rent your houses more easily, and you'll have happier tenants.

Tenant requests notification when landlord spends deposit.

Q. We have a tenant who is telling us that we must notify her when we spend some of her security deposit to repair a sink which she admits to having broken. She says she would have told us to buy a cheaper sink. I am sure she cannot dictate what we buy, but do we have to notify her?
—C.M., Ohio

A. Whoa! Wait just a trice here! You shouldn't be spending any of her security deposit to replace a sink which she broke unless you're replacing it after she moves out. Her deposit should be kept intact until she moves out. Only then should you use it if you must. It needs to be available then to pay for cleaning, damages, or unpaid rent.

While she is still living in your rental, you should bill her for a sink replacement necessitated by her carelessness and you should pester her to pay you if you have to. You don't absolutely have to notify her about the replacement, but you should as a matter of courtesy, and you should charge her only for a replacement which is similar in quality to the one she broke. If you want to upgrade the sink, you should pay the cost difference.

Tenant causes kitchen fire and must pay for it somehow.

Q. Four months after she moved in, one of my tenants accidentally started a fire in her kitchen while she was cooking. I had just remodeled the kitchen before she moved in. I installed new cabinets, put new ceramic tile on the counters, replaced the sink and faucet, and put new vinyl on the floor. I also repainted the whole apartment. Repairing the fire damage cost me over $700. Her rent is $550 per month, and she paid a $550 security deposit.

Should I ask her to replace her security deposit now that she owes me over $700 for the damages? What do I do if she refuses to pay?
—A.B., Montana

A. Itemize on paper the $700 cost of repairing the fire damage, and give this accounting to the tenant. Tell her that she owes you this sum and ask her how she wants to pay it, in a lump sum or in payments of at least $100 per month. If she says that you have her security deposit and should use it to cover the repairs, tell her that it is supposed to cover whatever she owes you for cleaning, damage, or rent when she moves out. It is not supposed to be used up while she is still renting from you. Tell her that if she moves out today, you will apply her security deposit to the cost of the repairs, but she will still owe you $150 to make up the difference between her deposit and the cost of the repairs. Tell her that if she chooses to stay, she must arrange to pay you the $700 now. Failure to do so will result in your giving her a notice to vacate.

Fire caused by tenant's printer complicates return of deposit.

Q. There was a fire in one of my apartments, and it did a lot of damage. The fire department determined that the printer connected to the tenant's computer malfunctioned and started it all. The tenant moved out so a crew could get in to repair the damage.

He informed me that he does not intend to move back into the apartment after the repairs have been made, even though they will be completed before the end of his lease. He lived there only five months and still had seven months to go on his lease. The lease says that he should not be held responsible for paying rent while the apartment is in disrepair, but it doesn't say anything about termination in an event of this nature.

I'd like to know how much of his deposit I ought to return to him. I required him to put up a deposit of $350 and agreed to let him pay it in installments. He paid two installments of $150 the first two months he was there, but he never paid the remaining $50. Three times he was at least five days late with his rent, but he paid the $25 late fee only once.

When I inspected the apartment after he moved, I found that there were a number of things damaged, but because of the fire, I couldn't tell whether he had damaged them or whether the fire or firemen had damaged them.

I think I should give him back a hundred dollars out of his deposit. I came up with this figure by dividing the $300 he paid by two, since his moving out was not something initiated by either of us, and subtracting the $50 in late fees he never paid. What do you think?
—L.C., Kentucky

A. Before you return any money to the tenant, take a look at two factors you might easily overlook, the rent owed and the deductible amount in your fire insurance policy.

Depending upon when the fire occurred during the month, you might find that the tenant owes you some rent money. Check to make sure that he paid his rent through the very day he moved out. If you find that he owes you rent money, subtract it from the deposit. If you find that he paid your rent for some days beyond the day he moved out, calculate what it is and add it to his deposit. Remember, your lease says that he does not have to pay rent when his apartment is in disrepair, and it was uninhabitable after the fire.

Also, check to see whether your fire insurance policy requires you to pay a deductible for any fire damage repairs. If it does, subtract the deductible from the tenant's deposit. Had the fire been your fault, you would be responsible for paying the deductible. In this case, the tenant's printer started the fire. He's at fault. He's responsible. He should pay the deductible. If he has renter's insurance, his insurance company may pay the deductible for him, but you don't know that now. You should subtract it now and settle

with him later if his insurance pays it.

The rest of your calculations are straightforward. He paid a $300 deposit and owes $50 in late fees. That leaves $250 you owe him. I can understand why you think that you and he ought to split the deposit, but you have no clear grounds for splitting it with him. He deserves to have it all returned after you take into account the rent and late fees owed and the deductible.

As for the lease obligating him to rent the apartment for a full year, you can't expect him to move back once the repair work is completed. It's major work requiring weeks to complete. Only if the repair work were minor and took a week or two to complete while he lived in temporary quarters in a motel or with a friend ought you to expect him to return.

The scope of the damage effectively terminated the lease.

Give him what he deserves to receive from his deposit and then find yourself a better tenant to rent the freshly decorated apartment, a tenant who will pay all of the deposit up-front, pay his rent on time every month, and pay for a renters insurance policy without your even asking.

New owner wants old tenants to put up deposits.

Q. I am in the process of purchasing a triplex. The sellers have informed me that they have returned the $100 security deposits to the two current tenants (one unit is vacant). So, at the time that I take possession, I will have two tenants with no security deposits. How should I handle this situation? Should I require a new deposit from each tenant? The rents are about $450, so a $100 deposit seems a bit low anyway.
—L.L., Minnesota

A. Trying to get current tenants to pay a security deposit is like trying to get a spouse to sign a prenuptial agreement after the wedding.

Don't even try to get a deposit from the current tenants because you will be starting your relationship on the wrong foot and because there really is no good way you can force them to pay if they choose not to.

Consider the previous landlord's having refunded the deposits as some indication that these people are good tenants and tell them so in a letter. Tell them that you have high expectations of them as tenants and that you are going to waive asking them for any deposits because you are confident that they will be good tenants during your ownership of the property just as they were when their previous landlords owned the property.

When any new tenants move in, of course, charge whatever you think they ought to pay as a deposit. With the rent at $450, the deposit ought to be $500-600.

Grease-loving tenant put up no deposit.

Q. I have a tenant who fries a lot and never cleans the stove. He even had a fire once and lost some pans. He doesn't listen to us when we ask him to clean, and I'm afraid that we'll have to buy a new stove when he moves.

He has no security deposit. We don't charge a deposit from our tenants because they can't afford to pay one in this area. This tenant is moving soon, and I'm wondering whether we might be able to get some help from the city's health inspector in this situation?
—J.K., Massachusetts

A. I would not call the health inspector. She might cite the tenant, but that's not too likely because she knows that she wouldn't be able to enforce a citation against a tenant. More than likely, she'd cite you, and you'd be responsible for cleaning up the place and extricating yourself from whatever bureaucratic mess you'd created by reporting the matter in the first place.

If you were holding a cleaning deposit for this grease lover, you could be sure that he'd be heeding your words about cleaning the stove so he could get his deposit back. Since you aren't holding a cleaning deposit, I'm afraid that you're just going to have to make the best of this bad situation and clean up after the guy or buy a replacement stove.

By the way, when I first started life as a landlord, all of my properties were where the po' folk lived, but I always charged, and always received, a security deposit. You may be surprised by what even the poorest applicants will pay as a deposit when required to do so.

Landlord worries about what he should have done years ago.

Q. I own a three-story triplex and live in the flat on the second floor of the building myself.

Four years ago I had a tenant at another property I own who moved out and left behind a big mess which cost me a lot more to take care of than she had given me as a security deposit. I didn't return her deposit and didn't give her a written accounting within the legal time limit as I was supposed to do because I was a new landlord then and didn't know what I was doing.

I made the mistake of renting to this same person again because I felt sorry for her. She was a friend of a friend and needed a place to live, and I let her move into the flat above where I'm now living. Somehow I knew that I'd have to evict her in time, and such was the case. She got three months behind in her rent and had to go. At least she did agree to move out before I had to evict her through the courts.

She paid me a $250 deposit when she moved in, and she owes me a lot more than that now. I will give her an accounting and keep her deposit, but I'm wondering whether I now ought to return that deposit of hers from four years ago since I didn't give her an accounting of it then.
—N.P., California

A. What happened four years ago is a dead issue today. You neglected to give the tenant an accounting of her security deposit then because you didn't know what you were doing, and you were lucky that your tenant didn't call you on it. You needn't compensate her today for something you should have done four years ago.

At least you do know enough now to give the tenant an accounting of her more recent security deposit. Give her the accounting but no money, and don't rent to her ever again. She has cost you twice now, and you're not in the landlording business to lose money, are you?

Wise up! Toughen up!

Tenants demand interest on their deposit.

Q. We have given some tenants a notice to terminate tenancy and they have agreed to move, but now they say that we owe them interest on their security deposit. Since they have been here nearly eight years, that could be a substantial sum if we really do have to pay them. Is there any law that says we have to pay them interest?
—V.J., California

A. California law does not require landlords to pay interest on security deposits. It does require landlords to account for deposits and return the balance within twenty-one days after the tenants move out. In states where landlords do have to pay interest on deposits, payment is made annually, so it's always a manageable sum.

Tenant wants payment for delay in deposit accounting.

Q. A tenant of ours has just moved out. She says that because she had an agreement with the previous owner to pay interest on her security deposit, we now have to pay the interest to her.

My mother purchased the property twelve years ago, and at one point she did pay this lady some interest because the lady misled my mother and said that the law required landlords to pay their tenants interest on deposits. My mother, being a first-time landlord, didn't know any better and never checked the law. She just paid the lady the interest.

My husband and I are now the owners. When we looked into the matter, we discovered that landlords do not have to pay any interest on security deposits in our state. The lady was lying. That's when she came up with the story about the agreement with the previous owner. She was lying again. There never was any agreement.

She left the place the biggest pigsty you could imagine in your wildest dreams. It was absolutely filthy. You'd think she never cleaned house once during the entire thirteen years she lived there.

She neglected everything so much that all the fixtures had to be replaced because they were corroded and couldn't be cleaned.

She actually owes us more than the amount of her measly deposit.

The law says that we have twenty-one days to provide her with an accounting of her security deposit. We tried our absolute best to send her the letter within the twenty-one day limit, but we had such an incredible mess to deal with that we couldn't. Getting the letter off to her took us twenty-three days.

Now she's saying that we have to pay her an automatic penalty of $600 because we were late in sending her the letter, and she's going to take us to small claims court to get the money out of us. We're not happy about going to court. We're worried that she may be right this time and that the judge will accuse us of ignoring the law and acting in "bad faith." Do you think the judge will award her this penalty when we missed the deadline by only two days?
—P.T., California

A. Let the tenant take you to small claims court and argue with you there. Bring photos and tell your story to the judge as honestly as you can. The judge is the law, and nobody can tell you in advance how the judge will decide the case.

15 Handling Evictions and Move-Out Problems

Tenants have "Deadbeat Tenants' Blarney Song" down pat.

Q. Our tenants have not been current on their rent for four months. They also have a dog on the premises even though there is a no-pets clause in their lease. We told them they had to move within thirty days. The thirty days have come and gone. They are now saying that we are not giving them enough time to make arrangements, and they are threatening to get themselves an attorney to sue us. Do we need to go through the courts to obtain an eviction?
—B.C., Missouri

A. Your tenants have the "Deadbeat Tenants' Blarney Song" down pat. Cover your ears. Don't listen to them. You know that you have given them enough time to vacate. You have given them four months. Most landlords wouldn't have given them four days. You know that they're not going to get an attorney to sue you. They're not going to get an attorney because they don't want to have to pay an attorney, and they know that any attorney they might consult would simply laugh at them anyway.

You're the one who needs an attorney, and you should get one right away or else school yourself in the eviction procedure and get busy with it right away. You are not going to get these deadbeat tenants to move by asking them nicely or even by yelling and screaming at them. You might get them to move by threatening them with physical violence, but that's illegal. Don't. You have to evict them through the courts, and the sooner you start, the sooner you'll be rid of them and their blarney.

They're classic deadbeats.

Q. My husband and I rented our 4-bedroom, 2-bath home to a couple with four kids. Two are hers and two are his. We pro-rated the rent the first month and charged them a $300 deposit and $350 for rent on a 6-month lease. This is very reasonable rent even for West Virginia, where we are. We did not get the first month's rent up front and gave them until the fourteenth of the month to pay it. On the seventeenth I called them. They paid $150 on the twentieth and said they would settle up the following week. When the following week came and went, I called them again, and they eventually paid $100, leaving a balance of $100 still owing.

Now their current month's rent is due, and they're giving me a major sob story. She didn't get her child support for the past two months. They had car repairs. He didn't work enough hours to get a full check. She is sick and can't work, but she doesn't get a disability check. They have his kids to look after, but he gets no child support for their expenses. They just received a final notice from the phone company, and if they don't pay their $130 bill within five days, they won't have a phone.

I told her that everybody suffers hard times now and then. That's understandable, but everybody has to live somewhere. Everybody needs a roof over their heads. Once they have a roof, they can have a telephone, but the roof comes first. I'm trying to be nice and don't want to kick them out. I was told by a friend that I couldn't kick them out if they have kids. What are my options? I don't think things are as hard for them as they say.
—J.L., West Virginia

A. You have rented to classic deadbeats, and you should understand right now that they are never going to pay you their rent on time, nor are they ever going to pay you anything at all without a hassle. Serve them with a notice to pay rent or quit as soon as possible so you can begin eviction proceedings against them. Kids are no shield against an eviction. If they were, nobody would be paying any rent.

She claims her delicate condition protects them from eviction.

Q. Can a pregnant woman be evicted?

After moving in and making her first rental payment, my tenant informed me that she and her husband had been trying for months to get pregnant and that they were finally successful. I was happy for them and gave them some slack about making their rental payments. What a fool I was! They took advantage of me. They owe me two months' rent now. I told them that I'm going to have to evict them if they don't pay up. She keeps screaming at me that I can't evict them because she's three months pregnant. She wasn't working when they moved in, but he was. To the best of my knowledge, he's still working and he's not pregnant.
—C.W., Alabama

A. Some old wives' tales are true, some are half true, and some are not true at all. Here are a few which are not true at all: pregnant women should not attend funerals; a knife placed under the bed during childbirth will ease the pain of labor; a dog's saliva will kill germs; and a pregnant woman need pay no rent.

A pregnant woman may indeed be entitled to certain special benefits, such as pickles and ice cream at three in the morning, but she is not entitled to any special legal benefits. She cannot, for example, kill her husband and get away with the murder by claiming she was pregnant. She cannot run up a credit card bill and get away without paying by claiming she was pregnant. She cannot run up a bill for rent and get away without paying by claiming she was pregnant.

A pregnant woman's legal obligations are not on hold during her pregnancy.

If a pregnant woman were to receive a "Get nine months of free rent" card at the onset of her pregnancy, no landlord would ever rent to women who could become pregnant.

Give this pregnant tenant of yours and her husband a notice to pay rent or quit today. It begins the legal process of eviction. Tell them that neither the cricket in their house nor the rabbit's foot in their pockets will bring them the luck they need to keep you from evicting them through the courts. It's inevitable. Tell them that when they move, they should make sure that they

do not take their broom along with them and that they should avoid stepping on the cracks in the front walkway.

O yes, ask this tenant of yours whether she's been eating any watermelon seeds lately. Tell her you've heard that a watermelon will grow in a woman's stomach if she swallows watermelon seeds. She may not be pregnant at all. She may just think she's pregnant.

Older couple split. He stays, contests eviction, and laughs.

Q. I have a tenant from hell who's living in a property I own in New York. Everything started a year ago when this older couple rented from me. Their credit was shot because each of them had been through a divorce, but records showed that they were trying to rebuild their credit. They deserved a second chance, I thought, so I decided to rent to them. They both signed the lease.

Well, a year went by without any problems. They paid the rent right on time, but when the year was up, the woman gave me a thirty-day notice stating that she wouldn't be renewing her lease. He gave no notice. She left when she said she would. He stayed on with no lease, and he stopped paying the rent. I gave him a notice, but he wouldn't leave, and I had to file an eviction. He is contesting the eviction and has decided to damage the whole property in the meantime. I'm afraid he's going to claim that the property isn't being maintained and that he shouldn't have to pay any rent.

By the way, he now has no job and has declared himself an indigent so that he can qualify for assistance from social services. He has no assets and probably will not have any in the future. I have tried offering to forgive him the rent that he owes me, provided that he leaves by the end of the month. His reply was "See ya in 90-100 days. Ha! Ha!"

Any suggestions for ways to deal with this guy would be greatly appreciated.
—M.S., New York

A. Not only do you have a tenant from hell, you have a property in hell, landlording hell! New York tends to treat landlords like netherworld creatures. Too bad! When landlords have good reason to believe that they won't be treated fairly in court, they will do strange things to compensate. Sometimes they will overcompensate, and they wind up on the six o'clock news.

Short of doing something unethical or illegal or just plain stupid in your case, you need to follow the legal methods available to you for dealing with a tenant from hell. Since your tenant has thumbed his nose at your every effort to evict him without going to court, you must press your case through the courts. You have no alternative. Once you have come to that conclusion, you will have to decide whether you want to enter the legal labyrinth alone or with an attorney. Ask other landlords in your area how they have handled similar situations, and learn from their mistakes rather than from your own. Some judges are more sympathetic to landlords than others. Find out who they are and do what you can to get into one of their courts if you decide to do the eviction yourself. Some attorneys are better schooled in handling evictions than others because they do little else. Find out who they are by visiting the courthouse and asking the court clerk who files the most evictions there. Those attorneys will know how to help you. Select one of them as your attorney if you decide to use an attorney.

The most important thing to remember is that you are losing money every day you allow that deadbeat tenant to remain in your rental property. Get him out legally, and get him out quickly. There is a legal method, even in New York. If that method fails you the first time, go back again and again until you succeed. You will.

Tenant given break is now three months in arrears.

Q. Last year I rented my parents' home to a single mother of two and her cousin. The rent was $750 per month, and her deposit was $1,400. She had the deposit, but she did not have the first month's rent. I felt sorry for her and let her move in without paying any first month's rent. Soon afterward the problems began. She wouldn't sign the month-to-month rental agreement, and she wouldn't pay the late fee whenever she paid her rent late. In one year she has paid her rent on time twice. Now her rent is three months in arrears, and she refuses to move. I served her a 3-day notice but have not gotten a response yet. I am sure she has not moved. I need to know how I can get her out and get the money she owes.
—J.M., California

A. You have made all the classic mistakes of a first-time landlord. I wrote the *Landlording* book

to help people such as yourself avoid these mistakes, and I would suggest you read the book if you decide to continue as a landlord.

Right now, you have only one choice. You must evict this woman as soon as possible. My eviction book explains how to do an eviction yourself, but if you have neither the time nor the inclination to evict this woman, get an attorney right away to assist you.

He lets tenants get two months behind in their rent.

Q. I rented my house out about two years ago. The tenants have been keeping the place up fairly well and haven't bothered me much.

Over the last six months they have been getting behind in their rent. Right now they are two months behind. I know that they have had financial problems and I have tried to be lenient, but now I would like some advice on good resources for writing a letter requesting them to attempt to catch up or move out. I have never been a landlord before.
—R.T., Minnesota

A. Your tenants are taking advantage of your big heart. Don't wait a moment longer. Fill out and serve a notice to pay rent or quit immediately, right now, today. You'll find such a notice in the back of my *Landlording* book and also on the "landlording.com" website. Use it or get one from your local rental property owners association. That will begin eviction proceedings. If the tenants haven't paid you in full or moved within the notice limit, file an eviction action against them and get them out.

They may not be professional deadbeats, but they're deadbeats all the same. They don't deserve your largesse. Get movin'.

Good tenant's son becomes bad influence on her.

Q. I rent an apartment in a triplex to a lady who's been living there for seven years. She was the best tenant I ever had until one of her sons, a cigarette and marijuana smoker, moved in with her.

Smoking is one of the things I do not tolerate. I talked to both her and her son about my rules, but the smoking went on. It became so bad that their neighbor threatened to call the cops because the marijuana smell was so strong. I persuaded him to let me deal with the problem.

I wrote the lady a letter giving her and her

son two months to leave. She confronted me about the letter and told me that she couldn't afford to leave. I told her that if she didn't tell her son to leave, they would both have to go. She told me that she would have no choice then but to move and she would start looking around for another place.

Two months later, after she had used her security deposit as her last month's rent, they were still there, and she was avoiding me. I had to go to her myself and ask about her plans. She said that she simply couldn't find a place to move to. I told her that she was going to have to move somewhere else and that she would have to pay the rent now that it was the first of the month. She told me that if she paid the next month's rent, she would stop looking around for another place.

What is my next step?
—M.D., Ohio

A. This lady may have been the best tenant you ever had before her son arrived, but now that she's under his influence, she's taken a turn for the worse. You, nonetheless, have continued to treat her graciously as if she were still a good tenant. You gave her two months to move out, and you let her use her security deposit as her last month's rent. She has taken advantage of your generosity.

Get this through your head. She is no longer a good tenant, and she should no longer be treated like a good tenant. She is allowing her son to defy your rule about smoking. She is ignoring your notice for her to move, even though you have given her plenty of time. She has not kept you informed about her progress in finding another apartment. She has used her deposit as her last month's rent, and she has given you a decree about her paying the next month's rent. Good tenants do not do such things.

You must decide whether you want to put up with her and her son's shenanigans or whether you want her to leave once and for all. If you want her to stay, accept her rent and be prepared to bend your no-smoking rule, and your other rules as well, for her and her son so long as they stay there. If you want her to move, do not accept her rent. Prepare the legal paperwork yourself to take the eviction into court and follow it carefully to its conclusion, or else hire an attorney to handle the eviction for you.

Should the tenant have a change of heart once

she understands that you mean business and really are going to evict her, listen to her and negotiate, but don't reduce the pressure on her until she produces. The least you should require of her at this point is her son's departure and a promise from her that if he comes to visit, he will not smoke on the premises; the rent as billed through the current month; the replacement of the security deposit; and the reimbursement of any costs you have incurred to evict her.

Apparently you didn't put enough pressure on her before to find another place to live. The very real threat of an all-out legal eviction will crank up the pressure and yield results. You'll see.

Solo woman with one car adds son and two more cars.

Q. I am writing you on behalf of my parents who are landlords.

They have been renting to a woman who signed a month-to-month rental agreement limiting vehicles to one and occupants to one. Since she signed the agreement, she has moved two additional vehicles onto the premises and has let her son move in with her.

What is the fastest way to evict her? She does pay on time, but money is not an issue here. She is also harassing other renters.
—R.Y., California

A. Please note that my remarks here are directed to your parents.

The fastest way to evict this woman would be to move her out bodily and throw her belongings out on the street, but doing so would be very illegal and very costly in terms of legal fees and onerous settlement costs. Don't resort to the fastest way.

The best way to evict her would be to approach her directly in person and tell her that "things" just aren't working out. Ask her how soon she can move out. Tell her that you will return all of her deposit money if she's completely moved out by whatever date you agree upon and if she leaves the place reasonably clean and undamaged. Urge her to give you a date within two to three weeks. If she says she can't move out for more than a month, tell her that you can't wait that long. You'd like her to move out within thirty days.

If she's somebody you "can talk to," this approach will work. If she isn't, you may have to offer her an incentive to move out. If that doesn't work, you may have to evict her through the courts.

No matter what agreement you make with her, you should give her a notice of termination of tenancy (prepared in advance). Every eviction must begin with some sort of a notice (unless it occurs when a tenant is holding over at the end of a fixed-term lease). You should serve the notice when you first approach her about moving out because she may not move when she says she will. If she puts you off for three weeks by saying she's going to move out and then she doesn't move, you will have to serve her a notice, and you will have lost three weeks in the process of forcing her to leave should you have to resort to evicting her.

If she's recalcitrant and you think you may have to evict her, emphasize that a court eviction will go on public record with the county and will be available to all who search those records looking for information about prospective tenants. Her having been evicted will make her getting credit or another place to live that much more difficult.

Nice, educated couple turn into squabbling, deadbeat couple.

Q. Two years ago we rented a house we own in Alabama to a nice, educated couple and their daughter on a lease-option. These past two months their lives turned upside down, and the police had to come out at least twice a week to quell some sort of domestic violence or other in their family. They got two months behind on their rent, and we just received written notification from them that they have vacated the property, although they apparently did leave a lot of their possessions behind. I suspect we'll have trouble getting inside because they changed the locks and added a security system. What should we be doing now?

—R.F., Tennessee

A. Count your blessings. Those tenants may have been two months behind on their rent, but at least they gave you written notice, so now you don't have to pursue an abandonment proceeding to regain possession of the property. You have legal possession.

Waste no time. Go over there with a witness, get inside, photograph and catalog everything they left behind, move their belongings to a self-storage unit or to a spare garage, and change the locks. Then, simultaneously prepare the house to rent or sell, and make every effort to find these people so you can return their belongings and pursue them for the rent they owe you.

Every state has a procedure you must follow for handling the belongings tenants leave behind. The procedure begins with notification and varies after that according to your estimate of the belongings' worth. If they're worth little, say, $300 or less, you may be able to dispose of them any way you see fit after holding onto them for several weeks. If they're worth more, you may have to advertise and hold an auction and turn the proceeds over to a public agency, after deducting your expenses. Check the Alabama legislature's website (legislature.state.al.us/) for the applicable laws on abandoned personal property, ask a local rental property owners association, or consult an attorney.

Tenant's biker boyfriend has bad attitude.

Q. Four years ago I rented a duplex unit to a single mother with two kids. They have been good tenants.

While visiting the property to do some yard maintenance recently, I discovered that she has a boyfriend living with her. My husband and the boyfriend exchanged words about the motor oil that was dumped in the back yard, the bald tires that had been leaning against a fence for two months, and the oil cans, buckets, and tools that were left lying around outside. I wrote the tenant a letter the next day and expressed my concern. She responded by cleaning up the yard herself.

Now I have learned that her boyfriend is parking his motorcycle in the basement. I know that there will be problems so long as she is involved with this man. He's got a bad attitude.

Do I have enough cause for eviction?

—O.L., Virginia

A. You have several causes for eviction. The number one cause is the boyfriend, this additional resident who's living there without your consent. The number two cause is the mess. You could charge ahead and evict everybody on these grounds, but it could become nerve-wracking, time-consuming, and costly, when what you really want is for him alone to leave.

Consider everything from your tenant's point of view. She's probably kicking herself for having let this devil-may-care biker move in with her, and she may feel she's not strong enough to tell him to leave. She may be looking for an excuse, and your notice could be just the excuse she needs to get rid of him.

Prepare the legal notice required to evict under these circumstances. It's called a notice to perform covenant. Serve it on her in person when you know that the boyfriend is out of the house, and tell her that the boyfriend has to go or else they all have to go. Explain the situation to her in few words. Listen to what she has to say, and leave.

Visit her again after several days to get an update in person. If she says that the boyfriend is staying, tell her that you have no choice then but to evict everybody. Tell her that if you do have to evict her through the courts, her eviction will remain on public record for all to see, including credit reporting agencies and landlords. Tell her that if she moves out on her own accord, she will avoid being branded as having been evicted.

She sounds like a responsible person. Give her some extra courtesy and see what she does, but do not delay in pursuing the court action against her unless you see evidence that he is moving or that they are all moving.

She is fed up with long-term tenant's bad housekeeping.

Q. I own a duplex and live in half of it. My tenant living in the other half has lived there for seven years, long enough for us to become friends. She's a nice person, and she's fun to be around, but she's a terrible housekeeper. I never go into her unit because I can't stand the odor and the mess. She doesn't seem to care what her unit smells like or looks like because it keeps getting worse and worse or so it seems when she greets me at her door and I glance at the inside over her shoulder. I suppose it wouldn't bother me so much if I weren't living next door to her and didn't have to be reminded every so often of her terrible housekeeping.

Recently I became so bothered that I decided to give her a 30-day notice to clean up her place or else. I don't know whether the notice was legal or not, and I don't know what the "or else" might mean. I was just so frustrated that I felt I had to do something. I really don't want to lose her as a tenant or as a friend, but I can no longer accept the growing accumulation of grime and junk in her unit. What do you suggest I do now? —N.N., New Mexico

A. People are so different. This tenant of yours who can't seem to keep her house in order is way different from the norm, and you can't know for sure how she will react to pressure from you as her landlord and friend to change a bad habit. Since you have decided to put pressure on her rather than continue to accept her slovenly way of living, you will have to follow through with your notice if she does not clean up her place.

"Or else" in notices which landlords give to their tenants generally means eviction, and that's what your notice implies, but since it doesn't state exactly what it means, it would not stand up in court were you to rely upon it to begin eviction proceedings. It must state the consequences in terms which are both legal and specific. "Or else" does not satisfy those requirements. Nonetheless, you could make it mean that if the tenant does not comply with the notice to clean up, you will serve her with the proper notice to begin eviction proceedings. That meaning would pass legal muster and make good sense. The notice you have given her already would essentially become a preliminary warning that you will take action to evict unless she takes action to clean.

Legal proceedings for an eviction resulting from a tenant's refusal to keep a clean and orderly house vary from state to state. If you do have to initiate an eviction, you may be able to evict for cause OR evict merely to terminate tenancy. Check your state's laws.

Most landlords will pursue an eviction to terminate tenancy when they're really evicting for cause because an eviction to terminate tenancy is more straightforward and not subject to a big burden of proof. All you have to do is complete the eviction paperwork properly and prove that the tenant received the paperwork as specified by law. Tenants defend themselves more frequently in evictions for cause than they do in evictions to terminate.

Let's hope that your slob of a tenant takes your notice as a wake-up call rather than as a challenge and that she complies with it and cleans up so that you don't even have to bother with an interpretation of "or else."

He wants to take tenants' possessions as collateral.

Q. Our tenants' lease expires at the end of January. I sent them a new lease for another year at the beginning of December, but they did not

contact me to reveal their intentions. At the beginning of January, I called to ask for that month's rent, and they informed me that they will be vacating the premises on the first of February. They did not give me sixty days' notice as required by the lease, and they still owe me $300 from a previous delinquent rent payment. When they move out, am I entitled to take some of their possessions, e.g., their TV, as collateral? I am certain that they have no intention of paying me anything before they leave.
—K.J., Kentucky

A. Your tenants seem to be calling the shots. The time has come for you to act.

Serve them with an appropriate legal notice to begin eviction proceedings for nonpayment of rent. The notice should demand only what they owe you for rent, nothing more. It should not even include the $300 they owe you from that previous delinquent rent payment unless it was clearly for December, the previous month.

Don't delay. Serve them now, for you cannot be sure that they will vacate on the first of February as they say they will. Lately they haven't been forthright with you in the least. They're liars and cheats. If they haven't vacated by the expiry date in the notice, file eviction papers with your local court. In doing so, you stand a decent chance of getting the money they owe you and of making sure that they will vacate. If they vacate before you file the court papers, go to small claims court and get a judgment against them. If they don't vacate before you file the court papers, follow through with the eviction. You will force them out and get a money judgment at the same time, a judgment which you might be able to collect. In addition, that money judgment will smirch their credit rating, and their having been evicted will be on their record as well. You must get tough or they will continue kicking sand in your face.

They want jailed boyfriend to pay girlfriend's rent arrearages.

Q. Last June we rented to a young man who was going to be living alone in our house. Soon after that, he allowed his girlfriend, who was kicked out of her own apartment, to move in without first telling us anything about her. He was a very good tenant and always paid his rent on time until his girlfriend had him arrested for battery. Since he had a prior record, which we did not know about, he was sentenced to jail for four years. She continued living in the house and did not pay any rent money after he was jailed, so we had to evict her. My question is this: Can we hold him responsible for the three months of rent that we lost even though he is in jail?
—S.G., Florida

A. You may hold the young man responsible for paying the three months of lost rent so long as you received a judgment against him when you evicted his girlfriend. If you didn't get a judgment against him then, you may file a separate action in small claims court for a money judgment.

The real question in this matter, however, is whether you can collect a judgment against this fellow at all. He's going to be detained in jail for four years, so his earning power is going to be limited during that time. Once he gets out, he may in time earn enough to pay you what he owes, but don't count on it.

My advice is this: If you already have a judgment against him, put it in the hands of a collection agency and then forget about it. If you don't already have a judgment against him, don't bother. Get on with your life. Your chances of collecting anything from this fellow are only slightly better than your winning the Florida Lottery.

First-time landlords have to evict their very first tenants.

Q. When we moved out of a condo we own, we decided to rent it rather than sell it. We had no experience as landlords, but we thought we could do as good a job as anybody.

We rented to a young couple and had nothing but trouble getting the rent out of them every month. We finally decided to evict them after their rent was late for two months in a row. At about the same time, they called to tell us that they were having financial problems and would have to pay their rent late or in installments over the coming months. We told them that we needed the rent on time and in one payment because we needed their rent money to make our mortgage payment.

We gave them a 3-day notice to pay their rent or move, and right away they told us they would move. They kept their word and moved, but they didn't move out completely. They left some large items behind, and now, a week following their departure, they're still using the unit for storage.

Every day they claim they will "come back tomorrow" to move the rest of their things, but they just keep making promises and breaking them.

Can we remove the items they left behind even though we did not evict them through the courts? We'd like to get the place ready to rent again, but we can't do much with their stuff still in there.

Do we have to give them back their security deposit? We have already decided to keep half of it to cover the rent they owe, but we're wondering whether they're entitled to get any of it back since we had to kick them out. We think we're going to have to do a lot of work in the place after they move out completely because they had an active house cat, even though they weren't supposed to have any pets according to their rental agreement. We're not sure how much all of that will cost us. We might even have to replace the carpet.

Should we send them a notice now that they're not going to get their deposit back, or should we wait until after we go in and work on the place?
—J.K., Ohio

A. You did the right thing in refusing to allow your tenants to pay their rent late or pay it in installments. First-time landlords tend to be too lax about collecting rents on time, and they wind up learning the hard way that tenants who are allowed to pay their rent late seldom catch up later. When the landlords wise up, they find that being lax about collecting rents has cost them thousands of dollars in lost rent, money they will never collect.

You did the right thing in giving your tenants a written notice to pay their rent or move. That notice is the first step required to commence a legal eviction for nonpayment of rent in every state. A verbal warning alone may have been enough to get the tenants to move, but it would

not have been enough to begin eviction proceedings had they not moved, and you would have lost valuable time in the eviction process because you would have had to serve the notice later and then wait the required number of days before you could file the court papers.

Getting the tenants to remove the rest of their things and getting their security deposit handled correctly are minor matters compared with getting them to vacate for nonpayment of rent without your ever stepping foot in court.

So far, you're batting a thousand. Congratulations!

There are any number of ways to get them to remove the rest of their things. Begin by asking them why they haven't moved everything out of the condo and asking them whether there's anything you can do to help them. You may find that they have a place to store the things, but they lack the funds to rent a truck or lack the brawn to move such big things. Find out,

ANDREW EXPECTED BOOT CAMP FOR LANDLORDS TO TEACH HIM HOW TO MAKE A MILLION

and help them if you can.

Tell them in your conversation that so long as they are storing things in the condo, they have possession of the condo and are incurring rent charges, and you have to charge them for every day the things are there just as if they were still occupying the unit themselves. The sooner they move their things out, the sooner their rent charges will end. Tell them that the rent charges will be deducted from their security deposit so long as there is any deposit left. When it's gone, you'll begin putting the charges on a moveout bill which you'll present to them as soon as you can itemize everything they owe.

What you charge them for rent must be based upon the number of days they have possession. It must not be an arbitrary figure. To arrive at the correct figure, divide their monthly rent by thirty to get the daily rent, and then multiply that figure by the number of days they have possession.

As for their security deposit, you may not keep all of it just because you had to kick the tenants out or just because they kept a cat when they had agreed not to keep any pets or just because they have cost you some sleepless nights. You may make deductions for rent owed, late fees, bad check charges, and missing items, and for cleaning and repairs resulting from wear and tear beyond the ordinary. That's all.

Don't tell them anything about their security deposit before they have removed all of their things from the condo, that is, nothing except that you will be itemizing everything you deduct from the deposit and you will be giving them a full accounting. Were you to tell them before they remove everything that they will get nothing back from their security deposit, you might as well be telling them to leave their things right where they are as long as they please and to trash the place whenever they please. Always give them hope that they will get some of their deposit back, and be generous when you do the itemizing so you don't have unhappy tenants who haul you into small claims court because you were so niggardly in your calculations.

You will continue batting a thousand in your dealings with these tenants if you are straight with them, even though they did throw you a few curve balls, and you will then feel confident enough in your landlording skills to continue being landlords.

Try to bat a thousand next time when you are selecting replacement tenants.

New owner wants to move into occupied unit.

Q. I just purchased a three-family apartment house and have decided to move into the first-floor unit. It is currently occupied. The tenants living there have trashed it and were refusing to let the previous owner in to make repairs. I did not know this before I became the owner.

On the day of the closing, I sent the tenants a 30-day notice to terminate tenancy. None of these people have a lease. They are all on month-to-month agreements. I have their security deposit and am contemplating not returning it because they have put holes in the walls and floors. I believe there are as many as eight people living in the two bedrooms. If they don't comply with the

certified letter, can I change the locks?
—B.W., Connecticut

A. You did the correct thing by giving the tenants a 30-day notice. Rather than trust that the notice will elicit the desired response, however, keep a line of communication open with them and put a human face on the notice, your face.

Visit them two weeks after giving them the notice and ask them how their plans to move are coming along. Ask them whether there's anything you can do to help them make their move. Do the same thing three weeks after you give them the notice, and if they still haven't moved when they're supposed to, pay them a final visit and ask them again what you can do to help them move. Tell them that you need a place to stay yourself and that you need to move there. If you see no evidence that they're planning to move, begin legal eviction proceedings immediately. Have them served with the papers, and let the process run its course.

Do not change the locks until after they move. Changing the locks while they are still in possession and not giving them keys will get you into big trouble.

Buyer wants house vacated.

Q. I am closing on a house that is currently rented to tenants on a monthly basis. I would like the tenants to clear out ASAP. I understand the laws in Texas are quite stringent when a notice to vacate is in order. What process do I take to evict so that I may occupy the premises soon after purchase?
—M.N., Texas

A. If I were purchasing an occupied house which I wanted to occupy myself, I would not complete the purchase until the current owner succeeded in removing the tenants.

After all, you don't want the tenants there. You want to occupy the house yourself. Why should you buy something which you cannot use? Why should you be responsible for removing the tenants? Get the current owner to remove them.

Remember this: if you assume the responsibility for removing the tenants, you cannot know how long the removal will take or what kind of condition they'll leave the place in. They could drag their feet. They could trash the house. Then what do you have? You have a house which you bought for good money, but you have to lay out more good money before you can occupy it.

Delivering the house to a buyer in good condition is the seller's responsibility.

If you choose to assume that responsibility, do so with your eyes wide open, and make sure that you're being compensated in the price for taking it on. Then approach the tenants directly and tell them your situation. Offer them a bribe, say $200, if they will vacate within two weeks. Put your offer in writing and pay them the money only after they have vacated. If neither talking nor bribery seems to be working with these tenants, go down to the courthouse and ask the clerks which attorney handles more evictions than any other. Hire that attorney to handle the eviction.

Seller wants to stay in house for one month after escrow closes.

Q. I am buying a house, and it's supposed to close escrow next week, but now the seller has informed me that she can't move out for another month. She wants to rent back the property until then.

I have to refuse her because I have already given my landlord notice, and I have to move out myself in another two weeks.

Can I evict the owner of the property after the close of escrow if she insists upon staying another month? What's the process? How long will it take, and can I sue her for my damages? —B.L., California

A. If you're working with a real estate agent, ask the agent for help in dealing with the problem. Agents face this kind of problem regularly and know how best to handle it.

If you're not working with an agent or if the agent isn't helpful, you should get together with the seller face-to-face and explore the possibilities. Don't even think about closing escrow and then evicting the seller. An eviction would take a minimum of sixteen days (more than likely much longer) and would cost you time, money, and aggravation, and then you'd have turned the seller into an adversary. Don't take that course.

Tell the seller quite frankly what your situation is and say that you can think of three possible solutions: 1) You close escrow as scheduled; the seller moves her things into storage temporarily and moves into temporary housing so you can move in as scheduled. 2) You close escrow as scheduled; you move your things into storage temporarily and move into temporary housing, but you are compensated for your costs plus 50%

for your trouble. 3) You delay the close of escrow for three weeks in exchange for the seller's agreeing to give you a credit in escrow of $1,000, plus $100 per day for every day she remains in the house. You would then have to find temporary accommodations and pay for them, but you'd be compensated when escrow closes.

Start with these three scenarios and try to work something out with the seller. There's always a way to settle problems without rushing into court. You won't win there, and neither will the seller.

Foreclosure apartment building has eviction in progress.

Q. I am purchasing a four-unit apartment foreclosure, and I just found out that one of the tenants is being evicted. The eviction is currently in progress. Everything seemed all right until today. The tenant who is being evicted is the sister of the ex-owner. Not only is she the sister of the ex-owner, but she was also acting as the manager of the property. As manager, she collected the rents and did small tasks around the apartments for her brother. When the bank took over the property, she put down that she paid only $122 in rent. The bank told her that her management services were no longer needed and that her rent would now be $450. She in turn stopped paying any rent at all. The bank then began the eviction proceedings, and when the case came to trial on Friday, the judge said that he had never seen a case like this and that he would need a couple of days to return his decision. The property is located in a rent-control area, and I'm afraid that it might be hard to evict this tenant. To make things worse, in order to qualify for the loan, I applied as an owner-occupant with the idea of living in the soon-to-be-evicted person's unit. What should I do? What are my options if the judge comes back with a decision against the bank? —J.C., California

A. You say that you are purchasing a four-unit apartment foreclosure. To me that means you haven't purchased it yet. If so, don't complete the transaction until the eviction matter has been resolved to your satisfaction. If you have already purchased it, hire an attorney to evict this former manager and sister of the ex-owner. The second time around, that is, when a first eviction has failed, is always easier because your attorney can take advantage of the paperwork created during the first failed eviction.

Dispossessed family aren't leaving without a fight.

Q. I bought a five-acre parcel of remote California land two weeks ago. On the property are an old, dilapidated bungalow, a water tank, two storage sheds, a small mobile home, and several recreational vehicles. The original elderly owners had not paid their county property taxes for eight years, so the county sold the parcel at a tax-lien auction, where a land company bought it. Later they held another auction, and that's where I bought it. At some undetermined time, both owners died, and their grown son and his two teenaged children moved onto the property (for all I know, they may have been there all along), and they don't want to leave.

Their position is that they were never notified of the tax problem. Therefore, the tax sale is illegal. They also appear to have emotional ties to the old family homestead. Naturally, I want them out. They appear to be neither tenants nor holdover owners. What are they then? Are they illegal squatters that the sheriff can haul away now, or do they have some sort of a residency claim through their deceased relations and their longevity at the property?

One of the teenagers has told me matter-of-factly that Aunt Patty will burn the place down if anyone tries to force them out. This is the same Aunt Patty who supposedly removed all of the surveyor's markers in the area, which made locating the correct parcel difficult in the first place. So, it appears that Aunt Patty also lives there, as well as someone who calls himself a caretaker of the property. At this point, I'm not really sure who lives there.

I am not interested in renting to these people, nor have I collected any rents from them. How do I get them out if neither talking nor bribing works? How can I prevent them from destroying the permanent improvements on the property? How can I prevent them from returning and moving back a week after they're evicted? I'm afraid that even if I am successful in getting them all out, they very well may burn the place down or destroy everything. Note that this remote property is two hours by car from my home, but there are neighbors nearby.
—T.G., California

A. When deciding upon your next move, you must keep three important facts in mind: 1) You live two hours away. 2) You bought the parcel cheap. 3) The improvements are easily transportable or virtually worthless.

Were you living near the property, you could do any number of things yourself, including extensive negotiations, a complete legal proceeding to evict the residents, and the monitoring of their comings and goings. Had you paid full "retail" for the property, you'd feel disinclined to hire help. Having paid less than "wholesale," you should consider legal help merely part of the cost of acquisition. Were the improvements all permanent and in good condition, you would want to be more concerned about preserving them.

Because you live two hours away and because there are any number of complications you could encounter in evicting these people yourself, not the least of which might be putting yourself in harm's way as a much-resented and distant absentee owner, you should hire a local attorney knowledgeable about evictions to handle the matter for you. Let the attorney determine the status of the residents and the best way to evict them.

As for the improvements, you should write them off in your mind. If anything halfway valuable is left after the eviction, consider it a bonus. Consider also that Aunt Patty, the amateur arsonist, may be doing you a big favor by torching everything, so you don't have to dismantle it and haul it off to the dump yourself. If that's not the case, tell the attorney to warn the residents that they will be charged with a criminal offense should they torch anything. That may deter them somewhat. Who knows? The situation is touchy. The people involved may think nothing of wasting the property or wasting you. Be careful, but do get busy.

Once the residents have been evicted, make arrangements with a neighbor to monitor the property and inform you should they return. If they do, have them arrested as trespassers.

Owner must fire and evict unprofessional manager.

Q. We have a 31-unit apartment building which requires an on-site manager. The current manager has been there for about ten years and is no longer doing his job in a professional manner. He may even be causing tenants to move. A good tenant who's been there for two years recently gave notice because he claimed that the manager was harassing him. The manager does not get along with my mother who is now the sole owner due to my father's death last year. Mom has never had to handle this business before and is at her wit's end.

What is the best way to fire him? We don't look forward to his last thirty days when he could wreak havoc on the building and tenants, not to mention all the keys, door codes, and files. His work contract states that either party may terminate the contract with a written 30-day notice. We will be requiring him to move out as well. Also, what is the best way to find and hire a new manager?

—K.S., California

A. The best way to terminate this burned-out manager is to go to the building with your mother in the early evening and surprise him with the announcement that the two of you have decided he must go. Since his contract requires a written 30-day notice of termination, bring a notice with you and give it to him. Specify in the notice that he is being relieved of his duties immediately and must vacate his apartment within thirty days. You do not need to give any written or verbal reasons for the termination, but he will undoubtedly ask. Be ready with some vague reason, perhaps that you have wanted to make some changes around the property ever since your father died. Tell him that even though you are relieving him of all management responsibilities immediately, you will continue compensating him for thirty days and you expect his cooperation during this period. Get all of the keys from him, all of the rent receipts, all of the files, and all of the tools. Bring new locks with you to change access to the office, if there is one, or else take everything home with you on a temporary basis. Change the locks on every garage, closet, room, access panel, machine, and storage area reserved for management use.

As soon as you have terminated the manager, visit the tenant you trust most and tell him (I'm using the masculine here; this trusted tenant may, of course, be feminine) you are looking to replace the manager you have just terminated. Ask him whether he would help you by looking after things on site temporarily and also whether he knows of someone living in the building who would make a good manager. In a building with 31 units, you and he should be able to identify several people, one of whom will take the job.

Before offering the job to anybody, identify the duties, calculate a fair wage, and make up a management agreement (the *Landlording* book has one to use as a model).

As soon as you identify a temporary manager, notify all of the tenants in writing of the change. Then call upon the good tenant who gave notice and ask him to reconsider his moving out in light of the management change.

Your mother cannot allow this monster of a manager to run the property according to his rules. He must be terminated now.

They're evicting Section 8 tenant.

Q. We started an eviction today. The tenant was behind in paying her rent and her deposit (we were stupid or naive, I know, to let her pay a little bit of the deposit each month; she still owes us a balance, even eighteen months after she moved in). She flooded the house twice, over-filled the septic tank twice, damaged the inside, and absolutely neglected the outside, not to mention what her dogs did to the place. She is Section 8, and half of the rent comes from the housing authority. They told me to give her a 30-day notice, which we did. It was up on the first of this month. Today is the third and still she hasn't paid any rent. She slammed the door in my face yesterday when I stopped by to ask about her packing and to tell her that we would have to evict her.

Here's my question. The eviction has already cost us $275. Can we deduct this sum from her deposit, even though we believe there will be nothing left of it with all the repairs we will have to do? She is on welfare and operates a day-care center in the house ("Community Connection for Child Care" is paying her). Do we have to let them know she is being evicted?

—M.L., California

A. Most Section 8 tenants want to protect their entitlement. They know that a screwup which results in an eviction from their rental dwelling will also "evict" them from the program. They'll no longer qualify for their government rent subsidy. Your tenant knows the rules, the Section 8 rules and your rules, and yet she chooses to ignore them and taunt you as well. You have to evict her.

Fortunately for you, the Section 8 program will continue its "supplemental assistance payments" during the eviction proceedings, and it will compensate you for some of the damage. Keep the housing authority informed of your situation, and ask them for a thorough explanation of what you are entitled to as a landlord evicting a Section 8 tenant who has damaged your property.

As for the tenant's deposit, you may most definitely deduct your eviction costs from it. You may also deduct the unpaid rent and the costs for the repairs. That's what the deposit is for. Keep a careful accounting, and tell the housing authority and the tenant how much you deducted from the deposit. Ask the housing authority to pay the balance.

As for the child care arrangement, you should advise the organization which is paying your tenant to care for children in the home. They need to know so they can prepare for the eviction to come.

They want to evict destructive, deadbeat tenant.

Q. My father's tenant is destroying his apartment and has stopped paying his rent.

What notice should we serve him? If we serve him a notice to pay rent or quit and he pays the rent before the notice expires, then he gets to stay because he has complied with the notice, doesn't he?

Because he is destroying the apartment, I want to give him a notice which tells him to pay his rent and still gives him no opportunity to stay on as a tenant even if he does pay his rent. What type of a notice do I give him and where can I get one?
—J.R., Illinois

A. Your father should serve him with two notices at once, a notice to pay rent or quit and a notice to terminate tenancy. To comply with the notice to pay rent or quit, the tenant must pay within just a few days. In Illinois, it's five days. If the tenant does not pay within that period of time, your father may begin eviction proceedings. If the tenant does pay, the other notice is still valid. It expires in the equivalent of one rental period, and the tenant must vacate by then.

Make sure that your father does not accept rent beyond the final move-out date determined by the notice to terminate tenancy. Accepting rent beyond this date invalidates the notice, and you'll have to serve a new notice.

The *Landlording* book has copies of these notices, but you should ask a local rental property association or a local attorney to supply you with local forms if they're available. They may have specially required verbiage.

They want to evict devil tenant.

Q. For the first time ever, I'm faced with the challenge of evicting a tenant who pays his rent regularly. He pays a week late every month, but he always pays the late fee without question when he pays. The trouble is that he breaks every rule in his rental agreement, and he's forever breaking things in his apartment, too. He's a thorn in my side. He plays loud music. He parks cars on the grass and destroys the lawn. He parks three cars in the building's parking lot where he has one assigned space. He complains when I don't repair something he wants repaired even though he refuses to move his belongings so I can have access to do the work, telling me that I ought to move them myself. His dog is damaging the apartment, and he won't acknowledge the damage or repair it. He broke a storm window and won't repair it. He broke the lock on his own front door when he left his keys inside. He replaced the lock, but he won't give me a copy of the new key. You get the picture. The list goes on and on.

I want him out, but I don't know how to get him out legally without a major hassle. I know that I can give him a 30-day notice, but he's just the type who will destroy the property and stay until the very last minute when an officer arrives to force him to leave. What do I do when he doesn't leave voluntarily after his thirty days are up?
—M.M., New York

A. You are right. This devil of a tenant of yours has got to go. Don't despair. There are ways to deal with such people, perfectly legal ways well short of making him a pair of custom concrete boots and throwing him feet-first into the nearest deep body of water.

One way you know already. Serve him with a 30-day notice to terminate tenancy and hope that he moves within thirty days. If he doesn't move, you proceed with an eviction through the courts.

A second similar way is to serve him with a notice to perform covenant. On the notice you list the various clauses in his rental agreement which he has broken, and you give him as much time as the law allows to mend his ways or move out. If he does neither, you prepare to prove his transgressions in court and proceed with an eviction through the courts.

A third similar way is to serve him with a notice to quit for waste, nuisance, or unlawful acts. This notice also lists his transgressions, but it does not give him a chance to mend his ways. It gives him a certain number of days to move out, and that's all. If he refuses to move out, you take him to court.

Each of these three legally sanctioned ways to evict a bad tenant varies according to location. To learn the specifics, research the landlord-tenant laws applicable to the jurisdiction where your apartment building is located or seek the advice of an attorney who specializes in landlord-tenant law and will know the specifics by heart.

Before choosing which one to use from these three obvious ways the law provides landlords for evicting a devil of a tenant, you need to consider some other options, especially because you believe your tenant will destroy what he hasn't already destroyed of your property when you challenge him with a legal eviction.

Instead of challenging him and making him think that you're on the offensive and he must defend himself, make him think that you're giving him a choice. He may stay or he may move. Give him some "wiggle room" rather than force him into a corner.

Raising his rent is the best way to get him to move and to think that moving is his decision, not yours. In this tenant's case, raising his rent is an especially appropriate way to get him to move because paying his rent appears to be the one thing he takes seriously. Capitalize on this characteristic of his. Raise his rent high enough for him to think that it's too high for him to want to stay, and wait for him to give you notice that he plans to move somewhere more reasonable.

An unreasonable rent might be fifty percent higher than he's paying now or several hundred dollars higher than the market rent or whatever other amount you think would make him move. When he screams to you about the increase, tell him that your costs keep going up and that you have to cover them by increasing the rent. You needn't be more specific than that. When he tells you that he can do better somewhere else, tell him that the choice is his to stay and pay the increased rent or find somewhere else where the rent is lower. Allow yourself a tiny smile now, but don't break out the champagne yet. Wait until he actually moves. Then celebrate.

Any landlord can succeed in evicting tenants by increasing their rent, but because of rent control, increasing rent is not always an option. When it is not an option and you want to avoid going to court, consider bribing the tenant to move or talking him into moving. They are less adversarial, less stressful, less costly, and less time-consuming ways to get rid of a bad tenant than going to court.

Take some kind of action now to get this devil of a tenant out of your apartment building and out of your life, and hope that he will find a devil of a landlord who will be a perfect match for him.

Threat of legal action puts scare into this landlord.

Q. We asked our tenants to move within thirty days and gave them a notice to vacate. They responded by threatening to take us to court. In light of their threat, we decided to give them an extra thirty days so they would have more time to find another place to live.

Do we need to draft a new notice? Do we have to state a reason for evicting them in the notice?

Over the past four years these tenants have consistently failed to report any problems or things that needed to be repaired even though we live next door to them. They live on one side of our duplex and we live on the other. We find out about problems when they finally impact us. This past fall we received a quarterly water bill of $1,700 instead of the usual $300! We found out from our plumber that their toilet had been running twenty-four hours a day for who knows how long! They never bothered to tell us. We are first-time landlords and find the situation frustrating.

Do you think we ought to offer to return their security deposit ahead of time if they will sign a letter stating that they will move out in forty-five more days? We are willing to pay their moving expenses to avoid having to pay legal fees. What do you think we should do?
—R.D., Massachusetts

A. Tenants who are asked to move sometimes respond just as yours have, with threats. They feel challenged and they want to lash out at you. They think you're pushing them around and they're angry. Giving them an extra thirty days to vacate might help defuse the situation. Then again, it might not. There's no one right way to respond to such threats.

You should definitely serve them with a new notice to vacate, one which gives the new date. Whether you must include a reason for the notice depends upon local laws. Generally, rent control jurisdictions require that notices to vacate do include a reason, and it must be a so called "just cause" reason, such as your wanting to move yourself or a relative into the unit, your wanting to rehabilitate the unit, your wanting to go out of business, your wanting to demolish or convert the unit, or their habitual failure to pay rent on time.

As for offering to return their security deposit before they move in exchange for a promise to move, don't. As for offering to pay their moving expenses, don't. That's bad business. Don't be cowed by their threat. Don't hesitate to take legal action against them if you have to.

Remember, you hold some pretty good cards in the poker game you're playing with your tenants right now. You can give them a bad recommendation when other landlords call for a reference, and you can smudge their credit rating. As a last resort, you can take them to court to force them to move. The resulting eviction will be a matter of public record which will haunt them for years to come.

Right now, take a wait-and-see approach. If they don't move when they're supposed to, file the legal papers required to evict them promptly. Sometimes you have no other choice. Don't shy away from evicting them judicially just because you hate to pay legal bills. These tenants have already cost you an extra $1,400 for the water they wasted. The average legal bill for evictions is much less than that. Resign yourself to accepting legal bills as part of the business of being a landlord. That's just what they are.

Much damage occurs after tenant abandons house.

Q. We own some rental houses and have never had any real problems until now. For the past three months we have been trying to collect the rent from one particular lady. We just learned that she has abandoned the property and that the utility company shut off her power three months ago. When we visited the house, we found frozen water pipes and water squirting all over. Supposedly she moved away to a new town, but she left some of her belongings behind. We have not heard from her in over a month and now we find

all this out. What should we do? What kind of recourse do we have when we don't even know where she is?
—J.E., Montana

A. First, look after the property. Turn off the water at the house's shutoff valve; open accounts with the gas and electric companies in your name and have the utilities turned on so you can keep the interior temperature at least forty degrees Fahrenheit; assess the damage caused by the broken water pipes; photograph the damage and the condition of the place just as the tenant left it; move the tenant's belongings into storage; submit a claim to your insurer for the repairs; repair the damage; clean everything inside and out.

Second, make some seat-of-the pants decisions to determine whether you should follow the legal proceedings for an abandonment of the property and also for an abandonment of her belongings. The big question is whether you think she will show up within a month or two, claim that she never intended to move out, and sue you because you moved her out and took possession. If you think she will, file for an abandonment of the property. In California, it's a non-judicial procedure which requires the preparation and mailing of a simple form called a "Notice of Belief of Abandonment" and a fifteen to eighteen-day waiting period. If you don't hear back from the tenant during that time, you gain legal possession. As for the belongings, in California you must follow another similar procedure which hinges upon whether you consider the belongings to be worth more or less than $300. You send a "Notice of Right to Reclaim Abandoned Personal Property" to the tenant's last known address, wait eighteen days, and do what you want with the belongings if they're worth less than $300. If they're worth more, you will have to advertise and hold a public sale and then turn the proceeds over to the county after subtracting your costs for storage and for holding the sale.

Third, determine whether this lady is worth pursuing for what she owes you. If she is, calculate what she owes, do a missing-person search (using the internet, you can do amazing things to find people), contact her and demand the money or sue her in small claims court for it. Another alternative is to join a credit bureau so that you can ding her credit for what she owes you without ever going to court.

Fourth, change the way you do business. You

or somebody who is looking after your interests must visit your rental properties regularly, at least every other month. When tenants stop paying their rent, visit them in person within four days and serve them with a notice to pay or quit. Then monitor them carefully. Never allow a tenant to get behind more than fifteen days without initiating eviction proceedings.

They want to charge tenants right amount for damage.

Q. Upon inspection of our rental house after the tenants moved out, we found cockroaches everywhere. The infestation was so bad that the exterminator, who charged us $250 for his initial visit and the three additional visits he had to make after that at weekly intervals, told me that the carpet and wallpaper would have to be removed in order for him to rid the house of the cockroaches properly. Then, he said, he would need to return on a monthly basis for approximately a year at a charge of $35 for each visit.

I know that I will have to take the tenants to small claims court to recover the costs we are incurring to make this house rentable again, but I'm not sure how much I ought to sue them for.

Exactly what should I claim for damages? Should I include loss of income due to the fact that it is going to be a while before we are able to rent the property again.

Also, the house has some hardwood floors. In one room there are two spots on the floor where the tenants put down strips of duct tape. When they removed the duct tape, they stripped the floor down to bare wood. There are spots where they spilled something, and there are big white spots, too. Since the whole floor will have to be stripped and redone, should I claim that as well?
—R.C., Iowa

A. These people have done major damage to your house by allowing the cockroach infestation to reach such a critical level that the carpets and even the wallpaper have to be replaced. You should be able to get a judgment against the tenants for the extermination costs, a portion of the wallpaper and carpet replacement based upon their useful life and how long ago they were installed, the cost to refinish the hardwood floors, and reasonable loss of use.

Collecting the judgment is another matter entirely.

People willing to share their living quarters with swarms of roaches aren't likely to have the money to pay a small claims court judgment. They're the kind of people who milk "the system" any way they can and get cash advances on their paychecks. They tend to be judgment-proof. You could go through all the trouble of suing them in small claims court, only to find that your effort was in vain because you couldn't collect.

Before you sue them, ask yourself what's important to you. Do you want to sue them to add an entry to their credit report so that other landlords and creditors would use caution before renting to them or extending them credit? Or do you want to sue them to collect what they owe you for damaging your house?

If you want to add an entry to their credit report, go ahead and sue. If you want to collect what they owe you, assess your chances of collecting the judgment before you take them to small claims court. If your chances of collecting are good, sue. If they're not good, get on with your life.

She wants to evict but can't find rental agreement.

Q. I'm in the process of trying to evict my non-paying tenants who refuse to leave. Never having done an eviction before, I'm finding the courts as difficult to deal with as my tenants.

I seem to have misplaced the initial rental agreement and am concerned that when I file the summons and complaint, my case will be thrown out due to a lack of documentation. Please advise me how to handle this situation.
—H.M., California

A. Evicting tenants is never easy and never cheap. Not evicting tenants who should be evicted is never easy and never cheap, either. Swallow hard and get busy evicting those deadbeat tenants of yours before they "steal" even more rent money from you. If you feel capable of handling the eviction yourself, you should, because there's nobody else who will pursue your eviction case as doggedly as you will. Go to your local law or public library and ask for a how-to-do-it book on evictions, or buy one through a local or online bookstore. Follow the procedure as outlined and be entirely truthful throughout. Although you ought to have the rental agreement handy to support your position in court, its absence will not sink your case. You will need to prove that you prepared and served the notice to pay rent or quit properly, and you will need to prove that the tenant is in arrears. Those are the most important aspects of your case. Prove them adequately and you will win. Get busy.

They wonder when judgment will show up on credit report.

Q. How soon after an eviction will the judgment show up on the evicted person's credit report? —R.B., Oregon

A. There's no set time. An eviction pursued to its conclusion through the courts becomes a matter of public record and will show up on a person's credit report within days after the judgment is recorded, depending upon how efficient the data gatherers are in a particular area. An eviction concluded between the principals themselves, that is, without court action, may or may not appear on a person's credit report at all, depending upon whether the landlord reports tenant payment records to a credit bureau. If the landlord does report such matters, it, too, will appear on the tenant's credit report within days. The big three credit bureaus want current and accurate information in their files, and they have their ways of getting it quickly. That's their business. That's what their clients pay to obtain.

Tenant calls landlord uncompassionate.

Q. My tenant who moved in six months ago has been late with her rent every month. I have extended her due date and even that has not changed things. Now she tells me that she has been laid off and that she has no idea when she will be able to pay. I did have her mother sign a co-signer agreement and will attempt to collect from her, but I would really prefer to end our agreement. She has given me excuse after excuse. I believe she is in over her head. She left her marriage to take this apartment, and her child support payments have been a problem. Now she is signing up for unemployment. I would like to know whether I can proceed with an eviction under the circumstances. I hate to seem heartless, but she has become hostile towards me and has repeatedly sent me letters informing me how uncompassionate I am. I sympathize with her situation, but I am not a social service agency and am tired of the stress and struggle I've endured because of her.
—C.T., Pennsylvania

A. Is a baker heartless for expecting a customer to pay for a loaf of fresh bread? Is a dentist heartless for expecting a patient to pay for extracting a sore tooth? Is a mechanic heartless for expecting a customer to pay for a tune-up? Is an attorney heartless for expecting a client to pay for drafting a living trust? Is a tattooer heartless for expecting a customer to pay for a heart-shaped tattoo on her rear end?

You are not heartless for expecting a tenant to pay for putting a roof over her head. You are in business, just as the baker, the dentist, the mechanic, the attorney, and the tattooer are in business. Your tenant is a customer, not a charity case. You have every right to expect payment for services rendered.

This tenant of yours is unclear on the concept of the landlord-tenant relationship. She thinks that you ought to let her pay only what she's able and willing to pay, not what you both agreed upon. That's not the way this business or any other business works. The customer pays the amount agreed upon or else.

For you and this tenant, the time has come for "or else." In the landlording business, "or else" is eviction. You aren't going to hear any sonorous voice from heaven telling you that the time has come to evict this lady. You aren't going to have friends and neighbors insist that you get busy and evict this lady. You have to come to that realization all by yourself, and you have to take the initiative. The time has come.

Wait no longer. Give her and her mother, as co-signer, each a notice to pay rent or quit, and you will be starting the eviction process. Put as much pressure as you can on the mother to pay the amount owed and talk some sense into her daughter about finding a more affordable place to live, but don't expect too much of the mother. She may be as lacking in good business sense as her daughter.

Find out what you do next to evict this tenant in your part of the country and do it.

Homeless couple move in and prey on old man.

Q. My 83-year-old uncle helped out a homeless couple by letting them stay with him for a while. They were arrested for drug use and put in jail, and when they got out of jail, they came back and let themselves into his house. We contacted the sheriff and he said that they are considered tenants since they have established residency at the house. They are not paying rent, and my uncle never made an oral or a written agreement with them. My uncle wants them to leave, and he has given my sister power of attorney to evict them.

My uncle is so stressed out that he is ill and doesn't even want to stay in his own house. These people do not work, and they take advantage of him by taking his money and making him drive them places.

My uncle is now living at my brother's house because he is afraid to go home, and he has hidden his car out of town so they can't force him to use it. He wants to move into an apartment and sell his house, but he can't sell it until these squatters leave. How can we remove them quickly and legally?

—R.A., Indiana

A. These people are predators. They are not tenants. They are taking advantage of a kind old man, and they should not be allowed to continue taking advantage of him.

You cannot rely on a sheriff to know and interpret the law for you. The sheriff told you what he did because it was a safe response for him to give. Sheriffs would rather leave matters for courts to decide than try to figure out which side is telling the truth in a given situation and then try to figure out which law applies and what they ought to do to apply the law. They're more concerned about the consequences of making a wrong decision in the field than they are about making a quick decision to help somebody in trouble. They don't understand urgency unless they witness actual violence or sense imminent violence.

The sheriff did not grasp the urgency in your uncle's situation. You do. Your uncle is ill and can no longer live in his own home. This homeless couple has taken over his home completely and could be removing anything and everything of value and selling it in order to get money for their drug habits. They could be inviting more people to stay with them in your uncle's home. They could be tearing the place apart. It might as well be theirs and theirs alone.

These people have no right to stay there. They are not tenants and never were. They never paid anything in rent, and they never had a contract. Staying there with your uncle for days on end while taking advantage of him and making him fearful for his safety does not transform them into tenants and does not give them the legal protec-

tions granted to tenants who are paying rent and have a contract with their landlord. Your uncle is not these people's landlord. He's their patsy.

These homeless people know something about practical measures used to achieve objectives. They used practical measures to gain access to your uncle's home in the first place. They charmed him into letting them stay. They represented themselves as homeless and needy and appealed to the goodness of his heart. They got to his heart, and he took them in. You should be using practical measures yourself to achieve your objective of getting them to leave.

The practical measures you might use to get them to leave are bold approaches. They require a physical presence and may necessitate asking friends to help. The first approach is none other than to go to the house, enter with a key, tell them forcefully to get their things and leave, and change the locks once they have left. The second approach is to go to the house, watch it from the outside, wait for them to leave, change the locks, box up their stuff, and leave it somewhere out in front with a note saying that you have changed the locks and will have them arrested if they try to re-enter. The third approach is to go to the house with as many willing friends as you can find, enter with a key, move in, make life miserable for the homeless couple until they move out, and then change the locks.

If they threaten a lawsuit, tell them to go ahead and sue. They won't. They don't look to courts for satisfaction. They look to drugs for satisfaction. They want quick and easy fixes to their problems, and they know that going to court wouldn't provide them with a quick and easy fix. It would only expose their own dirty deeds and get them nothing. They will move on and look around for another easy target like the one they found in your uncle.

Once you have forced them out and changed the locks, find somebody trustworthy to move in and stay there until the place is sold. You don't want the homeless couple to move back in themselves when they know the place is empty. They seem dense enough to try.

If you prefer not to take one of these practical approaches, check into your state's procedure for evicting lodgers, and evict them as lodgers. It takes far less time than evicting tenants and requires minimal paperwork. Legal aid may give you guidance if you need it.

Your uncle needs your help. Help him, and you will help to restore his faith in humanity.

They're too nice to evict elderly man down on his luck.

Q. I am writing on behalf of my parents. They rented an apartment to an elderly man some time ago. He used to pay his rent on time, but now he is two months behind and going for three. To make matters worse, the gas company shut off his gas and the pipes froze. Living conditions in the apartment are deplorable with piles of garbage everywhere. The apartment is virtually destroyed and will cost thousands of dollars to repair.

My parents are too humble and too nice to evict the man, but I am worried about his safety and worried that something might happen to him and that my parents might be held liable. I would like to initiate the eviction for them and help them through this ordeal. What is the best way to evict this person? Where do I get the forms needed to evict him? Can my parents file an insurance claim for the damages?
—J.G., Illinois

A. Whenever a good tenant goes bad, there's usually a reason, and frequently that reason is one of the six D's: divorce, depression, dementia, debts, drink, or drugs. You need to make every effort to find out why this tenant has gone bad at the same time you initiate the paperwork for a judicial eviction for nonpayment of rent. In this case, the poor fellow may have dementia, and you may want to contact the nearest of kin to enlist their help in taking charge of his health and welfare. If you cannot find anybody willing to take charge, contact the county health department. They will be concerned about him and about the filthy conditions he is creating. He is a living health hazard.

At the same time you pursue a humanitarian approach to this situation, you need to pursue a practical approach. You need to serve the tenant with the proper notice which begins eviction proceedings for nonpayment of rent. If you cannot locate a book outlining the procedure yourself, contact the local rental property owners association. If they have neither a step-by-step eviction guide available nor the necessary forms, they will surely be able to steer you in the right direction, be it to an eviction service, a legal document assistant, a forms supplier, an attorney, or a landlord services bureau.

Get busy today. The longer you wait, the worse the situation will become.

As for filing an insurance claim for damages, you should definitely file one. Call the company today and ask them whether they want you to file the claim right away or wait until the tenant has vacated.

Evicted nightmare tenant returns to haunt landlords.

Q. Our nightmare tenant finally moved out and handed us his keys three months ago after we went to court to evict him. Because of family pressures, we didn't take his eviction to its final conclusion and get a judgment against him for the $3,400 in back rent he owed us. We were just glad to be rid of him. We knew that he didn't have any money to pay us what he owed anyway, so we didn't bother going after him. Live and let live, we thought.

He's now decided that he's the one who ought to be going after somebody. He's going after us. He's had us served with a summons to small claims court. He's claiming that we owe him $4,200 because the house he rented from us was not safe to live in and because he wasn't paid for the work he had to do on the house.

His claim is completely outrageous, and he cannot back it up in any way other than with his own testimony. We never hired him to do any work for us, and the house he rented from us was very habitable. After all, there are new tenants living there right now, and they are perfectly happy. We suspect that his mother, who is a social worker, is behind the scenes urging him on.

We'd like to call him to find out what his real complaint is, but we can't because we have only a post office box as an address for him.

Might there be something in our landlord-tenant laws that we have overlooked, something he thinks he can use against us?
—E.M., California

A. If you failed to give your nightmare tenant an accounting of his security/cleaning deposit within the allowable time limits stipulated by law, generally fourteen or twenty-one days (the time frame is determined by state law) after he moves out, then you did overlook a significant landlord-tenant law. This law sometimes snags unsuspecting landlords who assume that they don't have to bother giving an accounting to tenants who are evicted or move out owing money. They assume wrong. Landlords must give a deposit accounting to every tenant who moves out, period. Deposit accounting is the law everywhere. It's also a good business practice because it forces you to document your costs linked to tenant move-outs and helps you adjust your deposit requirements.

Unless your tenant mentions something in his complaint about your not giving him an accounting of his deposit, the matter shouldn't come up in court, and you shouldn't bring it up.

At this point, don't despair about being unable to contact this former tenant of yours directly. He wouldn't give you any information, certainly nothing you'd want to hear. He's looking forward to his day in court to bring him a windfall. He's been watching too much court TV and listening to too many people sympathetic to him, and he thinks he's already won what he claims you owe him.

Instead of trying to contact him, read his complaint carefully and prepare to respond with relevant testimony and documents.

You want to prove to the court that the house was habitable while the tenant was living there, that you never agreed to pay him for any work he might do on the house, and that he moved out owing you $3,400 in back rent.

The judge wants solid proof, not rambling talk. Prepare your case. Organize your paperwork.

Gather together the rental agreement, rent receipts, repair receipts, work orders, written messages from the tenant, written messages to the tenant, and entries in the house logbook, and look around for photographs you may have taken of the house while the tenant lived there. Lacking any old photos, photograph the house now to show the judge how well it's maintained.

Ask neighbors whether they will testify on your behalf that the house was in good condition while the tenant was living there. If they can't or won't testify, ask them to sign a statement about the condition of the house which you have drafted for them.

Outline what you want to say in your opening and closing remarks and what you want to say about the evidence you intend to introduce in court.

Once in court, let the tenant make a fool of himself ranting and raving about what an ogre you are without providing any solid proof. Do not interrupt him. Stay calm. Wear the face of sincerity and truthfulness as you're listening to the tenant's lies.

The judge should see right through the tenant's claim and award him nothing.

16
Adapting to the Landlording Life

Landlording has more ups than downs for those who persevere.

Q. I don't really have a question. I have an observation about the landlording business which I would like to share with others who might be new landlords or might be considering becoming landlords.

With only nine years in this business under our belts, my wife and I have learned that landlording has more than its share of ups and downs.

One of the "downs" for us is having to do an eviction now and then, but we know how to do evictions, and we'll do one when we have to (thank heavens, we have had to do only two of them from start to finish). Another of the "downs" is having to deal with professional deadbeats. They require extra work, give us extra worries, cost us extra money, and make us more skeptical of people in general.

I am happy to say that the "ups" for us far outnumber the "downs." We now own a total of fifty-seven units. We work for ourselves, and we are financially independent. We have come to know and appreciate another side of life, having some people depend upon us as their housing providers and others depend upon us as their employers. We have experienced the joy of contributing in a meaningful way to the charities and causes which are dear to us. In addition, we have met some wonderful people whom we would never have met otherwise. Looking after our own rental properties has become a full-time job for both of us, and we enjoy it. We are upbeat about this business.

Being a landlord is hard for many people. They want to give up as soon as the going gets tough. When they become frustrated, they bail out and they avoid landlording ever after. Consequently, they miss out on all the benefits landlording has to offer people of average intelligence and aver-

age means who persist no matter what.

Our message to wannabe landlords and those new to the business is this: Don't ever give up when the going gets tough! Try your best to stay focused on the future instead of letting some ordinary setback throw you off course. Join a rental property owners association where you can get lots of advice from others in the business. Educate yourself as you go. Learn, adapt, and learn some more. You won't be sorry. We certainly aren't.
—R.R., Illinois

A. You have adapted well to the landlording life. Your sentiments are my sentiments exactly!

Wife tells husband to hire a property management company.

Q. Help! I'm at my wit's end! My wife and I own four rental houses, three apartment houses with a total of twenty units, and a trailer park with fifty-six spaces. The trailer park's no problem because we have an on-site manager looking after everything, but the other properties are taking up so much of my time that I can't do the things I really want to do.

My wife used to work with me on the rental properties. We would work together fixing and painting, interviewing tenants, and keeping the books. She even became good at pulling wobbly toilets, replacing the rotten subflooring, laying new vinyl tile, and resetting the toilets so they wouldn't leak. She's a big reason for our success. She's a trooper!

Now she's into other things like volunteer work and tennis and travel, and she isn't so eager to help me anymore. She says we should put everything in the hands of a property management company and take some month-long cruises on small luxury ships, fish for big halibut in Alaska, photograph Macchu Picchu at sunrise, sail across

Lake Titikaka, party during Mardi Gras in Rio, walk among the penguins in Antarctica, see the Wimbledon finals in person, visit the Louvre, dine at Taillevent in Paris, climb Kilimanjaro, observe wild game at Kenya's Treetops, swim in the Dead Sea, explore the Taj Mahal, ride an elephant in Nepal, trek through the Himalayas to Mt. Everest Base Camp, walk the Great Wall of China, sample durian in Kuala Lumpur, hike Mt. Fuji, and see an opera in Sydney.

I can't blame her for wanting to distance herself from the properties and travel to distant countries. I want more leisure time to travel and play, too, but I have heard so many horror stories about property management companies that I don't want to entrust our little empire to them. They charge a lot for a little and don't really care half as much as we do about our properties.

What should we do?

I don't mind spending some of my time on the rental properties, but I don't want to spend all of my time on them.

—O.M., California

A. Congratulations! You have arrived. You're in the third stage of landlording, and you ought to adapt to it. You are financially independent. You have already declared your independence from the workaday world. Now you need to declare your independence from your properties.

Your wife has already declared her independence. Follow her lead, but don't follow her advice about hiring a property management company.

Anybody who has worked as hard and as smart as you have to accumulate all of those properties would never be satisfied hiring a property management company to look after them. Continue being your own property management company. Just make some changes in your holdings and in your operations.

Look closely at your holdings.

Are there any which take more of your time or are more aggravating than the others? If so, exchange them into properties like your trailer park which are large enough to support full-time, on-site managers.

You may want to keep your whole collection of properties because you're sentimentally attached to them. You know everything about them. You know the neighborhoods. You know the tenants. You know the grounds. You know the buildings. You feel comfortable owning them,

and you don't want to give them up. That's understandable thinking, but it's not sensible thinking, not now when you're trying to free up more of your time.

You may want to keep a particular property because the tenants there are like family, and you don't want to desert them. You don't want to hand them over to another landlord who might treat them badly. That's understandable thinking, too, but it's not sensible thinking. You have to think about what's best for you, not what's best for someone else.

Do you think your tenants will refuse to desert you when they have the opportunity to move somewhere else better for them? No, they won't refuse. They'll move. They'll wish you well, but they'll move. You must do likewise. You must do what's best for you, and what's best for you at this stage of your landlording career is exchanging hard-to-manage properties for easy-to-manage properties.

You and your wife have worked like honeybees for ten or more years as landlords to accumulate properties, not so you could keep working like honeybees for the rest of your lives but so you could harvest the honey. The time has come for you to harvest the honey.

You ought to be spending five hours a week on your properties, not fifty. You ought to be taking four three-week vacations a year, not one.

If you insist upon keeping your smaller properties rather than exchanging them for larger, easier-to-manage properties, at least change your operations. Hire out everything except those things which you really have to do yourself or want to do yourself. Hire a maintenance person, a bookkeeper, a painter, a carpet cleaner, a house cleaner, a roofer, a plumber, an electrician, a carpenter, an attorney, and a gardener as you need them, and on-site managers as appropriate.

Select your most competent on-site manager to look after your rental houses and look after the work you hire out at all of your properties. That person will make sure that the work is done right, that it's done in a timely manner, and that it's done at a fair price. Show that person how to handle the tenant selection process, and let him or her oversee the process for all the properties. You're not the only one who can do it. You are replaceable.

Supervise your employees and contract workers as much as you feel you need to, and review your bookkeeper's work periodically. You are the only one who can do those tasks. They do require your personal attention.

Then figure out what you really want to do with all of your free time.

Tennis, anyone?

Did you say Everest Base Camp in April and Kilimanjaro in August?

Wannabe landlord asks what makes a "good landlord."

Q. I'm in my forties and thinking about becoming a landlord. I have some friends who have done very well buying rental properties and managing them. They're always telling me that I ought to follow their example unless I want to keep working for somebody else the rest of my life. They started four years ago and say they expect to be financially independent in another six to ten years.

They have told me how they found their properties and bought them, and they have even taken me under their wings to show me the ropes. They showed me the paperwork for the first rental property they ever bought and let me see what they go through when they fix up a property and select a tenant.

I know I can raise the money to buy a small rental property, but I'm a little reluctant to become a landlord because I know that many people look askance at landlords. They think that landlords are low-down despicable people.

I have to admit that I used to be a hippie when I was younger, and I never thought that I would ever consider becoming a landlord. Back then I thought that every landlord was a lowlife taking advantage of poor people who couldn't afford to buy a home of their own. Now I know better, but I still have a hard time thinking of myself as a landlord.

If I do become a landlord, I'd like to be a good one, that is, I'd like to treat my tenants the way I'd like to be treated. I'd like to keep the property in good repair, and I'd like to keep the rents reasonable. I wouldn't want to be called a rent gouger, and I certainly wouldn't want to be called a slumlord. That would really bother me.

How would you describe a "good landlord"? Do you think that I could become one?
—T.F., Illinois

A. Every occupation has its people who give the occupation a bad name, and every occupation has its detractors. Landlording has no more bad land-lords than teaching has bad teachers or the ministry has bad ministers or medicine has bad physicians, but landlording has more than its share of detractors, many of them very vocal.

These vocal detractors blame landlords for slums, housing shortages, high rents, crime, cockroaches, dark parking lots, toxic mold, racial discrimination, and everything else they think is wrong with rental housing today. They never blame tenants for anything. These detractors tend to be tenants who resent paying rent, idealists who think poverty is a virtue, socialists who believe private property is a vice, or students who rail against the status quo. You were once a hippie. You know.

You also know what makes a good landlord. You described one in your own question. You don't need me to come up with another description except that I would like to add a few things to your description.

A good landlord provides housing value for money and expects that money to arrive promptly as agreed. A good landlord understands that tenants will blame him for allowing them to get behind on their rent, so he doesn't allow his tenants to get behind on their rent. He evicts deadbeat tenants sooner rather than later.

A good landlord keeps track of the rental market and adjusts her rents accordingly, knowing that adjustments are necessary so that she can afford to pay for a new roof and new water heaters at today's prices.

A good landlord selects tenants carefully so that they will be good neighbors for the existing tenants.

There are good landlords and there are bad landlords, and there's no reason why you can't be a good one if you want to be. Landlords have to want to be landlords. Landlording is a big commitment, and you are right to do some soul searching before you commit yourself.

If you think you can adapt yourself to the landlording life, become a landlord. You'd make a good one.

He's ashamed to call himself a landlord.

Q. I guess you might say that I'm ashamed to call myself a landlord. Whenever I meet people I've never met before and they ask me what I do for a living, I tell them I'm a heavy equipment operator. That's what I used to be before I became a landlord. I never admit to being a landlord even though I believe I'm a decent landlord and have never knowingly taken advantage of anybody. I still won't admit to being a landlord unless I have to.

I admit that I've made a pile of money being a landlord, and I'm not ashamed of that, but I don't go around telling people what I'm worth and boasting about it. I keep a low profile. I don't want anybody to think that I made my money by being greedy and unscrupulous. If the truth were known, most of the money I've made has come from inflation in the price of real estate and not from being a landlord.

I bought seven rental houses and a twelve-unit apartment building from an older couple who were tired of looking after them and wanted out. I was living in one of their rental houses as a tenant, so they knew me and made me an offer too good to refuse. Within two years after I bought them, the houses had more than doubled in value, and I sold two of them for a profit of $200,000. Even after I paid the capital gains taxes, there was a substantial amount of money left over, so much that I had to deposit it into two separate bank accounts in order for the whole amount to be federally insured.

I still can't believe my good fortune. I sold the two houses and have five houses and the apartment building left, and I'm worth a million dollars, more or less. I don't mean that my properties are worth a million. I know better than that. I mean that my equity in the properties and my money in the bank are equal to a million.

I never could have saved up that kind of money when I was a heavy equipment operator. I was making good money, enough to live on and squirrel away a few thousand for a rainy day, but I never needed to worry about exceeding the federally insured limit in my savings account. I must admit that I feel as if I'd won a lottery jackpot.

My best friend has told me that I'm being too sensitive about not referring to myself as a landlord. He says that landlords no longer have the bad reputation they once had and that I should just tell people the truth about what I do.

You're a landlord. Do you admit to being a landlord when you meet new people?
—D.L., Montana

A. Your friend is right. You are being too sensitive. You have nothing to be ashamed of. You're earning an honest living providing rental hous-

ing. You have tenants who depend upon you for their most basic needs, a watertight roof over their heads, indoor plumbing, a heater to keep them from freezing in those cold Montana winters, and an electrical socket for their TV. They're paying you a market rent, maybe even a below-market rent, to provide them with a decent place to live.

You could call yourself a rental property owner, a rental property investor, a rental housing provider, or a landlord, whatever suits you. They all mean the same thing. I use the terms interchangeably to refer to myself, but I use landlord more often than I use the other terms because it's shorter. It's easier to get out of my mouth. It's two syllables rather than seven or eight.

Unless you socialize with people who are prejudiced against landlords, who think the words "greedy" and "landlord" are as inseparable as "proud" and "grandparent," who consider all landlords to be slumlords, who blame landlords for the homeless problem, and who believe that rent control would solve the homeless problem, go ahead and admit to being a landlord whenever the subject of occupations arises. I do.

People who have a head for business will think you're smart for being a landlord, and if you tell them you used to be a heavy equipment operator but now you're a semi-retired landlord and you live off the income from your rental properties, they will think you're very smart indeed. People who have no head for business will think you're lucky to have the rental properties and even luckier to be semi-retired.

You might even find that some of those people you are meeting for the first time are landlords themselves, no matter what else they do for a living, whether it be cutting hair, building bridges, preaching, teaching, or seeking a cure for cancer.

"Landlord" is a good word. It's not pejorative. It's descriptive. Think of yourself as a landlord. Refer to yourself as a landlord. Hold up your head when you tell someone you're a landlord. It's what you are. It's what I am. Be the best landlord you can be, aware of your tenants, aware or your properties, aware of the market, and aware of yourself. Be comfortable calling yourself a landlord. I am.

He penalizes students who fail to meet his expectations.

Q. My wife and I rented a three-bedroom house we own in a resort area to some college students for a week over the New Year's holiday. They signed the contract we gave them and paid everything up front, the rent, the non-refundable cleaning deposit, and the security deposit.

One of the restrictions in the contract was a limit on the number of people who could stay there. We came up with a figure of eight people because that's all the sleeping accommodations there are.

We have owned the house for twelve years. We bought it to use ourselves on weekends and during vacations, but because we aren't using it much anymore and don't want to sell it, we decided to rent it out to help cover some of our expenses. Until now, we have rented it only to people we know, and we have never had any problems. They treat it as if it were their own home.

We didn't know these students as well as we knew the other people we rented to. One of the students is the daughter of somebody I know casually at work. That's how they found out about the house.

I met the girl and thought she was sensible enough and would treat the house well. She seemed like a nice kid from a good family, and we expected no problems. Little did we know!

Everything seemed all right for the first few days, but on New Year's Day the neighbors called to tell us that at least twelve people had stayed at the house the night before. I called and spoke to the girl who rented from us. She admitted that more than eight people had stayed there. She said that she knew about the eight-person limit, and she apologized for exceeding it. She said that she let the extra people stay the night because it was late when they were ready to leave and she was afraid that they might have had too much to drink. She didn't want to kick them out and then worry that they might get in an accident or get picked up for drunk driving, so she let them sleep on the floor.

What she said sounded reasonable enough, but I told her that because she had broken the agreement, we would have to keep her security deposit. She wasn't happy about that.

There were no other problems except for one. Even though I told her she wouldn't get her security deposit back, she did make sure that the place was clean. It was, but then I found a cracked window when we were there the next weekend. I hadn't noticed it before. I decided that somebody in her group must have cracked it, and they

should have to pay for it.

Since the cleaning deposit was non-refundable and the security deposit was all used up because she had broken the agreement by having more than eight people stay there overnight, I sent her a registered letter with a bill for the cost to replace the dual-glazed window. I told her that we expected immediate payment or we would take her to court to force her to pay the bill and pay our legal expenses.

It's been a week now since I sent the letter, and there's been no answer.

What should I do? Should I follow through and take her to court, or should I drop the matter and never again rent to people I don't know and trust completely?
—R.D., Nevada

A. You have not adapted well to being a landlord. Your tenant expectations are too high for anybody who owns rental property.

The students who rented your vacation home were acting prudently when they exceeded your eight-person limit. They had a good excuse for doing so. When you confronted them, they admitted what they had done, and they told you why. They didn't try to deceive you. They were honest with you. They also took the time to clean up before they left, even though you told them they wouldn't be getting any of their deposit back. They didn't have to do that. They could have left it dirty. They could have trashed it. They could have stolen everything. They didn't do any of those things.

You were luckier than you know. You rented to responsible kids. You incurred no extra expenses as a result of their having allowed four people to sleep on the floor New Year's Eve, and you should have shown some understanding for how they handled the situation. You should have chided them for exceeding your occupancy limits and told them that you expected them to follow every one of your rules during the remainder of their stay or else you would have to penalize them.

Even if you were inclined to penalize them for what they did that one night, you should have told them that you would withhold only a portion of their deposit rather than the entire amount. Their infraction didn't warrant withholding the entire amount. After all, you suffered no consequences because they exceeded your eight-person limit.

Also, you as a landlord put yourself in a vulnerable position when you told tenants who were still in possession that they would have nothing to lose if they tore the place apart, and that's just what you did when you told them you would be keeping their entire deposit. They could have torn the place apart, and you would have had no recourse other than a courtroom challenge to recover your costs. You might have secured a judgment against the kids, but you would never have collected a cent from them because they have no assets for you to attach.

As for the cracked window you discovered, you must be quite certain that the students were responsible for cracking it before you accuse them and bill them for it. You cannot be certain of that unless you have some written or photographic proof that the window was flawless when they arrived for their stay. The crack could have been there before they arrived and you didn't notice it, or it may have resulted from a temperature change or an errant stone. You don't know.

Without proof, you aren't going to win in small claims court, especially not when the judge learns that you charged a non-refundable cleaning deposit (contradictory and illegal), that you retained all of the security deposit because of a minor infraction (unreasonable and arrogant), and that the students cleaned up after themselves even knowing that you weren't going to return their deposit (considerate and well-mannered). You'd be lucky to leave the courtroom without hearing the judge berate you and tell you that you must return all of the students' security deposit.

Because of ignorance and unrealistic expectations, you have committed some cardinal landlording sins. You were lucky. They cost you nothing. Don't push your luck by renting that perfect vacation home of yours to less-than-perfect people. Rent only to people you know and trust completely, or don't rent to anybody.

Index

Order Forms

ExPRESS, P.O. BOX 1639, EL CERRITO, CA 94530-4639

Dear ExPress:

    I'm a scrupulous property owner, and I'd like copies of your materials for my very own. Hurry up with my order. I need all the help I can get right now.

    Please send me:

_____ copies of *Landlording*	@ $27.95	$_____
_____ copies of *What's a Landlord to Do?*	@ $21.95	$_____
_____ copies of *The Eviction Book for California*	@ $24.95	$_____
_____ copies of *Landlording® on Disk (The Forms)*	@ $39.95	$_____
_____ copies of *Eviction Forms Creator*™	@ $79.95	$_____
_____ copies of *Pushbutton Landlording®*	@ $149.95	$_____
> > > > SALES TAX FOR CALIFORNIA RESIDENTS > > > >		$_____
	Shipping and handling	$ 4.00

My computer disk format is Windows___, Macintosh___   TOTAL $_____

PLEASE SEND TO

_____

_____

_____

ExPRESS, P.O. BOX 1639, EL CERRITO, CA 94530-4639

Dear ExPress:

    I'm an unscrupulous property owner who's merciless, lowdown, and greedy, and I'll pay double the usual price for your stuff just to lay my hands on all that great information. It may even reform me. Who knows?

    Please send me:

_____ copies of *Landlording*	@ $55.90	$_____
_____ copies of *What's a Landlord to Do?*	@ $43.90	$_____
_____ copies of *The Eviction Book for California*	@ $49.90	$_____
_____ copies of *Landlording® on Disk (The Forms)*	@ $79.90	$_____
_____ copies of *Eviction Forms Creator*™	@ $159.90	$_____
_____ copies of *Pushbutton Landlording®*	@ $299.90	$_____
> > > > SALES TAX FOR CALIFORNIA RESIDENTS > > > >		$_____
	Shipping and handling	$ 8.00

My computer disk format is Windows___, Macintosh___   TOTAL $_____

PLEASE SEND TO

_____

_____

_____

ExPRESS, P.O. BOX 1639, EL CERRITO, CA 94530-4639

Dear ExPress:

    I'm not a property owner yet, but I think I'd like to be one some day, and I'd certainly like to know what I'm doing. Show me.

    Please send me:

_____ copies of *Landlording*	@ $27.95	$_____
_____ copies of *What's a Landlord to Do?*	@ $21.95	$_____
_____ copies of *The Eviction Book for California*	@ $24.95	$_____
_____ copies of *Landlording® on Disk (The Forms)*	@ $39.95	$_____
_____ copies of *Eviction Forms Creator*™	@ $79.95	$_____
_____ copies of *Pushbutton Landlording®*	@ $149.95	$_____
> > > > SALES TAX FOR CALIFORNIA RESIDENTS > > > >		$_____
	Shipping and handling	$ 4.00

My computer disk format is Windows___, Macintosh___   TOTAL $_____

PLEASE SEND TO

_____

_____

_____

Use one of these forms and mail it with your check or money order, OR call ExPRESS at 800.307.0789 and charge to your MasterCard, Visa, or American Express. Our pricing changes periodically. Visit our website (landlording.com) for current pricing.